Working toward Sustainability

Working toward Sustainability

ETHICAL DECISION MAKING
IN A TECHNOLOGICAL WORLD

Charles J. Kibert

Martha C. Monroe

Anna L. Peterson

Richard R. Plate

Leslie Paul Thiele

WILEY

John Wiley & Sons, Inc.

100%
TOTAL RECYCLED PAPER
100% POSTCONSUMER PAPER

This book is printed on acid-free paper. ∞

For general information on our other products and services, or technical support, please contact our Customer Care Department within the United States at 800-762-2974, outside the United States at 317-572-3993 or fax 317-572-4002.

Wiley publishes in a variety of print and electronic formats and by print-on-demand. Some material included with standard print versions of this book may not be included in e-books or in print-on-demand. If this book refers to media such as a CD or DVD that is not included in the version you purchased, you may download this material at http://booksupport.wiley.com. For more information about Wiley products, visit www.wiley.com.

Library of Congress Cataloging-in-Publication Data:

Working toward sustainability / Charles Kibert . . . [et al.]. – 1st ed.
    p. cm. – (Wiley series in sustainable design ; 35)
  Includes index.
   ISBN 978-0-470-53972-9 (hardback), ISBN 978-1-118-10438-5 (ebk.); IBSN 978-1-118-10440-8 (ebk.);
ISBN 978-1-118-10589-4 (ebk.); ISBN 978-1-118-10603-7 (ebk.); ISBN 978-1-118-10604-4 (ebk.)
 1. Sustainable development. 2. Environmental ethics. 3. Environmental economics. 4. Sustainable development–Case studies.
5. Environmental ethics–Case studies. 6. Environmental economics–Case studies. I. Kibert, Charles J.

HC79.E5W662 2011
338.9'27–dc23

                                                                                          2011026067

Printed in the United States of America

Contents

Chapter 2
The Technology Challenge

Chapter 3
Introduction to Ethical Concepts

Preface

Sustainability balances economic, ecological, and social values in the principled pursuit of long-term welfare. It continues to gain importance and adherents 20 years after entering the lexicon with the publication of the 1987 Brundtland Report. Since then, nations, institutions, corporations, many other types of organizations, and individuals in both their professional and personal lives have adopted this framework for ethical decision making. As a result, for example, corporations are acknowledging that their social and environmental behavior, not just their financial bottom line, should be considered in judging their performance. Governments at all levels use the concept of sustainability to guide the allocation of resources, structuring of taxes and subsidies, and planning of cities and infrastructure.

Technology is an important arena for applying sustainability because the design and deployment of novel processes, materials, and products affect life on Earth in an ever more profound manner. Climate change, for example, is largely a by-product of transportation and power generation technologies that convert fossil fuels into other forms of energy and generate the enormous quantities of the atmospheric carbon dioxide that is increasing global temperatures. Developing and deploying other forms of energy, especially renewable ones, is now a global priority. We face similar challenges regarding emerging technologies such as genetic engineering, nanotechnology, robotics, and computer technology. Applying sustainability criteria to guide our choices—balancing potential benefits with risks and dangers—is both an ethical and practical task. The main purpose of this book is to provide principles and a process to ground sustainability-based decision making. Although this volume highlights technological concerns and developments, the general approach described here may be applied to a much wider variety of issues.

Acknowledgments

The authors would like to acknowledge the support of the National Science Foundation (NSF) in bringing this book from discussion to reality. The NSF kindly provided a grant to four of the authors (Charles Kibert, Martha Monroe, Anna Peterson, and Leslie Thiele) to develop teaching resources related to the ethics of sustainability for what the NSF refers to as the "STEM" professions (science, technology, engineering, and mathematics). We produced a course book and other materials for this purpose, which were then piloted and refined as part of a multidisciplinary graduate course at the University of Florida. When the opportunity arose to publish this work as a book, we were fortunate to have another colleague, Richard Plate, join us and take the lead in recasting the original materials into the present form.

The authors were assisted by a very capable and motivated group of graduate students, who not only performed many important tasks such as research and editing, but also pushed us by asking thoughtful and useful questions, challenging us to provide a consistent and clear message throughout the writing. We would like specifically to thank the following graduate students for their invaluable support: Kelly Biedenweg, Kristin Grey, Evgenia Ilieva, Chris Manick, Greg McElwain, Patricia McKetchey, Dana Shaut, and Deborah Wojcik, In addition, Kelly Biedenweg and Deb Wojcik authored the majority of the teaching activities that accompany this text in the Instructor's Guide, and Annie Oxarart assisted with the pilot course evaluation.

Finally, we would like to express our appreciation to Paul Drougas, the John Wiley & Sons acquisition editor, who supported the idea of this book from the beginning, Nancy Cintron, the Production Editor, and Michael New, editorial assistant to Paul Drougas.

The Authors
Gainesville, Florida

Introduction

New technologies abound, and they are being developed at an ever-increasing pace. Rapid technological advances sweeping through society have become the norm. Much of the technology that has reshaped society in the last century has become so commonplace that many hardly recognize it as technology at all. Cars, computers, and cell phones have become such integral parts of day-to-day life that their absence in a given situation is often more remarkable than their presence. As a result, it is easy to overlook the profound impact technology has had on the global community. Through technology, human beings have reached a larger population size and had a greater impact on global environmental systems than could have been imagined just a mere century ago, when urban travel for the majority was limited to a horse-drawn carriage and communiqués between continents were sent by ship.

This book is about making good decisions about the development and use of technology. More specifically, it is about making decisions that promote sustainability, a concept that has achieved broad support, yet remains difficult to implement. In this book we define sustainability as the balanced pursuit of three goods: ecological health, social equity, and economic welfare. It is grounded in an ethical commitment to the welfare of contemporary populations as well as the well-being and enhanced opportunities of future generations. The scientific and technical professions have a special responsibility in this regard because the knowledge and technologies they develop and employ have immense impacts on natural environments, economies, and the empowerment of citizens and societies. Moreover, their efforts and achievements can continue to produce effects, for good or ill, well into the future.

Sustainability is inherently ethical, as it requires decisions to be rooted in moral principles, rather than based solely on economic calculation or convenience. Broadly speaking, sustainability requires that we do not undermine opportunities for others as we strive to meet our own needs. The others whom we must take into account include future human generations and the least well off contemporary citizens and societies, as well as natural creatures and place. This book provides natural and social scientists, engineers, architects, builders, and other professionals with a clear description of the meaning of sustainability and a practical guide to the ethical challenges involved in its promotion and achievement.

MAKING CONNECTIONS

The relations among ethics, sustainability, and technological development are complex and extremely varied. A number of important issues recur, however, including most significantly the problem of balancing different goods and values when not all can be maximized or prioritized equally. Sometimes, in fact, the pursuit of one good conflicts with or harms the possibility of pursuing another, also important, good. Environmental health or social justice, for example, may be compromised by the pursuit of economic security. In addition, differences in values, access to information, and available resources and technology can cause diverse constituencies—all of whom value sustainability—to approach the challenge in different ways. In order to explore some of these issues in more detail, we offer two examples that highlight some of the challenges facing professionals and policy makers in search of greater sustainability.

For the first example, we turn to the Democratic Republic of Congo (DRC), an African country with the second largest block of tropical forest in the world, covering 62 percent of the nation's territory. Tropical forests are considered valuable ecologically because of their high biological diversity, and the forests in the eastern region of the DRC are particularly diverse. Currently, they provide habitat to a number of endangered species, including mountain and lowland gorillas and elephants, In addition, they are home to many of the 71 million Congolese, who are dependent on the forests for their livelihoods. All of these factors make the DRC a fitting subject for inquiry into environmental management and sustainability. What makes this topic particularly pertinent to this book is that the DRC also has some of the largest tantalum reserves in the world.

Coming in as number 73 on the periodic table, tantalum may not get a lot of attention in chemistry classes. However, it is a rare and vital resource in the production of a wide variety of electronics, including cellular phones and computers. As demand for electronic products soared in the 1990s, so did the demand for tantalum. The DRC has been mired in military conflict since the mid-1990s, including a civil war that involved troops from several African nations and a United Nations peace-keeping force 17,000 strong. The death toll has reached over four million. The presence of tantalum is central to the conflict.[1]

In addition to the tremendous hardships felt by the people of the Congo, the lack of governmental control over mining activities has resulted in significant ecological damage. The increase in prices produced a gold-rush mentality in the DRC, with people shifting from other activities—including gold mining and farming—in order to search for coltan, the dark gray ore that contains tantalum. The shift brought many people within the boundaries of the Kahuzi-Biega National Park, one of the five UNESCO Natural Heritage sites in the country. The process of coltan mining itself can have significant impacts to the landscape and streams. In addition, the people attracted to the coltan-rich area have hunted the wildlife, including thousands of lowland gorillas and elephants, for food and other uses, resulting in the loss of the vast majority of gorillas and all of the elephants in the park.[2]

Clearly this is an example of unsustainable development. From an economic perspective much of the local revenue that could be raised has been lost through black market trade of coltan through neighboring Rwanda and Uganda. From a social perspective, the presence of the valuable resource exacerbated existing tensions and contributed to the creation of a social climate characterized by fear and aggression. In this socioeconomic climate, ecological concern (which has historically been higher in DRC than other African countries) became a very low priority. This is not just a story about occurrences in a faraway place, however. Each of us may contain a small piece of this story in the cell phones, laptop computers, DVD players, and other electronics that we use every day.[3]

In 2010, the United States passed legislation requiring companies to demonstrate that their products are not fueling the conflict in the DRC.[4] Certainly this is part of the solution, but tracking the source of tantalum can be difficult. Some have suggested a more comprehensive approach, namely regulating the coltan industry in the DRC in order to harness long-term economic gains, foster social improvements, and keep mining activity out of national parks and other ecologically sensitive areas.[5] However, in the context of the current political instability of the region, such a solution presents daunting and long-term challenges.

The issue of tantalum in the DRC is an unfinished story. While some recent developments are positive, much of the challenge still lies ahead. This example illustrates the profound and unexpected effects that technological developments and our collective behavior as consumers can have. The point is not to stop using or developing electronics. The challenge is to develop sustainable alternatives to ecological, social, and economic relationships that jeopardize long-term welfare. One need not go to faraway lands to find examples of unsustainable practices and the ethical responsibilities that they demonstrate. At home and abroad, we are faced with the challenge of securing better ways to meet basic needs and pursue prosperity.

SHIFTING TOWARD SUSTAINABILITY

A second example illuminates further issues involved in pursuing sustainability, this time in the context of a particular business enterprise. In 1994, Ray Anderson, the founder of Interface, Inc., a company that produces carpets, was preparing a talk for his sales staff on the company's approach to the environment. He realized two things: first, his company's approach to the environment up to that time was focused merely on compliance with the law, and second, his company was in his words "plundering the earth." More than that, he realized that this was the accepted way of doing business.

Anderson decided that he wanted to change the way his company did business in order to make it a "restorative enterprise" with zero waste and zero harm to the biosphere, and he wanted to do this by 2020. It was an ambitious goal. As a carpet company, Interface, Inc. was dependent on fossil fuels not only for its energy but also as a raw material in its carpets. Anderson developed what he called seven fronts of sustainability to guide his company towards its goal.[6]

- *Eliminate waste*: Eliminate all forms of waste in every area of business.

- *Benign emissions:* Eliminate toxic emissions from products, vehicles, and facilities.

- *Renewable energy*: Operate facilities with renewable energy sources.

- *Closing the loop*: Redesign processes and products to close the technical loop using recovered and bio-based materials.

- *Resource-efficient transportation*: Transport people and products efficiently to eliminate waste emissions.

- *Sensitizing stakeholders*: Create a culture that uses sustainability principles to improve the lives and livelihoods of all our stakeholders—employees, partners, suppliers, customers, investors, and communities

- *Redesign commerce*: Create a new business model that demonstrates and supports the value of sustainability-based commerce

As of 2007, the changes implemented in Interface, Inc. resulted in a 45 percent reduction in fossil fuel use and an 80 percent reduction in the waste stream to landfills.

Perhaps more importantly for stockholders, profits were up 49 percent. Anderson considered himself 45 percent of the way toward his goal for 2020.[7] Interface employees attribute their successes to a combination of Anderson's determination and consistent vision of sustainability, as well as a bottom-up approach that allowed all employees to play a role in determining specific approaches to the seven fronts.[8] Clearly his answer to sustainability is not only what is accomplished but also how it happens.

As a result of this success, Anderson has become in much demand as a speaker on industrial sustainability, and he has opened up a separate consulting division of Interface, Inc. devoted specifically to assisting other companies make similar changes. Of course, the measures taken by Interface, Inc., while admirable, are far from achieving full-scale sustainability. Interface does not control what happens further up the supply chain. And even within the company, Anderson acknowledges that several of the changes are only temporary measures (e.g., offsetting carbon emissions by planting trees) undertaken until more sustainable processes can be implemented (e.g., a complete shift to renewable energy). Still, Interface has become an impressive example of how sustainability can be profitable for a company and spur innovation.

THE STRUCTURE OF THIS BOOK

The pursuit of sustainability is grounded in value judgments. Often discussions about sustainability neglect this important fact. It is tempting, particularly for those with a technological background, to view sustainability primarily as a technological issue. To be sure, technology will play a significant role in meeting the challenges that lie ahead, but technology addresses the question: What can we do? There is a prior question that goes to the issue of values: What should we do? This book explores the ethical foundations and concepts involved in answering this latter question. In turn, this book describes a number of the tools and skills involved in implementing decisions that reflect our values.

Chapters 1 through 3 provide the context for this discussion. Chapter 1, "A Context for Sustainability," introduces basic concepts and provides an overview of some of the most pressing challenges we face today.

Chapter 2, "The Technology Challenge," explores the role of technology as it shapes— and is shaped by—society. It provides an overview of the history of technology as well as discussion of the impacts—both positive and negative—that it has on society.

Chapter 3, "Introduction to Ethical Concepts," provides an overview of the field of ethics. The ethics of sustainability is in many ways a continuation of conversations held over millennia regarding what it means to do good or lead a good life. This chapter explores some major themes in ethical thought from religious and philosophical traditions that are particularly relevant to a discussion of sustainability.

Chapters 4 through 7 explore the three pillars of the ethics of sustainability. Chapter 4,

"The Social Dimensions of Sustainability Ethics," focuses on ethical relationships and responsibilities between people and communities. It explores core principles and the challenge involved in concretely realizing these principles with regard to people around the globe and in future generations.

In Chapter 5, "The Ecological Dimensions of Sustainability Ethics," we examine the relationships between people and the environmental systems that support them. Incorporating nonhumans and even ecosystems or biomes into an ethical framework has had a profound impact on the way people view ethics. In this chapter, we explore the ethical components of ecological relationships.

Chapter 6, "The Economic Dimensions of Sustainability Ethics," explores the development, insights and shortcomings of the neoclassical economic model. We focus specifically on the development of the study and practice of ecological economics, where scholars are attempting to include biophysical aspects of natural resources in economic analyses.

Chapter 7, "Integrating the Dimensions of Sustainability Ethics," discusses the challenge of combining the social, ecological, and economic facets of sustainability. It presents the concept of complex adaptive systems as a tool for developing a framework of sustainability that can integrate its various dimensions.

Chapters 8 through 10 turn to the more practical issue of applying the ethics of sustainability to decision making. In Chapter 8, "Improving Our Thinking about Sustainability," we investigate how making good decisions requires changing the way that we think and learn. We identify a number of common patterns people fall into when processing information that can lead to misconceptions regarding sustainability, and we discuss how to change these patterns.

Chapter 9, "The Process of Changing Behavior," grapples with the problem that a sound ethical foundation and a clear understanding of the issues are still not enough to bring about behavior that fosters sustainability. It identifies several other factors that influence people's decisions, including structural barriers, attitudes, force of habit, and what other people think.

Chapter 10, "Creating Change with Groups," describes the importance of collective action and institutional change. Whether working with a handful of employees or government leaders from around the globe, the dynamics of orchestrating change with groups follow similar patterns. Facilitating communication among people possessing different perspectives and goals is a daunting challenge central to the task of pursuing sustainability.

Chapter 11, "Applying an Ethic of Sustainability," reviews the ideas and concepts addressed in earlier chapters. In addition it describes current approaches to putting concepts of sustainability into practice. Finally, it provides the Case Study of the Ford Corporation to illustrate how the ethics of sustainability have been (or could have been) applied.

In our attempts to move toward sustainability, there are myriad paths and directions that we might take. In order to succeed, we must approach the challenge thoughtfully, guided by both a sound ethical framework and a realistic understanding of human behavior. The goal of *Working toward Sustainability* is to provide readers with (1) an understanding of the meaning of sustainability, (2) a sound ethical foundation for navigating the difficult challenges associated with pursuing sustainability, and (3) a practical assessment of processes and problems associated with decision making and being agents of change. Throughout the book, we provide short case studies and examples that help us meet these goals by illustrating concepts, ideas, and practical issues.

REFERENCES

All Party Parliamentary Group on the Great Lakes and Genocide Prevention. 2002. *Cursed by Riches: Who benefits from resource exploitation in the Democratic Republic of the Congo?* www.savethechildren.org.uk/en/docs/cursed_by_riches.pdf.

Hayes, Karen and Richard Burge. 2003. *Coltan Mining in the Democratic Republic of Congo: How tantalum-using industries can commit to the reconstruction of the DRC.* Washington, DC: Flora and Fauna International. www.vodafone.com/etc/medialib/attachments/cr_downloads.Par.74638.File.dat/FFI_Coltan_report.pdf.

Dean, C. 2007. "Executive on a mission: Saving the planet." *New York Times* on the Web May 22. www.nytimes.com/2007/05/22/science/earth/22ander.

Montague, D. 2002. "Stolen goods: Coltan and conflict in the Democratic Republic of the Congo." *SAIS Review* XXII(1): 103–118.

Stubbs, W. and C. Cocklin. 2008. "An ecological modernist interpretation of sustainability: the case of Interface Inc." *Business Strategy and the Environment* 17: 512–523.

United Nations. 2001. *Report of the Panel of Experts on the Illegal Exploitation of Natural Resources and Other Forms of Wealth of the Democratic Republic of the Congo.*

ENDNOTES

1. See United Nations (2001).
2. All Party Parliamentary Group on the Great Lakes and Genocide Prevention (2002).
3. A United Nations (2001) report discusses letters that link Rwandan companies that allegedly finance military operations in the Congo with illicit coltan to clients from the United States and Western Europe, but it is very difficult at this point for the consumers to know where the coltan came from in a particular electronic device. In this book we discuss changes at the individual level (e.g., making socially, ecologically, and economically responsible choices) and the institutional level (e.g., providing individuals with information necessary to make those choices).
4. See Dodd-Frank Wall Street Reform and Consumer Protection Act H.R. 4173.
5. Hayes and Burge (2003).
6. The following bullets are quoted from Interface's website: www.interfaceglobal .com/Sustainability/Our-Journey/7-Fronts-of-Sustainability.aspx
7. Dean (2007).
8. Stubbs and Cocklin (2008).

Working toward Sustainability

CHAPTER 1

A Context for Sustainability

Sustainability is a concept that, over the past two decades, has continued to gain traction in a wide range of institutions and sectors, from national to local governments, from agriculture to tourism, and from manufacturing to construction. Domestically and internationally, sustainability is employed as a key criterion in governmental and business decisions, in consumer choices, and in individual lifestyles. As a concept and practice, sustainability is invoked to address issues as diverse as energy production, building design, waste disposal, urban planning, social welfare, and local and national economies. Universities and schools are applying sustainability to guide changes to their campuses, curriculum, governance, investments, procurement policies, and relationships to their local communities. In short, sustainability is a framework upon which increasing numbers of individuals and organizations ground their decisions and policies. In this chapter, we take a closer look at the concept of sustainability and the context in which it has developed.

THE RATIONALE FOR SUSTAINABILITY

There are at least 70 documented definitions of *sustainable development* or its sister term *sustainability*. Our goal here is neither to list all the contenders nor to add to their numbers. Rather, we provide a sense of the basic principles of sustainability, first through a series of hypothetical scenarios and second through a brief explanation of how the concept was developed.

Sustainability Interlude

At its most basic, the concept of sustainability is relatively straightforward. In our first scenario, our hero—call him Lucky—has been given a trust fund of one million dollars that receives 10 percent interest a year. This gives Lucky an annual income of $100,000 in interest. In order to use this trust fund sustainably, Lucky must take out no more than $100,000 from the fund each year. If he does that, then the fund will never diminish, and the original million dollars will continuously produce income for Lucky and his descendents. Thus, we have identified the essence of sustainability: using a resource no faster than the resource can replenish itself.

For our second scenario, suppose that the fund is no longer something as static

1

BOX 1.1   Sustainability Is Being Adopted by a Growing Number and Variety of Organizations

One can see increased focus on sustainability in political and corporate contexts. Several countries have articulated policies centered on sustainability, using it as a framework on which to base integrated strategies covering the environment, the economy, and quality of life. For example, the United Kingdom embraces sustainability as part of its national policy as articulated in "Securing the Future—The UK Sustainable Development Strategy." Similarly the European Union Sustainable Development Strategy describes the EU's approach to sustainable development and the seven key challenges facing its implementation.

A significant number of Fortune 500 corporations, including Nike, Coca-Cola, Dell Computer, and Starbucks Coffee are embracing sustainability as a strategy in the form of corporate social responsibility (CSR). Sustainability is a framework for ecological, economic, and social policies and programs that continues to grow in importance and is finding application in an ever wider range of circumstances. For example, the highly successful green building movement started by the U.S. Green Building Council in the United States is based on the concept of sustainability, providing a useful template for implementation in other sectors.

and homogenous as a pile of cash. Instead, it is a mixture of resources each with different and varying growth rates, and those growth rates prove very difficult to predict. Some years the interest could be well over $100,000. Other years it could be much less. In this case, Lucky must watch the fund closely to be able to respond to any unforeseen changes. The added complexity of the fund makes the prospect of withdrawing beyond sustainable levels more likely when the needs for these resources are great.

For our third scenario, suppose a much larger fund was left to Lucky and seven billion of his closest relatives and friends—call them collectively the Global Population. In this situation, responding to changes in the growth rates of the fund's resources becomes much more difficult, as communication between all the recipients and coordination of activity is well nigh impossible. In turn, not everyone will agree about which of those resources or benefits are important or about who has a claim to them. Under such circumstances sustaining the original capital in the fund and receiving a fair share of the interest for each of the seven billion participants is a mighty challenge.

The concept of sustainability itself is fairly straightforward. Achieving sustainability in the real world presents a daunting and complex challenge.

A Response to a Crisis

The concept of sustainability has its roots in what might be called "the crisis of development," that is, the failure since World War II of international development schemes intended to improve the lot of impoverished peoples around the world. The proportion of those living in abject poverty has remained relatively steady over the past 60 years, around 1 in 5 people. The poor continue to live on the edge of survival, with shortened lifespan, abominable living conditions, malnutrition, disease, and little prospect for a better future. Often they live in countries crushed by the burden of debt, with poor infrastructure, almost no educational system, the lack of a functioning justice system, and in the shadow of omnipresent violence. Simultaneously the world is facing environmental crises and resource shortages that compound the problem for the world's poorest and place stress on even the wealthier nations as energy prices rise, climate patterns shift, and the Earth's store of biodiversity dwindles.

In 1983 the United Nations convened the World Commission on Environment and Development to address these problems. This Commission (later called the Brundtland Commission after its chair, Norwegian Prime Minister Gro Harlem Brundtland) set about the task of developing ways to address the deterioration of natural resources and the decrease of the quality of life on a global scale. In its 1987 report, the Brundtland Commission described this problem as stemming from a rapid growth in human population and consumption and a concomitant decline in the capacity of the earth's natural systems to meet human needs (see Figure 1.1).

After describing the problem, the Brundtland Commission identified two main imperatives needed to correct this imbalance. First, the basic needs of all human beings must be met and poverty eliminated. Second, there must be limits placed on development in general because nature is finite. The commission also provided a definition for sustainable development that is still widely cited today: "Sustainable development is development that meets the needs of the present without compromising the ability of future generations to meet their own needs."[1]

The Brundtland definition provides a new vision of development—optimistic in tone but laced with challenges and contradictions. It suggests that we have a moral responsibility to consider the welfare of both present and future inhabitants of our planet—a serious task indeed. It would mean that wealthier, more technologically sophisticated societies would have to contribute through a wide range of assistance programs to help poorer nations develop the capability to provide the basic needs of their population. However, we cannot use up the world's resources in the effort. Future generations have to be considered, as well.

Most definitions of sustainability propose that the welfare of present and future generations can be achieved only by balancing environmental protection and restoration with a healthy economy and social justice. The following section briefly describes some of the issues that are forcing a rethinking of conventional approaches to policy, production, and consumption with this balance in mind.

FIGURE 1.1 The report of the Brundtland Commission was published in 1987 with the title *Our Common Future,* and it was responsible for popularizing the sustainability concept.

BOX 1.2 Some Additional Definitions of Sustainability

Although the Brundtland definition of sustainability is the one most often cited, there are a wide variety of other variants, some short and some long, A few of these are listed here to give a flavor of the different points of view of its meaning.

"A transition to sustainability involves moving from linear to cyclical processes and technologies. The only processes we can rely on indefinitely are cyclical; all linear processes must eventually come to an end."

Dr. Karl Henrik-Robert, MD, founder of The Natural Step, Sweden

"Actions are sustainable if:

There is a balance between resources used and resources regenerated.

Resources are as clean or cleaner at end use as at beginning.

The viability, integrity, and diversity of natural systems are restored and maintained.

They lead to enhanced local and regional self-reliance.

They help create and maintain community and a culture of place.

Each generation preserves the legacies of future generations."

David McCloskey, Professor of Sociology, Seattle University

"Clean air, clean water, safety in city parks, low-income housing, education, child care, welfare, medical care, unemployment (insurance), transportation, recreation/cultural centers, open space, wetlands . . ."

Hazel Wolf, Seattle Audubon Society

"Leave the world better than you found it, take no more than you need, try not to harm life or the environment, make amends if you do."

Paul Hawken, *The Ecology of Commerce*

"Sustainable development is a 'metafix' that will unite everybody from the profit-minded industrialist and risk-minimising subsistence farmer to the equity-seeking social worker, the pollution-concerned or wildlife-loving First Worlder, the growth-maximising policy maker, the goal-oriented bureaucrat and, therefore, the vote-counting politician."

Sharachchandra Lélé

CONTEMPORARY CHALLENGES

Numerous books and articles have been devoted to each of the challenges covered in this section. The content provided here is a brief overview of each of the issues discussed. We encourage the interested reader to review the notes and references for further reading suggestions. However, the information provided here should be sufficient to understand the discussion and examples in the later chapters. Many of these examples appear to be primarily about the environment. However, approaching these problems in the context of sustainability requires looking at the social and economic impacts of any attempts to address them.

Population and Consumption

In recent decades, global population has grown at an astonishing rate. The world's population doubled in about 44 years, from 3.4 billion in 1965 to 6.8 billion in 2009, and is projected to reach 9.4 billion by 2050.[2] Much has been said about the role of population growth as the cause of many global problems (see Figures 1.2 and 1.3). The resources required to feed, clothe, and house the earth's still rapidly growing human population are enormous. To make matters more complicated, per capita consumption has also been growing even faster than population, so that even if population growth slows, each generation of human beings uses more resources than the last.

In general, developing countries tend to have higher population growth, while industrialized countries tend to have higher per capita consumption. However, per capita consumption

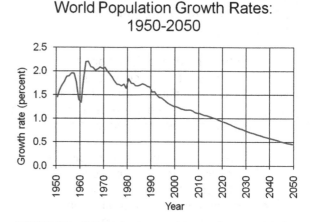

FIGURE 1.3 If there is any good news about population growth, it is that the rate of growth is decreasing, from over 2.0 percent in 1970 to about 1.1 percent at present. Projections are that the rate of growth will continue to fall to under 0.5 percent in 2050. *(Source: U.S. Census Bureau, International Data Base, June 2010 Update)*

in developing countries, especially India and China, has been climbing in the past few decades. The higher level of consumption not only diminishes global natural resources but also increases waste production and pollution. Indeed, the world's wealthiest countries have less than 20 percent of the world's population, yet contribute roughly 40 percent of global carbon emissions and are responsible for more than 60 percent of the total carbon dioxide that fossil fuel combustion has added to the atmosphere since the Industrial Revolution began. To pursue sustainability, the so-called "twin horns of the dilemma," population and consumption, must both be addressed.

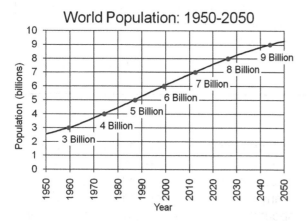

FIGURE 1.2 World population in 2011 is about 7 billion, increasing by about 75 million people each year. *(Source: U.S. Census Bureau, International Data Base, June 2010 Update)*

Climate Change

In 1988, the World Meteorological Organization (WMO) and the United Nations (UN) established the Intergovernmental Panel on

BOX 1.3 The Challenge of Decreasing Population Growth: Thailand

In the 1970s Thailand had one of the highest rates of population growth in the world—roughly twice the global average. Understanding the strain that this rate of growth would put on national resources, the government in coordination with the nongovernmental organization the Population and Community Development Association (PDA) began a provocative and innovative campaign to encourage its citizens to adopt contraceptives. One challenge was making the technology— including condoms, oral contraceptives, and injectable contraceptives—available to the population. This challenge was addressed with government financing to make these contraceptives available for free.

The larger challenge, however, was getting the people to use these technologies. Thai citizens were reluctant to talk openly about matters regarding sex. These inhibitions proved to be barriers to education about—and adoption of—contraceptives. The response to this challenge was an aggressive social marketing campaign led by economist Mechai Viravaidya, who has come to be known as Mr. Contraception. Viravaidya explained, "I wanted to remove the taboo, take birth control out of the realm of the secretive and make it fun" (Sexes 1981). To that end, the government and the PDA developed a public awareness campaign that included balloon-blowing contests in which public officials would inflate and pop condoms, a distribution program in which police would distribute condoms during traffic jams (which Viravaidya called "Cops and Rubbers"), and a contraceptive-themed chain of restaurants used to finance family-planning services. In addition, family-planning services were closely linked to economic development programs to emphasize the connection between family planning and economic welfare.

The program has been quite successful, reducing Thailand's growth rate to less than a quarter of its peak rate in the 1970s. In addition, the program has been credited for greatly reducing the spread of HIV/AIDS. In 2007, the PDA received a Gates Award from the Bill and Melinda Gates Foundation in recognition of its accomplishments in the area of family planning and HIV/AIDS reduction. The methods were unorthodox, but Thailand's family planning program has become an internationally admired example of how public awareness campaigns can be used to address the challenges of sustainability. We will discuss these ideas in greater detail in Chapters 9 and 10.

Climate Change (IPCC) to assess the scientific, technical, and socioeconomic information relevant to climate change. The Fourth Assessment Report of the IPCC, published in 2007, concludes that the globally averaged surface temperatures have increased by 0.3 ± 0.1°C (0.6 ± 0.2°F) over the twentieth century. The globally averaged surface air temperature is projected by models to warm 0.8 to 3.2°C (1.4° to 5.8°F) by 2100.[3]

At first glance, these temperatures may not seem like much, but they would result in major environmental and social changes. Sea level rise is perhaps the most discussed with models projecting 0.30 to 2.9 feet (0.09 to 0.88 meters) increase by 2100, which would put low-lying coastal areas, such as the Mississippi River delta, most coastal cities, and many island nations at risk. Many cities and nations (e.g., The Netherlands) already devote considerable resources to flood control. Sea level rise exacerbates this problem. The temperature shift would also change regional climactic patterns.

IPCC projections indicate that the warming would vary by region and be accompanied by both increases and decreases in precipitation. Ecologically, such changes would place added stress on many of the world's most highly valued ecosystems (e.g., coral reefs). In a social and economic context, even slight temperature increases would mean a shift and even decreases in agricultural production (see Figure 1.4). No doubt some of those changes would be positive, such as longer growing seasons in northern regions. However, traditionally fertile regions may become too hot or too dry to continue to support agriculture. Adjusting an agricultural system in response to these climactic shifts would be a major undertaking. As ecosystems change, insect populations will shift as well. Some projections suggest that mosquito-borne diseases will become problems in many new areas of the world.

Changes in the Earth's climate are the rule rather than the exception, and there is ample evidence that, over the past several million years, there have been significant shifts in the Earth's average annual temperature. Such a historical perspective can perhaps provide some comfort. On a geological scale, atmospheric greenhouse gases are likely to go back to pre-industrial levels over the next several million years. However, human beings do not live at a geological scale, and the potential for climate change has profound implications for every aspect of human activity on the planet. Shifting temperatures, diminished agricultural output, more violent storms, rising sea levels, and melting glaciers will displace people, affect food supplies, reduce biodiversity, and greatly alter the quality of life.

Nonrenewable Resource Depletion

Evidence to date seems to indicate that we have maximized our ability to extract oil and

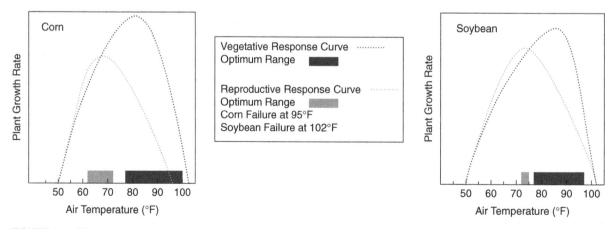

FIGURE 1.4 Rising temperatures have the potential to dramatically affect food production. As indicated in this graphic, growth of corn and soybeans drops off with higher temperatures and reproduction ceases at temperatures above 95°F for corn and above 102°F for soybeans. (*Source: U.S. Department of Agriculture*)

that we are in an era of probably far higher prices for oil-based products, among them gasoline, diesel, jet fuel, and oil-based polymers. A similar scenario is playing out with other key nonrenewable resources, most notably metals. Researchers Robert Gordon, M. Bertram, and Thomas Gradel suggest that the supply of copper, zinc, and other metals—even if recycled—may soon fail to meet the needs of the global population.[4] In other words, even the full extraction of metals from the Earth's crust and extensive recycling programs may not meet future demand if all countries try and attain the same standard of living enjoyed in developed nations.

Gordon and colleagues found that all of the copper in ore, plus all of the copper currently in use, would be required to bring the world to the level of the developed nations for power transmission, construction, and other services and products that depend on copper. Globally, the researchers estimate that 26 percent of extractable copper in the Earth's crust is now lost in nonrecycled wastes, while lost zinc is estimated at 19 percent. While copper and zinc are not at risk of depletion in the immediate future, the researchers believe scarce metals, such as platinum, are at risk of depletion in this century because there is currently no suitable substitute for their use in devices such as catalytic converters and hydrogen fuel cells. Further, because the rate of use for metals continues to rise, even the more plentiful metals may face similar depletion risks in the not too distant future. While there is a renewed emphasis on recycling and efficiency, such measures will only slow down the rate of depletion.[5]

Loss of Biodiversity

Biodiversity can be measured on several scales. For example, ecologists talk about a diversity of habitats (e.g., wetlands, hardwood forests), a diversity of species, and the genetic diversity within one population. Thus, biodiversity expresses the range and variety of life on the planet, considering the relative abundance of ecosystems, species, and genes. Human diversity includes cultures and languages as well. These diverse ecosystems and species provide numerous services and resources, such as protection and formation of water and soil resources; nutrient storage and cycling, pollution breakdown and absorption, food, medicinal resources, wood products, aquatic habitat, and undoubtedly many undiscovered applications.[6] Thus, one might view biodiversity as a stock of potential solutions to problems—past, present, and those not yet encountered or even predicted. From this view, preserving biodiversity has a high priority. Once lost, species cannot be replaced by human technology, and potential sources of new foods, medicines, and other technologies may be forever forfeited.

Most of the time when people talk about loss of biodiversity, they mean loss of species. Species loss occurs primarily because of habitat loss or degradation, as humans burn down, plough up, build upon, pave over, or pollute massive acreages of forests, scrublands, grasslands, wetlands, and coral reefs. Over half the world's wetlands and original tropical and temperate forests are already gone. Rainforests, which support 60 percent of the world's species, are disappearing at a rate of 15 million hectares per year.[7] Of course any harvesting of re-sources for consumption involves changing the original ecosystems. Resource manag-ers work to restore or maintain **ecosystem services** and biodiversity, while still utilizing products from these systems. If all species are not retained in the managed system, are there enough? Given the vast number of species, we probably do not even know what we are losing.

Loss of biological diversity is also occurring because of the introduction of exotic (inva-sive) species, which overtake and outcom-pete indigenous flora and fauna. Pollution of air, land, and water as well as overfishing, overhunting, and overharvesting are also major problems. Finally, as noted previously, climate change increasingly appears to be playing a significant role in species decline, and its contribution will likely increase pre-cipitously in the near future.

An estimated 1.7 million species have been scientifically documented out of a total es-timated number of between 5 million and 100 million species. However, habitat loss and climate change are causing such a rapid extinction of many species that some biolo-gists are predicting the loss of 20 percent of existing species over the next 20 years. Given these trends, some suggest that half of all living mammal and bird species today will be extinct within 300 years. Other stud-ies are even more alarming: potentially half of *all* species may become extinct within the next century.[8] Species extinction on such a massive scale undoubtedly will jeopardize the welfare of future generations, and will severely constrict their opportunities.

Overfishing

The Earth's ocean ecosystems contain the majority of all life found on earth, including 22,000 species of fish and ocean mammals, ranging in size from the 150-ton, 40-meter long blue whale to very small fish that feed on microscopic phytoplankton. Oceans were once thought to hold inexhaustible resources. Historical accounts of the seas' bounty abound. For example in the waters off of Newfoundland, early explorers re-ported fish populations so large that they could catch them simply by dipping weighted baskets over the side of the ship. Another account from the same period describes the number of cod in those waters as seeming "to equal that of the grains of sand which cover this bank."[9] Despite this richness, the Newfoundland fishery collapsed in the 1990s leading to a fishing moratorium, putting a severe economic strain on the region where the only employment, and much of the food, was related to fishing. The fishery has still not recovered and may never return to en-able fishing to return to Newfoundland.

This pattern is not unusual in fisheries. When overharvesting decreases populations of particular fish to a point where further fish-ing was no longer profitable, new fisher-ies would be sought.[10] The approach was commercially viable at least in the short term until no more unexploited fisheries could be found. In the 1980s geographical expansion could no longer make up for the loss of pro-ductivity in overexploited fisheries.

There is some disagreement regarding the pervasiveness and severity of collapse in commercially important marine species, but there is broad agreement on the tendency for these species to be overexploited.[11] In a report published by the UN Food and Agriculture Organization, scientists reported that 52 percent of fish stocks are fully exploited, meaning that catch rates are at or near the populations' estimated reproductive rate. Another 17 percent are overexploited, meaning that fish are being caught at rates faster than the populations can reproduce. Seven percent are depleted (i.e., no longer able to support fishing industries), and 1 percent are recovering from depletion.[12]

BOX 1.4   Indirect Effects of Overfishing: Jamaica

When a population of fish becomes overfished, the ability of that population to reproduce decreases, which means that the ability for fishers to benefit economically in a future from those species also decreases. The impact of overfishing goes further, however. For example, in Jamaica decades of fishing pressure has resulted in the decrease of a number of herbivorous fishes, which graze on algae growing on corals. These fishes perform the ecological function of keeping the algae levels on coral reefs low. The long-spined sea urchin (*Diadema antillarum*), prominent on most Caribbean reefs in the early 1980s, performed this same function.

With several species performing similar ecological functions, a coral reef is said to be resilient because changes to any one of the grazing species will not significantly change the reef as a whole. In the case of Jamaica, when the numbers of herbivorous fish decreased because of fishing pressure, the long-spined sea urchins were still able to keep the reefs from becoming overcome with algae. However, as the reefs became more and more dependent on grazing from just one species, they also became less resilient. In other words, a change in the long-spined sea urchin population would mean major changes to the reefs. That change happened in 1983 when a disease broke out killing up to 97 percent of the long-spined sea urchins in the Caribbean (Lessios 1988). The reefs lost the only grazer left, and as a result, corals were smothered by algae growth (Hughs 1994).

In this case, fishing pressure caused the reefs to lose resilience, becoming more susceptible to natural disturbances, such as disease. These impacts—combined with others, including hurricanes and increased nutrients from development—resulted in highly degraded ecosystems. It is not difficult to see how such changes can translate into social and economic changes as well. While Jamaica has a rich fishing history, the most significant economic benefit that Jamaica's reefs provide today comes from tourism, which accounts for more than half of Jamaica's gross domestic product. Many of Jamaica's tourists value seeing high-quality reefs through SCUBA, snorkeling, or glass bottom boat rides. As Jamaica's reefs continue to degrade, those tourists are likely to choose different destinations with healthier reefs, resulting in the loss of income for Jamaica.

The example of Jamaica's reefs remains a much studied case of how subtle changes to an ecosystem can decrease resilience, making that system more susceptible to major problems in the future. The importance of resilience, in ecological, social, and economic contexts, is addressed in more detail in Chapter 7.

The methods used by large commercial fishing are destructive in two ways: they result in overfishing and they degrade the ocean bottom. While overfishing reduces fish numbers directly, the damage done by bottom trawling can destroy habitat, decreasing a fish population's capacity to recover. In addition, declines in specific species of an ecosystem can cause widespread changes in the entire system. Box 1.4 illustrates how these changes can ripple through an ecosystem and affect social and economic systems as well. Other stresses on marine systems, such as increased pollution and climate change, can further decrease an ecosystem's ability to persist in the face of increased fishing pressure.

Eutrophication

One of the most serious forms of pollution affecting waterways and marine systems is the overenrichment of water bodies with nutrients from agricultural and landscape fertilizer, urban runoff, sewage discharge, and eroded stream banks. Nutrient oversupply fosters algae growth, or algae blooms, which block sunlight and cause submerged vegetation to die. This ecological response to the overabundance of nutrients is called eutrophication. Decomposing algae further absorb dissolved oxygen, depriving aquatic species such as fish and crabs. Eventually, algal decomposition in a completely oxygenless, or anoxic, water body can release toxic hydrogen sulphide, poisoning organisms and making the lake or seabed lifeless.

Eutrophication has led to the degradation of numerous waterways around the world.

Perhaps the most famous example is the "dead zone" in the Gulf of Mexico at the mouth of the Mississippi River. Flowing for more than 2,000 miles through the eastern United States, the Mississippi River picks up sediment, fertilizer, and sewage from the agricultural heart of America. When those nutrients reach the Gulf of Mexico, the process of algal growth and decomposition creates an area of almost 6,000 square miles—an area about the size of Connecticut—in which oxygen levels are too low to support most animals (see Figure 1.5).

The reversal of eutrophication in the Black Sea provides a hopeful example. In a situation not unlike the Gulf of Mexico dead zone, the Danube River flows through 11 countries,

FIGURE 1.5 Nutrients from farming and sewage are transported down the Mississippi water shed to the Gulf of Mexico, resulting in eutrophication and the creation of an enormous dead zone, with very low oxygen levels and which is very inhospitable to life. As shown in this satellite image, the dead zone stretches from the southernmost coastal region of Texas as far east as Florida's Gulf Coast (*Source: National Oceanic and Atmospheric Administration*)

carrying a high level of nutrients from agricultural and industrial waste and urban run-off into the Black Sea. Nutrient levels from the Danube increased dramatically from the 1960s to the 1980s largely because of the adoption of industrial farming techniques involving heavy use of fertilizer. The resulting eutrophication created the largest dead zone in the world. However, in 1989 the collapse of the communist regimes in Eastern Europe meant that many of the farmers on the Danube could no longer afford to purchase such large quantities of fertilizer. As a result, the nutrient load coming from the Danube decreased, and within six years the dead zone itself began to decrease. Recovery remains gradual, but it provides researchers with cautious hope regarding the ability to dead zones to become biologically viable again.[13]

Desertification and Acidification

In arid and semiarid regions, land degradation can result in the destruction of natural vegetative cover, which promotes desert formation—a process called desertification. As a result of this process, soil fertility decreases, putting strain on ecosystems as well as agricultural production. Loss of vegetation may reduce an area's ability to absorb water, resulting in flooding or the siltation of water supplies in nearby areas. The United Nations Convention to Combat Desertification, formed in 1996 and ratified by 179 countries, reports that over 250 million people are directly affected by desertification.[14] Furthermore, drylands susceptible to desertification cover 40 percent of the Earth's surface, putting at risk a further 1.1 billion people in more than 100 countries dependent on these lands for survival. For example,

China, with a rapidly growing population and economy, loses about 300,000 acres of arable land each year to drifting sand dunes.

Acidification represents another form of degradation. In this process, air pollution in the form of ammonia, sulphur dioxide, and nitrogen oxides, mainly released into the atmosphere by burning fossil fuels, is converted into acids. The resulting acid rain is well known for its damage to forests and lakes. The acidity of polluted surface and groundwater dissolves minerals in soil and rinses them away. This reduces the amount of nutrients available to vegetation. In addition, acid rain can release substances in the soil that are toxic to vegetation. The decreased nutrients and increased toxics can result in slowed growth or death. Many species of animals, fish, and other aquatic animal and plant life are sensitive to water acidity. The toxic substances released by the acid rain also flow into nearby water bodies and can harm microorganisms and affect the food chain.

As with eutrophication, acid rain is often produced in an area different from the one it affects. Therefore, reducing the effect of acidification often requires a regional approach. Europe experienced a significant decrease in acid rain in the 1990s as a result of European directives that forced the installation of desulphurization systems and discouraged the use of coal as a fossil fuel. Nonetheless, a 1999 survey of forests in Europe found that about 25 percent of all trees had been damaged, largely because of the effects of acidification. As you will see in Chapter 6, the United States has also taken great measures to decrease acidification.

Poverty

Poverty describes the absolute or relative lack of basic goods and services. While poverty is a very broad and variable term, it is helpful as a starting point for discussion of the human social and economic needs that are part of our definition of sustainability. In particular, we find useful the concept of *"absolute* poverty,"* which is "a condition characterized by severe deprivation of basic human needs, including food, safe drinking water, sanitation facilities, health, shelter, education, and information."[15] Absolute poverty can be defined as the absence of any two of the following eight basic needs:[16]

- *Food*: Body Mass Index must be above 16.

- *Safe drinking water*. Water must not come solely from rivers and ponds, and must be available nearby (less than a 15-minute walk each way).

- *Sanitation facilities*: Toilets or latrines must be accessible in or near the home.

- *Health*: Treatment must be received for serious illnesses and pregnancy.

- *Shelter*. Homes must have fewer than four people living in each room. Floors must not be made of dirt, mud, or clay.

- *Education*: Everyone must attend school or otherwise learn to read.

- *Information*: Everyone must have access to newspapers, radios, televisions, computers, or telephones at home.

- *Access to services*: Access to typical services such as education, health, legal, social, and financial (credit) services.

For the purpose of global aggregation and comparison, the World Bank defines absolute poverty as an income of less than $1.25 per day. Poverty estimates released in August 2008 showed that about 1.4 billion people in the developing world were living on less than $1.25 a day in 2005, down from 1.9 billion in 1981.[17] This amounts to a reduction of absolute poverty from 1 in 2 people in 1981 to 1 in 4 people in 2005.[18] This is significant progress. The challenge is to continue with this progress without continuing to degrade ecosystems.

Overall poverty goes beyond absolute poverty to include social discrimination and lack of participation in decision making. This is an important aspect in the context of sustainability. Reducing overall poverty will not simply require more resources reaching those who do not have enough. It will also require adequate political systems that empower people to make choices that affect their own lives.

Ecosystem Services and Quality of Life

Ecosystems provide a wide range of goods and services to humankind at no cost. These goods and services would otherwise be technically difficult and costly to replace. They include production of food and potable water, control of climate and disease, support from the major global-geochemical and nutrient cycles, crop pollination, spiritual and recreational benefits, and the maintenance of biodiversity. In a study conducted by Robert Costanza and his colleagues in 1997, the economic value of these services was estimated to be almost double the global Gross Domestic Product.[19] The conversion of forests and habitat by agriculture, extraction, and development, together with human impacts on seas, oceans, lakes, rivers, and other bodies of water causes a reduction in the wide range of services provided by ecosystems.

THE ETHICAL CONTEXT OF SUSTAINABILITY

The directive of the Brundtland Commission to meet "the needs of the present without compromising the ability of future generations to meet their own needs" proposes a novel ethical concept. It frames the rights of both present and future peoples, juxtaposes the rights of future versus present generations, and suggests that everyone's needs should be fulfilled before the wants of some are addressed. This view raises several questions. For example, can future individuals have rights? How is it possible to address the needs of future peoples when the needs of the vast majority of the world's present population are not being met? What exactly are the "needs" that must be met, and how might these be prioritized?

Another lens through which to view the issue of future generations is that our ancestors have greatly benefited us and that we have a similar obligation to the future. The Japanese concept of *On* is close to that of obligation. *On* requires that one make past payment to one's ancestors by giving equally good or better conditions or things to posterity. Future persons may be thought of as proxies for past generations to whom present people owe debts. These debts are repaid by providing as much or more to future generations as our ancestors did for us.[20]

In addition to the positive benefits that must be passed on to future generations, harmful consequences must not be passed on. Many of the present day's technologies are likely to pose ominous threats to future generations: genetic engineering, nanotechnology, chemicals, antibiotics, pesticides, and nuclear reactors and their fuel cycles, to name but a few. The resources we take, the products we make, and the resulting waste streams pose enormous challenges for future generations. Consequently if sustainability suggests an obligation to the well-being of future generations, how to deal with technology development and application must be an issue of great concern.

THE THREE-LEG MODEL OF SUSTAINABILITY

It should be clear by now that sustainability is a broad term encompassing a number of different concepts and goals. While the key to sustainability is integrating all of these concepts and goals, the concepts must first be understood before they can be integrated. To facilitate that process, we have divided them into three sets of interconnected concepts: social, ecological, and economic. Social sustainability generally refers to the consequences of a process to the social fabric of a community. It involves culture, justice, decision-making opportunities, and equity. Ecological sustainability focuses on the health of the ecosystems that support both human and nonhuman life. Economic sustainability focuses on the economic viability of a process, project, enterprise, or community.

Sustainability can be considered on a wide range of scales, from a single development to multinational or global policies. To better understand these three legs, consider a proposed tourism development in a developing country. To assess the development's social sustainability, one would look into the impacts of tourism on the local community. How will the influx of tourists disrupt or enhance local traditions and values? What are the social costs associated with the development, and who will have to bear those costs? Will the wealth generated be distributed so as to foster social justice? Who will run the businesses, and will the community have decision-making power?

To assess the development's ecological sustainability, one would focus on the impacts of the development on the local ecosystem. How will new construction and added visitors affect the quality of the ecosystems that support local life? How will such a development affect nonhuman species in the area? Changes in water, air, noise, lights, soil composition, or migration routes could have direct and local impacts as well as indirect and regional impacts.

To assess the economic sustainability, one would focus on the economic viability and impact of the project. Will the enterprise be profitable in the long term? Will these profits be secured without externalizing costs to local, regional, or global stakeholders? What

types of jobs and business opportunities will be created, and what will their long-term impacts be?

For sustainability to be the outcome, these three systems must be balanced. Hence the popular depiction of sustainability as a three-legged stool: to serve its function well, the three legs of the sustainability stool must be roughly of equal length (see Figure 1.6).

The ecological, economic, and social legs of sustainability are easy enough to distinguish in theory. In reality, the social and economic component are fully embedded in Earth's ecological systems and could not exist without a thriving global environment. Therefore, the three-legged stool metaphor is perhaps most useful if it is not viewed in an overly rigid way, but simply as a tool for beginning to understand the vast and complicated topic of sustainability. Its faults notwithstanding, the three-legged stool provides a way of breaking up the concepts that comprise sustainability

FIGURE 1.6 The three-legged stool model is one of the more popular models used for understanding and exploring the concept of sustainability. *(Source: Texas State Energy Conservation Office)*

into understandable—if not mutually exclusive—parts. Therefore, Chapters 4 through 6 of this text are organized according to these three components. Before focusing on the ethical issues relevant to sustainability, however, we will take a closer look at the role of technology in the development of society and the role, or roles, it will likely play in the context of sustainability.

CONCLUSION

Sustainability is a concept and practice that has been applied to guide citizens, organizations, government, and corporations onto a path where both present and future generations have the opportunity for a high quality of life. At its core, sustainability is about ethics. It calls on us not only to consider the condition of those less fortunate than us who share the planet, but also the potential condition of future populations who cannot participate in our decision-making processes.

Clearly we are at a significant fork in the road, with the consequences of climate change and resource depletion on the horizon. Our welfare and the fate of future generations are on the line. Sustainability forces us to think through the consequences of our behavior and act responsibly.

REFERENCES

Costanza, R., d'Arge, R., de Groot, R., Farber, S., Grasso, M., Hannon, B., Limburg, K., Naeem, S., O'Neill, R., Paruelo, J., Raskin, R.G., Sutton, P., and van den Belt, M. 1997. "The value of the world's ecosystem services and natural capital" *Nature*, 387, pp. 253–260.

Essington, Timothy, Ann Beaudreau, and John Wiedenmann. 2006. "Fishing through the marine food webs." *Proceedings of the National Academy of Sciences* 103(9): 3171–3175.

Food & Agriculture Organization of the United Nations. 2006. "State of the World Fisheries and Aquaculture Report 2006," www.fao.org/docrep/009/A0699e/A0699e00.htm.

"Global Environmental Problems: Implications for U.S. Policy," 2003. Watson Institute for International Studies, Brown University (January 2003), available at www.choices.edu.

Gordon, David R. 2005. "Indicators of Poverty & Hunger," *Expert Group Meeting on Youth Development Indicators*, United Nations Headquarters, New York, pp. 12–14 December. Available at www.un.org/esa/socdev/unyin/documents/ydiDavidGordon_poverty.pdf.

Gordon, R. B., M. Bertram, and T. E. Graedel. 2006. "Metal stocks and sustainability," *Proceedings of the National Academy of Sciences*, 103(5), January 26, pp. 1209–1214.

Hutchings, Jeffrey. 2000. "Collapse and recovery of marine fishes." *Nature* 406: 882–885.

Jackson, Jeremy. 2001. "Historical overfishing and the recent collapse of coastal systems." *Science* 293:629–638.

Lessios, H. A. 1988. Mass mortality of *Diadema antillarum* in the Caribbean: What have we learned? *Annual Revue of Ecology and Systematics* 19:371–393.

Levin, Phillip and Donald Levin. 2003. "The real biodiversity crisis." *American Scientist* 90(1): 6.

"Materials Prices Dictate Creative Engineering." 2006. May edition of *Engineeringtalk*, an online publication at www.engineeringtalk.com/news/lag/lag102.html.

Mee, Laurence. 2006. "Reviving dead zones." *Scientific American* 295(5):78–85.

Myers, Ransom and Boris Worm. 2003. "Rapid worldwide depletion of predatory fish communities." *Nature* 423:280–283.

Ravallion, Mark, Shaohua Chen, and Prem Sangraula. 2008. *Dollar a Day Revisited*, Research Working Paper 4620, Washington, D.C.: The World Bank.

Roberts, Callum. 2007. *The Unnatural History of the Sea*. Washington, DC: Island Press.

Securing The Future—The UK Government Sustainable Development Strategy. 1995. Command Paper 6467. Available at www.defra.gov.uk/sustainable/government/publications/uk-strategy/index.htm.

"Sexes: Thailand's Mr. Contraception." 1981. *Time Magazine*. March 23.

Sharachchandra Lélé. 1991. "Sustainable Development: A Critical Review," *World Development* 19(6), pp. 607–621.

Shrader-Frechettte, K.S. 1981. *Environmental Ethics*, Pacific Grove, CA: The Boxwooed Press.

"Tropical habitats disappearing fast," 2008. ScienceAlert Australia & New Zealand, June 26, 2008. Available at www.sciencealert.com.au/news/20082606-17560-2.html.

United Nations. 1995. *Report of the World Summit for Social Development*. http://daccess-dds-ny.un.org/doc/UNDOC/GEN/N95/116/51/PDF/N9511651.pdf?OpenElement.

World Council on Economic Development, The. *Our Common Future*, 1987. Oxford: Oxford University Press.

World Watch Institute, The. 2008. *State of the World 2008: Innovations for a Sustainable Economy*, Washington, DC: The World Watch Institute.

Worm, Boris, Edward Barbier, Nicola Beaumont, J. Emmet Duffy, Carl Folke, Benjamin Halpern, Jeremy Jackson, Heike Lotze, Fiorenza Micheli, Stephen Palumbi, Enric Sala, Kimberly Selkoe, John Stachowicz, and Reg Watson. 2006. "Impacts of biodiversity loss on ocean ecosystem services." *Science* 314: 787–790.

ENDNOTES

1. The Brundtland Report (1987) was published by the World Council on Economic Development (WCED) under the title *Our Common Future*. The report is named after Gro Harlem Brundtland, then prime minister of Norway and chair of the Brundtland Commission. Four years after its establishment, the Brundtland Commission produced the final report that provided the classic definition of sustainable development.
2. United States Census Bureau, Population Division: www.census.gov/ipc/www/idb/worldpopgraph.php.
3. The Fourth Assessment Report of the IPCC (2007) can be found at www.ipcc.ch.
4. Gordon, Bertram, and Graedel (2006).
5. "Materials Prices Dictate Creative Engineering," (2006).
6. See "Global Environmental Problems: Implications for U.S. Policy," (2003).
7. "Tropical habitats disappearing fast," (2008).
8. Levin and Levin (2002).
9. Roberts (2007).
10. Myers and Worm (2003).
11. See for example, Hutchings (2000), Jackson (2001), Essington et al. (2006), and Worm et al. (2006).
12. FAO (2006).
13. See Mee (2006).

14. The website of the United Nations Convention to Combat Desertification is www.unccd.int.

15. United Nations (1995).

16. Gordon (2005).

17. It was not until 1993 that the World Bank established the absolute poverty level at a certain number of dollars per capita per day, about $1.08 at that time. Extrapolating this back to 1981 would result in absolute poverty of $0.90 per person. As noted in the text, the 2005 rate was $1.25 per day. See Ravallion, Chenm and Sangraula (2008) for more details on the World Bank methodology used for this purpose.

18. Ravallion, Chenm, and Sangraula (2008).

19. Costanza et al. (1997).

20. Shrader-Frechette (1981).

CHAPTER 2

The Technology Challenge

The most general ethical principle underlying sustainability is a conviction that human beings need to live within the carrying capacity of the planet. To achieve this goal will require, first, determining the carrying capacity, and then, ultimately, slowing population growth and reducing per capita consumption of resources. Technology is inextricably connected both to these problems and to their potential solutions. Without agricultural, energy, and medical technologies, it would not be possible for human beings to approach the planet's carrying capacity in the first place. Without technology, human beings will not be able to reduce population, increase consumption for those populations whose basic needs are not being met, and decrease the consumption of natural resources by industrialized nations in a way that promotes welfare and equity. Technology will be required to reduce resource consumption, emissions, and waste; develop chemicals, materials, and processes that are environmentally benign; and facilitate the shift from nonrenewable to renewable resources as the basis for the economy.

Thus, technology is a central concern for organizations and individuals intent on facing the world's most difficult and persistent problems. Any effort to analyze technology for the suitability of its deployment inevitably encounters ethical dilemmas, many of them linked to sustainability concerns. Technology also provides its own twin-horned dilemma or paradox, being both a significant cause of problems and a potential source of solutions. In this chapter, we explore this dual role of technology.

OVERVIEW OF TECHNOLOGY

Although technology, science, and engineering are related and often used interchangeably, there are distinct and important differences worth noting before focusing on technology itself. **Science** can be defined as the investigation of phenomena that humans observe in the natural world by using a formal approach known as the **scientific method** to elaborate laws and principles that are universally applicable. Kepler's observations of planetary motion and his discovery of the laws of this motion are an example of what would classically be described as science. Sustainability science is now in development. Some of its endeavors include work on: (1) ecosystem resilience, (2) industrial ecology, (3) earth system complexity, (4) yield-enhancing, land-saving agriculture, (5) nature-society interactions, (6) renewable energy systems, and (7) biomimicry.[1]

Engineering is the application of these laws and principles, discovered through scientific methods, to produce processes and tools that utilize science for human needs. For example, scientist Daniel Bernouli published his principle describing how pressure decreases as the velocity of fluid flow increases (now called Bernouli's principle) in 1738. Many years later, that principle was applied in the development of an airplane wing, which generates lift by creating higher air velocity (and, therefore, lower air pressure) above the wing and slower velocity (higher air pressure) below.

Defining Technology

Technology may be defined in different ways:

1. *Technology as objects*: The physical artifacts such as cell phones and refrigerators

2. *Technology as knowledge*: The know-how of scientists, engineers, and designers

3. *Technology as activities*: The application of skills of people such as machinists and computer programmers

4. *Technology as process*: Finding solutions based on a problem

5. *Technology as a social-technical system*: The interaction of people and artifacts in manufacture and use.[2]

In this book, we define *technology* as the combination of science and engineering to produce the artifacts of human society, including computers, automobiles, stainless steel, and polymers. In short, technology is the ultimate outcome of science and engineering. Interlaced with science and engineering, technology can be considered a problem-solving process in which the designer applies science and engineering to move from problem to solution. The iPhone and iPad are examples where designers applied science and engineering to solve the problem of how to create small devices to store, communicate, and display information in a wedding of physics and creative design.

A Brief History of Technology

Much of the technology that people notice and are familiar with has evolved in the last century. This includes computers, airplanes, electronic communications of every type (e.g., television, radio, cell phones), nuclear power, plastics, electric power grids, superhighways, nanotechnology, biotechnology, genetically modified organisms, robotics, and information technology. However, each of these is based on other prior technologies. The history of technology can be said to date back over 2.5 million years when the first evidence of tool making, the Olduwan tools of the late-Paleolithic period, appeared to aid in butchering dead animals.

In the ninth millennium Before Common Era (BCE), copper was first extracted and used for tools. It was also in this millennium that agriculture emerged as a technology that enabled human beings to subsist beyond hunting and gathering.

The wheel appeared for the first time in the fifth millennium BCE, bronze around 3300 BCE, and iron around 1500 BCE. The Egyptians invented the ramp, which enabled the construction of the pyramids, and the sail, which allowed the exploration of the seas and the navigation of rivers. At the same time, the ancient Chinese were inventing the pump, gunpowder, matches, the magnetic compass, and the iron plough. The Romans, considered the greatest engineers of the time, developed roads, aqueducts, domes, harbors and reservoirs, the book, glass blowing, and concrete.

BOX 2.1   Agriculture and Technology

Agriculture provides a useful context for thinking about the range of items and techniques that fit into the category of technology. Early agricultural technology included hand tools such as digging sticks and hoes for planting seeds and stone-bladed sickles for harvesting grains. Some tools and techniques developed independently in several regions around the globe. Various irrigation techniques were developed as a way to increase production through the control of a water supply. Animal-drawn ploughs greatly increased the amount of land one person could cultivate. Other developments depended on the specific needs of the farmer. For example, Mayas and Incas began using terracing in order to produce crops on steep slopes.

Conventional agriculture today is industrially based with heavy dependence on chemical inputs—including petroleum-based fertilizers, pesticides, and herbicides—as well as a large investment in capital equipment such as heavy machinery. Using these technologies, farmers have been able to decrease the need for labor, while increasing production. Of course, each of these technologies involves a number of social and ecological impacts, some quite far-ranging. For now the important thing is to understand that the category of technology includes a broad array of developments. Agricultural tools, including everything from computer-programmed combine threshers for harvesting grains to the digging sticks used by the first farmers millennia ago, all represent technological innovations. Indeed, the very decision to shift from gathering food to growing it represents one of the most significant technological innovations in human history.

Some even consider the crops themselves to be forms of technology. Most of the agricultural products we think of today are quite different from the wild varieties first domesticated by early agriculturalists. Farmers would plant seeds from individual specimens that exhibited desirable traits, placing selective pressure on the crops, which over time resulted in significant morphological differences. For example, domestic varieties often provide an increased yield and have characteristics preferable for harvesting. In other cases, changes represent consumption preferences. For example wild bananas contain large, hard seeds unlike the domestic varieties, which have either very small seeds or no seeds at all. Farmers have been placing this sort of evolutionary pressure on crops since the beginning of agriculture, and there is some debate as to whether domesticated varieties qualify as technology. Conversely, scientists have in recent years applied quite sophisticated technology to genetically engineer crops with industrially desirable traits. We discuss the impacts of this practice later in this chapter.

In medieval Europe (500 Common Era (CE) to 1450 CE), the windmill, clock, pointed arch, and cannon were invented. The Renaissance (starting in about 1450 CE) experienced the many inventions of Leonardo DaVinci, Johann Gutenberg's movable type presses, improved navigation tools and ships, the pocket watch, and flush toilets. During the same time frame, the Incas and Mayans developed potatoes, corn, and the calendar, and reshaped the landscape.

Technological developments accelerated in the seventeenth century with Isaac Newton's discovery of calculus and the invention of the submarine, telescope, steam turbine, adding machine, and air pump. The eighteenth century saw the replacement of human labor by machines, and Thomas Newcomen invented the steam engine, which revolutionized manufacturing and transportation. The nineteenth century experienced the invention of usable electricity, steel, and petroleum products, the growth of railways and steamships, and the development of faster and broader means of communication. It was also during this century that the steam locomotive, reaper, sewing machine, refrigerator, telegraph, photography, bicycle, plastics, typewriter, phonograph, automobile, diesel engine, vacuum cleaner, and revolver all made their appearances.

As enormous as the advances of the nineteenth century were, the pace of technological development dramatically increased in the twentieth century as automobiles, airplanes, cell phones, wireless technology, genetic engineering, the Internet, nuclear technology, biotechnology, nanotechnology, space travel, and a host of other technologies appeared.

The development of biological, chemical, and nuclear weapons of mass destruction also occurred, along with aircraft and missiles. Based on the pattern of the past, it is probable that the pace of technology will continue to accelerate even more. In the twenty-first century, we have already seen the emergence of a wide range of other compact information display, storage, and communication devices. The hybrid automobile, translucent concrete, highly advanced and versatile video game systems, YouTube, and countless other products and processes have already emerged in just the first decade.

In short, the pattern throughout human history is that technological development has steadily accelerated. It is probable that this pace will continue to increase, the result being even more products, processes, and services, some designed to improve quality of life, others that may support military operations, and still others that produce novelties and gadgets of little lasting value. When technology develops so quickly, both producers and consumers tend to focus on technological advance as its own end. From this perspective, the primary questions are about what is technologically possible to develop and how those new developments might prove profitable for the developer or convenient and entertaining for the consumer. It is easy to focus on the specified design goal without considering the social and ecological impacts a new development could have. In this book, we shift the focus from "What can we do?" to "What should we do?" Answering this latter question means looking more closely at the impacts of technology beyond its intended use and profitability.

THE TECHNOLOGY PARADOX

Technology is a two-edged sword. On one hand, it has provided numerous advantages and comforts in a wide array of areas. Particularly in industrialized countries, few today could argue that modern technology does not contribute to their quality of life. However, the benefits of technology have not come without a cost. Much of our present technology is based on unsustainable use of resources and results in negative impacts on the environment and society that receive little notice from technology users. But while technology has played a central role in creating or exacerbating the problems described in Chapter 1, it will likely also play a central role in addressing those challenges.

Technological Optimism versus Technological Pessimism

People generally have one of two opposing views when thinking about technology, and their perception of it dictates the levels of risk they are willing to accept. So-called technological optimists have the point of view that virtually every problem has a technical solution, and given the resources and minimal government regulation, scientists and engineers will find a solution. They suggest that in key areas such as food production, environmental quality, and energy, technology will sustain the quality of life even as human population increases unabated. In this school of thought, running out of oil is not a cause for concern because an as yet unidentified source of energy will be found. Indeed climate change, caused in part by the depletion of oil, can also be resolved by technological

fixes. For example, the carbon dioxide can be extracted from the atmosphere and stored in caverns, or dikes can be built that will prevent widespread flooding resulting from rising sea levels.

Alvin Toffler, author of *The Third Wave* and *Future Shock* and a proponent of technological optimism, posited the notion that technological developments have led to a sequence of so-called "waves" over the centuries.[3] The First Wave was agrarian society in which farming replaced hunting-gathering. The Second Wave was industrial society, from the start of the Industrial Revolution in the seventeenth century through the mid-twentieth century. Toffler referred to the Third Wave as the postindustrial era or Information Age (see Figure 2.1). He was confident that technology would increase wealth with a better life for all being the result. In a similar vein, Alvin Weinberg, the technological

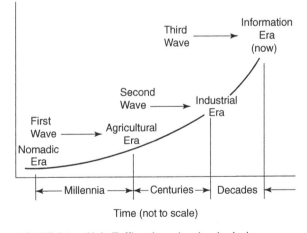

FIGURE 2.1 Alvin Toffler viewed technological progress as a series of three waves, which advanced at an accelerating pace over time. *(Photograph Courtesy of The Harbinger, nonprofit organization in Mobile, Alabama.)*

optimist who invented the phrase "technological fix,"[4] proposed nuclear energy as the substitute for rapidly depleting fossil fuels and as a means of converting seawater into fresh water. In general, technological optimists do not focus on reducing consumption but on the technological means of increasing consumption and dealing with its effects.

While new technology will no doubt present new opportunities for addressing contemporary challenges, many find the optimism of Toffler and Weinberg to be misguided in predicting the continual emergence of breakthroughs at ever-increasing rates while failing to acknowledge any limits. On the other end of the spectrum, pessimists tend to focus on the problems that technology has caused. Technological pessimists include such notables as the population biologist Paul Ehrlich.

In his 1968 book, *The Population Bomb*, Ehrlich predicted that the world would experience widespread famine in 1970s. His remedy for countering this looming catastrophe was population control. The "bomb" never exploded, however. Industrialized agricultural systems were able to increase food production to meet rising demand. In fact, the number of famines and resulting deaths fell steadily during the 25-year period after the book was written (and with a 50 percent increase in world population). As you will see in later chapters, this increased capacity of industrialized food production came with a cost. At the time, however, industrial agriculture's ability to meet the nutritional needs of a growing population was seen as support for the technological optimist point of view.

Ehrlich also gained notoriety for a bet he made with Julian Simon, a technological optimist, in 1980 (see Figures 2.2 and 2.3). Simon suggested that if Ehrlich's population predictions were correct, the price

FIGURE 2.2 Paul Ehrlich, a Stanford professor, biologist, and author of *The Population Bomb*, was the technological pessimist in the 1980 bet with Julian Simon. *(Photo by John Ogden)*

FIGURE 2.3 Julian Simon was an economist and professor of business administration at the University of Illinois and University of Maryland. His optimism about the human species weighed heavily in his winning bet with Paul Ehrlich. *(Courtesy of University of Maryland)*

of commodities would rise over time because of enormous demand for increasingly scarce resources. Simon believed in human ingenuity and technology, and he bet Ehrlich that for any basket of five commodities selected by Ehrlich, the total price would fall by 1990. Ehrlich took the bet and selected tin, tungsten, copper, nickel, and chrome as the commodities and purchased $200 worth of each, a total of $1,000. If the price rose, Simon would owe Ehrlich the increased value of the commodities. If the price fell, Ehrlich would owe Simon the decrease in value. In 1990 Ehrlich wrote Simon a check for $576. The price of all five metals had fallen. Here again Ehrlich had underestimated human ingenuity, namely, the ability to more efficiently extract and refine or replace these metals.

A few years after the appearance of *The Population Bomb, Limits to Growth* was published in 1972 as an exploration of the consequences of exponential growth among five variables: world population, industrialization, pollution, food production, and resource depletion.[5] Using a massive computer program, the authors modeled change on the planet assuming these variables continued at the present pace. Although not intended to predict future resource scenarios, it did provide ammunition for its critics by hypothesizing scenarios for oil depletion, among other resource issues. For oil, it could be interpreted that depletion would occur between 31 and 50 years from the time of the report, that is, as early as 1992. Technology and behavioral changes have clearly changed the scenario by extending existing resources and developing alternatives.

Developing a More Nuanced View of the Impacts of Technology

Technological pessimists tend to overlook the ways in which technology is innovative and can play a role in pursuing sustainability. Conversely, technological optimists tend to underestimate the importance of nontechnical approaches to sustainability, dismiss natural limits, and ignore the problems that new technologies create. Optimists may be tempted to dismiss the ethical issues raised by sustainability, believing that someone somewhere will invent a technological solution for every problem, but let us take a broad look at some of the limits within which technology must work.

It is clear that the Earth is a finite planet with finite resources, and at some point in time, if population and consumption continue to grow, collapse will occur. If one were to assume the current annual population growth rate of about 1.7 percent were to continue indefinitely, there would be a human being standing in every square meter of the Earth within five centuries. Clearly this would not be a utopian future, nor would any of these people be able to grow enough food to sustain them. Similarly, consumption per capita is also growing at about 1.7 percent annually and the combination of human population growth and consumption would consume the entire planet—every rock, tree, and drop of water—in the time frame.

Given these physical and social limits, we know that we cannot continue to increase our impact on global environmental systems, but this is exactly what most technological advances have done. In previous centuries, before the Industrial Age, human technology was relatively rudimentary. Nonetheless, as Jared Diamond has demonstrated in his bestselling book, *Collapse*,[6] many rudimentary technologies—coupled with short-sightedness—led to disastrous consequences. Simple iron, bronze, or even stone axes produced the deforestation of a number of ancient lands and the demise of entire peoples, such as those occupying Easter Island. Agriculture based on primitive mechanical methods of plowing and planting, prior to any use of artificial fertilizer and machinery, may have led to the widespread erosion and salinization of soil, and helped bring about the collapse of other ancient societies, such as the Anasazi of southwestern North America and the Maya of Central America.

Diamond underlines that environmental destruction is not the sole, or sometimes even predominant, factor that leads to the collapse of civilizations. Coupled with overpopulation, however, environmental destruction has played a decisive role in many instances. While technology is certainly implicated in these cases of social collapse, the technology involved was not particularly advanced. A little technology can go a long way in bringing agricultural, economic, and military benefits and in producing environmentally and socially disastrous consequences.

Of course, modern technology has increased our ability to effect widespread changes that few could have imagined just a century ago. Paul Ehrlich proposed the IPAT equation as a means of recognizing the increased impacts allowed by technological advance. First introduced in the early 1970s, the IPAT equation suggests that environmental impact is the result of a combination of social and technological factors. The formula proposes that ecological impact (I) is the product of population (P), affluence (A), and technology (T).

Although the IPAT formula is useful, it may give the misleading impression that technology contributes to increasing the ecological impact. Historically, that has often been the case, but some technologies (e.g., solar panels, air emission controls) have been designed with the purpose of decreasing human impact on the environment. These technologies have varying degrees of success, but they will certainly play an important role in the pursuit of sustainability.

CONSEQUENCES OF TECHNOLOGY

New technologies have consequences, some of them known, others that are suspected, and many that are unknown or unexpected. In general, technological consequences can be categorized as *anticipated* or *unanticipated*. Anticipated consequences can be (1) intended and desired, (2) not desired but common or probable, or (3) not desired and improbable. Similarly, unanticipated consequences can be (1) desirable or (2) undesirable. For example, the development of hybrid automobiles brings with it the anticipated, intended, and desirable outcomes of extending the supply of petroleum, reducing air pollution, and reducing carbon emissions into the atmosphere. An anticipated, undesired, but probable outcome, based on the appeal of hybrids, could be more automobiles on the road, more miles driven, and more accidents (given more vehicles driving more miles). An anticipated, undesirable, and improbable outcome is the significant issues connected with disposal of vast quantities of batteries needed by hybrid cars.[7]

The challenges of anticipating the consequences of technology are of course the wild card. It is true that unanticipated but desirable consequences can occur. There have been several pleasant outcomes from the DNA sequencing of the human genome, such as a richer understanding of how we are all related to one another. It has also opened the doors to relatively easy genetic testing for predisposition to breast cancer, liver disorders, and many other diseases. In contrast, this same technology can result in unanticipated and undesirable outcomes, such as health insurance companies cherry-picking genetically favorable patients to insure, thus reducing their payments.

Predicting Consequences of Technology

The consequences of technology, both good and bad, are often not well understood, partly because the technologies themselves have features that make it difficult to comprehend their full effects. Several kinds of features can contribute to the problem of grasping the consequences of technology, including complexity, dynamics, intransparence, and ignorance and mistaken hypotheses.[8]

Complexity addresses the many parts of a system and the wide range of interconnections, many of which are not obvious and

may be unknown. For example, ecosystems are extremely complex and only a small fraction of the enormous number of ecosystem relationships is known. Consequently, when ecosystems are disturbed by human activities, the extent of the damage may be unknown because the interconnections are not known. Complexity has evolved into a theory of its own—which we will explore further in later chapters.

Dynamics describes the property of continuous and sometimes spontaneous change that takes place in systems that often cannot be fully described and comprehended. The movement of information across the Internet, the flow of electricity through the grid, and the behavior of high-definition televisions all exhibit dynamic behavior. The dynamics of a system increase, often exponentially, as the number of actors in the system increases. For example, the dynamics of traffic on an interstate highway increases as the number of drivers increases, each driver with his or her own driving style, behavior, attitudes, and state of mind.

The fact that many of the components of a system cannot be seen is the property called **intransparence**. The more complex a system is, the greater its degree of intransparence. Ecosystems, the economic system, and the Internet are systems that exhibit a high level of intransparence. As a result of these difficulties, sometimes human beings simply get it wrong and the resulting model is badly flawed because of **ignorance and mistaken hypotheses**. For example, the U.S. economic problems of 2008–2011 can be at least attributed in

BOX 2.2 GM Crops—Technology with Potentially Huge Impacts on the Global System

Genetic engineering provides the techniques needed to remove, modify, or add genes to a DNA molecule in order to change the information it contains. The result is the alteration of the genetic material of cells or organisms in order to make them capable of making new substances or performing new functions. Supporters of this technology claim it can lead to more abundant food supplies, inexpensive medicines, and cures for currently untreatable diseases. Its detractors suggest that it would lead to plagues, diseases, or other catastrophic environmental disasters.

The potential downside is especially daunting because new life forms, whose behavior and consequences would be largely unknown, may be introduced either accidentally or deliberately into the biosphere. Amory and L. Hunger Lovins suggest that the term itself is misleading: "'Engineering' implies understanding of the causal mechanisms that link actions to effects, but nobody understands the mechanisms by which genes, interacting with each other and the environment, express traits. Transgenic manipulation inserts foreign genes into random locations in a plant's DNA to see what happens. That's not engineering; it's the industrialization of life by people with a narrow understanding of it" (Lovins and Lovins 2000). Of course, a great deal of technology is developed by way of experimental methods.

Genetic engineering of agricultural products to produce genetically modified (GM) crops brings with it several ethical challenges. First is the possibility of creating health problems for human beings consuming genetically altered foods. For example, splicing peanut genes into other plant DNA to produce an enhanced species has already been shown to affect people with peanut allergies. In addition, these new life forms may cause future agricultural problems. For example, herbicide-resistant genes may end up creating "superweeds." (see Figure 2.4). Finally, the new genetic combinations may result in ecological problems. The modified bacterial genes of GM crops allow them to make their own pesticides, which may result in the death of harmless insects such as monarch butterflies.

On the other side of the debate, proponents of GM crops say they are not different in any important way from their natural counterparts. U.S. officials cite this reasoning in support of the decision not to require labeling of food products that contain GM products. Such labeling is required in many European countries. The potential for negative effects to human health as well as to agricultural and ecological systems raises ethical issues about the continued production of GM foods.

FIGURE 2.4 The use of genetically modified plants can easily backfire as was the case when corn modified to be herbicide tolerant (HT) was planted in Arkansas to encourage the use of herbicides. The result has been an explosion of herbicide-resistant giant pigweed plants that are ravaging the corn crop, with over 1 million acres infested in Arkansas alone. *(Source: US Department of Agriculture)*

Another ethical issue concerns attempts to encourage poor farmers in developing countries to grow genetically modified crops. Corporations such as Monsanto and Novartis own patents on these altered plants and the farmers using them must buy new seeds each year at premium prices rather than reusing seeds from the previous year's crop as they have traditionally done. Marketing GM seeds to developing countries increases the profits for multinational companies while not addressing the poverty and inequality that are the real roots of world hunger.

Still GM proponents suggest that GM crops offer the world's best chance to end or greatly reduce hunger and malnutrition. For example, blindness caused by a deficiency in Vitamin A continues to be a widespread problem among the poor in developing countries. Some point to "golden rice," a genetically engineered variety designed to provide extra vitamin A, as a way to address this problem. As we can see, assessing the potential impacts—desirable and undesirable—of new technologies can be difficult.

part to the belief that the economy and the demand for housing would continue to grow unabatedly and that highly speculative hedge funds and financial instruments based on the growth in demand for housing would provide huge returns to the financial institutions that created them. The hypothesis that the risk of these instruments was manageable turned out to be false, and the collapse of banks, insurance companies, stock brokerages, and other financial institutions ensued.

Reducing the Uncertainty of Technology

When judging technologies, society is faced with difficult choices. The technology developers are not the best people to ask whether or not there is a reasonable level of risk associated with technology because their judgment, as the inventors, may be clouded. Yet because inventors best understand technology, society must often turn to them to determine the likely outcomes. It is crucial to remedy this situation by better understanding the

consequences of technology. Society could decrease the uncertainty and unintended consequence of technology through four strategies: (1) increasing knowledge, (2) combining uncertainties through large-scale organization, (3) increasing control of the situation, and (4) slowing the march of progress.[9]

Increasing knowledge by additional research, studies, and independent evaluations should provide a better understanding of consequences. However, there is no perfect knowledge and any effort to gain additional insights will inevitably run into time and cost constraints. Combining uncertainties through large-scale organization refers to the potential for providing some type of insurance that will help protect society from catastrophic consequences. This is plausible to some degree, because, if there are potentially high risks, the cost of deploying the technology could be prohibitive and effectively block its implementation. Nuclear power plants exemplify this concept because the government has invested heavily in research on safety systems that hopefully prevent Chernobyl-type catastrophes from occurring. Additional strong regulatory oversight by the Nuclear Regulatory Commission was designed to provide additional insurance that a reactor accident will not occur.

Government can increase its control of technologies and factor in probable costs to society by imposing taxes that shift the burden of mitigating the impacts of technologies with negative effects to the producers and effectively reduce the rate of their uptake. Finally, the rate of change can be slowed to allow more time to effectively study and understand the situation. In its extreme form, this could take the form of a moratorium that would freeze development until the risk could be adequately studied or understood. Immediately after it was announced that Dolly, the cloned sheep, had been born in 1996, President Clinton declared a moratorium on cloning until more was understood about the implications of this technology.

Technology Risk Assessment, Acceptance, and Management

Virtually every technology is accompanied by some form of risk, and the assessment of the risk is essential for government and society to determine if the technology is suitable for deployment. The transformations of matter and energy that occur as a result of the application of science and engineering, although intended to benefit human beings, can have a wide range of consequences with negative impacts, some of which in fact damage qualities that humans value, such as their health. For example, the pesticide DDT proved effective during World War II at controlling disease-spreading insects, and was

used to wipe out malaria in the United States. However, it was also found to have undesirable effects on environmental systems.

Most often technology is a tradeoff between benefits and costs that may be technical, social, economic, and/or environmental. When the impacts are known, the decision is a matter of deciding whether the benefits of the technology are worth the costs that come with it. In most cases, however, the impacts are not entirely known. Therefore, one must also consider the possible impacts. That is, one must assess the risk involved with the development and use of a technology.

Risk assessment and the resulting decision to implement or shelve a technology represent the intersection of an ethics of sustainability with technology. Weighing short-term, contemporary benefits against the welfare of future people is characteristic of this challenging type of ethical decision as are assessments of the merits of technology that benefit wealthier people at the expense of vulnerable populations. For example, a nuclear power infrastructure based on the uranium fuel cycle is likely relatively short-lived, perhaps under 150 years total from its inception in the early 1950s until uranium is essentially depleted as a fuel resource. Nuclear power's benefits of relatively cheap, reliable, and low carbon energy for contemporary society will burden future people with a vast array of dangerous radionuclides that must be contained for millennia before they decay to harmless levels.

Certainly the assessment of risk must be based in science and research, but much of the assessment relies upon statistical

BOX 2.3   Nanotechnology

The American physicist, Richard Feynman, is credited with the notion of manipulating individual atoms and molecules to make designer molecules in a speech he made at a meeting of the American Physical Society at Caltech on December 29, 1959. He described a process of creating tools that could manufacture ever smaller versions of themselves, ultimately reaching the size of individual molecules and atoms that could be rearranged by the smallest set of tools. The term **nanotechnology** was first used by Professor Norio Taniguchi in 1974, and he defined it as processing single atoms or molecules for some end purpose such as creating new materials.

Nanotechnology encompasses a wide range of technologies and processes. It can be defined as the branch of engineering that deals with things smaller than 100 nanometers, about 1/100,000th the thickness of a human hair. At this scale, fundamentally new compounds can be created. For example, carbon in its pure state exists in two forms: diamonds and graphite, the latter being the stuff of pencil lead. By rearranging the carbon atoms into a novel structure, new materials called **carbon nanotubes** can be created that are 30 times stronger than steel but that have only one-sixth its weight. Carbon nanotubes were one of the first practical results of nanotechnology, and they are ubiquitous in everyday products such as tennis racquets, aircraft wings, and bicycle frames.

The use of nanotechnology in electronics makes possible virtually every consumer electronic device, from MP3 players to cell phones, digital cameras, video game consoles, and of course, computers. Applications of nanotechnology also include the ability to devise self-replicating machines, robots, and computers that are molecular-sized, nano-delivery systems for drugs, and quantum and molecular computing—the next generation of computation.

While nanotechnology offers a number of exciting possibilities, the risks are virtually unknown. There is the potential for nanoparticles to end up in the environment, soil, food, and many other places that can affect health and life (see Figure 2.5). The small size of nanoparticles means that, when inhaled, they can penetrate into tissues, the bloodstream, and cells far more efficiently and quickly than typical airborne particulates and that they can contribute to the mutation of DNA, directly

FIGURE 2.5   Some applications of nanotechnology have potential health and safety threats. Titanium dioxide in nanoparticle form is being used in sunscreens. The Australian Therapeutic Goods Administration (TGA) is monitoring the use of nano-titanium-dioxide in sunscreens because of the potential for these particles to be absorbed by the skin. Although there has been no evidence of harm, the TGA requires that products carrying nanoparticles be labeled to indicate this content. *(Courtesy Australian Therapeutic Goods Administration)*

(continued)

affecting the evolution of living organisms. The potential consequences of self-replicating and nano-scale materials and devices have raised more concern, including the potential for the self-replicating attribute to go awry, leading to the consumption of all matter on earth as the self-replicating nanorobots turn all matter into copies of themselves. Eric Drexler coined the term *grey goo* in *Engines of Creation* to describe this scenario.

Still little effort has been expended on characterizing these risks for humans and other species. Even the process for how to measure exposure to nanoparticles is still unknown. The Project for Emerging Nanotechnologies (PEN) was formed in 2005 as a result of a collaboration of the Woodrow Wilson International Center for Scholars and the Pew Charitable Trusts to identify and close gaps in knowledge about nanotechnologies. PEN is helping to foster public discussion about a topic that is predicted to become a far-reaching issue as the value of manufactured goods in the global market that incorporate nanotechnology are expected to increase in value from $150 billion in 2008 to $2.6 trillion in 2014. (See www.nanotechproject.org.)

probabilities, which many people find difficult to judge. For example, pressurized water reactors (PWRs), the most common variety of nuclear power plant in the United States, have a very low probability of a serious accident. A 1975 report by the U.S. Nuclear Regulatory Commission (NRC) put the probability of a worst-case accident with core meltdown and the failure of containment at 1 chance in a billion or about 1 in 10 million for 100 operating nuclear reactors.[10] Four years after the NRC report, the Three Mile Island PWR in Pennsylvania suffered a core meltdown, calling into question the low probabilities cited in the report. Yet government, and by extension, society, have opted for the benefits of nuclear power in spite of the risk.

When society gambles that a technology will have a favorable outcome, it is deciding the risk is acceptable. Technology is, of course, not the only source of risk. Where people live, their lifestyles, where they work, how they travel, what they consume, and the waste they generate all carry risks. Natural disasters, terrorism, and the weather also have risks associated with them. However, the risks associated with technology are in a special class because, unlike natural disasters, technological risks are avoidable. In theory, societies can decide to avoid these risks if people decide that they are too great and have the power to change the process, but in practice assessing and regulating risks raises ethical and logistical questions. We will discuss risk assessment in more detail in later chapters. For now, the important point to remember is that no technology, even those designed specifically to address sustainability, comes entirely without risk.

ALTERNATIVE, APPROPRIATE, AND SUSTAINABLE TECHNOLOGY

One approach to managing technological risk is to allow those technologies that are inherently beneficial to people and the environmental to have an advantage in their deployment. Through the use of regulation, fees, taxes, or incentives, society can exercise control over which technologies are permitted to enter the marketplace, allowing only those that are very low risk to be implemented. Two categories of technologies that are often described as having these attributes are **alternative technology** and **appropriate technology**.

The term *alternative technology* was first used by Peter Harper from the Centre for Alternative Technology in Wales in the 1970s and is still commonly used as label to describe technologies that are relatively benign. In general, it refers to those types of technologies that produce a minimal impact on the environment. Technologies that mimic nature or that rely on natural processes are often labeled as alternative technologies. Technologies that use resources sparingly, foster recycling, use renewable and local resources, and limit the use of fossil fuels are also examples of alternative technologies. Composting, solar hot water heating, anaerobic digestions, solar ovens, biofuels, and wind energy generators are examples of technologies that fit this description.

Appropriate technology includes the concept of alternative technology, but in addition to considering the environmental attributes of a technology, also considers its ethical, cultural, social, and economic aspects. Amory Lovins, E. F. Schumacher, and Buckminster Fuller are considered to be among the originators of the concept. It can refer to technologies that are either the most effective for addressing problems in developing countries or that are socially and environmentally responsible in industrial countries. In the context of developing countries, it often refers to the simplest type of technology that can be used to accomplish a given end, with low capital cost being an objective. This is in contrast to the complex and often capital-intensive technologies prevalent in the industrial world.

Appropriate technology should not be confused with primitive or low technology, however. Solar photovoltaic panels that are used to power nighttime lighting systems in rural India in support of microeconomic ventures would be considered appropriate. Compact fluorescent bulbs and LED lights can also be considered appropriate technology because they use minimal energy, are durable, and provide a substitute for otherwise dangerous and unhealthy lighting systems. Food production systems that involve intensive gardening, hydroponics, no-till farming, permaculture, and drip irrigation would fit the description of appropriate technology. Mahatma Gandhi and his colleagues invented the compact spinning wheel, introducing it to Indian villages as a means of assisting their economic development and freeing them from British colonial rule. As a result, he is often associated with the emergence of the appropriate technology movement. At the same time, he opposed the adoption of Western industrialized agriculture and its associated technologies because they would destroy India's villages, where 80 percent of its population lives. He felt that the large-scale agriculture did not match the scale at which people lived and survived and that its technology was largely inappropriate because of the displacement of human labor in favor of machinery.[11]

BOX 2.4   Biomimicry

An excellent example of technology that fits very well into the sustainability framework is **biomimicry**. Defined by its originator, Janine Benyus, as "the conscious emulation of nature's genius," biomimicry provides an approach to creating an enormous range of materials and processes from nature that can be adopted in the human sphere and that have the attributes of being biodegradable, originating from local resources, and being less harmful to the environment (Benyus 1996). In other words, biomimicry is the process of adapting the lessons from 4.5 billion years of trial and error by nature and applying them to industrial processes.

For example, natural mother-of-pearl inside seashells is surprisingly tough. Scientists are using the composition of seashells as a model to produce strong, lightweight ceramics for use in cars, strong insulating materials for buildings, and even bulletproof vests. The powerful adhesives secreted by mussels and the ability of plants to convert sunlight to other energy forms via photosynthesis are other examples of natural system materials and processes that are effective and benign and have application in the human sphere. Indeed, as scientists learn more about the natural world, they will be able to provide more ideas for the sustainable products and processes that perform better than their predecessors but with fewer negative impacts on environment and human health.

THE ETHICAL IMPLICATIONS OF TECHNOLOGY

The development and implementation of technology almost always results in ethical dilemmas. Some of the ethical issues are fairly straightforward and are simply variants of age-old problems. The Internet and email, for example, have opened up a Pandora's box of information security and confidentiality problems. Although serious, these are not actually new ethical issues, the technology simply multiplies the opportunity for problems beyond the current capacity of our legal system.

Other technology issues are strictly about right and wrong, classic ethical issues. For example, the decision of a Union Carbide subsidiary to build a pesticide plant in a densely populated area around Bhopal, India, proved to be disastrous when the plant exploded in 1984, with approximately 20,000 deaths, at least 100,000 injuries, and 5 million people affected directly or indirectly by this tragedy. The Bhopal disaster has many ethical dimensions and serves to illustrate the need for ethical principles that can cope with decision making about technology implementation.

The Union Carbide plant was originally conceived with the intent of supporting India's Green Revolution, a plan to dramatically increase India's agricultural output through the use of technologies such as pesticides. This plant produced carbaryl, a highly toxic and dangerous pesticide listed by the U.S. Environmental Protection Agency as a likely human carcinogen. However, the full range of its toxicity has never been determined, and while it is illegal in the UK, it continues to be used in the United States and elsewhere. In addition, the chemical required equally dangerous ingredients such as the highly reactive chemical methyl isocyanate (MIC).

One question that arises, then, is whether it is ethically acceptable to produce chemicals whose toxicity is not fully understood.

The location of the plant within a densely populated area raises a second ethical issue. Bhopal itself was a city of 900,000 people at the time of the incident. Siting the plant there ensured that such an explosion would result in many casualties. In addition, the people who died were from the nearby shantytowns of Jayaprakash Nagar, Kazi Camp, Chola Kenchi, and the Railway Colony, so it was the poor who suffered the brunt of the event.[12] A final ethical dimension of this disaster was the lack of information and transparency. It took at least two hours to sound the alarm after the workers detected the MIC leak, and by that time over 40 tons had leaked out and spread through the air in a plume 8 kilometers long that spread out over the city (see Figure 2.6)

FIGURE 2.6 A man blinded by the Bhopal gas tragedy. On June 7, 2010, about 26 years after the disaster, an Indian court issued a shocking verdict that provided minimal compensation for the victims and essentially no punishment for the Dow chemical managers. (© Greenpeace / Raghu Rai)

Some of the ethical questions that must be considered when a technology has been developed and considered for widespread implementation can be summarized as follows:

- Under what conditions is the technology acceptable?
- At what point in the development of the technology is widespread use acceptable?
- How should society weigh the associated risks against the possible benefits?
- Who should make decisions about the development and use of technology?
- Are there cases where a particular technology should be considered unacceptable even though it has potential benefits?

The development of general ethical principles that support the sustainability framework is vital to our ability to confront the twin challenge of technology. The issue of obligation to present and future generations and to other species, as well as issues of fair distribution of resources, must all be answered for this framework to be successfully applied to many of our contemporary technological problems and solutions.

SUMMARY AND CONCLUSIONS

Technology provides the capability for humans to increase or decrease their impact on environmental systems, the quality of life, and the equitable distribution of resources. New technological innovations (e.g., genetic engineering) promise to increase the potential for human impact in each of these areas in unpredictable ways.

If indeed there is an obligation to future generations, as well as to the present poor of Earth, then technology needs to be examined and used in a manner that will produce manifest benefits and minimize negative outcomes. Risks and benefits to multiple stakeholders must be weighed and decisions made. Clearly ethics is central to this process. An ethics of sustainability is needed that can help technology developers, policymakers, and technology consumers make sound decisions regarding technology. In the following chapters, we will look more closely at the ethical concepts useful in making these decisions.

REFERENCES

Asaro, Peter M. 2006. "What Should We Want from a Robot Ethic?," *International Review of Information Ethics*, Vol. 6, available online at www.i-r-i-e.net/inhalt/006/006_full.pdf.

Asimov, Isaac. 1942. "Runaround," originally published in 1942 and included in the 1968 collection of the author's short stories in *I, Robot*, published by Grafton Books, London.

Asthana, Praveen. 1994. "Jumping the Technology S-Curve," *IEEE Spectrum*, June.

Beniger, James. 1986. *The Control Revolution: Technological and Economic Origins of the Information Society*, Cambridge: Harvard University Press.

Benyus, Janine. 1997. *Biomimicy: Innovation Inspired by Nature*, New York: William Morrow.

Capurro, Rafael, et al. Eds. 2006. "Ethics in Robotics," *International Review of Information Ethics*, Vol 6, available online at www.i-r-i-e.net/inhalt/006/006_full.pdf.

Clark, William C. and Nancy M. Dickson. 2003. "Sustainability Science: The Emerging Research Program," *Proceedings of the National Academy of Sciences*, 100(14), July, pp. 8059–8061.

Dorner, Dietrich. 1989. *The Logic of Failure: Why Things Go Wrong and How We Can Make Them Right*, New York: Metropolitan Books.

Drexler, K. Eric. 1986. *Engines of Creation: The Coming Age of Nanotechnology*, New York: Anchor Books.

Drexler, K. Eric. 1992. *Nanosystems: Molecular Machinery, Manufacturing, and Computation*, New York: Wiley Interscience.

Ehrlich, Paul. 1969. *The Population Bomb*, New York: Sierra Club Publishers.

ETC. 2003. "Nanotech Unglued: Is the Grey/Green Goo Brouhaha the Industry's Second Blunder?" *Communique*, ETC Group, Issue #80, July/August. Available for download at www.etcgroup.org/en/materials/publications.html?pub_id=154.

Foster, Richard N. 1986. *The Attacker's Advantage*, Orangeville, Ontario: Summit Books.

Joy, Bill. 2000. "Why the future doesn't need us," *Wired*, Issue 8.04, April.

Lovins, Amory B. and L. Hunter Lovins. 2000. "A Tale of Two Botanies," *Wired*, Issue 8.04, April.

Knight, Frank. 1921. *Risk, Uncertainty, and Profit*, Boston: Houghton-Mifflin Company.

Koepsell, David. 2007. "The Ethics of Genetic Engineering," a position paper from the Center for Inquiry, Office of Public Policy, August. Downloadable at www.centerforinquiry.net/uploads/attachments/genetic-engineering-ethics_2.pdf.

Meadows, Donella H., Dennis L. Meadows, Jorgen Randers, and William W. Behrens III. 1972. *The Limits to Growth*. New York: Universe Books.

Pearson, Greg and A. Thomas Young, Eds. 2002. *Technically Speaking*, Committee on Technological Literacy, National Academy of Engineering, National Research Council, Washington, DC. Downloadable at the website of the National Academies Press at www.nap.edu/catalog .php?record_id=10250.

Rogers, Everett. 1964. *Diffusion of Innovations*, Glencoe: Free Press.

Sandler, Ronald. 2009. *Nanotechnology: The Social and Ethical Issues*, Project on Emerging Nanotechnologies, Woodrow Wilson Center for International Scholars, PEN 16, January. Available for download at www.nanotechproject.org/ process/assets/files/7060/nano_pen16_final.pdf.

Shepard, Mark. 1990. *Gandhi and His Myths*, Los Angeles: Shepard Publications.

Thayer, Robert. 1994. *Gray World, Green Heart,* New York: John Wiley & Sons, Inc.

Toffler, Alvin. 1980. *The Third Wave*. New York: Morrow.

WASH-1400. 1975. *The Reactor Safety Study.* The U.S. Nuclear Regulatory Commission.

Weinberg, Alvin M. 1966. "Can Technology Replace Social Engineering?" *Bulletin of the Atomic Scientists* 22(12), December, pp. 4–8.

ENDNOTES

1. From "Sustainability Science: The Emerging Research Program" by William C. Clark and Nancy M. Dickson (2003).
2. From the website of Learning Alive at http:// atschool.eduweb.co.uk/trinity/watistec.html.
3. From The Third Wave by Alvin Toffler (1980).
4. From "Can Technology Replace Social Engineering" by Alvin M. Weinberg (1960). Although a technological optimist, Weinberg did note that technology and social engineering should be used together and that technology that ignores social reality will not work.
5. Limits to Growth (1972) was authored by Donella Meadows, Dennis Meadows, Jorgen Randers, and William W. Behrens III. A 20-year update called Beyond the Limits based on the original material was written by Meadows, Meadows, and Randers in 1992.
6. Jared Diamond, Collapse: *How Societies Choose to Fail or Succeed* (New York: Viking Press, 2005).
7. This outcome is unlikely because the valuable materials in the high-tech batteries emerging from industry will need to be recovered to "sustain" battery production. There is also considerable pressure to prevent environmental problems resulting from the disposal of large quantities of difficult to dispose of materials. Examples are electroscrap and tires.
8. From The Logic of Failure: Why Things Go Wrong and How We Can Make Them Right by Dietrich Dorner (1989).
9. From *Risk, Uncertainty, and Profit* by Frank Knight (1921).
10. The Nuclear Regulatory Commission report on reactor safety is commonly referred to as the Rasmussen Report, after the chair of the committee, Norman Rasmussen, professor at Massachusetts Institute of Technology. The committee started its work in 1972 and issued its final report in 1975.
11. From *Gandhi and His Myths*, Mark Shephard (1990)
12. We will discuss the disproportionate level of risk borne by the poor in more detail in the context of environmental justice.

CHAPTER 3

Introduction to Ethical Concepts

Chapter 1 provided background necessary to understand the context in which individuals, communities, and business and political leaders are now considering matters of sustainability as they attempt to identify the right action to take, policy to develop, or technology to implement. Of course, attempting to identify the right, proper, or just action is nothing new. Those doing so today have the advantage of insights offered by some of the world's most influential minds over the last several thousand years. This chapter provides a look at those insights in the field of ethics, introducing and examining how different ways of thinking about ethics can help people sort through some of these complex issues and make more sustainable choices.

While ethics, in general, explores problems of good and evil, there exist countless ways to specify what this means, according to diverse interests and perspectives. For many philosophers, ethics is about individual conduct or character, and thus defined by questions such as "How shall I live?" or "What does it mean to be a good person?" For others, ethics refers to universal values and thus poses questions such as "What is the Good?" or "What rules can rightly apply to all moral actors or agents?" Still other ethicists focus on the process of moral decision making, the characteristics of a good society, or the relationship between human goodness and the divine, among many other questions.

These differing approaches depend in part on varying foundational assumptions about, for example, whether goodness stems from a transcendent power such as God or whether the source of value is nature, human conscience, or reason. A further source of divergence is the question of whether it is possible to identify a universal, absolute good or if, to the contrary, values are inevitably subjective or relative in nature. Differences in ethical frameworks also emerge from divergent attitudes toward rationality, emotion, and science, among other matters. What unites different schools of ethics is a conviction that it is both possible and worthwhile to identify good, or at least better, ways of acting and being in the world. (Ethics in this sense is identical to "morality," although some scholars distinguish between ethics as an academic area and morality as personal or cultural codes of conduct. The two terms are used interchangeably in this book.)

We begin this chapter describing some important religious and secular approaches to ethics and how these approaches can be applied to the process of decision making. The concepts introduced here will provide a foundation for the discussion in subsequent chapters. We then take a closer look at the three legs of sustainability, introducing each leg in more detail.

RELIGIOUS ETHICS

Probably the earliest, and still the most prevalent, way of thinking about values is religious. Religion involves ritual, symbol, community life, institutions, doctrines, and many other factors, but moral values are a central aspect of religious identity for both individuals and groups. Through religion, people think about what it means to be a good person and what a good society would entail; they find resources, support, and guidance in their efforts to live up to these values and to improve their communities.

Many discussions of sustainability do not refer to religion explicitly but rather define the problems of sustainability only in relation to technical, economic, or otherwise secular concerns. This is an unfortunate omission, not because sustainability is inherently religious, but because so many people in the world think about values—including the social, economic, and environmental values that help define sustainability—in religious terms. This is why we focus here on both religious and secular ethical traditions in relation to the ethical dimensions of sustainability.

Common Ideals

While people follow dozens of different religions, the vast majority belong to what are commonly called "world religions." Most of these first emerged in the Middle East – Judaism, Christianity, and Islam – South Asia – Hinduism, Buddhism, and Jainism – or China – Daoism and Confucianism. Christianity and Islam are by far the largest religious groups in the world, together including over 3.6 billion adherents, more than half the world's population (see Figure 3.1). The largest Asian religion by far is Hinduism, with around a billion practitioners, mainly in India, followed by Buddhism, with more than half a billion followers. Another billion profess no religion. After these large groups, the religious arena is extremely diverse, encompassing the oldest monotheistic Western tradition, Judaism, and diverse indigenous and tribal religions in Africa, Asia, Australia, and the Americas, as well as new religious movements such as Spiritism and the Baha'i faith, among many others.[1]

In discussing religious ethics in relation to sustainability in this chapter, we focus on the Western traditions, which have been most influential in North America, while also presenting a diverse range of perspectives from around the world. Many of the ethical perspectives and issues related to sustainability emerge in more than one tradition, such as a concern with social justice, care for the least well off, and stewardship of nonhuman nature.

Most religions have sacred texts that shape their ethics, although the role and significance of these texts vary widely. In the

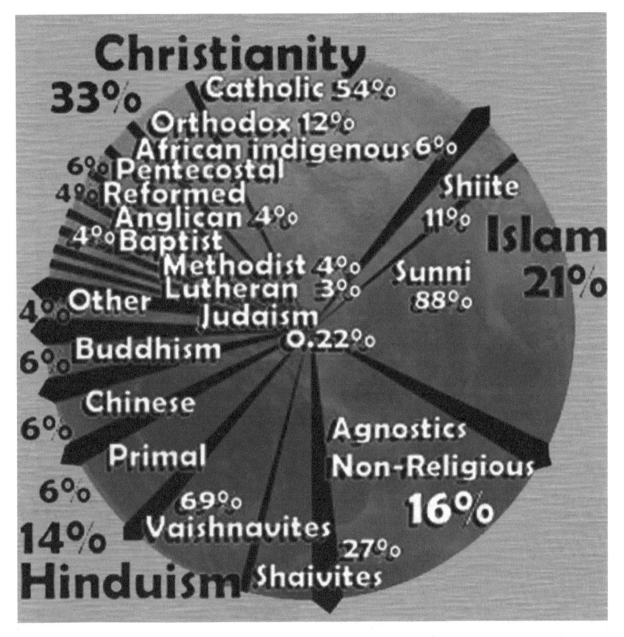

FIGURE 3.1 An estimate of world religion statistics based on data from 2005. *(Figure by Ingrid Shafer; usao.edu/~facshareri/ shafer_pluralism_final.htm)*

Western monotheistic traditions of Judaism, Christianity, and Islam, ethical thinking is strongly influenced by their respective sacred texts: Hebrew scriptures (the Old Testament); Christian scriptures (the New Testament); the Qu'ran; and various commentaries on and additions to these books, such as the rabbinic texts in Judaism or the sayings of the prophet Mohammed (*hadith*) in Islam. These texts were written over many centuries by different people with different goals in vastly different cultural and historical settings.

Textual scholars emphasize the presence of diversity and the importance of context in any effort to understand the ethical (or other) dimensions of scriptures. Still, it is possible to identify some common concerns in Western religious texts that have particular bearing on contemporary discussions of ethics and sustainability. Asian, indigenous, and new religious movements tend to be less focused on scriptural sources than Western traditions, although Hinduism and Buddhism, in particular, have vast and important sacred texts, which offer important guidelines for personal and social morality.

In relation to the ethics of sustainability, perhaps the most important theme in the major Western religions is an emphasis on social justice, which emerges strongly in Jewish, Christian, and Islamic scriptures. For example, Hebrew prophets such as Amos, Jeremiah, and Isaiah repeatedly and stridently call on their contemporaries to care for the least well off, symbolized by widows, orphans, and refugees—categories of people who were especially vulnerable in ancient Middle Eastern societies and are among those who

remain vulnerable today. The words of the Hebrew prophets remain important for many religious social justice advocates today (see Figure 3.2). In relation to these groups, and in wider social interactions, some important ethical guidelines include hospitality, protection of the weak from the strong, forgiveness of debts, and prohibitions on usury.

Similar themes can be seen in other traditions as well. For example, social justice and charity are central to the Qu'ran and the

FIGURE 3.2 Emphasizing social justice, Martin Luther King Jr. echoed the biblical prophet Amos in his "I have a dream" speech: "... until justice rolls down like waters and righteousness like a mighty stream." *(Source: Library of Congress)*

sayings of the prophet Mohammed, which are the foundational sources of Islamic ethics and important reference points for contemporary Muslim thinking about sustainability. Asian religious traditions such as Hinduism and Buddhism also encourage practitioners to practice charity and compassion for the most vulnerable members of society, both because compassion is an important duty (*dharma*) and because individuals' own spiritual development is influenced by their treatment of others.

Views of Human Nature

In many of these religious traditions, injunctions to charity and social justice rest on a social view of human nature: people are related to and dependent upon one another and are thus responsible for one another's well-being. This is expressed most clearly in the Buddhist concept of "no self" (*anatman*), which asserts that there exists no autonomous individual self. Instead people are constituted by their webs of relationships. Buddhist ethics emphasize charity and compassion, which should be social as well as individual characteristics. For many of the world's religious traditions, a good society is one in which no one falls through the cracks, well-off people take care of those in need, and cries for help are answered promptly, generously, and without rampant self-interest. This poses a challenge to secular Western moralities that sometimes emphasize the individual pursuit of happiness and prosperity over the well-being of the larger whole.

This challenge is especially explicit in Roman Catholic social thought, which offers a strong critique of individualism and consumerism. For example, in a 1986 pastoral letter on the economy, titled "Economic Justice for All,"[2] the U.S. Catholic Bishops assert that economic decisions and institutions should be judged on whether they protect or undermine "the dignity of the human person." This dignity, they add, "can be realized and protected only in community."

People are social beings, and their most important goods require collective support and enactment, which in turn are the responsibility of all social groups and classes. This responsibility can be fulfilled only with widespread participation in both the economic and political processes, which must be equitable and open. Finally, the bishops assert that all members of society, and especially the most powerful, have a special obligation to "the poor and miserable." This obligation can be understood, in part, as the demand to fulfill the basic human rights of all people to food, clothing, shelter, and other economic and material conditions for human dignity, as well as political and civil liberties. The economic values outlined in "Economic Justice for All" build on centuries of Catholic social thought and are reaffirmed in Catholic statements today, not only in the United States but also globally.

Few other religious traditions in both West and East are as centralized as the Catholic Church, which means they cannot issue globally authoritative statements on various issues. Nonetheless, it is possible to identify some common themes regarding social and economic ethics among diverse religious traditions. A concern for social justice and care for the poor and vulnerable, for example, is central to Buddhist political movements in Sri Lanka, to Gandhian-influenced Hindu groups in India, and to many Muslim community organizations in the Middle East and elsewhere.

As we discuss in more detail in Chapter 5, contemporary religious thinkers and leaders are paying increasing attention to environmental issues. Of particular interest to many religious leaders is the impact of environmental problems on poor and minority populations. Environmental concerns, in other words, are linked to traditional faith-based social and economic values. This inclusion of environment rests upon the social view of human nature that is common to many religious traditions, as discussed above. According to this view, people are connected to, dependent upon, and responsible to each other and to the larger society, in direct contrast to the highly individualistic approach to human nature that dominates mainstream secular understandings.

Unlike religious approaches, contemporary thinking about sustainability rarely makes explicit its definition of human nature. In many cases, understanding stakeholders' varying definitions of human nature can be helpful in framing challenges regarding sustainability. One contribution that religious ethics might make to the ethics of sustainability, then, could come in the form of explicit reflection on the foundational assumptions that underlie moral, political, and economic claims.

Despite commonalities, significant differences exist among and within religious groups on many ethical issues related to sustainability, including the value of nonhuman nature, the role of government, the responsibility of individuals and families, the moral status of capitalism and other economic systems, and a range of other matters. Still, at least in their ideals, most world religious groups largely agree that justice, charity, and environmental stewardship are important principles for evaluating specific social decisions, institutions, and processes. There remains, of course, great diversity both in the details of how these principles are interpreted and in the ways and extent to which they are applied. In the case of religious ethics, no less than secular values, a wide gap often exists between expressed ideals and concrete practices.

SECULAR AND PHILOSOPHICAL ETHICAL TRADITIONS

Not all ethical traditions, of course, are religious in nature. Contemporary Western culture, including its efforts to become more sustainable, is strongly influenced by philosophical ethics. The secular tradition in Western ethics begins with the classical Greek thinkers, especially Plato and Aristotle. The moral issues of concern to these philosophers are primarily social, with a special focus on the characteristics of a good society.

Plato and Aristotle asked explicitly what the good life is for human beings and provided answers that continue to influence both scholarly and popular thinking about ethics. Their reflections began with the notion that human beings are social animals whose good is only fulfilled in community. Their work does not display much interest in the issues that preoccupy many popular discussions of morality such as preoccupations with sexual behavior, family arrangement, and so forth, but rather focuses on problems of public virtue, right relationships, and justice.

Justice

One of the most important classical philosophical themes for sustainability is **justice**, which is also one of the most important virtues discussed by Aristotle. Justice involves giving to each his or her due, which implies a careful weighing both of what is possible and what is deserved, as well as comparisons among different relevant cases. For Aristotle, justice is both **procedural**—concerned with fairness in decision making and other social processes—and **substantive**—concerned with the proper distribution of actual goods. Both kinds of justice are central for sustainability today since a sustainable society requires both just political institutions and mechanisms, on the one hand, and distribution of necessary goods that avoids extremes of poverty and social inequality on the other.

Deontological Ethics

The most influential thinker in the Western ethical tradition is Immanuel Kant (1724–1804), the father of **deontological ethics**, which defines good practices as those that identify and follow the correct rules or uphold correct duties (deontology comes from the Greek *deon*, meaning duty). For deontological ethics, the likely consequences of actions do not matter in moral decision making, and the actual consequences do not affect evaluations of the moral worth of an action. Rather, ethical judgments are based on the moral actor's intentions and adherence to duties or rules. For example, people typically value honesty. Indeed, politicians go to great lengths to establish a reputation for honesty. Few elections are run on the slogan: "He lies, but he has his reasons." With this in mind, most people feel an obligation to exhibit honesty in their interactions with others. One might say that as a rule, honesty is the best policy.

Kant insisted that human reason was competent to determine ethics, and that ethics should be based and critiqued on rational grounds. Most famously, Kant articulated his ethical thesis in the form of several "**categorical imperatives**," moral statements that are objectively and universally true because of their intrinsic qualities (rather than because of their source or consequences). The most famous articulation of Kant's categorical imperative is to "Always act according to that maxim whose universality as a law you can at the same time will."[3] In other words, to be ethical an action must be able to be made universal. Returning to our example of honesty, we consider lying morally unacceptable, because we do not want to live in a world where everybody lies all the time. If it is not good for all people to act in this way, it is not good for a single actor to act in this way. While there are countless critiques of Kant's approach, his emphases on rationality, consistency, and universality remain highly influential in Western philosophical ethics.

Rights

Perhaps most notably, Kant's deontological model has strongly shaped theories about rights, one of the most important concepts in modern political and social ethics. **Rights** are moral claims that certain categories of persons can make on other persons who are, in turn, duty bound to respect those claims. For example, in the *Declaration of Independence* Thomas Jefferson referred to unalienable rights to life, liberty, and the pursuit of happiness. His argument here is that men, simply by virtue of existing as men, had a moral claim to these things. Of course, historians have pointed out that we took some time to extend similar rights beyond the rather narrow focus of white men. Indeed the issue of exactly who or what can make claim to a right has become a vibrant ethical discussion, as we shall see in Chapter 5.

For now, the key is to understand that theories of rights depend on Kant's insistence that morality requires treating other persons as ends in themselves and never simply as means to other ends. In other words, Kant argues that persons have intrinsic value that is independent of their instrumental use to others. This distinction between intrinsic and instrumental value is worth dwelling on a moment.

A hammer has instrumental value. It is quite helpful when one wants to hang a picture. Similarly, human beings can be said to have instrumental value. A plumber is a valuable person to have around when the kitchen sink is leaking. In contrast, a hammer does not have intrinsic value. If the hammer fails to serve a useful function (e.g., driving a nail), we typically discard it, caring very little about the hammer's welfare from that point on. Not so with the plumber. Few would abide killing the plumber simply because he has been unable to perform plumbing duties. While the hammer is merely a means to driving a nail, the plumber is an end in himself.

The assertion of intrinsic value is necessary to declarations of human rights, which assert that simply by virtue of being human, persons have certain rights that require no further justification. This is well expressed in Article One of the United Nations Universal Declaration on Human Rights, which states that "All human beings are born free and equal in dignity and rights. They are endowed with reason and conscience and should act towards one another in a spirit of brotherhood."[4] While the UN offers no transcendent justification for human rights, there are also religiously-based rights positions, such as that of the Roman Catholic Church, which asserts that because God created human beings with intrinsic dignity, all persons have the duty to respect and preserve this dignity through the fulfillment of rights claims.

Rights advocates differ not only regarding the source of the intrinsic value that justifies the attribution of rights but also about exactly what form these rights should take. The major disagreement, among both philosophers and politicians, is between "civil-political" and "socioeconomic" rights. The former include rights to freedom from torture and arbitrary arrest, freedom of expression, freedom of religion, and similar protections. Socioeconomic rights include rights to adequate housing, food, and water, free education, and a minimal standard of living. While civil and political rights are protected in the U.S. Bill of Rights, many Americans do not accept the concept of inalienable rights to social and economic welfare.

While both types of rights are included in the Universal Declaration on Human Rights (1948), the more comprehensive International Bill of Human Rights included two different "covenants," one on "Economic, Social, and Cultural Rights," and the other called "Civil and Political Rights" (both 1966). The United States did not sign the covenant on socioeconomic rights until 1979 (under President Jimmy Carter), and it still has not been ratified by the U.S. Congress. Civil and political rights may be more widely accepted in the United States, but social and economic rights are the most pertinent to sustainability, especially when those rights are expanded to include environmental rights such as clean water and air.

One of the most important principles for sustainability is the principle of Distributional Justice, according to which all people have a right to a fair share of basic resources—including food and water—that provide them with at least the chance of a quality of life that supports their actualization and not just mere survival. Distributional Justice does not require a theory of rights to support it, but it is greatly strengthened when allied to principles of intrinsic value and universal human dignity. We discuss the principle of Distributional Justice further in Chapter 4.

In addition to Distributional Justice, other human rights are often important when considering sustainability. Many of the social, environmental, and economic dimensions of sustainability are related to different rights, and sustainability projects and policies can be bolstered when allied to rights that are already widely accepted and even legally protected in a particular society. On the other hand, in some cases sustainability goals can conflict—in theory or practice—with other rights, such as individual claims to private property. Further, there are cultural, religious, and national differences in conceptions of rights, which can affect the reception of sustainability projects conceived in one setting and applied in another. This is particularly important for Westerners working on "sustainable development" projects in Asia, Africa, Latin America, and North American indigenous communities.

At the same time, it is important to remember that rights are a thoroughly Western philosophical concept, based on the concept of an autonomous individual with preexisting dignity and intrinsic value. Many non-Western and indigenous cultures and religious traditions do not understand human nature in this way. Thus, development and sustainability specialists might face the dilemma of trying to protect the rights of particular groups while at the same time broadening their own understanding of ethics beyond a focus on individual rights. For example, the Buddhist concept of the interdependent self encourages on respectful and compassionate behavior through relationality, and not on a commitment to individual rights.

BOX 3.1 Bioprospecting and Different Cultural Conceptions of Rights

While the concept of rights is central to Western ethics and legal systems, rights are not universally agreed upon. First, not all cultural and religious groups agree that rights are the most appropriate way to think about moral obligations and social relations. Some critics point out that rights theory is based on individualistic understandings of human nature, which assume that people will enter into conflicts with each other over the distribution of goods. From this perspective, framing morality in terms of rights can provoke conflict and competition.

In addition, even groups that share a commitment to rights language differ about which rights are most important and who holds them. In many Western nations, for example, individual rights to own property, including land, water, and other natural resources, are taken for granted and legally protected. In some cultures, however, land and other resources are held collectively, and cannot be bought or sold by individuals. This has led to abuses such as the appropriation of Native American lands by white settlers in the western United States during the nineteenth century, along with similar cases affecting other indigenous communities.

The notion that rights can be held collectively, by a cultural group, also creates challenges for contemporary rights theory, which generally focuses on individuals as rights holders. The problem of "bioprospecting" or "biopiracy" illuminates some of the ethical, legal, and political issues connected to philosophical questions about who has rights and to what. As defined by the national park service, biodiversity prospecting, or bioprospecting, is "scientific research that looks for a useful application, process, or product in nature." (For more information on these issues see www.nature.nps.gov/benefitssharing/whatis.cfm.)

Scientists, explorers, and entrepreneurs of all sorts have undertaken bioprospecting for centuries, but the issue has become more contentious in recent years as many bioprospectors have not shared the benefits with local populations or even the source country. The process is made more common and more problematic today as a result of technological developments (such as genetic modification), ecological threats to many biodiversity-rich regions of the world, and the political and economic challenges faced by many of the indigenous groups that inhabit such areas.

Bioprospecting is an important issue for sustainable development in many areas of the world today. A number of products native to indigenous regions of Latin America, Africa, and Asia have been identified by Western researchers and corporations, some of whom hope to profit from the products themselves or from products based on them (synthetic or genetically modified versions). The ethics of sustainability must provide a framework for thinking about these problems in practical and theoretical terms. Is rights language the best way to begin this process? Often the indigenous groups involved in these issues do not think of their relationship to each other, to the land, or to outsiders in terms of rights. Placing the issue in a rights framework may change the identities, relationships, and values of the native groups.

Once that framework is imposed, a number of more specific questions arise. Does anyone have a right to the special qualities of native plants that live only in a particular region? If so, does this right belong to individuals or to the group as a whole? Who protects this right legally? What are the moral obligations of foreign individuals or companies who want to investigate and use, in research or commerce, these natural resources? Rights theories from philosophical and religious ethics can help sustainability advocates sort out these questions.

Rights theories are also important in relation to the ethics of human treatment of non-human animals. A number of philosophers and activists have asserted that nonhuman animals have certain rights, such as the minimum right to avoid unnecessary suffering and untimely death. This idea is discussed more thoroughly in Chapter 4.

Consequentialist Ethics

Deontological ethics, which include rights theories, has received its share of criticism. Most notably, critics take aim at the idea of moral laws seen as coming from universal reason. What Kant saw as universal reason might instead be seen as merely a matter of subjective opinion. By what grounds is one to distinguish universal reason from personal or culturally based reasons? Indeed, some have argued that the concept of universal reason has led at times to the promotion of one authoritative voice (say, white European males) to the exclusion of all other voices.

In light of this kind of criticism, many contemporary ethicists favor the other major model in Western philosophical ethics: **consequentialist**. In consequentialist ethical systems, decisions about what to do and subsequent evaluations of the morality of an action are based on the expected or actual consequences of a behavior. Whether or not a person or action is good is based not on the intrinsic qualities of a person or on the rules he or she is following, but rather on the outcome of particular actions.

Returning to our ideal of honesty, is it really the best policy? Imagine being treated to a home-cooked meal only to find that the food tastes awful. How would people respond when prompted by the proud cook for their honest opinion about the meal? Some might lie outright: "That was delicious." Others might cleverly try to skirt the issue: "I have never had anything quite like it." Almost no one would respond with complete honesty: "This was quite possibly the worst meal I have ever had." Under a deontological system of ethics, the potential consequence of hurting the cook's feelings is immaterial. However, in the consequentialist model outcomes not only matter but are central to the decision.

The most prominent consequentialist model is **utilitarianism**, first articulated by English philosophers Jeremy Bentham (1748–1832) and his protégé John Stuart Mill (1806–1873). Bentham, who is regarded as the founder of utilitarianism, claimed that the ultimate goal of ethics should be to create the greatest good for the greatest number of people. Bentham defined good as happiness, and his "greatest happiness principle" focuses on happiness, defined largely as pleasurable feelings. Bentham devised a hedonistic or pleasure-based calculus to aid in determining whether an action contributed positively or negatively to the overall good or happiness.

Mill popularized and expanded upon Bentham's utilitarianism but disagreed with his mentor's belief that all pleasures were on a relatively level plane based on how well they contributed to one's happiness. Mill disagreed with this basic hedonistic form of happiness and claimed that there were higher pleasures (intellectual) and lower pleasures (sensual). The higher pleasures should be favored and encouraged over the lower pleasures. For example, the pleasure of learning something new would be more valuable or higher good than eating a tasty meal. This led to Mill's effort to instill a moral education in the public sphere that would teach people how to value and promote the higher pleasures or good in society.

Classical utilitarianism generally claims that an action's utility is determined by whether it produces more benefit or harm to the overall good, including pain and pleasure (or negative and positive feelings).[5] For utilitarianism, as for all consequentialist ethics, ends are more important than means, in contrast with deontological methods. As some rights theorists have pointed out, this means that a variety of questionable moral actions—especially involving minority groups—could be justified in relation to their positive outcome for majorities. For example, a decision to place all of the United States' hazardous waste facilities in New Jersey might be supported by the vast majority of people in other states. However, New Jersey residents might rightly object that this was unfair treatment.

As a result of dilemmas such as this, some philosophers have promoted a form of rule utilitarianism or consequentialism, which uses the principles of utilitarianism to determine which rules should be followed in order to promote the greatest good. In this view, rules could be developed for siting hazardous waste facilities and compensating affected local residents in order to avoid injustices. Rule utilitarianism is similar to deontology because it uses rules to evaluate moral

decisions, but it focuses on rules that create certain outcomes rather than on the intrinsic value of the action itself.

A final significant form of utilitarianism is **preference utilitarianism**, which claims that one's best interest is based in the satisfaction of individual-specific preferences and desires. This has most notably been championed by Peter Singer in relation to animals through the idea that rights cannot be conceptualized outside of the satisfaction of interests of all species, not just human beings, which is mainly the minimization of suffering. Singer's work, building on Bentham's earlier interest in reducing animal suffering, has made utilitarianism an important resource for advocates of animal welfare.

Objectivism and Ethical Relativism

Many approaches to sustainability implicitly, if not explicitly, follow a utilitarian ethical model. They aim to maximize selected goods for the largest number of individuals or groups without the need to specify philosophical foundations. Utilitarianism is especially appealing in culturally or religiously diverse settings where participants in environmental or social projects may have diverse founding principles while still agreeing on specific goals.

In this sense, utilitarianism overlaps with **pragmatism**, a school of philosophical ethics that originated with the work of American philosophers C. S. Peirce (1839–1914), William James (1842–1910), and John Dewey (1859–1952). Pragmatists assert that knowledge and meaning emerge from practical experience and that, in regards to ethics, values must be judged by practical consequences rather than intentions or relations to abstract goods. A pragmatist might argue that people possess inalienable rights, but this argument would not rest on any fundamental view regarding the value of human beings. Rather, the pragmatist would point to the ways that society breaks down when such rights are not bestowed on its members. For many social and environmental ethicists, and thus for people concerned with sustainability, pragmatism is appealing because it represents an effort to achieve concrete, positive results without the need to find consensus about abstract philosophical issues in advance (or ever).

While both pragmatism and utilitarianism emphasize practical consequences as the measure of moral worth, they differ in their understanding of what defines the good and how people can know it. Pragmatism rejects efforts to uncover ultimate meaning, truth, or other philosophical foundations for ethics. It is, thus, more relativist than utilitarianism since pragmatism requires no objective justifications for moral behavior. Utilitarianism, on the other hand, may insist that goods such as the reduction of pain and the maximization of pleasant feelings can be valued on objective bases.

Ethical relativism asserts that moral value must always be defined in light of a particular context, which may include cultural, historical, or individual differences as well as the social, economic, and political relations that create an understanding of goodness in a particular situation. For example, a relativist could decide that something is right for *a* but wrong for *b*. In contrast, **objectivism** in ethics asserts that judgments of good and evil rest on absolute foundations, which may be religious, philosophical, or scientific in origin.

One of the most prominent philosophers of sustainability, Bryan Norton, argues that people who seek a more sustainable society must join together to establish and achieve practical environmental and social improvements.[6] Norton writes from the perspective of environmental pragmatism, which finds many of the more abstract arguments in environmental philosophy insignificant and sometimes destructive to these larger goals insofar as they distract attention away from the urgent need for tangible results.

For example, a city may be considering converting part of a city forest to a parking lot. One group opposing such a change may focus on the economic value of the forest in terms of tourism dollars or an increased quality of life for local residents. A second group opposing the change may point to the intrinsic value of the wildlife. Pragmatists believe that such groups spend too much effort arguing with each other over WHY the green space is valuable, rather than focusing on their common interest in preserving that green space. They urge that diverse environmental groups look past their foundational differences toward practical goals that are based on the best environmental science and management available, and that well-reasoned action is the best course in enacting change and overcoming these differences.

BOX 3.2   Coca Production and Ethical Relativism

Mention the word "coca" to many people around the world, and you will conjure up visions of dangerous criminals and illicit drug trafficking. For many others, the word is part of a way of life centuries old. The wide and often contentious range of perspectives associated with coca production is represented in not only personal perspectives but also international policy.

Archaeological evidence indicates that the growing and chewing of coca plants in South America dates back to the sixth century CE and was prevalent throughout the Incan period. Coca is traditionally grown in many places throughout Latin America, from the high altitude Andes to the Amazon Basin, the Caribbean to Argentina. In the Andes, the coca plant is an integral part of traditional cultures, particularly the Aymara and Quechua in which coca is linked with special symbolism and rituals. Coca leaves are found both with ancient Andean mummies and in the mouths of high Andes pastoralists of today. Coca leaves, chewed directly or made into teas, possess medicinal properties that assist with ailments associated with life at high altitudes, stomach discomfort and fatigue. The leaves contain caffeine, which is used as a stimulant for the strenuous physical activity necessary to cultivate subsistience crops. Some traditional producers also trade coca for goods from other producers and regions. (For more information on cultural history of coca, see www.drugs-forum.com.)

From the perspective of an ethical relativist, there is nothing wrong with the coca production described. Coca is deeply integrated into this cultural and historical context and is part of the social and economic relations of the people and places involved in its traditional cultivation. In this context, it is not morally "wrong." The same ethical relativist may believe the export of coca outside of that cultural context or its transformation into cocaine, for example, is morally wrong.

In contrast with this ethical relativism, the policies and actions of many national governments reflect an objectivist belief that there is nothing "right" about coca production of any kind. Coca is a primary component in cocaine, and while coca is not produced in large quantities in North America and Europe, the demand for cocaine in those places is very large. Cocaine is highly addictive, and the cocaine trade is associated with extreme criminal acts and harmful impacts on end users. Foreign aid policies often include an absolutist stance, requiring assurance by recipient governments that they will eradicate coca production. The "war on drugs" and eradication efforts stemming from this perspective affect not only large-scale producers involved in the drug trade but also small-scale producers pursuing traditional uses. Eradication is severe and swift, often done with fire or chemicals and at great cost—in financial terms as well as impacts on human and ecosystem health, social structures, cultures, and livelihoods.

This presents a challenging ethical dilemma linked closely with all three dimensions of sustainability—environmental, economic, and social. What is seen as innocuous and integral to the lives and culture of some appears, from a different ethical perspective, to be evil and destructive of larger goods.

Objectivism and Relativism in Sustainability

The debate between objectivism and relativism is important for scientists and others concerned with sustainability in several ways. Most scientists share a commitment to the pursuit of what they understand to be objectively verifiable truths, which may be modified when better evidence is uncovered but are still judged according to objective standards. In contrast, some contemporary humanistic scholars, including some philosophers and ethicists, have adopted **postmodernist** approaches. Postmodernism is an umbrella term used for a diverse array of scholarly approaches in the humanities and social sciences. In philosophy, postmodernists reject the conviction that people can, through the use of reason, attain objectively true knowledge or identify absolute values. Consequently, some heated debates have erupted over these questions between scientists and other scholars (especially in literary or cultural studies).

The debate between relativism and objectivism has implications for sustainability in both its social and environmental dimensions. If there is no objective standard by which to judge the health of a natural ecosystem, for example, then it is not clear why individuals are justified in rejecting some uses of natural resources and preferring others. The groups opposed to replacing the green space with a parking lot might be seen as merely expressing their personal preference, and there is no reason that their preference should carry more weight than those who would like to see more parking available.

Similarly, if social and political values such as equality, democracy, or human rights are always culturally relative, there are no solid grounds to identify some policies, institutions, or societies as more or less ethical. These questions have been important in some related fields, such as environmental philosophy. However, they have not played a central role in scholarly discussions of sustainability, which—with their general focus on identifying and achieving practical goals—have tended more toward a preference for pragmatist or utilitarian ethical approaches.

ETHICS AS A TOOL FOR MAKING DECISIONS

Ethical traditions, both religious and secular, provide tools for thinking about difficult issues in a complicated world. They are thus a vital element of effective and successful decision-making processes. This is especially important for sustainability, which seeks to integrate diverse and sometimes conflicting ethical and practical goals.

Ethics can help people identify the values that are most important to them and analyze possible actions or outcomes in relation to these values. However, ethics is not simply about applying preestablished rules to clear-cut situations. First of all, multiple values are involved in many decisions, and certainly in those that aim toward sustainability. Thus, the choice is never just between good or evil but rather among various goods. Further, the relationship among different goods is almost always complex. Rarely do genuine goods stand in such stark opposition to each other that the choice is a simple one between, for example, jobs or endangered species. Anyone who frames complicated decisions in such dualistic terms is usually obscuring or ignoring important pieces of the problem.

Framing Ethical Problems

The issue of how to frame ethical problems in constructive and fruitful ways is especially relevant for problems of sustainability, where popular discourse often defines problems as stark choices between economic or environmental goods. In such situations, one of the most important tasks of ethics is asking questions that help lead to good solutions. The philosopher Anthony Weston notes that "if we are to find the best solutions to our ethical problems, we first need to find the best *problems.*"[7]

Better framing of ethical issues makes it possible to avoid obstacles that frequently prevent people from arriving at solutions that maximize diverse goods. For example, false dualistic choices like those mentioned previously are likely to impede sound decision making. When people stop thinking in terms of dualistic choices, they may engage in creative searches for alternative solutions that do not require the sacrifice of important values.

In searching for sustainability, it may be possible both to preserve wildlife habitat and to increase economic security for local residents, for example, by thinking creatively about developing more sustainable kinds of jobs, adopting different farming methods,

or protecting land through innovate means such as wildlife corridors. Such expansive solutions will not be possible, however, if decision makers believe economic and environmental goods are mutually exclusive and, thus, see their moral choices as between two diametrically opposed alternatives.

Another common obstacle to good ethical solutions is reactive thinking, or what Weston calls "freezing." In such cases, people simply try to cope with and adapt to a problem after it has developed. Instead of responding after the fact, Weston proposes that people think preventatively, asking whether ethical problems can be changed, made less serious, or even eliminated.[8] This call for proactive thinking is especially relevant for sustainable planning and design, endeavors that can help maximize both environmental and social goods. Rather than cleaning up after people have made bad choices, in other words, an ethic of sustainability can help make good choices more affordable, attractive, and convenient.

Conflicting Values

Maximizing goods is not always possible, of course. In real life situations, people often face decisions about what goods to prioritize, given multiple values and limited resources with which to pursue them. Ethical questions arise, in other words, not when there is an easy choice between a good solution and a bad one but rather when real values conflict and it is not possible to preserve them all to the extent desired. Such situations arise frequently in the context of sustainability, which strives to incorporate a range of social,

BOX 3.3 Conflicts between Human Needs and Wildlife Preservation

Wildlife have been hunted for food since people began using spears to make up for our lack of claws, fangs, and speed. Relatively small or nomadic human populations posed little threat to wildlife populations. New forms of technology, however, allowed people to kill more animals, devastating populations such as bison on the North American plains and cod on the Great Banks of the Atlantic. Technology in the form of trains provided a means and market incentive for people to ship barrels of dead passenger pigeons to be eaten in Chicago and New York in the late 1800s, driving this species to extinction. It is hard to imagine what the enormous flocks of literally millions of birds looked like, darkening the sky for hours while migrating or breaking tree limbs from the weight of their collective nests in roosts.

Aldo Leopold mourned the loss of the passenger pigeons by comparing the event with the advent of technologies: "Our grandfathers were less well-housed, well-fed, well-clothed than we are. The strivings by which they bettered their lot are also those which deprived us of [Passenger] pigeons. Perhaps we now grieve because we are not sure, in our hearts, that we have gained by the exchange. The gadgets of industry bring us more comforts than the pigeons did, but do they add as much to the glory of the spring?" (1949, p. 109).

In the United States today, conflicts between wildlife and people lie less in the realm of hunting for sustenance and more in the need for land. As cities sprawl into rural areas, there are fewer streams, woodlots, and fields for thrushes, garter snakes, and cottontails. As the paper industry converts forests to plantations or farmers till more fields for crops, some species cannot find the requisite prey or nesting areas to remain viable.

Grizzly bears in the western U.S. are large predators requiring large ranges to feed, breed, and survive. These ranges, required to maintain biodiversity, extend beyond the scope of designated protected areas and parks and are threatened by land-use change. In addition to the drastic development that often occurs at the edges of protected lands, problems from adjacent lands can include invasive species, poaching, pollution, and altered flood and fire regimes (Hilty et al. 2006). Changes destroy habitat which can isolate populations and make the bears more vulnerable to losses in genetic diversity and thus render the species and the ecosystem less resilient and adaptable to change.

Wildlife corridors between isolated protected lands can help to reverse the loss the biodiversity by making gene sharing more likely and decentralizing species populations. In the case of grizzlies, this could connect disparate populations in the western United States through designated pathways, or "wildlife highways," that allow relative freedom of movement between protected areas through unprotected ones. To properly implement a wildlife corridor program, it must be specifically developed and tailored to the needs of the ecosystem, which includes the human community.

A truly functional corridor will take into consideration the historical conditions that led to the establishment of the reserve, such as Yellowstone National Park, and the settlement history of the surrounding area, including the displacement of people, especially indigenous groups. The design then combines this awareness of human history

(continued)

and values with the scientific understanding of the ecosystem and focal species. There are, of course, challenges with this approach, as boundaries of the corridors are often informal, and grizzlies may interact with human beings along their way.

While we may know a great deal about animals such as grizzlies, conflicts between people and wildlife may only become evident when wildlife populations fall perilously close to endangerment. At that point, federal laws (such as the Endangered Species Act in the United States) or international treaties (such as the Convention on Biological Diversity) can be used to protect habitat or halt proposed projects, if an advocacy group is willing to get involved. Research funds may become available to determine how best to promote breeding, alter fishing quotas, or redirect development (as with research to better manage blue crabs in the Chesapeake Bay). Finally, local communities may be more amenable to changing their practices when confronted with data they trust about the decline of culturally valuable species (Blanchard and Monroe 1990).

economic, and environmental goods in complex situations.

Not infrequently, for example, environmental values such as the preservation of wildlife habitat conflict with social or economic goals such as the production of a larger food supply or low-cost housing. In such situations, the goal of ethics is to help resolve conflicts as constructively as possible. In such cases, the best decisions will be based on a number of factors, including good knowledge (scientific, economic, and cultural), an understanding of the history of the situation, accurate information about the likely outcomes of various decisions, a careful weighing of the different values involved, and efforts to frame the problem in a way most likely to maximize as many important values as possible.

All these factors, in turn, will be facilitated by wide participation by the different individuals and groups affected by the decision. Democratic processes and open, fair political institutions are not only goods in themselves but also prerequisites for achieving a host of other goods. We will go into more detail on incorporating these aspects into decision making in Part III of this text. First, however, we will take a closer look at the ethical concepts used to analyze decisions regarding sustainability.

THE THREE LEGS OF SUSTAINABILITY

With this basic discussion of general ethical principles, we are now ready to explore how these ideas apply specifically to the challenge of sustainability. In Chapter 1, we described the three-legged stool model of sustainability. This model provides the structure of the following three chapters with each chapter focusing on one leg of sustainability.

However, as we will continue to stress, understanding the concepts explained within the context of each leg requires an understanding of how the three legs are integrated into one framework. The following section provides a brief discussion of the ethical issues central to each of the three legs in order to provide a sense of how these legs relate to each other before isolating each leg for a more in-depth discussion of the concepts. The objective here is to help the reader maintain a sense of this larger picture while reading about the individual legs in Chapters 4, 5, and 6.

Social Ethics

We focus here on the ways that a community, society, or even a nation can be organized so as to achieve common goods that are not reducible to the sum of personal aims and interests. Sustainability is social both because it looks primarily at decisions and actions that are collective rather than individual and personal, and because it is concerned with goods that are collectively defined and achieved.

In contrast, more personal or individualistic ethical systems may be concerned with actions that do not directly affect larger groups of people, such as personal choices about sexual identity or behavior. Certainly even the most apparently personal of decisions have larger implications, if only for the people close to the individual concerned. Further, even intensely personal moral decisions are made within a larger social context and on the basis of values and attitudes that are the result of social learning, social experiences, and social relations. Thus, the line between personal and social ethics is never hard and fast. Still, it is possible to distinguish between moral issues that are primarily personal and those that have immediate and unavoidable social implications. The

latter is most relevant for sustainability, because it is a quality of groups, including local communities, institutions, and entire societies.

An ethic of sustainability is a particular sort of social ethic. While individual decisions and actions may have important ramifications for sustainability, they do so because they contribute to—or detract from—efforts to create and maintain more sustainable collectives. In other words, the goal of sustainability is a vision not simply of private benefit but rather of a common good.

Traditional topics of concern to social ethicists include the morality of war and peace, the benefits of different forms of governance, civil and human rights, and the proper role and treatment of vulnerable social groups, along with many other issues. Perhaps most important, social ethics has addressed the relations between individuals and larger groups, including the rights and responsibilities of the former and the beneficial as well as oppressive potential of the latter. This ethical analysis is conducted in light of social goods, which are defined differently in various times and places but which, in the modern West, often include justice and fairness, equity and equal opportunity, concern for vulnerable groups, stability and security, and protection of individual liberties.

Today, social ethicists continue to reflect on these longstanding questions. while also expanding the discussion to important contemporary issues, including many related to science, medicine, and technology. These topics receive attention from many different

---

BOX 3.4   Cloning and Social Ethics

Cloning, a technology in which an exact copy of a biological organism can be made through the manipulation of DNA fragments, has been used to create individuals of a number of nonhuman animal species—most famously Dolly the sheep, who in 1996 was the first cloned mammal. Many of the ethical debates about cloning focus on the possibility of cloning human beings, for purposes that may include creating infants for infertile couples, treating genetically based diseases, supplying organs for transplants, or even replicating "great" individuals. All these purposes raise ethical questions, some of which concern the personhood of clones (including their rights and legal protection), the possible harm or suffering caused to cloned individuals, and the responsibility of scientists, businesses, and society generally for the welfare of cloned individuals (See McGee 1998; Nussbaum and Sunstein 1998).

In addition to these issues, the cloning of other species raises important and often troubling moral questions. These include how we set limits on human manipulation of nature, the possible reduction of genetic diversity because of widespread cloning, and the morality of creating organisms for purely instrumental ends. Social justice concerns are also important, as raised, for example, by some gay advocates, who fear that cloning may lead to efforts to eliminate traits labeled as "undesirable" or "unnatural." Finally, cloning raises environmental issues, especially in relation to the possible loss of biological diversity, if cloning largely replaces the sexual reproduction of, for example, endangered species. Many more ethical and practical issues are entailed in cloning.

---

perspectives, of course. What distinguishes their treatment by social ethicists is attention to the values that are explicitly or implicitly upheld in a given position or practice and to the moral consequences of collective decisions and actions.

The boxed example here describes a social ethics analysis of cloning. Similar analyses can be conducted on a wide range of other contemporary issues: How should the traditional just war requirement to minimize civilian casualties be modified in light of new weapons technologies that make it impossible, often, to avoid civilian deaths? Who will benefit and who will be harmed by agricultural innovations such as genetically modified crops or new pesticides? What moral duties does a society have in relation to new immigrant groups, and vice versa? The examples are endless, and social ethics raises and answers distinctive questions about a range of concerns, sources, and criteria.

Environmental Ethics

Ethical issues focused on the ecological leg of sustainability can be discussed largely in the context of **environmental ethics**, a subfield of ethics defined as philosophical reflection on and arguments about the value of nonhuman nature. Environmental ethics may be concerned about entire ecosystems or regions, or with smaller units such as species, individual nonhuman animals or plants, or landscape features such as mountains or forests. Questions about the value of nonhuman nature and its relations to other moral goods have been important to philosophers, theologians, and naturalists for centuries.

The relationship between environmental ethics and ethics of sustainability takes several different forms. Sometimes "environmental" is treated as a synonym for sustainability, in which case an ethic of sustainability would be virtually identical to environmental ethics. This is the case for some environmental philosophers, including Bryan Norton, whose book *Searching for Sustainability* is subtitled *Interdisciplinary Essays in the Philosophy of Conservation Biology*.[9] Norton's more recent book, called simply *Sustainability*, is subtitled *A Philosophy of Adaptive Ecosystem Management*. For Norton, and for a number of other environmental philosophers, sustainability is first and foremost about conservation of and attitudes and practices toward nonhuman nature.

Another view would define sustainability as a subset of, or specific approach within, environmental ethics. In this approach, an ethic of sustainability would be identified with environmental philosophies that emphasize social and economic issues, such as environmental justice and human health issues. Some of the more **anthropocentric** (human-centered) approaches in environmental ethics, thus, might be understood as "sustainability" ethics.

One example of this is the work of Ben Minteer, a pragmatist who argues that environmental ethics should be identified as a kind of "civic philosophy" that emphasizes "long-term human interests, such as a concern with the well-being of future generations."[10] Minteer rejects **nonanthropocentric** (**ecocentric** or **biocentric**) ethics, which find intrinsic value in nonhuman nature apart from its usefulness to or appreciation by humans. While nonanthropocentric environmental ethics often focus on wilderness and other aspects of nature apart from human goods, pragmatists such as Minteer make social, economic, and political concerns central.

While both these approaches can be found in the literature on environmental (and sustainability) ethics, neither is adequate for the goals of this book. Here, it is most accurate to understand environmental ethics as one part or subset of sustainability, corresponding to the environment as one of sustainability's three key dimensions. This approach is evident in the organization of Part II of this text, in which social, economic, and environmental ethics are discussed as distinctive subfields, all of which contribute to the integrative whole that constitutes an ethic of sustainability.

Economic Ethics

We can see that sustainability raises a number of new moral questions. Perhaps the most important of these come in relation to the integration of social goods with economic and environmental values. Economics, by definition, involves collective decisions and processes. Even individual financial decisions are made only in relation to the influence of larger economic forces. Economic ethics is concerned with the moral foundations, characteristics, and consequences of economic activities and institutions. The focus here may be on specific business practices or industries or on broader issues, such as the moral values, implicit or explicit, that undergird economic policies and practices.

When considering the ethical dimensions of economic systems, institutions, and decisions, a number of significant questions related to sustainability must be taken into account. One question concerns the definition of economic goals such as productivity, efficiency, and security. Efficiency, for example, is usually defined as the maximization of output in relation to certain inputs, and is a primary goal of many economic practices, systems, and institutions. The inputs at stake can vary, and depending on which ones are selected—for example, labor time, energy, or capital investment—judgments of economic efficiency will vary.

Contemporary North American agriculture provides an illuminating example of the way differing economic approaches entail particular ethical consequences. Agriculture, like sustainability more generally, is often assumed to be a practical, scientific, and technical undertaking rather than an ethical and cultural one. Any agricultural system, however, involves implicit or explicit efforts to live according to a particular definition of the good in the standards or rules that farmers and ranchers follow, the goals they seek, and the constraints by which they abide. Making explicit the values that underlie an agricultural system enables us to evaluate agriculture in relation to other values that are important for sustainability. This process is necessary in order to identify and transform unsustainable practices.

Efficiency, for example, is usually defined as the maximization of output in relation to certain inputs, and is a primary goal of many economic practices, systems, and institutions. In Western agriculture, efficiency is defined as a minimization of human labor—fewer "man-hours"—used to produce ever larger harvests. The drive to reduce human labor has led to tremendous increases in the use of energy, mainly fossil fuels, and to the establishment of a particular type of farm.

First, contemporary North American farms have become very large, often over 2,000 acres. Such farms usually grow one or at most a few crops or raise only one species of animal. This reduction of diversity maximizes efficiency because you need fewer types of machines, but it can create additional challenges, including the use of large amounts of artificial fertilizers and pesticides for plant production, and large amounts of waste in animal production. These farms, such as the massive chicken facility pictured above, usually employ very few people to work very large areas or care for large numbers of animals (see Figure 3.3). Most of these farms rely heavily on large tractors and other machines.

FIGURE 3.3 Large-scale facilities like this chicken house in Florida can increase some types of efficiency (e.g., saving processing time) but often at the cost of increased fuel and chemical use. *(U.S. Department of Agriculture)*

These trends, which stem largely from the drive for a particular kind of efficiency, have led to a number of secondary consequences. These include the depopulation of rural communities, the loss of topsoil and biological diversity, and the contamination of soil, water, and air. A number of observers have criticized the social, environmental, and economic consequences of the industrial model for modern agriculture.[11] These critics point out that this kind of farming, along with its effects, has arisen not accidentally, but because of a particular view of what values to prioritize and what goals to seek.

It is possible to define efficiency in different terms, for example, in relation to the use of energy. Aiming for that sort of efficiency might lead to smaller, more diverse, more labor-intensive farms that have much smaller **carbon footprints.** Such farms succeed according to economic values that are not dominant in Western agriculture today.

This example shows how economic and social goals are intertwined. Decisions about economic processes and institutions inevitably favor one social good or another, which can ultimately favor one social class over another. The social and economic values of sustainability are not currently priorities in contemporary U.S. society (or many other societies). Unless those values are made explicit, it is impossible to evaluate concrete practices and institutions or to develop alternatives. Simply establishing standards does not, of course, necessarily lead to real-life changes. It may, however, constitute a necessary step in the movement toward more sustainable practices and ultimately toward more sustainable societies.

Integrating the Three Legs

This effort at integration is one of the most distinctive, and sometimes most difficult, aspects of sustainability. The attempt not only to include but also to integrate social, economic, and environmental values makes the ethics of sustainability both especially challenging and especially promising. In its moral as well as practical dimensions, sustainability does not mean simply accumulating a list of divergent goals. Rather, it requires efforts to find common ground when possible and to adjudicate between different values and goals when necessary. Difference does not necessarily mean incompatibility or competition, and in fact sustainability rejects simplistic dualisms between social and environmental goods. Thus, a sustainable ethic is holistic, in theory, insofar as it is guided by a vision in which social, economic, and environmental values not only coexist but, in many cases, reinforce each other.

In many concrete situations, however, different ethical concerns and goals cannot be integrated harmoniously, and choices must be made about which to prioritize. This is perhaps especially true for an ethic of sustainability, which explicitly takes into account distinctive and sometimes conflicting goals of social justice, economic efficiency, and environmental integrity. In order to address conflicts and ambiguities constructively, it is not enough simply to have ethical principles or rules. A clear and well-considered process of ethical decision-making is also required in order to understand the issues at stake, the options available, and the potential consequences of various decisions.

CONCLUSION

A distinctive aspect of sustainability is the attempt to integrate a diverse set of ethical principles and goals in both theory and practice. Sustainability is not simply a patchwork of disparate values but an integrated system in which the parts work together to reinforce each other. In the case of potential conflicts between, for example, environmental and social principles, an ethic of sustainability should not simply choose one or the other but rather should attempt to maximize both values to the extent possible. This may require considering a wider range of options than usual, including some that might not normally seem desirable or feasible. It may require engaging in dialogue and reaching compromises with individuals or groups who are not one's usual conversation partners. Implementing the values of sustainability might even demand considerable sacrifice of other interests, both private and collective.

In this delicate and difficult task, established traditions of ethical thinking offer invaluable resources and insight. They can help to identify the values at stake and clarify the knowledge and assumptions that undergird and justify these values. On a practical level, ethics provides tools that can help people seeking sustainability to adjudicate conflicts, set priorities, and seek consensus or compromise. In Part II of this text, we will explore in more detail the issues and approaches regarding these goals.

REFERENCES

Berry, Wendell. 1977. *The Unsettling of America: Culture & Agriculture*. San Francisco: Sierra Club Books.

Blanchard, K. A. and M. Monroe. 1990. "Culture and conservation: Strategies for reversing population decline in seabirds," *Endangered Species Update* 7(3/4): 1–5+.

Hilty, Jodi, William Lidicker, Adina Merenlender, and Andrew Dobson. 2006. *Corridor Ecology: The Science and Practice of Linking Landscapes for Biodiversity Conservation*. Washington, DC: Island Press.

Jackson, Wes. 1994. *Becoming Native to this Place*. Lexington, KY: University Press of Kentucky.

Kant, Immanuel. 1990. *Foundations of the Metaphysics of Morals*. 2nd ed. Trans. L. W. Beck. New York: Macmillan Publishing Company.

Leopold, Aldo. 1949. *A Sand County Almanac*. Oxford: Oxford University Press.

McGee, Glenn. 1998. "Primer on Ethics and Bioengineering." www.actionbioscience.org/ biotech/mcgee.html#primer.

Midgley, Mary. 1991. *Can't We Make Moral Judgments?* New York: St. Martin's Griffin.

Minteer, Ben. 2006. *The Landscape of Reform: Civic Pragmatism and Environmental Thought in America*. Cambridge, MA: MIT Press.

Norton, Bryan. 2002. *Searching for Sustainability: Interdisciplinary Essays in the Philosophy of Conservation Biology*. Cambridge: Cambridge University Press.

———. 1991. *Toward Unity Among Environmentalists*. Oxford: Oxford University Press.

Nussbaum, Martha C. and Cass R. Sunstein, Eds., *Clones and Clones: Facts and Fantasies about Human Cloning*. New York: Norton.

United Nations. "Universal Declaration on Human Rights." United Nations. www.un.org/en/documents/udhr/index.shtml.

United States Catholic Bishops. "Economic Justice for All: A Pastoral Letter on Catholic Social Teaching and the U.S. Economy." Office for Social Justice. www.osjspm.org/economic_justice_for_all.aspx.

Weston, Anthony. 1997. *A Practical Companion to Ethics*. Oxford: Oxford University Press.

ENDNOTES

1. For a list of major religions ranked by number of adherents, refer to www.adherents.com/Religions_By_Adherents.html.
2. United States Catholic Bishops, "Economic Justice for All: A Pastoral Letter on Catholic Social Teaching and the U.S. Economy," Office for Social Justice, www.osjspm.org/economic_justice_for_all.aspx.
3. Kant (1990).
4. United Nations, "Universal Declaration on Human Rights," United Nations, www.un.org/en/documents/udhr/index.shtml.
5. Note that the focus here is on the sum of individual feelings—the greatest good for the greatest possible number. "Overall good" refers to that sum, not to a holistic sense of community benefit or harm.
6. See for example Bryan Norton, Toward Unity among Environmentalists (Oxford: University Press, 1991).
7. Weston (1997).
8. Ibid
9. Norton (2002).
10. Minteer (2006).
11. Wes Jackson and Wendell Berry, mentioned earlier in this chapter, are two of the most vocal critics.

CHAPTER 4

Social Dimensions of Sustainability Ethics

In Chapter 3, we highlighted the challenge and the promise of an ethics of sustainability: the integration of social, environmental, and economic concerns in a coherent, plausible, and practical way. The next three chapters explore these three sets of concerns in more detail, beginning here with the social dimensions of an ethics of sustainability.

Social ethics, as noted in Chapter 3, addresses the characteristics of a good society, including economic and political institutions as well as the relations between individuals and larger social structures and the integration or balancing of different, sometimes competing, values. This sets it apart, as a subfield of ethics, from a more individualistic morality. In this chapter, and the book as a whole, we ask about a good society that is sustainable in social, environmental, and economic terms. The social dimensions of the ethics of sustainability or of a sustainable society are not identical to social ethics, at least as traditionally developed in the West. However, they have many overlapping concerns and themes. The social dimensions of sustainability ethics are shaped, in a constitutive way, by their relation to environmental and economic themes and to the construction of

an overarching ethic that brings together all three dimensions.

This chapter explores some of the specifically social dimensions of sustainability. We focus on justice and interdependence as two of the most important and inclusive social values that appear in most discussions of sustainability. Before entering into a more detailed discussion of these themes, we briefly discuss their relationship to more general moral themes that undergird their expressions in sustainability ethics—justice, fairness, and reciprocity.

JUSTICE, FAIRNESS, AND RECIPROCITY

Sustainability involves intrinsically collective questions about the shape of a society, the relations among social groups, and the mechanisms by which public decisions are made. A number of different values and approaches from social ethics are relevant to these discussions. Among the most important values in traditional Western thinking about social ethics and in contemporary discussions of the social aspects of sustainability is justice. Justice has been defined in many different ways but the most common description, at least since Aristotle, is that justice entails "giving to each his due." Justice is a collective value, concerned not only with individual behavior but also with social relationships, including the distribution of goods, procedures and institutions of governance, and mechanisms of judgment and punishment, among other issues.

Justice provides a procedural and sometimes substantive value for organizing both entire societies and the relations among individuals. It was the most important social and political value for Greek philosophers, beginning with Plato and Aristotle, and has remained important in Western thought since then. Since the Enlightenment, justice has been closely linked to discussions of rights, which today encompass not only natural and human rights but also the rights of minority groups, women, nonhuman animals, and even the natural world itself.

Justice is not always linked to a philosophical perspective based on rights. More broadly, justice is a good that societies can achieve through deliberate steps, which often include the establishment of rights for individuals and groups and rules and procedures to guide governments and other institutions. Justice is central to many other individual thinkers and social groups involved in sustainability discussions, including utilitarian, feminist, environmental, and social democratic groups. Despite differing priorities and definitions, for all these groups justice provides a lens for thinking about fair distribution of resources, democratic governance, and the preservation of goods for future generations. One of the most important themes in these discussions, especially in relation to sustainability, is the notion of reciprocity, often expressed in terms of the "Golden Rule."

The Golden Rule

One of the most common statements of ethical concern, found in many religious and cultural traditions dating back thousands of years, is the "Golden Rule." Many different versions of this rule exist, both secular and religious in perspective (see Figure 4.1). Sometimes called an "ethic of reciprocity," golden rules generally call on people to consult their own needs and wants and extend to others the same treatment that they would want to receive. In other words, golden rules call for reciprocal or mutual treatment. In contrast to justice, golden rules provide guidelines for individuals rather than descriptions of social institutions or collective practices. Nonetheless, they are relevant for an ethics of sustainability, which involves attitudes and practices at many different levels, from individuals to the largest collectives.

One of the earliest versions of a golden rule was articulated by the foundational Chinese thinker Confucius (551–479 BCE). His *Analects* contains the following dialogue: "Tzu-kung asked, 'Is there a single word which can be a guide to conduct throughout one's life?' The Master said, 'It is perhaps the word "shu" [empathy, or consideration]. Do not impose on others what you yourself do not desire.'"[1] Statements reflecting a similar ethics of reciprocity written at approximately

FIGURE 4.1 Ideas akin to the Golden Rule can be found within many systems of faith *(Poster by Paul McKenna and Scarboro Missions)*

the same time period can be found in the *Mahabharata* of the Hindu tradition, and in Buddhist texts. The Jewish sage, Hillel, when challenged to teach the holy scriptures or Torah briefly said, "What is hateful to you, do not do to your neighbor, that is the whole Torah, while the rest is the commentary thereof; go and learn it."[2] In the *New Testament* of the Christian Bible, the Golden Rule is articulated in slightly different ways in the different gospels, but its basic formulation is the same: "Always treat others as you would like them to treat you."[3]

Some people view the golden rule as a complete and sufficient ethics, maintaining that all moral duties can be inferred from it. The Golden Rule is not without its detractors, however. The nineteenth-century British writer George Bernard Shaw suggested that the Golden Rule mistakenly assumes that one's own wishes provide a good measure of what others actually want. "Don't do to others as you want them to do unto you," Shaw wrote. "Their tastes may be different."[4] Shaw was a satirist, but his criticism foreshadowed contemporary discussions. Feminist thinkers, for example, point out that ethics based on the values or interests of a generic individual—such as the "you" of the Golden Rule—usually assume a typically male perspective and fail to account for the qualitative differences that gender makes in desires and interests.

In addition to gender, many other factors, including socioeconomic status, generation, religious commitments, and cultural traditions make any straightforward implementation of the Golden Rule problematic. For example, an independently wealthy person may prefer a low-taxing, hands-off government. Such a person, if elected to office, might strip away welfare programs with the Golden Rule in mind, to the detriment of economically disadvantaged members of the society.

Likewise, it is always dangerous to enact the Golden Rule literally when crossing cultural boundaries. For example, attempting to stimulate the local economy and local food production by starting an environmentally friendly hog farm may constitute an effort to treat others economically and ecologically as you would wish to be treated. However, such good intentions will be misplaced if the local community in question is predominantly Jewish or Muslim, where the eating of pork is forbidden, or if residents belong to a vegetarian religion, such as the Jain or Krishna traditions.

With these concerns in mind, we might adjust the Golden Rule to read: "Always treat others as you would like them to treat you if, and only if, you share preferences for commonly accepted elements of the good life." With these concerns in mind, some endorse what is called the platinum rule: always treat others as they would like to be treated. Of course, this leaves us with the very demanding task of clearly articulating other people's desires and identifying commonly accepted elements of the good life. It also leaves open the question of whether individual preferences, however carefully calibrated, can simply be added together in order to achieve an adequate social ethic. This presupposes that a good society is merely the sum of its parts.

More likely, however, a collective good—such as sustainability—require something beyond the discernment and satisfaction of a bunch of individual desires.

The Golden Rule can, however, make some contributions to an ethic of sustainability. At a minimum, it gives us a strong reason to assume that, like us, our local and global neighbors want and deserve to have their basic needs met—needs for physical security, health, nutritious food, decent housing, education, a meaningful livelihood, and a life-supporting, beautiful, and biologically diverse planet. In turn, we can assume that they, like us, want and deserve the right and opportunity to participate in the decision-making processes that determine how these basic goods are defined and distributed. Also, we can assume that they, like us, want and deserve to receive a proportionate share of these basic components of the good life.

Ethics of Care

Some political philosophers and ethicists have noted weaknesses in theories based on procedural principles such as reciprocity or justice. A number of feminist thinkers, for example, argue that while justice is an important principle, it cannot by itself define or guide a society that is good for all its members, or in all the ways that matter. They highlight the notion of "care," which "emphasizes responsiveness to particular persons in their uniqueness, and commitment to them as such." By contrast, they note, "the so-called 'justice' perspective emphasizes adherence to moral rules, values and principles, and an abstractive treatment of individuals, based on the selected categories which they instantiate."[5]

The abstractness of justice rests in part on an assumption that morality is primarily concerned with relationships between equals. Good societies, however, involve a wide range of kinds of relationships, including those between women and men, children and adults, able-bodied and disabled people, and people of different economic classes, among many other forms of diversity. Many, perhaps most, of the relationships in which people engage are not between rational, autonomous equals. We need a social ethic that can account for and help guide these relationships as well. This is especially important for sustainability, since it entails a host of structurally unequal relationships, including those across generations and with nonhuman nature, as well as between people and nations whose economic and political status varies widely. An ethic of care promotes the idea that individuals are socially interdependent and that we have to pay special attention to the decisions and choices that affect the most vulnerable members of society.

An ethic of care, as well as perspectives from environmental ethics (examined in the next chapter), can help us adapt theories of fairness and justice to accommodate concern for sustainability. With the need for such adaptations in mind, a number of specific issues come to the fore. Among the most important are distributional questions, including distribution of goods and risks, within and among contemporary social groups and also between generations.

BOX 4.1   Social Justice, an Ethics of Care, and Sustainability

Kenule "Ken" Saro-Wiwa (1941–1995) a Nigerian author and environmental activist, was president of the Movement for the Survival of the Ogoni People. The Ogoni are an ethnic minority living in the Niger Delta, where a long history of crude oil extraction has produced extreme environmental damage. Saro-Wiwa was an outspoken critic of the Nigerian government and the multinational corporations responsible for the degradation of his ethnic homeland. His nonviolent campaign for social justice called for the end of the toxic pollution of the Ogoni territory and extensive remediation of degraded lands and waters, as well as economic reparations and a more equitable sharing of resources.

Saro-Wiwa's unflagging efforts to care for a vulnerable people and pursue social justice led to a lengthy imprisonment, a hasty trial, and his subsequent hanging, along with eight other members of the Movement for the Survival of the Ogoni People. The charges against Saro-Wiwa were widely recognized as unfounded, and his execution by the military regime, which outraged the international community, led to the suspension of Nigeria from the Commonwealth of Nations for three years. Those who testified against Saro-Wiwa later admitted to being bribed to offer false accusations.

In 1995 Saro-Wiwa was a nominee for the Nobel Peace Prize and the winner of the Goldman Environmental Prize for his pursuit of social justice and his efforts to protect his people from environmental ravages. His efforts remain an example of the close interconnections between social and environmental issues. American environmental justice scholar and advocate Bunyan Bryant writes: "We can no longer afford to champion the rights of trees and nonhuman life without also championing the rights of all people, regardless of race, sex, income, or social standing. We can no longer afford to treat certain categories of people as if they were not part of a biodiverse community." (Bunyan 1995, p. 217)

DISTRIBUTIONAL PRINCIPLES

Both the interpersonal principle of reciprocity (or the Golden Rule) and more collective notions of justice ask people to consider the distribution of goods and harms. In the context of sustainability, we might interpret this in terms of fair distribution of social, environmental, and economic benefits, costs, risks, and opportunities. But what does fair distribution entail? In order to address this issue, it would help to have a firmer grounding regarding what we might think of as an ideal distribution of both advantages and disadvantages.

For insight into our ideal distribution, we can turn to the ideas of philosopher John Rawls, who defines justice in relation to the determination of rights and duties and the fair distribution of social advantages.[6] In a just society, Rawls argues, basic civil rights are upheld and the social advantages of education and economic opportunity are equitably shared. However, justice also requires the fair distribution of social *dis*advantages, such as environmental risks. In turn, justice requires a fair distribution of power and decision-making power. These (political) goods determine how and to whom other social advantages and disadvantages will be distributed. This is a very important component of justice, and Rawls is sometimes faulted for paying insufficient attention to the underlying causes of maldistribution that result from power differentials, discrimination, and oppression.[7]

Distribution in a Just Society

Why should a government or state be involved in the distribution of social goods? Why not allow each individual (or family) to be on his or her own, to benefit from or suffer the full consequences of his or her actions, to succeed or fail based solely on his or her own efforts and resources? One reason is that no one—and certainly not the most powerful people of any society—ever truly succeeds on his or her own. All benefit from the basic infrastructure and services that society provides, such as elementary and secondary education; roads, bridges, and highways; the administration of civil justice and police forces; and national defense. No one would be able to gain much in the way of knowledge or economic opportunity without this basic infrastructure. Given that social advantages can only be obtained by way of a foundation provided by society at large, there is reason to insist that these advantages be distributed fairly within society.

A *fair* distribution of social advantages does not necessarily mean an *equal* distribution, however. Absolute equality in the distribution of social goods would be very difficult to achieve and maintain. Further, it is not clear that such a distribution would be fair or just. Arguably, fairness and justice entail the appropriate rewarding of effort. Since unequal individual efforts may be involved in the pursuit of social advantages, a fully equal distribution of these advantages may be unjust and unfair to those who exerted more effort.

Employing a Kantian framework, Rawls suggests that justice can best be conceived by asking how we would order society and distribute the benefits and costs of social life from what he calls the **original position**.[8] In the original position, standing behind a **veil of ignorance**, we would not know our socioeconomic status, or any of our personal attributes or history. We would not know whether we were black skinned or white skinned, tall or short, healthy or ill, employed or unemployed, powerful or weak, rich or poor, American or Chinese or Haitian. Unaware of our class position and social status; our race, religion, and nationality; our abilities, predispositions, and propensities, we would not design principles of justice that favored a particular social or personal condition. Not knowing what position in society—or on the planet—we occupied, we would establish principles of justice that were as fair as possible to everyone.

Rawls argues that people behind the veil of ignorance would insist that basic civil rights be safeguarded. That is to say, they would insist on equal liberty. They would also insist on equality of opportunity. This would ensure that individuals were not prevented from seeking education or competing for jobs or offices. In this context Rawls develops what he calls the **difference principle**, which permits unequal distributions of social and economic benefits only when these inequalities can be demonstrated to benefit the least advantaged in society and are (in accordance with the equal opportunity principle) attached to offices or positions that are open to everyone.

In other words, everyone's civil rights must first be secured, with equality of opportunity, ensuring that everyone is able to seek education and compete fairly for jobs, positions, or offices. In turn, inequalities that arise out of this competition are considered acceptable if, and only if, these inequalities benefit the least advantaged in society. For instance, if everyone in society benefits from the most knowledgeable, most skilled, and hardest-working scientists and engineers filling the most important positions in their respective institutions or corporations, and if paying higher salaries can be shown to ensure that the best scientists and engineers apply for and retain these positions, then inequalities in income would be considered acceptable.

This type of system, in which individuals are rewarded according to their ability and talent is called a meritocracy. To generalize, a meritocracy that rewards the best people the most may produce acceptable inequalities if the least advantaged in society benefit from that meritocratic organization more than they would benefit were rewards (salaries) equally distributed regardless of merit. In this case, distributing rewards equally might result in a dearth of talented scientists, engineers, and the like and make everyone worse off.

Distributing Disadvantages

The question now is whether social disadvantages should be shared equitably. Consider environmental risks. We have observed

that risk in life cannot be eliminated, only comparatively assessed and mitigated. Managing risks justly entails reducing the gravity and frequency of adverse events. It also entails ensuring that those who produce environmental risks remain responsible for justifying their acceptability and compensating those who suffer harm. Another important feature of risk management is "spreading risks across a group such that particular individuals or sub-classes are not inequitably subject to non-compensated risk."[9] In other words, just as the advantages that come with collective life ought to be equitably shared, so, too, must the disadvantages.

The poor and powerless members of society—those without the economic or political means to meet their needs—also tend to be the most vulnerable to environmental risks. As sociologist Ulrich Beck argues, wealth tends to accumulate at the top of the socioeconomic spectrum, while risks accumulate at the bottom.[10] These risks are not limited to health hazards from increased exposure to pollution or waste. Nongovernmental organizations also address what is being called **climate justice**.[11] Those people already living near subsistence levels around the world will undoubtedly bear more than their fair share of the effects of climate change, such as decreased agricultural yield, flooding and other effects of weather pattern changes, increased desertification and water scarcity, and sea-level rise with its accompanying displacement of residents and farmers of low-lying coastal lands.[12]

A meritocratic approach is less likely to yield acceptable results in the arena of environmental risks than it is in regards to economic compensation and opportunity. There is no reason to believe that the least advantaged in society benefit from bearing more than their fair share of environmental risks. If anything, efforts to limit or eliminate the environmental hazards would be increased if the most advantaged members of society bore more environmental risks.

The chief means of ensuring that advantages and disadvantages, including risks, will be more equitably distributed in society is to ensure that political power and decision-making processes are themselves more equitable. However, developing such processes in a fair way that ensures everyone has a voice is a significant challenge—one that becomes even more complicated in the context of a globalized world. As we have seen, debates regarding the ethical treatment of community members have been going on for millennia, but for most of that time, the communities in question have been rather narrowly defined. Within the context of sustainability, the idea of community must expand across former geographic and temporal boundaries to account for the effects our actions have on people around the globe and members of future generations. We will spend the remainder of the chapter exploring these broader connections.

EXPLORING INTERDEPENDENCE

Thomas Friedman, the *New York Times* columnist and author, has employed the metaphor of a "flattened" world to describe the growing levels of interdependence that characterize contemporary life.[13] Friedman highlights social, cultural, and business linkages through the Internet, computers, cell phones, and other media, transnational business operations that spread supply chains, workloads, and customers across multiple continents, and growing cultural and political connections that make independence and isolation increasingly unworkable.

While Friedman's metaphor is instructive, it may obscure many of the very real differences in cultures and in opportunities that exist in a world characterized by growing disparities in wealth and power. There is no doubt, however, that the contemporary world, more than ever before, is characterized by what scholars of international affairs describe as "**complex interdependence**."[14] The complexity arises from the multiple forms of interdependence involved in a vast web of connections.

The intermeshing of the world's economic, scientific, technological, social, political, cultural, and ecological systems has created both benefits and burdens for human stakeholders. These burdens and benefits are not evenly or equitably distributed, and such unevenness and inequity contributes to the complexity. For example, a small island state and a large mountainous country may contribute equally to global warming, but the expected rise in sea levels will leave only one nation without a homeland. While human and natural systems may enjoy or suffer differentially from their interconnectedness, historian Donald Worster maintains that there is no exception to "the reality or extent of the interdependency itself."[15] The cross-cutting and multilayered linkages that characterize the contemporary world are undeniable and inescapable. In today's world, interdependence is "a strict fact of life."[16] Sharing equitably the burdens and benefits that our relationships of interdependence create is a core feature of sustainability.

Thinking Globally, Acting Locally

To pursue sustainability is to think and act inclusively, with the welfare of a larger community in mind. Chapter 3 discussed Aldo Leopold's description of widening circles of ethical concern. According to Leopold's view, one might be primarily concerned with the sustainability of one's family, neighborhood, business, or civic association. At times, concern might extend to one's town, city, county, state, or nation. Where the specific boundaries of one's "community" lie is a complicated question.

For some sustainability advocates, the main focus of both thought and action should lie with local communities, natural and social. From this perspective, as Wes Jackson puts it, "the majority of solutions to both global and local problems must take place at the level of the expanded tribe, what civilization calls community."[17] From this perspective, in order to pursue sustainability effectively people must concern themselves first and foremost with the local communities in which they live and work. As Wendell Berry writes:

> The real work of planet-saving will be small, humble, and humbling, and (insofar as it involves love) pleasing and rewarding. Its jobs will be too many to count, too many to report, too many to be publicly noticed or rewarded, too small to make anyone rich or famous.[18]

Jackson and Berry are two of the founding thinkers of **bioregionalism**, a set of principles that insists on the priority of local commitments and caretaking. Sustainability is chiefly grounded in the actions of countless people looking after their own human and biological communities.

However, all such "local" actions, if uninformed by a global perspective that illuminates ever larger, more encompassing webs of interdependence, may prove counterproductive and shortsighted. Critics of bioregionalism, and indeed many bioregionalist advocates themselves, note the potential for parochial or insular tendencies. Encouraging people to focus on local problems may lead them to ignore the larger contexts in which those problems have developed. Thinking globally entails becoming aware of and responsive to the webs of interdependence that connect us to distant peoples, cultures, and ecosystems. These relationships of shared duties, rights, risks, and opportunities are not dissolved, though they may be attenuated and complicated, by distinctions or divisions arising out of differences in class, race, gender, ethnicity, belief systems, and nationality.

In response to these challenges, some environmental thinkers have called for a **cosmopolitan bioregionalism** that is concerned and informed about the wider world while embedded within local ecological constraints and cultural traditions.[19] Ultimately, the pursuit of sustainability must always be

BOX 4.2 Global-Local Connections: The Case of Forests

Forests serve as carbon sinks, holding carbon dioxide in the form of biomass so that it does not migrate into the atmosphere to form a greenhouse gas. It is estimated that 20 percent of global greenhouse gas emissions are currently caused by deforestation and forest degradation. As much as 5 percent of global greenhouse gas emissions result from deforestation in Indonesia alone, where the world's second largest tropical rainforest is rapidly being destroyed. With deforestation taken into account, Indonesia has been identified as the world's third largest emitter of greenhouse gases (Rainforest Action Network 2010).

Beyond their impact on climate change, the world's forests constitute the most diverse terrestrial ecosystems. While forests cover only 6 percent of the planet, they account for 90 percent of its land-based biodiversity. The vast majority of the planet's endangered terrestrial species live in forests. Many forest species go extinct each day, and tens of thousands are threatened. In turn, forests provide fuel, timber, medicinal products, and subsistence income for billions of people across the globe. Countless communities depend upon surrounding and adjacent forests for their survival. Protecting the world's forests and forest communities is a crucial sustainability concern.

In May 2003 the European Union (EU) proposed its first Forest Law Enforcement, Governance, and Trade (FLEGT) action plan to address the unsustainable practice of illegal logging in developing countries. Oftentimes, developing nations are hard-pressed to monitor or control illegal logging operations, as the demand for wood products from consumers in developed nations provides an overpowering economic incentive. FLEGT facilitates bilateral and multilateral voluntary partnerships and financial support agreements (FLEGT 2007).

In 2008, the EU and the government of the African nation of Ghana initiated the first ever Voluntary Partnership Agreement (VPA) based on FLEGT (European Commission 2010). VPAs were subsequently established with other African nations and have been initiated with Asian nations (Congo 2010 and European Commission 2010). The VPAs license, track, monitor, and verify compliance with sustainable logging practices. They also educate consumers about forest conservation and the hidden costs of unsustainably produced wood products.

FLEGT efforts complement programs aimed to Reduce Emissions from Deforestation and forest Degradation (REDD), which include financial incentives for developing countries to protect their standing forests not only from logging but also from slash and burn (swidden) agriculture and other threats. The United Nations' REDD program promotes national action, supported at regional and global levels. Such programs must strike a delicate balance between addressing global concerns of climate change and attending to the subsistence needs of local forest-based communities. Increasingly important is the development of livelihood opportunities for local communities grounded in the sustainable harvesting of nontimber forest products, such as mushrooms, wild berries and other foods, medicinal plants, and other marketable goods.

International nongovernmental organizations (INGOs) such as Rainforest Action Network (RAN) also play roles in protecting the planet's forests and forest communities. RAN has worked to protect indigenous forest-based communities from across the developing world as well as in certain developed nations such as Canada. It has also pressured companies such as Boise Inc., the largest American forest products company, Lowes, and Home Depot to cease marketing wood products from endangered forests (e.g., Eris 2000).

Janus-faced, with one eye turned toward the local community and one eye turned toward the world community. Bioregionalists believe, however, that people can turn meaningfully toward the world community only if they have already fulfilled their commitments to their local communities.

The broadening of community boundaries can be seen not simply in terms of the advancement of civilization, as Leopold framed it, but also in terms of an individual process of moral maturation. It is hard to imagine moral concern for an expanding circle of fellow citizens developing in a person who was not, as a youth, devoted to family and friends and morally educated by them. As Edmund Burke, the eighteenth-century political theorist, wrote: "To be attached to the subdivision, to love the little platoon we belong to in society, is the first principle (the germ as it were) of public affections. It is the first link in the series by which we proceed towards a love of our country and of humankind."[20] A similar focus on interpersonal relationships grounds the feminist ethics of care developed in recent years as a counter to the overly rationalistic and individualistic traditions in Western social ethics.[21] Concern for the near and dear, and being cared for by kith and kin, is generally the prerequisite for broader, more encompassing relationships of moral concern.

Of course, care for the near and dear—conceived of in bioregionalist, feminist, or other terms—does not inevitably extend to a broader community. Parochialism remains a challenge to the ethics of sustainability, as to other efforts to develop broadly inclusive ethical frameworks. Burke, a conservative and patriot, knew well that loving one's own platoon did not always produce a more encompassing embrace of others. Not infrequently, it produced a fearsome hatred of other platoons, other armies, and the other nations they defended. Much of the history of the world, after all, is written with the blood of the victims of tribal conflict, ethnic feuds, and national wars. More immediately, care for local communities, family, and other loved ones can lead to a retreat from larger commitments just as easily as it can lead to wider circles of concern. The key, for the ethics of sustainability, is to link personal commitments to natural and social communities, on the one hand, to a politically informed understanding of the larger forces that affect them.

Life on Spaceship Earth

While typically grounded in local actions, sustainability is generally planetary in its broadest visions. This planetary vision is occasionally described as **globalism**, a term that means different things to different people. It often has negative connotations. For some, it signals the cultural imperialism of Western power and values as the planet's diverse peoples become increasingly connected—and homogenized—through modern media and technology. For others, it represents the threat of a unitary world government, a globeocracy, that erodes individual freedoms and the sovereignty of nation-states. Still other people see globalism in terms of the growing power of multinational corporations and the integration of economies and consumption patterns across the planet, creating a so-called

McWorld, where everyone marches—and eats—to the same corporate beat.

Globalism can also hold more benign meanings and effects, however. It can indicate the weakening of dangerous forms of nationalism and tribalism, increased transparency through media, greater interaction and connection of the world's peoples and cultures, and greater opportunities for mobility, employment, and education. It also suggests, as international relations theorist Paul Wapner writes, "a heightened sensitivity to the fragility of the life-support system of the planet and a sense of human solidarity in a world of increasing interdependence."[22]

FIGURE 4.2 With this photograph of an Earthrise taken in 1968, people for the first time had an image to help them see the Earth as a single system rather than a collection of nation states. *(NASA)*

This latter, benign understanding of globalism can be traced back to the 1960s, when U.S. ambassador to the United Nations Adlai Stevenson popularized Kenneth Boulding's notion of **Spaceship Earth**. This conception gained great power from the images of our planet taken from space, including the famous photograph of an Earthrise taken in 1968 (see Figure 4.2). In his last speech to the U.N., delivered in 1965, Stevenson said:

> We travel together, passengers on a little spaceship, dependent upon its vulnerable reserve of air and soil; all committed for our safety to its security and peace; preserved from annihilation by the care, the work, and I will say, the love we give our fragile craft.

On Spaceship Earth, ecological interdependence sows a common fate and a common task for the human species.

Many appreciate this unifying vision, but there are problems associated with the Spaceship Earth metaphor. Although the planet's peoples are, in an important sense, "in the same boat," the image of all of us as passengers on a single craft sharing a single fate may be deceptive. Not all passengers on Spaceship Earth enjoy the same privileges or suffer the same deprivations. The majority, those with little power and wealth, sweat and all too frequently starve in the smoke-filled engine room. A small percentage enjoys fine dining and issues orders from the air-conditioned bridge. Benefits and risks aboard the planetary craft are not equally shared, and Stevenson was well aware of this inequity. Echoing Abraham Lincoln's famous "House Divided" speech given a century earlier where Lincoln announced that the American "government cannot endure, permanently half slave and half free," Stevenson continued his speech to the U.N. with these words:

> We cannot maintain [the spaceship] half fortunate, half miserable, half confident, half despairing, half slave to the ancient enemies of mankind and half free in a liberation of resources undreamed of until this day. No craft, no crew, can travel safely with such vast contradictions. On their resolution depends the security of us all. [23]

Stevenson's notion of Spaceship Earth links caretaking of the global commons with social justice. It might be considered an early precursor to the ethics of sustainability, as it envisions a single, just global community to which everyone belongs.

Environmental Justice

Acknowledging a global community requires reassessing domestic relationships as well as international ones. In 1982, more than 500 people were arrested in North Carolina for civil disobedience. The protestors were objecting to the disposal of toxic wastes in a landfill located in a primarily African American community. The following year, a U.S. government report documented that African Americans comprised the majority of the population in the counties of a number of southeastern states where hazardous waste landfills were located. Over the following decade, numerous reports, articles, books, and summits documented and debated the extent and nature of such "**environmental injustice**." [24]

Academic research confirmed that communities that ended up holding the short end of the toxic stick tended to be populated with minorities. The political and economic powerlessness of these minority communities left them vulnerable to "**environmental racism**." [25] In response to this charge, the Environmental Protection Agency set up an **Office of Environmental Justice**, and a presidential order directed all federal agencies to ensure that minority communities were not disproportionately burdened with environmental ills and risks.

While environmental injustice and environmental racism were originally understood as identical concerns, the notion of environmental justice was soon broadened to include concern for the environmental risks and burdens borne by any disadvantaged communities, such as Appalachian coal miners or subsistence farmers on low-lying coastal lands in an era of climate change, regardless of their racial composition. Advocates of environmental justice addressed various forms of environmental inequities beyond the increased exposure to toxic contamination suffered by disadvantaged communities.

Environmental justice advocates have addressed hardships produced by environmental catastrophes that fall disproportionately on the disadvantaged, such as the effects of Hurricane Katrina on the poorer and typically black communities of New Orleans. They have addressed the "climate injustice" suffered by those communities, peoples, and nations that will bear the brunt of global warming. They have also addressed the "stealing" of genetic material from indigenous populations by pharmaceutical companies that subsequently enforce intellectual property rights through the patenting of living organisms or DNA sequences.[26]

According to environmental ethicist Kristin Shrader-Frechette,

Environmental injustice occurs whenever some individual or group bears disproportionate environmental risks, like those of hazardous waste dumps, or has unequal access to environmental goods, like clean air, or has less opportunity to participate in environmental decision-making. In every nation of the world, poor people and minorities face greater environmental risks, have less access to environmental goods, and have less ability to control the environmental insults imposed on them.[27]

If we expand Shrader-Frechette's definition to include *social* as well as *environmental* risks, goods, and decision-making opportunities, then we arrive at the broader category of social justice. Robert Bullard, whose 1990 book *Dumping in Dixie* brought the issue of environmental racism to widespread attention, maintains that the concern for environmental justice is indeed an extension of the broader concern for social justice.[28] Within the sustainability framework, the fair distribution of environmental benefits, costs, risks, and opportunities is understood as intrinsic to the commitment to a fair distribution of social, economic, and political benefits, costs, risks, and opportunities.

However, acknowledging our connections to people who are geographically or cultural distant from us does not satisfy all the requirements of sustainability. Recall the Brundtland Commission's call to meet "the needs of the present without compromising the ability of future generations to meet their own needs."[29] If we are to follow this mandate, then simply extending ethical consideration to everyone alive today is not enough. The following section focuses on the temporal aspect of sustainability and what it means to extend ethical concern into the distant future.

OBLIGATIONS TO FUTURE GENERATIONS

Many of the people that we might care about are not yet born. These people will be the beneficiaries—perhaps the chief beneficiaries—of an ethics of sustainability.

There are nearly seven billion human beings currently living on this earth. Assuming that no massive catastrophes occur, however, the vast majority of people the planet will ever have known are yet to arrive. They will be our descendants—our children, grandchildren, great-grandchildren, and their progeny. Indeed, more people will be born in the lifetimes of the younger readers of this text than currently inhabit the earth.[30]

The decisions we make and the actions we take today will affect the lives and livelihoods of these billions of future human beings. Every discovery we make and every innovation we produce is a gift we bestow on future generations. Our learning, moral and social development, economic prosperity, and technological progress provide our legacy to them, but we not only provide benefits—we also bestow burdens. Every nonrewable natural resource that we consume leaves less for future generations. Every pound of carbon that we emit into the atmosphere contributes to the warming of a planet they will inherit. Every species we cause to go extinct they will never know, except as a loss. If we weigh the moral significance of an action by the number of people it potentially affects, then the impact of our actions on future generations ought to be of paramount concern. This is the realm of intergenerational justice, and it sits at the core of any ethics of sustainability.

It is easy enough to acknowledge our responsibility to future generations. In practice, however, it is the present that typically claims our attention. Former Vice President Al Gore, who produced the academy-award-winning film, *An Inconvenient Truth*, and won a Nobel Peace Prize, observed that we deplete the earth's natural resources and live unsustainable lives because "the future whispers while the present shouts."[31] A sustainability framework attempts to give equal voice to the future. It prompts us to consider the burdens we thrust upon our progeny as well as the benefits we bestow upon them.

Intergenerational Justice

At the heart of most ethical traditions lies a preoccupation with how moral concern is extended in social space. The individual is held responsible to care not only for his or her own interests but also to consider the welfare of family, of neighbors, of fellow townspeople or citizens, and perhaps of humanity at large. Recall from Chapter 3 Immanuel Kant's categorical imperative, stating that the rules or axioms guiding one's actions must be universalizable. That is to say, these rules of practice must remain consistent and applicable when extended across an indefinitely wide population.

Jeremy Bentham's utilitarian ethics, although traditionally opposed to Kant's duty-based reasoning, also assesses action according to its capacity to be extended in social space. In turn, the ethic of the Golden Rule, variations of which are found within most religious and moral traditions, simply states that we should treat our neighbors the same way that we ourselves would want to be treated by them. This model also extends concern beyond the self to larger populations in social space. Potentially, the world may be understood as our neighborhood.

While most ethical traditions focus on the extension of moral concern across social space, a parallel—if historically less salient—issue has been the extension of moral concern across time. Justice is often thought to entail a fair distribution of resources between members of a particular generation with duty, utility, or a Golden Rule determining how these resources ought to be allocated. This might be thought of as **intragenerational justice**. By contrast, and as an extension of this, **intergenerational justice** is concerned with the fair distribution of resources among generations.

Most contemporary ethicists insist that a person's moral worth should not depend upon chance. We would think it wrong, for instance, to privilege people who were born with blond hair while punishing those born with black, brown, or red hair. The date of one's birth is

---

BOX 4.3 Intergenerational Justice and the Chain of Obligation

The principle of intergenerational justice can be understood by considering the interdependent relationships we have within families and communities. Clearly, children depend upon parents for their welfare, just as future generations depend upon current generations to pass on a world without diminished resources and opportunities. Richard Howarth (1992) refers to a "chain of obligation" that stretches from the present into the indefinite future. Parents have obligations to their children, and these children, in turn, will have obligations to their own offspring.

Howarth observes that "unless we ensure conditions favourable to the welfare of future generations, we wrong existing children in the sense that they will be unable to fulfill their obligation to their children while enjoying a favourable way of life themselves." Parents are obligated not only to satisfy the basic needs of their children but also to educate them as to the obligations that they themselves will have to their offspring. The key sustainability concept of intergenerational justice, therefore, includes parental responsibility to meet their moral responsibilities to their children such that an unbroken chain of obligation might link current and future generations across the ages.

Yet, in many respects, present generations also depend upon future generations—upon progeny and future communities—to give their lives continuity and meaning. Lisa Newton (2003) articulated this concept in the following manner:

Communities and family ground us in space and time. They contain our records, the history of what we have done, assuring us of our own existence and continuity, and the receptacles for our future actions and existence. It is the community (however designated and circumscribed) that remembers us, holds our past, and therefore can recall us to ourselves; it is the community that expects us in the future and calls out (when it is working as it should), the very best that is in us. We are always performers on the stages of our kinship, local, professional, or otherwise chosen communities, measuring ourselves by their reaction to what we are and what we do, projecting our future selves in relation to them. As we love ourselves, and are essentially related to one or more communities that we call our own, we must desire their future existence.

Expanding from parental relationships to broader community relationships, we can see that intergenerational justice is grounded in this intergenerational interdependence.

---

equally a matter of chance. The day, month, year, decade, or even century in which a particular individual is born might be considered as morally irrelevant as the color of his or her hair. It follows that any form of justice that we deem appropriate between the members of one generation might also be applicable between members of different generations.

More specifically, the life prospects of members of future generations, given their equal moral worth, should not be worsened by us without some morally defensible reason. It is not at all clear that making ourselves better off today is morally defensible if these actions worsen the prospects of future generations. From this perspective, *inter*generational justice is simply a logical extension of *intra*-generational justice: if the prospects of our descendents are worsened by our actions, we bear the burden of proof for justifying these actions. It is incumbent upon us to explain why we choose not to extend across time the same principles, rights, and responsibilities that we deem appropriate to extend across space.

John Rawls employs this sort of reasoning in making the case for intergenerational justice.[32] Recall that from Rawl's original position behind a veil of ignorance we would not know any of our persona attributes, including socioeconomic status, race, or religion. Behind the veil of ignorance, we would also be ignorant of our date of birth. We might, for instance, have been born 50 years ago or only arrive in the world next century. It follows that we would design an ethic that was equitable to both current and future generations. In adhering to the principles of justice, Rawls writes, "we are not allowed to treat generations differently solely on the grounds that they are earlier or later in time."[33] In order for the ethical rules or axioms guiding our actions to be truly universalizable, they must be acceptable to future as well as existing generations.

A Look Back at Looking Forward

While an expanded time horizon is central to an ethics of sustainability, looking to the future has a long and venerable history that far predates contemporary sustainability concerns. Edmund Burke, the conservative eighteenth-century British political thinker and parliamentarian, maintained that the state was "a partnership not only between those who are living, but between those who are living, those who are dead, and those who are to be born."[34] Given this partnership, Burke argued that current generations ought to be mindful of "what is due to their posterity" and must, above all, refrain from wasting their inheritance. We have no right, Burke insisted, to pass on to future generations a "ruin" rather than a "habitation."[35]

In the United States, and with a very practical bent, the founding fathers also voiced their sense of obligation to future generations. Thomas Paine insisted that future generations should not be saddled with the repercussions of former generations' choices. Both George Washington and Thomas Jefferson maintained that each generation must pay its own debts and that the failure to do so burdened posterity with deprivation and the threat of war.

Early national environmental laws and policies were explicitly grounded in ethical obligations that spanned generations. In the United States, for example, the landmark National Environmental Policy Act of 1969 issued the mandate to "Fulfill the responsibilities of each generation as trustee of the environment for succeeding generations."[36] This intergenerational ethics became a cornerstone for environmental thought and action. Of course, the Brundtland Commission provided one of the first official linkages of intergenerational ethics to the language of sustainability in 1987, aptly titling their report *Our Common Future*.

In 1997, the General Conference of the United Nations Educational, Scientific and

Cultural Organization (UNESCO) endorsed a *Declaration on the Responsibilities of the Present Generations towards Future Generations*. Explicitly employing the language of sustainability, the Declaration held that "present generations have the responsibility of ensuring that the needs and interests of future generations are fully safeguarded." Taking this responsibility seriously required that "each generation inheriting the Earth temporarily shall take care to use natural resources reasonably and ensure that life is not prejudiced by harmful modifications of the ecosystems and that scientific and technological progress in all fields does not harm life on Earth."[37]

The UNESCO declaration was grounded in a sense of moral responsibility, but it was clear that such a statement of moral purpose demanded empirical foundations. Accordingly, the U.N. initiated the largest study to date of the status of the earth's natural resources and ecosystems. After five years of research by more than 1,300 scientists from 95 countries, the **Millennium Ecosystem Assessment** was completed in 2005.[38] The full report, over 2,000 pages, laid out in great detail how and why the planet's ecosystems may prove incapable of being sustained owing to the strains placed on them by contemporary humanity. The Millennium Ecosystem Assessment was grounded in a sense of responsibility to future generations.

Future Quality of Life

The decisions we make and the actions we take today will affect the health and welfare of future generations and their opportunities to meet their needs and satisfy their wants. With this in mind, it is important to recognize that the rights of future generations are not limited to mere existence. Intergenerational justice asks us to protect the rights of future generations to the same level of well-being and the same opportunities as are currently enjoyed by present generations.

To maintain such a quality of life across the generations, the use of natural resources must not exceed the earth's capacity to regenerate them. Consider the loss of ecological diversity that is now occurring on a massive scale across the globe. As you learned from Chapter 1, species extinction today occurs primarily because of human activity. This loss certainly will severely degrade the web of life that human beings depend upon for their own sustenance, health, recreational pleasure, and spiritual renewal. Once the current generation allows a species to disappear, future generations—to the end of time—will be deprived of the opportunity to enjoy its presence or otherwise benefit from its existence.

The biologist E. O. Wilson has said that "The one process now going on that will take millions of years to correct is the loss of genetic and species diversity by the destruction of natural habitats. This is the folly our descendants are least likely to forgive."[39] This folly, Wilson predicts, "will be remembered by generations a hundred years from now, a thousand years from now."[40] Conservation biologist Michael Soulé observes that the problem is not solely the destruction of living species but also the elimination of sufficient

BOX 4.4   Wildlands Network

While the negative consequences of environmental destruction may quickly become obvious and urgent, the measures best suited to safeguarding and renewing the biosphere often require extended time horizons.

The field of conservation biology developed as scientists began thinking of habitat in terms of the scale most relevant to the long-term sustainability of species. Michael Soulé, a founder of conservation biology, realized that none of America's protected spaces were large enough for the long-term protection of many of its species. He knew the dynamic migration and movement patterns of some animals could not be adapted to "postage stamp parcels of nature." In 1991, Soulé's vision for a vast connected landscape of wildlands that could provide a viable long-term habitat for threatened species took organizational shape as the Wildlands Project, now called the Wildlands Network.

On the Wildlands Network website can be found a quote from Edmund Burke, which reads, "No man made a greater mistake than he who did nothing because he could only do little." This quote speaks to the methodology of the organization, which works daily in small ways toward grand goals with extended time horizons. Connectivity is key to this method. A key strategy of the organization is to establish "wildlife corridors" that will allow animals to move freely between larger, protected conservation areas. Likewise, Wildlands Network links conservation teams and projects around the world so that they can be more effective working together. The only way such a large-scale initiative can meet with success is through the collaboration of many teams, each working toward specific goals.

Many smaller successes have fortified the grand vision of Wildlands Network, garnering widespread support and growing the network in the process. As a result of the Room to Roam Campaign, Wildlands Network has worked with various partners and stakeholders to protect wildlife. One initiative brought together the New Mexico Department of Transportation, the Federal Highway Administration, the city of Albuquerque and private landowners to virtually eliminate Wildlife-Vehicle Collisions on I-40 in the Tijeras Canyon (the connection between the Sandia Mountains and Manzano Wilderness) by integrating wildlife crossings and signage into a highway maintenance project. Another effort of the Room to Roam Campaign focused on the need for a wildlife bridge across I-70 at West Vail Pass to protect wildlife movement between major United States Forest Service core areas. The Colorado Department of Transportation received a $500,000 federal grant to begin the monitoring and design process for the wildlife bridge, and a national contest for that design was initiated.

Sustainability issues often demand a scale of thinking and acting that is both temporally and spatially expansive. The Wildlands Network exemplifies scalable approaches to environmental protection through collaboration across organizations, conservation across borders, and goal setting across lifetimes. Each small success by the Wildlands Network can be celebrated in its own right and as incremental steps toward the larger goal of developing a continental conservation community.

wilderness space to allow for the evolution of new species. "For the first time in hundreds of millions of years," Soulé writes, "significant evolutionary change in most higher organisms is coming to a screeching halt."[41] Environmental scientist Norman Myers similarly maintains that:

> In addition to eliminating large numbers of species, we are also causing evolution to lose its capacity to come up with large numbers of replacement species. . . . [W]e are effectively saying that we are absolutely certain that people for the next 5 million years can do without maybe half of all of today's species. That's far and away the biggest decision ever taken by one generation on the unconsulted behalf of future generations since we got up on our hind legs.[42]

Of course, future generations can never be consulted as to whether they want or appreciate biological diversity or any other good. We shall address this difficulty in a subsequent section. For now, the point is simply that we hold the prospects of future generations in our hands. At an ecological level, many of those prospects are diminishing.

With this in mind, sustainability-oriented individuals and organizations have generally made a "future focus" central to their efforts. A popular slogan—"We do not inherit the Earth from our parents, we borrow it from our children"—underlines this sense of obligation.[43] Advocates for sustainability ask us to safeguard our children's natural inheritance, an inheritance that took hundreds of millions of years to evolve. Few who adopt

the sustainability framework look that far into the future, but, at least in some cases, the future focus is quite expansive.

The Wildlands Network, for example, was conceived with the aim of preserving and expanding viable populations of the indigenous flora and fauna of the American continent through the creation of wilderness areas and corridors. The goal is to preserve or reclaim 25 percent of the land area of the continent, a goal project administrators acknowledge will only be achieved slowly, with 200- to 500-year projections for recovery in some areas.[44] The legacy of such conservation efforts is meant to endure for millennia.

Beyond Seven Generations

Prior to the European arrival in North America, a confederacy formed by the Mohawk, Oneida, Onondaga, Cayuga, and Seneca tribes in what is now Upstate New York. These confederated "People of the Longhouse," who came to be known as the Iroquois nation (and were later joined by the Tuscarora tribe), developed a "binding" oral constitution called the *Haudenosaunee* or "Great Law of Peace." The Great Law stipulated that one must consider the impact on future generations in every deliberation. Not only immediate effects but also long-term risks, costs, and benefits extending over multiple generations were to be considered before taking any action. Decision makers, the "mentors of the people," were described as having "endless patience" and skins with a thickness of "seven spans." This latter phrase has been interpreted to mean that their decisions attended to the welfare of seven generations. Within sustainability circles, this measure of moral responsibility often goes by the name of a **"seventh generation" ethic**.

The Great Law asks all mentors and decision-makers to "Look and listen for the welfare of the whole people and have always in view not only the present but also the coming generations, even those whose faces are yet beneath the surface of the ground—the unborn of the future Nation."[45] Benjamin Franklin and James Madison, two of the founding fathers of the United States, were said to have studied the Great Law of the Iroquois and looked to it in their own efforts to craft an enduring constitution for the young American nation.

Given the Iroquois's level of technological development (and population density), seven generations—approximately 150 to 200 years—would be an appropriate time scale for sustainable decision making. It would be difficult to imagine any action that these tribal peoples might take whose effects beyond 150 years would not already be apparent within 100 or even 50 years. If the actions they took had no negative repercussions for seven generations, it was likely that they would have no negative repercussions for 70 or 700 generations.

The same cannot be said today. As we learned in Chapter 1, technology can make our impact on future generations potentially more potent and of longer duration. Our technology has advanced in its power and scope, and with these advances come repercussions that extend their shadows across time. Technologies that produce greater and longer-lasting impacts would presumably demand greater oversight in development and use if we take our ethical responsibilities to future generations seriously. Consider a few examples.

Chlorofluorocarbons (CFCs) were invented in the late 1800s. In the 1920s, an American engineer, Thomas Midgley, improved the synthesis of CFCs, allowing for their widespread, commercial use as refrigerants (and later as solvents and propellants). In 1974, it was discovered that CFCs significantly contributed to the destruction of stratospheric ozone, a band of gas 9 to 22 miles above the planet that protects the biosphere from harmful ultraviolet radiation (UV-B). In the United States, CFCs were banned in nonessential aerosol products in 1978. Concerted action to stem CFC production and use, however, was not taken until scientists had discovered a growing "ozone hole" over the Antarctic. Photographs taken from space, helped both scientists and activists understand the extent of the problem (see figure 4.3). In 1987, an international treaty called the Montreal Protocol on Substances That Deplete the Ozone Layer was written. Two years later, the **Montreal Protocol** came into force and advanced industrial nations committed to producing no more CFCs beginning in 1996.

Production of CFCs fell markedly after the Montreal Protocol. Still, ozone depletion may get worse before it gets better sometime in the mid-twenty-first century, as existent chlorofluorocarbons continue to work their way up to the stratosphere, where they may persist in their ozone-destroying reactions for

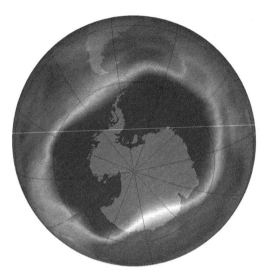

FIGURE 4.3 This image from NASA taken in 2006 shows the largest ozone hole ever recorded *(NASA)*

many years before becoming inactive. That is why stratospheric ozone has continued to decline by about 4 percent per decade since the late 1970s. And there has been a much larger, seasonal decrease in ozone over polar regions—reaching up to 60 percent—during this same period. As a result, photosynthetic processes will continue to be disturbed, aquatic plankton will be killed, and many of the earth's creatures, including human beings, will experience higher rates of skin cancer, eye cataracts, and other ailments for many more decades.

The international treaty developed in Montreal is an inspiring example of international cooperation and foresight. Over 195 nations signed either the original document or its subsequent revisions. It has been very successful, and will eventually allow for the restoration of stratospheric ozone. Nonetheless, the fact remains that in little more than

half a century, a life-protecting atmospheric layer that the Earth required 1.9 billion years to produce was significantly depleted.[46] The damage caused by this depletion of stratospheric ozone harms us today, and will continue to exert its negative effects upon future generations. The technology involved in producing CFCs effectively extended an ecological shadow across seven generations.

The stakes are even higher and the dangers are of longer duration when we examine the impact of radioactive waste. Radioactive waste is produced in the process of building nuclear weapons and making nuclear energy. Radioactive waste is highly toxic and must be isolated for many thousands of years to prevent contamination of the ground water, the earth's surface, and the air. Plutonium-239, the primary material used in nuclear weapons, takes a quarter of a million years to decay to safe levels—that is 50 times longer than any civilization has yet survived, and longer even than *Homo sapiens* have walked the earth. Other radioactive isotopes, such as iodine-129, take 100 times longer than Plutonium-239 to decay.

When the U.S. Environmental Protection Agency regulates the storage and disposal of radioactive waste, it must concern itself with timescales spanning ten thousand to one million years. With the decision in 2009 to discontinue exploration of Yucca Mountain in Nevada as a permanent storage site, the United States remains without a home for its growing stockpile of radioactive waste, which currently sits in temporary, above-ground depositories. Inevitably, to produce radioactive isotopes today is to saddle future generations with the responsibility of disposing and monitoring a vast tonnage of hazardous material.

The most serious consequences of many contemporary environmental problems, including climate change, the depletion of natural resources, and the eradication of species and habitats, will develop long after present generations are gone. The amount of time before its repercussions make themselves fully felt determines whether we are obligated to concern ourselves with the welfare of seven generations or seven thousand generations. Of course, the capacity of technology to affect the future is not always negative—far from it. Enduring benefits, not just risks and costs, must be considered when assessing the impact of technological developments.

CONCLUSION

People in power sometimes ignore the voices of stakeholders whose voices are most difficult to hear, including those of low socioeconomic status, indigenous peoples, and future generations. As you have seen in this chapter, stakeholders' concerns cannot be dismissed simply because of cultural, geographical, or temporal distance between them and ourselves. Principles of social justice demand that these people be given a voice.

An ethic of sustainability suggests that all people living in the global community deserve consideration. Moreover, with its future focus, the sustainability framework insists that another group, future generations,

should also be placed within the circle of concern. In the following chapter, we will see another key addition, marking the culmination of Leopold's land ethic.

REFERENCES

Adlai Today. "CONNECT." Adlai Today. www.adlaitoday.org/ideas/connect_sub2_engage.html.

Afeiguejet. 2010. Congo, EU Sign Agreement to Fight Illegal Wood Export. Afrique en Lignei. July 5th. www.afriquejet.com/news/africa-news/congo,-eu-sign-agreement-to-fight-illegal-wood-export-2010051949556.html.

Athanasiou, Tom. 1996. *Divided Planet: The Ecology of Rich and Poor*. Boston: Little, Brown.

Babylonian Talmud, Tractate Shabbath, Folio 31a. www.come-and-hear.com/shabbath/shabbath_31.html.

Baier, Annette. 1995. "The Need for More than Justice." In Virginia Held, Ed. *Justice and Care: Essential Readings in Feminist Ethics*, Boulder, CO: Westview Press, pp. 47–58.

Beck, Ulrich. 1986. *Risk Society: Towards a New Modernity*. Thousand Oaks, CA: Sage Publications.

Berry, Wendell. 1981. *The Gift of Good Land*. San Francisco: North Point Press.

———. 1993. *Sex, Economy, Freedom and Community*. New York: Pantheon Books.

Bhalla, Surjit S. 2002. *Imagine There's No Country: Poverty, Inequality, and Growth in the Era of Globalization*. Washington DC: Institute for International Economics.

Bromley, Daniel and Kathleen Segerson, Eds. 1982. *The Social Response to Environmental Risk: Policy Formation in an Age of Uncertainty*. Boston: Cluwer Academic Publishers).

Brower, David. *Let the Mountains Talk, Let the Rivers Run: A Call to Those Who Would Save the Earth*. New York: Harper Collins.

Brown, Lester R. 2009. *Plan B 4.0: Mobilizing to Save Civilization*. New York: W. W. Norton.

Bullard, Robert. 1994. *Dumping in Dixie: Race, Class and Environmental Quality*. Boulder: Westview Press.

Bullard, Robert, Ed. 1993. *Confronting Environmental Racism: Voices from the Grassroots*. Boston: South End Press.

Bullard, Robert, Ed. 1994. *Unequal Protection: Environmental Justice and Communities of Color*. New York: Random House.

Bunyan Bryant. 1995. "Summary," in Bunyan Bryant, Ed., *Environmental Justice: Issues, Policies, and Solutions*, Washington, DC: Island Press, 1995.

Burke, Edmund. 1961. *Reflections on the Revolution in France*. Garden City, NY: Doubleday and Company.

Chawla, Ambika. 2009. Climate Justice Movements Gather Strength. In *State of the World 2009*, Robert Engelman et al. New York: W. W. Norton.

Colborn, Theo, Diane Dumanoski, and John Peterson Myers. 1996. *Our Stolen Future*. New York: Dutton Books.

Confucius. 1979. *The Analects*. New York: Penguin.

Congo, "EU Signs Agreement to Fight Illegal Wood Export." 2010. *Afrique en Lignei*. July 5. www.afriquejet.com/news/africa-news/congo,-eu-sign-agreement-to-fight-illegal-wood-export-2010051949556.html.

Di Chiro, Geiovann. 2007. "Indigenous Peoples and Biocolonianism." In Ronald Sandler and Phaedra Pezzulo, Eds. *Environmental Justice and Environmentalism: The Social Justice Challenge to the Environmental Movement*, Cambridge, MA: MIT Press, pp. 251–283.

Dryzek, John S. 1997. *The Politcs of the Earth: Environmental Discourses*. Oxford: Oxford University Press.

Environmental Careers Organization. 1992. *Beyond the Green: Redefining and Diversifying the Environmental Movement*. Boston: Environmental Careers Organization.

Eris, Mona El. 2000. The Home Depot-Rainforest Action Network Dispute: A Lesson on Issues and Stakeholder Management. *Corporate Environmental Strategy* 7 (2): 185–193.

European Commission. 2007. Forest Law Enforcement, Governance, and Trade Briefing Note 1. September. http://ec.europa.eu/development/policies/9interventionareas/environment/forest/forestry_intro_en.cfm#F1.

———. 2008. Conclusion of Negotiations of the First Voluntary Partnership Agreement Between Ghana and the European Union on a Forest Law Enforcement Governance and Trade. Press Release. Accra-Brussels, 3 September. http://ec.europa.eu/development/icenter/repository/FLEGT_VPA_Ghana_signature.pdf.

———. 2009. EFI *Policy Brief 3 – What is a Voluntary Partnership Agreement?* http://ec.europa.eu/development/policies/9interventionareas/environment/forest/forestry_intro_en.cfm#F1.

———. 2010. Press Release: Conclusion of Negotiations of a Voluntary Partnership Agreement Between Cameroon and the European Union on Forest Law Enforcement Governance and Trade in Forest Products to the European Union. Press Release. Yaoundé-Brussels, 6 May 2010. http://ec.europa.eu/development/icenter/repository/Flegt_vpa_Cam_Press_release_negoc.pdf.

French, Hilary F. 1997. Learning from the Ozone Experience. In *State of the World 1997*, eds.

Lester R. Brown et al., New York: W. W. Norton, pp. 151N171.

Friedman, Marilyn. 1995. "Beyond Caring: The De-moralization of Gender Held." In Virginia Held, Ed. *Justice and Care: Essential Readings in Feminist Ethics*, Boulder, CO: Westview Press, pp 61–77.

Friedman, Thomas. 2006. *The World Is Flat: A Brief History of the Twenty-first Century*. New York: Farrar, Straus and Giroux.

Gilligan, Carol. [1982] 1993. *In a Different Voice*. Cambridge, MA: Harvard University Press.

Gore, Al. 1992. *Earth in the Balance: Ecology and the Human Spirit*. Boston: Houghton Mifflin.

Gottlieb, Robert. 1993. *Forcing the Spring: The Transformation of the American Environmental Movement*. Washington, DC: Island Press.

International Union for the Conservation of Nature and Natural Resources. 1980. *World Conservation Strategy: Living Resource Conservation for Sustainable Development*. Gland, Switzerland: International Union for the Conservation of Nature and Natural Resources.

Jackson, Wes. 1994. *Becoming Native to this Place*. Lexington, KY: University Press of Kentucky.

Kaplinsky, Raphael. 2005. *Globalization, Poverty, and Inequality*. Cambridge: Policy Press.

Keohane, Robert O. and Joseph S. Nye. 1989. *Power and Interdependence: World Politics in Transition*. Boston: Little, Brown.

MacNeill, Jim, Pieter Winsemius, and Taizo Yakushiji. 1991. *Beyond Interdependence: The Meshing of the World's Economy and the Earth's Ecology*. Oxford: Oxford University Press.

McKibben, Bill. 2003. *Enough: Staying Human in an Engineered Age*. New York: Henry Holt.

MacNeill, Jim, Pieter Winsemius, and Taizo Yakushiji. 1991. *Beyond Interdependence: The Meshing of the World's Economy and the Earth's Ecology*. Oxford: Oxford University Press.

Milbrath, Lester. 1996. *Learning to Think Environmentally (while there is still time)*. Albany: SUNY Press.

Millennium Ecosystem Assessment (MEA). 2005. *Ecosystems and Human Well-Being: Synthesis*. Washington D.C.: Washington.

Myers, Norman. 1993. *Ultimate Security: The Environmental Basis of Political Stability*. Washington, D.C.: Island Press.

National Environmental Policy Act of 1969, 102 U.S.C. 4332 (1970).

New Jerusalem Bible. 1985. New York: Doubleday.

Noddings, Nel. [1984] 2003. *Caring*. Berkeley, CA: University of California Press.

Ophuls, William and A. Stephen Boyan Jr. 1992. *Ecology and the Politics of Scarcity Revisited: The Unraveling of the American Dream*. New York: W. H. Freeman.

Partridge, Ernest, ed. 1981. *Responsibilities to Future Generations*. Buffalo: Prometheus Books.

Rain Forest Action Network. 2010. "Indonesia, Climate Change, and Rainforests." Rain Forest Action Network. http://ran.org/content/indonesia-climate-change-and-rainforests.

Rawls, John. 1999. *A Theory of Justice*. Cambridge: Harvard University Press.

———. 2005. *Political Liberalism*. New York: Columbia University Press.

Roberts, J. Timmons. Globalizing Environmental Justice. In Ronald Sandler and Phaedra Pezzulo, Eds. *Environmental Justice and*

Environmentalism: The Social Justice Challenge to the Environmental Movement, eds Cambridge: MIT Press, pp. 285–307.

Shaw, George Bernard. 1903. *Man and Superman: A Comedy and a Philosophy*. Westminster: A. Constable.

Shiva, Vandana. 2005. *Earth Democracy: Justice, Sustainability, and Peace*. Cambridge: South End Press.

Shrader-Frechette, Kristin. 2002. *Environmental Justice: Creating Equality, Reclaiming Democracy*. Oxford: Oxford University Press.

———. 1991. *Risk and Rationality: Philosophical Foundations for Populist Reforms*. Berkeley: University of California Press.

Sikora, R. I. and Brian Barry, eds. 1978. *Obligations to Future Generations*. Philadelphia: Temple University Press.

Soulé, Michael. 1980. Thresholds for Survival: Maintaining Fitness and Evolutionary Potential. In Michael Soulé and Bruce Wilcox, Eds. *Conservation Biology: An Evolutionary-Ecological Perspective*, eds. Sunderland, MA: Sinauer Associates, pp. 151–170.

Thomashow, Mitchell. 1999. "Toward a Cosmopolitan Bioregionalism." In Michael Vincent McGinnis, Ed. *Bioregionalism*, ed. Berkeley, CA: University of California Press, pp. 121–132.

Trombulak, Steve, Reed Noss, and Jim Strittholt. "1995/1996. Obstacles to Implementing the Wildlands Project Vision." *Wildearth* Winter.

United Church of Christ Commission for Racial Justice. 1987. *Toxic Wastes and Race in the United States*. New York: United Church of Christ Commission for Racial Justice.

Vaughn, Jacqueline. 2007. *Environmental Politics: Domestic and Global Dimensions*. Belmont, CA: Thomson Wadsworth.

Wapner, Paul. 1996. *Environmental Activism and World Civic Politics*. Albany, NY: State University of New York Press.

Weiss, Edith Brown .1987. *In Fairness to Future Generations*. Tokyo: The United Nations University.

Wilson, Edward O. 1984. *Biophilia*. Cambridge, MA: Harvard University Press.

World Commission on Environment and Development. 1987. *Our Common Future*. Oxford: Oxford University Press.

World Wildlife Fund. 1993. *Focus*, May/June.

———. 1996. *Focus*, March/April.

Worster, Donald. 1994. *Nature's Economy: A History of Ecological Ideas*. Cambridge: Cambridge University Press.

Young, Iris Marion. 1990. *Justice and the Politics of Difference*. Princeton: Princeton University Press.

UNREDD. 2008. UN Collaborative Programme on Reducing Emissions from Deforestation and Forest Degradation in Developing Countries (UN-REDD) Program Framework Document. February 2010. www.un-redd.org/AboutUNREDDProgramme/tabid/583/language/en-US/Default.aspx.

ENDNOTES

1. Confucius (1979).
2. Babylonian Talmud.
3. Mathew 7:12; Luke 6:31, New Jerusalem Bible.
4. Shaw (1903).
5. Friedman (1995).
6. Rawls (1999).
7. See, for example, Young (1990).
8. Rawls (1999).
9. Bromley and Kathleen (1992).

10. Beck (1986).
11. Chawla (2009).
12. Quoted in Vaughn (2007).
13. Friedman (2006).
14. See Keohane and Nye (1989); MacNeill et al. (1991).
15. Worster (1994).
16. Myers (1993).
17. Jackson (1994).
18. Berry (1993).
19. Thomashow (1999).
20. Burke (1961).
21. For example, see Noddings ([1984] 2003) and Gilligan ([1982] 1993).
22. Wapner (1996).
23. Quoted from Adlai Today.
24. United Church of Christ Commission for Racial Justice (1987); Bullard (1994).
25. See, for example, Gottlieb (1993); Environmental Careers Organization (1992); Bullard (1993).
26. Di Chiro (2007); Roberts (2007).
27. Shrader-Frechette (2002).
28. Bullard (1994).
29. World Commission on Environment and Development (1987). The term sustainable development may have first been employed in the 1980 publication of the International Union for the Conservation of Nature and Natural Resources (1980).
30. Currently, there are approximately 136 million births per year. A young reader with 67 years of life ahead of her would live through the birth of well over 9 billion people. See the World Health Report at www.who.int/whr/2005/media_centre/facts_en.pdf.
31. Gore (1992).
32. See Rawls (1999). The extension of Rawls' framework to intergenerational justice is clarified in Rawls' subsequent work (2005).
33. Rawls (1999).
34. Burke (1961).
35. Burke (1961).
36. NEPA (1970).
37. Accessed at http://conf.diplomacy.edu/human-rights/decleration.htm.
38. MEA (2005).
39. Wilson (1984).
40. World Wildlife Fund (1993).
41. Soulé (1980).
42. World Wildlife Fund (1996).
43. The original version of the phrase has been attributed to Brower (1995).
44. Trombulak et al. (1995/96).
45. See www.ratical.org/many_worlds/6Nations/EoL/index.html#ToC and www.indigenouspeople.net/iroqcon.htm.
46. See French (1997).

CHAPTER 5

Environmental Dimensions of Sustainability Ethics

In Chapter 4, we explored the first and second of Leopold's concentric circles of ethical evolution—ethics between individuals and between communities—and we redefined community to include future generations. In this chapter, we redefine community yet again, exploring Leopold's third circle: the land. Recall that Leopold uses the term land to represent all of nonhuman nature. What does it mean to extend moral consideration to nonhuman nature? What does it mean not to? These questions are central to the second pillar of sustainability: the environment.

Environmental ethics in the most general sense—philosophical reflection on the moral value of nonhuman nature—has a long and varied history. In this chapter, we will explore this history and provide an overview of theoretical approaches in environmental ethics. Issues of special interest include the role of scientific, especially ecological, principles and ideas in environmental ethics, as well as the relationships between social and ecological communities in relation to environmental justice. We will also address arguments about the ethical status of nonhuman animals, both as individuals and as parts of species or populations. And finally, we address the moral status of domestic animals and their relationship to an ethic of sustainability, using the notion of a "mixed community" in which humans coexist with nonhuman, and particularly domestic, animals.

THE EMERGENCE OF ENVIRONMENTAL ETHICS

Nature's value and its relation to human life are important themes from the very origins of both religious and secular ethics, appearing in the work of foundational Western philosophers such as Aristotle and Ptolemy, as well as in the sacred texts of most world religions, both Asian and Western. While nature is a continuous concern, it has been highlighted in the work of certain thinkers, whose work provides a reference point for many contemporary environmental philosophers. For example, as mentioned in Chapter 2, Western thinkers such as Saint Francis of Assisi, Henry David Thoreau, Ralph Waldo Emerson, and John Muir made important contributing to the ethical consideration of nature.

The Birth of Modern Environmental Ethics

Recall from Chapter 3 that contributions of earlier thinkers notwithstanding, the birth of modern environmental ethics is generally attributed to the work of Aldo Leopold. Born in Iowa, Leopold worked for many years for the U.S. Forest Service, first in the southwestern United States and then in Wisconsin. In 1933 he became a professor of game management at the University of Wisconsin in Madison, where he lived until his death fighting a forest fire on a neighbor's land. Leopold's career coincided with the early development of the field of ecological science, which was just emerging, and he had great influence on a range of fields from ecology and wildlife management to philosophical ethics.

Leopold's greatest and most lasting impact came through his essay "The Land Ethic," part of a posthumously published collection of essays titled *A Sand County Almanac* (1949). "The Land Ethic" revolutionized philosophical thinking about the value of nonhuman nature and paved the way for the emergence of environmental ethics as a distinctive subfield. The land, for Leopold, was not merely soil, but what we now think of as an ecosystem, or "a fountain of energy flowing through a circuit of soils, plants, and animals."[1] This interconnected web of inorganic elements and living beings, asserted Leopold, deserves to be treated with love and respect, for it has not only instrumental but also intrinsic value.

The goal of environmental ethics, in Leopold's vision, is to encourage people to think about how they use land as not simply an economic concern but also an aesthetic and especially a moral issue. The land ethic provides a basic guideline by which people can judge the moral correctness of different attitudes and actions regarding nature. Leopold writes: "A thing is right when it tends to preserve the integrity, stability, and beauty of the biotic community. It is wrong when it tends otherwise."

Although Leopold's land ethic is a very simple premise, extending the circle of moral concern to the land, it was revolutionary and counter to the prevailing notions of his day. The land ethic called for a shift from *land as resource* to *land as community*, with the proper role of humans as "plain members and citizens" rather than conquerors. Leopold made a move away from a more anthropocentric (human-centered) view of the land to a more ecocentric (nature or ecologically centered) one. His ecocentrism is considered to be holistic in that what is best for the land, or nature, is what best preserves the ecological integrity of the entire community and not just for individual elements—human or otherwise. As a result, environmental decisions must be made in light of what best preserves the integrity of nature and not on what is most convenient, useful, or economically expedient to people.

Although the academic field of environmental ethics has grown exponentially in the past 60 years, Leopold's land ethic continues to be one of the major models. The "land ethic" is the best known example of a holistic, ecocentric ethic, which has spawned many variations and modifications—and not a few critiques.[2] Leopold's work remains a reference point and touchstone even for philosophers who ultimately advocate different sorts of ethics, for example, those that are more individualistic or more anthropocentric than Leopold's vision. In part, the power of the land ethic lies in its brevity: it sets out an agenda for an entire field in just a few short pages, with enough specificity to prompt lively debate while also leaving most of the work of practical systematizing still to be done.

BOX 5.1   Leopold and the Ocean: A Sea Ethic

Leopold's ideas have had a major impact on how people view natural systems, but Leopold was a professional forester, focused on terrestrial systems. Likewise, most explorations of Leopold's ideas have been primarily land-based. To echo Leopold, there is as yet no ethic dealing with human's relation to the sea and to the animals and plants which grow within it. Recall from Chapter 1 that the impacts on marine systems from fishing are now measured on a global scale. Large pelagic trawlers—which track fish with sonar, catch them in nets with openings as large as 90 m x 50 m, and process and freeze them onboard—are seen by many as a symbol of the *ocean as resource* attitude.

Given the vastness of the ocean, it is perhaps easy to understand how one might view it as an inexhaustible store of resources. Even Rachel Carson once thought the ocean was too vast for humans to have any real impact—a misconception she corrected earlier than most. Now that we are more aware of the ability for humans to have significant impacts on ocean systems we can see the wisdom of an *ocean as community* attitude.

Many of the points Leopold makes in developing his land ethic apply equally as well to marine systems. For example, in a famous passage from *A Sand County Almanac*, Leopold explains how he once considered wolves an enemy and describes the moment he came to understand their importance as top predators, controlling the deer population in a forest ecosystem. Without them, the deer become overabundant and can cause major damage to a forest's undergrowth. "Such a mountain," says Leopold, "looks as if someone had given God a new pruning shears, and forbidden him all other exercise." Such sights taught Leopold a lesson about thinking ecocentrically. He explains, "I now suspect that just as a deer herd lives in mortal fear of its wolves, so does a mountain live in mortal fear of its deer."

The same point can be made with sharks in an marine system. For example, large reductions in large shark species in the North Atlantic has been linked to increased populations of their prey species, including cownose rays. With the depletion of several large shark species in the North Atlantic, cownose ray (a type of stingray) populations have increased as much as 1000 percent in some places. Cownose rays feed largely on mollusks, including scallops. Scientists have suggested that the collapse of the scallop industry in Chesapeake Bay can be attributed to the increased predation pressure from cownose rays. In addition, water quality has declined in part because there are fewer scallops and other shellfish around to filter algae from the water.

Sharks and wolves both evoke fear, but both have important roles to play in their respective ecosystems. Leopold urged readers to think like a mountain. We might also consider thinking like an ocean. As the importance of marine conservation grows, we will likely see more of Leopold's insights applied to a marine context.

Environmentalism Becomes Mainstream

Following on "The Land Ethic," environmental ethics—and **environmentalism** generally—reached another major turning point with the 1962 publication of *Silent Spring*, by Rachel Carson (1907–1964). Carson, a biologist and writer for the U.S. Fish and Wildlife Service, wrote *Silent Spring* as an impassioned and detailed attack on the destructive ecological consequences of pesticide use, but it is also an attack on the notion that scientific progress is always beneficial. Sometimes, Carson argued—as in the case of pesticide use—scientific progress is more destructive than anyone could have anticipated.

Carson especially criticized the widely used chemical known as DDT (dichlorodiphenyltrichloroethane). At the time *Silent Spring* was published, DDT was already heralded for its role in stopping the spread of malaria and typhus during World War II. After the war, chemicals such as DDT were used more widely as efficient and economical ways to eradicate pests and increase crop yield, but they also had unintended consequences to humans and the environment alike.

One of the key ecological problems of DDT is that it is soluble in fat but not in water, which leads to **biomagnification**. This means that the chemical can be picked up in plankton and stored in fatty tissue, then transferred to plankton-eating fish. Those fish, again, store the chemical in fatty tissue and pass it to fish-eating animals. Each time the chemical moves up the food chain, the concentrations increase

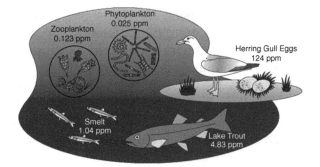

FIGURE 5.1 Biomagnification in the Great Lakes–even low concentrations of some chemicals in the water can result in the presence of toxic concentrations at high levels of the food chain. *(Source: U.S. EPA)*

drastically so that a body of water with very low levels of DDT can still result in high levels of the chemical in the body tissue of animals high on the food chain (see Figure 5.1).

Initially, these links were only suspected. In the absence of detailed studies, not only farmers but also public health officials—seeking to reduce mosquitoes—continued to use DDT widely, in the United States and other parts of the world. Carson made the case that chemicals like DDT could become concentrated enough in animals high in the food chain (e.g., birds) to affect their health. Furthermore, she noted that human beings are also high in the food chain and, therefore, susceptible to the same high concentrations of chemicals. The dangers and damages reported by Carson in *Silent Spring* led to both an outcry against pesticide use by the public and defenses of the agricultural necessity of pesticides by the manufacturers of the chemicals. Although these companies vigorously tried to discredit Carson and invalidate her claims, the book was widely praised and mobilized many Americans against the dangers of DDT.

More generally, *Silent Spring* is recognized as having launched the environmental movement in the United States. As a result of the book's popularity, many Americans became more aware of the interconnections between human beings and nature and how human technologies can have wide-ranging effects that cannot be bargained against the health and well-being of our planet, human or nonhuman. DDT was banned in 1972 for agricultural use in the United States, in no small part because of Carson's work. The banning of DDT in the United States is one of the major reasons for the recovery of the bald eagle, among other endangered bird species. (The chemical is still used in some countries.)

Undertones of the Sacred

Carson and Leopold wrote primarily as scientists, drawing on their professional experience and training as the foundations of their moral attitudes toward the nonhuman world. For each, however, the natural world seemed to hold a sacred status. Leopold explains, "Our ability to perceive quality in nature begins, as in art, with the pretty. It expands through successive stages of the beautiful to values as yet uncaptured by language."[3]

For Carson, approaching nature with a sense of wonder was a fundamental aspect of her studies and writing. She explained to a group of women journalists:

I am not afraid of being thought a sentimentalist when I say that I believe natural beauty has a necessary place in the spiritual development of any individual or any society. I believe that whenever we destroy beauty, or whenever we substitute something manmade and artificial for a natural feature of the earth, we have retarded some part of man's spiritual growth."[4]

This type of spiritual or religious sentiment has played no small role in the development of environmental ethics.

RELIGION AND ENVIRONMENTAL ETHICS

One of most important documents in the development of environmental philosophy is a 1967 article by historian of science Lynn White, Jr. In "The Historical Roots of Our Ecologic Crisis," published in the journal *Science*, White argued that human values deeply condition human practices and, specifically, that religion deeply conditions environmental practices. The claim was a provocative one. At a time when many considered science—rather than religion—to have primary influence over how humans characterize their relationship with nature, White illustrated the fundamental influence that religion has on modern Western society by using modern science as an example. His argument is worth revisiting in relation to the ethics of sustainability.

Religion and Nature

White attributed much of the "ecological crisis" to specific beliefs that lie at the heart of modern scientific and technological pursuits—most notably a belief in perpetual progress, as well as human separation from and transcendence over nature. He then traced these beliefs to the Christian world-view that dominated medieval Europe. With this move, White drew direct connections between Christianity and deleterious environmental practices throughout history. Moreover, he described Christianity as the most anthropocentric religion in the world, citing a belief (held by some manifestations of the religion) that it is God's will for humans to dominate and subdue the earth.

According to White, the belief that Creation existed to serve human purposes made it easy to justify increasing exploitation of nature as technology advanced over time. In light of the strong correlation between certain deleterious Christian ideas of nature and environmental degradation in certain historically Christian societies, White asserted that "What people do about their ecology depends on what they think about themselves in relation to things around them. Human ecology is deeply conditioned by beliefs about our nature and destiny—that is, by religion."[5]

White's article has stirred much debate not only about the relationship between Christianity and environmentalism but also about the role of religion in shaping attitudes and practices toward nature more generally. We focus here on this more general relevance of White's argument. At the root of White's thesis is the claim that environmental attitudes and practices are inherently religious issues, even for those who are not religious.

This is true, he claims, because religion has so pervaded history and society that it cannot become disentangled from general views on nature. "What we do about ecology depends on our ideas of the man-nature relationship. More science and more technology are not going to get us out of the present ecological crisis until we find a new religion, or rethink our old one."[6]

White, thus, posed environmental problems as essentially social and moral problems rather than scientific and technical ones. The attitudes and principles that guide our scientific research and technological developments, in other words, are more important than the science and technology themselves. This is an important claim for people concerned with sustainability today, which involves continuing debates about the relative roles of technology and culture (including religion). White's argument about the religious and cultural underpinnings of environmental problems has led to one of the central claims of environmental ethics: there can be no purely technical solution to environmental problems.

More recently, a number of environmental scholars have agreed with White's assertion that religion holds a singular place for many people as an overarching narrative that guides and shapes both beliefs and practices. This speculation is upheld by empirical research that has found that even individuals who do not invoke God in other contexts do so in order to talk and think about nature. Willett Kempton and a team of researchers found that people use the concept of divine creation to "express the sacredness of nature" in particular. Kempton et al. observe, "Regardless of whether one actually believes in biblical Creation, it is the best vehicle we have to express this value."[7] For many, speaking of nature in terms of "creation" seems a powerful way to describe its intrinsic value, even if they are not members of monotheistic religions. More generally, the ways that religious narratives define the human position in relation to nature often have a dramatic impact on people's environmental attitudes and practices.

This influence, as White noted, can be extremely negative. For White, the roots of the ecological crisis lie in the cultural assumptions that held sway during the early development of science, namely the Roman Catholic beliefs of thirteenth-century Western Europe. Among these beliefs, according to White, was the divinely ordained separation from—and dominance over—nature. While White believed that Christianity fostered particularly destructive attitudes toward the environment, other religions do not appear exempt. A number of scholars have examined the influence of traditional Asian religions on environmental practices in India, China, and Japan. Stephen Kellert has found that presumably positive views of nature in Japanese Buddhism have not prevented widespread environmental destruction. Yi-Fu Tuan has made similar claims regarding China.[8]

Greening Religion

White's article also elicited discussion regarding the notion of green religion. Early entries into this discussion revolved around the issue of which religion is greenest, or, most likely to result in environmentally responsible behavior.[9] However, scholars now generally agree that no one religion can be seen as necessarily eliciting environmentally responsible behavior. Rather than promoting any one religion as the greenest and suggesting mass conversion, the discussion has turned toward developing green interpretations within religious traditions already held dear. In recent years, a wide range of religious groups have issued statements on the environment. Some of these are very general, such as Pope John Paul II's calls for "ecological conversion" and his naming of Francis of Assisi as the "Patron Saint of Ecology." Other religious statements address specific problems, such as climate change, a topic to which American Evangelical Protestants have recently given a great deal of attention.

Among the many other environmentally beneficent approaches to nature within Western monotheistic traditions, perhaps the most important is the notion of stewardship. According to this view, creation belongs to God, and human beings are not owners of nature but rather its stewards or, in Islamic theology, "vice-regents." People are entrusted to care for the planet as part of their duties to God. They have special privileges but also special duties in relation to the rest of creation. Stewardship perspectives tend to prioritize human goods, while also constraining human freedom to act in destructive ways.

The great value of stewardship ethics, as secular philosopher Baird Callicott explains, is that they solve the problem of where nature's inherent value comes from—God's act of creation—while at the same time acknowledging humans' special role in the creation. This special role requires people to treat nature respectfully, as good caretakers, rather than as despots.[10] Stewardship ethics are especially important for agricultural societies, in which the land must be protected for human survival. This concern is evident, for example, in the Jewish tradition of the Jubilee Year, which falls at the end of seven 7-year cycles (either 49 or 50 years). The Jubilee is a kind of year-long Sabbath, during which the land and animals are to rest. Thus, fields are left fallow and draft animals are not worked.

Even within monotheistic traditions, there is a range of opinion. Stewardship represents a generally human-centered ethic, but many Christian, Muslim, and Jewish thinkers have developed more ecocentric ethics, in which nature has value not simply for its usefulness to human beings. Some religious thinkers speak, for example, of the "integrity of creation," or the notion that because God

---

BOX 5.2 Environmental Interpretations of Christianity

In addition to stewardship, the Catholic and Anglican natural law tradition provides a strong foundation for some Christian environmental ethics. Within the natural law tradition, God created the earth according to principles that guide every level of creation, from the movement of the planets to the behavior of individual creatures. Thus, all of creation, including humanity, is related in harmonious and hierarchical ways. A Christian environmental ethic based on natural law locates moral value in a relational account of common good of humans and nonhumans and the cosmos, rather than in the more dualistic view of stewardship ethics.

However, both stewardship and natural law models remain anthropocentric insofar as they ascribe to a hierarchy with humans above nonhuman nature (though below God). From both perspectives, human beings are justified in using nature instrumentally. Natural law and stewardship traditions are both important in Islamic environmental ethics. The western monotheistic traditions seem to offer less support for ecocentric models, such as Deep Ecology, in which human beings and nature enjoy more egalitarian relationships.

Thomas Berry, a Catholic priest and cultural historian (he preferred the label "geologian"), famously integrated his Christian beliefs with an egalitarian worldview. Berry gained fame among theologians and scholars from many fields for his ability to integrate ideas from worldviews that appear to be at odds with each other. In his work *The Dream of the Earth*, Berry provides a scientifically accurate account of the history of the universe expressed in mythical language, presenting the evolution of the universe as an ongoing story of creation. From this perspective, Berry interpreted his Christian beliefs in the context of a sense of kinship to the nonhuman world. He asserts in *The Great Work*, "Of one thing we can be sure: our own future is inseparable from the larger community that brought us into being and which sustains us in every expression of our human quality of life, in our aesthetic and emotional sensitivities, our intellectual perceptions, our sense of the divine, as well as in our physical nourishment and bodily healing" (1999, p. 162).

created the natural world as well as human beings, nature has its own intrinsic value and is not meant only to serve short-term human interests.

In non-monotheistic religions, including Buddhism, Daoism, and many Native American traditions, interdependence rather than stewardship is a major theme guiding discussions of religious duties and attitudes toward nature. Because human beings are related to all of nature and dependent upon other creatures and the Earth itself, according to some of these worldviews, principles of humility, moderation, and compassion should guide environmental practices. More specifically, the Buddhist concept of the interdependent self de-centers humans, just as Buddhist principles of compassion and nonviolence may encourage more caring and enlightened respect for human beings and nature alike. Similarly, many environmental philosophers find promise in Native American cultural emphases on "walking lightly" on Earth and respecting the agency of other creatures. The problem posed for an ethic of sustainability is how these ideas, valuable as they may be, can have a significant impact in contemporary Western societies.

ECOLOGICAL PRINCIPLES IN ENVIRONMENTAL ETHICS

Religious ideas, practices, and institutions have undoubtedly had a powerful influence on attitudes toward nature throughout the world, including supposedly secularized Western societies such as the United States. For many scientists and technology professionals, however, as for many environmental philosophers, scientific principles are the most important factor in determining ideas about nature and the world in general. This section focuses on the influence science has had on environmental ethics.

Development of Ecology

The relationship between ecological science and environmental ethics is intimate and complex. Ecology is the study of the interactions between living organisms (plants and animals) and their surroundings, including physical landscape features and climate. It began as a serious scientific endeavor in the nineteenth century, with the work of Alexander von Humboldt (1769–1859), Charles Lyell (1797–1875), and Alfred Russel Wallace (1823–1913), among others.

The history of ecological science reflects not a single unchanging agreement but rather continual debates within an ever-changing historical consensus. In his influential book *Nature's Economy: A History of Ecological Ideas*, historian of science Donald Worster documents both the development of scientific ideas in ecology and their interactions with wider cultural forces. Among the earlier models that Worster describes is the "Romantic" view, which stresses harmony and balance in nature. This view parallels themes found more generally in art and literature of the Romantic era in the eighteenth and nineteenth centuries. For example, poets such as William Wordsworth in Europe and Walt Whitman in the United States expressed the popular notion of nature as pure, a perfect world that becomes sullied by civilization.

By the turn of the nineteenth century, the work of Charles Lyell, Alexander von Humboldt, and Charles Darwin brought conflict and competition to the forefront of ecology. Here again, we can see the parallel in the art and literature of the Victorian period of the late nineteenth century, where a tranquil and harmonious nature had been replaced by one "red in tooth and claw" to quote Alfred Tennyson's famous description. By the early twentieth century, the work of Frederic Clements (1874–1945) helped shape a new approach, focused on the dynamics of ecological succession in plant communities (Worster 1994, p. 209). In this view, an ecosystem goes through a series of stages before reaching a more stable set of conditions, often referred to as a climax community.

In each of these shifts, we can see the interplay between the prevailing cultural views in general and the ecological models in particular. No doubt, these scientists were viewing nature through the cultural lenses of their times. However, they were also seeing ecosystems in new ways that would greatly influence subsequent interpretations of the behavior of ecosystems. And the interplay continues. While these models have been subsumed in many ways, all have contributed elements to contemporary ecological science and more generally to contemporary perspectives on nature. Newer themes that are important for ecology include work in

physics on complexity, resilience, unpredictability, and chaos.

CARICATURES OF NATURE

One way to view these historical views of ecology and their current significance is as what Lance Gunderson and C. S. Holling refer to as caricatures of nature,[11] underlying assumptions we make regarding how natural systems work. Gunderson and Holling identify five such caricatures, emphasizing that none of them are wrong, but all of them are incomplete.

In the first view, Nature Flat, nature is a blank slate, "infinitely malleable and amenable to human control and domination." The second caricature, Nature Balanced, is similar to Worster's Romantic view, in which nature is characterized as maintaining an equilibrium condition. Any disturbance to the system will cause a temporary change of conditions, but stabilizing forces return the system to equilibrium. While this second caricature is characterized by stability, the third caricature, Nature Anarchic, emphasizes instability. In this view, nature is seen as incredibly volatile. Any disturbance to the system will result in spiraling change that causes major shifts in the system.

Before reviewing the final two caricatures, let's focus for a moment on the ethical responsibilities and subsequent policies that coincide with each of the first three. In a Nature Flat world, nature is seen largely as a construct of human action. Gunderson and Holling describe a "cornucopian" view, "where human ingenuity and knowledge surmount all obstacles." This is the view of neoclassical economics, one which we will explore in more detail in the next chapter.

Gunderson and Holling identify the Brundt-land Commission, as well as the International Institute for Sustainable Development, as subscribers of the Nature Balanced view. They cite these institutions as "some of the most effective forces of change," but criticize them for what they see as a static view of sustainability. The same criticism could hardly be aimed at Nature Anarchic subscribers. This view, however, goes too far the other way, focusing on "hyperbolic processes of growth and collapse." In this caricature, held by many radical environmentalists, any impact to natural systems by human beings will be amplified by the system itself. Subscribers to this view oppose centralization, as staying small and localized means that the inevitable collapse will be localized, too.

Gunderson and Holling emphasize that each of these views has something to offer. Certainly, human ingenuity will play no small role in efforts to move toward sustainability. And both stabilizing and destabilizing forces are inherent parts of natural systems. But a more useful view of nature will have to encompass all of these aspects. The last two caricatures, Nature Resilient and Nature Evolving, account for the changing behavior of natural systems. Nature Resilient can be understood as focusing primarily on short-term changes, while Nature Evolving encompasses slow changes that occur over longer periods of time.

The key insight provided by these last two caricatures is that nature is not a blank slate, nor is it essentially stable or essentially unstable. The behavior of a natural system depends largely on the context, on the details specific to a particular time and place. These dynamic and mercurial aspects of natural systems raise serious questions for environmental ethicists. Recall the discussion from Chapter 2 on ethical relativism. The latest models in ecology raise similar issues, what might be called ecological relativism. If an ecosystem is already in a constant state of change, then which version of the environment should one work to sustain?

A Closer World

If ecology has at times seemed to complicate matters, it has also provided a number of concepts that have had special impacts on the development of environmental values. Consider the theory of evolution. There is a reason why Donald Worster calls Charles Darwin "the single most important figure in the history of ecology over the past two or three centuries."[12] While some responded to Darwin's ideas with trepidation, others have come to see the idea of evolution as an epic story that unifies not only all people but all life on earth.

Let's look at how the picture of evolution offered by science might inform an environmental ethic. First, it might instill in human beings a greater sense of humility. The idea that the world as it exists today was not created solely, or even primarily, for use by humans may indeed have a transformative effect on one's sense of entitlement to resources. If we realize the pie was not baked just for us, we might be inclined to cut ourselves a smaller slice.

Second, evolution offers a world of familial connection. It is admittedly a strange kind of family, hardly a loving one. Writer Edward Abbey describes a wilderness that frightens "not through danger or hostility, but something far worse—its implacable indifference."[13] If the evolutionary process as depicted by science is red in tooth and claw, it is not so out of hostility, but out of utter indifference to the individual. Nonetheless, in an evolutionary world nonhumans are more than just fellow travelers or neighbors. They are kin. Leopold explains, "It is a century now since Darwin gave us the first glimpse of the origin of species. . . . This new knowledge

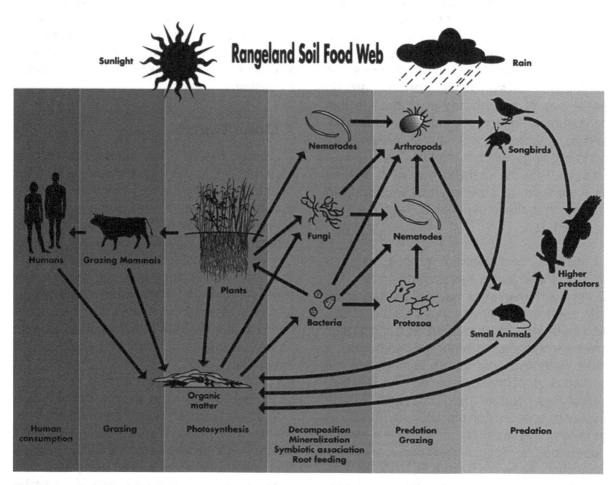

FIGURE 5.2 Rangeland Soil Food Web: the science of ecology illustrates humans' physical and biological connection to other species (*Source: US Bureau of Land Management*)

should have given us, by this time, a sense of kinship with fellow creatures; a wish to live and let live; a sense of wonder over the magnitude and duration of the biotic enterprise." [14]

Evolution, then, offers us a picture of connections to other species that reach far back through time. Ecology offers a similar picture of the present. Ecologists study the multilayered, interactive relationships between organisms and their environments that form the dynamic webs of connections called ecosystems. Conflict and competition between individual organisms is intrinsic to such systems. But so is symbiosis, as the life-supporting activities of one species complements or supplements the life-supporting activities of another species. It is the dance of competition, conflict, cooperation, and symbiosis that create the relationships of interdependence between the diverse organisms comprising an ecosystem.

Informed by these ecological insights, social scientists have explored the conflict, competition, cooperation, and symbiosis that create webs of interdependence between and within economic, scientific, technological, social, political, and cultural systems (see Figure 5.2). In the previous chapter, we focused on interdependence as it exists between people. However, the concept of interdependence between species is central to the science of ecology and probably the most important element of ecological understanding for the general public.[15] Nonhuman species are also riding aboard the lifeboat, and in many cases, they play an integral role in keeping it afloat.

CONTEMPORARY APPROACHES IN ENVIRONMENTAL ETHICS

Now that we have an understanding of the religious and scientific concepts commonly used in developing an environmental ethic, let's take a closer look at some contemporary approaches to the topic. Environmental ethics shares many common themes and approaches with other subfields within ethics and draws upon many of the same thinkers. What distinguishes environmental ethics is that attention is directed primarily toward nonhuman nature. Thus, the lens and the resources of philosophical ethics are brought to bear upon an area that, some argue, challenges certain foundational assumptions of Western philosophy.

In other words, part of what makes Western (especially Enlightenment-based) philosophy distinctive is its **humanism**, which places human beings in a position of primary importance. Environmental ethics questions and sometimes rejects this assumption. Because of this, some philosophers argue that environmental ethics, at least in its ecocentric, or ecosystem-based versions, represents what land ethicist Baird Callicott has referred to as an effort "to build, from the ground up, new ethical (and metaphysical) paradigms."[16] Environmental ethics, in this view, does not merely add a new topic but rather transforms established ways of thinking about ethics. Taking nonhuman nature seriously is such a radical step that traditional philosophical and moral models are inadequate to the task, and entirely new approaches are necessary.

It is not clear whether the same is true for the ethics of sustainability, which integrates its concern for nonhuman nature with more traditional moral concerns such as social justice and economic equity. Precisely because sustainability integrates environmental and social concerns, more anthropocentric (human-oriented) ethics are generally more congenial than ecocentric approaches. We will discuss this question in more detail later in this chapter when we turn to the relations between environmental and sustainability ethics. In this section, our goal is to outline some of the major theoretical approaches that have emerged in environmental ethics, as a necessary foundation for understanding its role in and relationship to the ethics of sustainability.

Getting the Scale of Ethics Right

All ethics pose the question: "What is of primary moral concern?" In environmental ethics, this question is first and foremost about the value of nonhuman nature. However, this focus allows for many different approaches. One of the most important variables for thinking about the moral dimensions of nonhuman nature—and for human social life—is whether the main unit of concern is individuals or larger collectives, such as communities or societies.

For some thinkers, the individual being is the only measurable unit that can be accounted for in any moral equation. This is especially true for many advocates of animal welfare, who focus on the rights or interests of individual sentient beings. Both rights-based (deontological) and utilitarian (consequentialist) approaches have been used in arguments about the moral status of individual nonhuman animals. Precisely because of this individual focus, animal welfare is sometimes considered an issue separate from environmental philosophy. However, animals' moral status is linked to thinking about the value of nonhuman nature more generally, and thus it must be addressed in any consideration of environmental ethics. This is especially true for reflections on the ethical dimensions of sustainability, because sustainability entails economic and social issues in which the fate of nonhuman animals is inextricably caught up with that of humans.

In contrast to the individual-based morality common to many (though not all) treatments of animal welfare, a number of environmental philosophers adopt a more holistic approach. One of the most influential holistic models is Leopold's land ethic, especially as interpreted by J. Baird Callicott, who claims that with slight scientific and philosophical modifications, the land ethic is compatible with contemporary scientific models of ecology and is the most appropriate model for contemporary environmental ethics.

Callicott has developed a form of the land ethic that is evolutionary in nature and ecologically holistic: the ecosystem and its species are primary and the individual is of secondary concern. Ecological holism has been criticized for subordinating the interests of individuals or minorities to those of the larger group, a criticism also leveled at utilitarianism.

BOX 5.3 Individual and Ecocentric Ethics: Hunting

Hunting offers a good example of a case in which holistic and individual ethics appear to clash. For holistic environmental ethicists, hunting of prey species such as deer or elk is not only acceptable but sometimes necessary in order to preserve fragile habitats. Human hunters of these large herbivores replace the ecological function of the predators, including wolves, cougars, and grizzly bears, which human hunters largely eliminated decades earlier. Environmental holists argue that the suffering and death of individual animals caused by hunting is either irrelevant or perhaps even morally positive—a "painful good," as environmental ethicist Holmes Rolston puts it: "We endorse a painful good" (1988, p. 59). Because pain exists in nature and because individual pain often contributes to the well-being of larger wholes such as species or ecosystems, it is not just sentimental but morally wrong to try to eradicate or reduce the pain of individual nonhuman entities.

Environmental philosopher Eric Katz makes a similar argument: "If the primary ethical goal or principle of an environmental ethic is the well-being of the ecosystemic natural community as a *whole*, then the well-being of individual animals in the community will sometimes be sacrificed for the communal good. The problem is that ecosystems function, develop, and survive by means of the life and death struggle of competing natural forces, competing living beings" (Katz 1997, pp. 26–27).

Environmental holists such as Katz and Rolston argue against the more individualistic ethics that prioritize individual welfare over the good of the whole—at least in ecological contexts. They do not extend the same holism to human societies, where consideration of individual interests and rights still trumps collective benefits. They would be appalled at calls to "cull" human beings when their numbers become too great, as we might do for deer, elk, or elephant herds. Advocates of the rights of individual nonhuman animals find this dualism problematic. Tom Regan, for example, calls ecological holism a form of "environmental fascism," which allows and even encourages the destruction of sentient individuals for abstract collective goods (Regan 2004, p. 362). Regan echoes the arguments of human rights advocates concerned about ethical and political systems that focus on the well-being of the whole—which can include democratic, utilitarian, religious, and socialist models, among others.

Deep Ecology, Ecofeminism, and Social Ecology

One of the most thoroughly and explicitly holistic types of environmental ethic is **Deep Ecology**, a strain of environmentalism that was first developed in the 1970s by Norwegian philosopher Arne Næss. Næss was already well-known both as a mountaineer and a philosopher when, in the 1960s, he became a radical environmentalist—influenced, he said, by *Silent Spring*. His systematic reflections on environmentalism began with a 1973 article, "The shallow and the deep, long-range ecology movements," in which he defined "Deep Ecology" over and against "**shallow ecology**."

Næss defined shallow ecology, which he saw as the predominant trend in environmentalism, as the anthropocentric practice of protecting resources and fighting pollution primarily for the sake of the quality of life of the "well-off" in society. Here the natural world is seen as the environment in which humans operate, and the goal of its protection is human well-being. Næss contrasted this view with Deep Ecology, an ecocentric (nonanthropocentric) venture that places humans squarely in the natural world as beings who are interdependent with—and morally equal to—other life forms on the planet. According to Næss's "**biospherical egalitarianism**," all organisms have an equal right to live and flourish.[17] Deep Ecology is thus more holistic, viewing nature as a large community that must be protected and valued for its own sake because it has intrinsic value.

Næss and the many subsequent advocates of Deep Ecology argue that human beings should live in harmony with nature by realizing their selves in relation to nonhuman nature. With an expanded sense of self, humans are defined not as isolated individuals but by their interactions and relations with the many facets of nature. In this, some have seen the parallels between Deep Ecology and certain forms of religion, such as Buddhism and New Age religions.[18] Næss himself was influenced by Buddhism, as are later Deep Ecologists such as the Australian John Seed and the American Joanna Macy. Deep Ecology is considered a form of radical environmentalism and exists today in a number of forms that are distinguished according both to spirituality and to political militancy.

Another form of radical environmentalism is **ecofeminism**, which argues that human

destruction of nature is linked to gendered dynamics of dominion, subordination, and power. Just as men have subordinated women, human beings (particularly males) have subordinated and dominated the natural world, especially in the West. Carolyn Merchant helped launch ecofeminism with her 1983 book *The Death of Nature*, which documented parallels in the history of patriarchy and the domination and subordination of nature.

Today ecofeminism takes many different forms, including some with a strong spiritual bent and others that are more philosophically or politically oriented. Like other environmental ethicists, ecofeminists draw on longstanding philosophical schools, including rights theories and utilitarianism. They also look to more recent intellectual developments, such as feminist care ethics, which find moral guidance in relationships and emotions, as well as (or sometimes instead of) reason and abstract principles.

Ecofeminism tends to be ecocentric in orientation, affirming ecological interdependence and the intrinsic value of nonhuman nature. Rather than prioritize either gender inequities or ecological problems, ecofeminists often believe that both emerge from the same problematic ways of thinking and acting and, therefore, must be analyzed and resolved together.

Along with ecofeminism and Deep Ecology, another radical branch of environmental philosophy is **social ecology**, which has roots in earlier social justice movements, such as anarchism and socialism. Its founding thinker is Murray Bookchin, an anarchist who began writing about these issues in the 1960s. Bookchin and other social ecologists argue that environmental problems are rooted in unjust, hierarchical social, economic, and political relations. Because it prioritizes social causes and solutions to environmental problems, social ecology tends to be more anthropocentric than Deep Ecology or ecofeminism. In this sense, it is more akin to sustainability than these more ecocentric approaches to environmental ethics. However, few sustainability advocates adopt social ecology's radical critique of economic and social institutions.

Pluralistic Approaches

A less radical way to link social principles to environmental concerns has been developed by thinkers working within the pragmatist tradition of philosophy. As discussed in Chapter 2, philosophers Dewey, Peirce, and James developed pragmatism with a focus on moral pluralism and practical goals in an effort to overcome some of the problems of monistic philosophical thought. Philosophical monism presents a universal ethical framework, which provides the only (true or accurate) way to look at all formulations and situations. Many of the major models in environmental ethics, including Deep Ecology, ecofeminism, and social ecology, tend toward monism insofar as they attempt to explain environmental problems (and sometimes social and gender dynamics) through one overarching analytical lens.

In contrast, pluralistic approaches such as pragmatism explore a number of theories and values, with the understanding that more than one model or formulation of ethics may provide a feasible solution. Pragmatism is a concrete and particularistic form of ethics that looks at individual circumstances in order to evaluate the best possible routes to achieving goals. For this reason, it is especially valuable for sustainability, which is less a single analytical approach than it is an attempt to pursue practical goals.

Environmental pragmatists such as Bryan Norton argue that people whose reasons (philosophical foundations) for action differ can still work together for the same goals. Pragmatists acknowledge that environmentalists often disagree about the bases for environmental action and practices. Some claim, for example, that nature has value in itself (inherent value), while others argue that nature is simply here for human use. However, in these opposed views, there often reside similar goals, such as preserving a park or keeping water free of chemical runoff. Environmental pragmatists argue that these goals are important in and of themselves, and that the search for shared theoretical foundations is often unnecessary and sometimes destructive.

Ben Minteer, another important environmental pragmatist mentioned in Chapter 2, has developed a "civic philosophy" in which social, economic, and political concerns are central to environmental ethics.[19] Minteer brings the importance of a well-functioning democratic civil society for environmental protection to the center of philosophical discussions about how to value nature. Pragmatism has become increasingly influential within environmental ethics because of its emphasis on concrete action and policy, its advocacy of democratic deliberation, and its respect for scientific evidence.

Bioregionalism

Bioregionalism, which we covered last chapter in the context of social ethics, is another growing and action-oriented approach addressed within environmental ethics. Particularly relevant to this discussion is the bioregionalist claim of the value of local cultural knowledge—including knowledge about native animals and plants, agricultural traditions, and landscape features—as a guide to living within ecological limits. Such local knowledge is thought to have enabled some Native American tribes, along with other small-scale indigenous societies, to have cultural practices more adapted to local resources.

This local knowledge was not important to European immigrants, who rarely learned about or cared for their local places, according to bioregionalist critics. Instead, they lived according to a "frontier mentality" that has had disastrous environmental and social consequences, argues Wendell Berry in his influential 1977 book, *The Unsettling of America*, a founding bioregionalist text (see Figure 5.3). Unlike most Native Americans, according to Berry, European immigrants "did *not* look upon the land as a homeland."[20]

Bioregionalists call for people—especially Americans—to become native to their "little places" as a necessary first step toward becoming native to—and living sustainably in—their larger place.[21] Living as much as possible within the limits of a bioregion both

FIGURE 5.3 Wes Jackson and Wendell Berry: two of the leading advocates of bioregionalist and agrarian values are plant geneticist Wes Jackson (L) and farmer and author Wendell Berry, shown here at the old schoolhouse in Matfield Green, Kansas.

reduces energy and resource usage and increases knowledge, care, and efficacy. Further, beginning at the local level makes it possible to solve environmental and social problems that are overwhelming at larger scales. A focus on the local enables people to develop both knowledge of and attachment to their particular region, including the land and its nonhuman inhabitants as well as local human cultures.

Bioregionalist thinkers have paid special attention to food and agriculture. Many argue that the move away from local knowledge and culture and from the ecological constraints of a particular watershed has been especially marked in food production and distribution. Most Americans today eat foods that have been transported many miles, burning fossil fuels and other resources in both production and transportation. They do not eat what is grown locally and in season but expect year-round availability of many products.

These products are grown not only far away from their ultimate destinations but also, in many cases, with methods that are not sensitive to local conditions. Mass-produced and transported food is often grown in large farms with a single crop (monocrop), using high doses of artificial pesticides and fertilizers. To counter these trends, a number of movements have emerged in the United States, Europe, and elsewhere in recent years, often drawing heavily on bioregionalist ideas. This is particularly true of the local food (**locavore**) movement that is growing in the United States.

The New Agrarian Movement

Bioregionalists and locavores often advocate not only environmental but also economic and cultural shifts, toward farms and businesses that are not only locally oriented but also smaller in scale and more diversified. Similar values are important to the New Agrarian movement, which like bioregionalism emphasizes the importance of land and place. **Agrarianism**, according to one of its leading advocates, "is a deliberate and intentional way of living and thinking that takes seriously the failures and successes of the past as they have been realized in our engagement with the earth and with each other. Authentic agrarianism, which should not be confused with farming per se . . . represents the sustained attempt to live faithfully and responsibly in a world of limits and possibilities."[22]

Like bioregionalism, contemporary agrarianism looks to the values of local rural cultures, based on reliance and connection to the land,

as appropriate for urban as well as rural dwellers today. However, agrarianism may highlight cultural and moral issues more explicitly, especially with its focus on the dual character of cultivation: cultivation of the land and cultivation of character. Agrarians rail against the destructive popular commercial farming practices of the West, citing the damage that monocultures and synthetic chemicals have caused across the globe. For agrarians, one of the most sustainable lifestyles is a self-sufficient, communal, and "simple" life that revolves around hard work and respect for nature as well as attachment to neighbors and local institutions.

Both bioregionalism and agrarianism are relevant to sustainability in particular because they explicitly link social, economic, and environmental problems and solutions in the light of an overarching moral analysis. They differ from many other environmental ethics in that they take social and economic problems just as seriously as ecological ones. Issues such as food and agriculture show how environmental, social, and economic systems and values are connected, suggesting, according to bioregionalist and agrarian analyses, that they cannot be solved separately. While not all sustainability ethics share the local orientation that is central to bioregionalism and agrarianism, these approaches are important models for any ethic that aims to bring together the social, economic, and environmental dimensions in a coherent way.

The approaches to environmental ethics discussed here do not by any means exhaust the variations within the field. We have not discussed a number of theoretical models, including some that are very influential within environmental philosophy, because they are exceedingly abstract and, thus, less relevant to sustainability.[23] Many introductions to environmental philosophy are available that outline the different kinds of ethics, major thinkers and works, and central issues.

ENVIRONMENTAL ETHICS AND NONHUMAN ANIMALS

The themes from religion and science are also central to contemporary philosophical work on the value of nonhuman animals. The evolutionary continuity among species suggests that species share not only physiological but also behavioral similarities, as well as intertwined histories and futures. If nonhuman animals share many of the same capacities and feelings with human beings, some argue, their moral status cannot always be sharply distinguished from that of human beings. This raises questions about many of the ways that both wild and domestic animals are treated, in contexts including agriculture, scientific laboratories, park management, and even urban development and building construction.

For example, animals are generally treated very poorly in modern Western agriculture and often in research situations, where their intrinsic value and interests in goods such as free movement, social interactions with other animals, and even continued life are not primary concerns. Urban buildings and development often harm or destroy habitat

necessary for different nonhuman species. Further, sometimes the well-being of individual sentient animals can conflict with larger ecological goals, which necessarily arise when wild individuals of an endangered population are captured for breeding or when feral animals of an exotic population are killed. The philosophical debates about human treatment of nonhuman animals are related to discussions about the natural environment more generally but also include a number of specific issues, mostly regarding the moral value of individual creatures.

Making a Case for the Individual

Ethical thinking about individual animals is often very different from that about the environment more generally. Environmental ethicists are historically more concerned with ecological wholes, while those concerned with the interests of nonhuman animals are generally more concerned with individual beings. Moral considerability, some argue, cannot be attributed to generalities such as ecosystems, but rather inheres in individuals—whose interests are overlooked in holistic perspectives. More specifically, values come from individual characteristics such as intelligence or the capacity to suffer and social relationships among individuals. The moral value of individual creatures may be described in deontological perspectives, in terms of rights, as developed in the writings of Tom Regan who argues that mammals have specific rights to life, liberty, and nonharm, among others.[24]

Other philosophers approach the topic from the perspective of utilitarianism, most notably the influential Australian philosopher Peter Singer. Singer argues that individual sentient animals have an interest in avoiding pain and in having their basic needs met (e.g., for food and shelter), regardless of species. Singer uses the term "**speciesism**" to suggest a parallel between racial discrimination among human beings and the equally arbitrary (to Singer) discrimination among species. While Singer and Regan disagree about philosophical foundations, they share a common commitment to the welfare of individual animals and an opposition to holistic approaches to ethics.

The work of Regan and Singer hints at the diversity and complexity of debates about the moral status of animals. Equally lively are the debates between advocates of animal welfare and environmental ethicists. Many philosophers in both camps perceive the two subfields as not just distinct but conflicting, because of the individualistic focus of most animal ethics and the holism of many environmental philosophies. These distinctions raise a number of issues that are relevant for sustainability.

Some of these distinctions entail fairly abstract questions about matters such as the role of science in ethics or the validity of rights theories. Other issues are more concrete, such as those involving the relations between domestic (or feral) and wild species in a given ecosystem or the environmental consequences of particular agricultural methods. Many of these practical issues involve social and economic problems as well. An ethic of sustainability might help sort through debates about, for example, the relative

social, economic, and environmental benefits of agricultural methods that are more humane for the domestic animals involved, such as free-range organic farming.

Mixed Communities

This leads us to some of the additional questions raised when we think about domestic animals and their social and economic, as well as environmental, roles. For all of our species' history, human communities have included both wild and domestic animals and plants. English philosopher Mary Midgley uses the notion of a "**mixed community**" as the context for human cultural evolution.[25] Here "community" includes both domestic and wild animals, both of which play integral roles in human experience. Midgley argues that because humans are biologically similar to other animals and have evolved together with them, we have a direct capacity "for attending to, and to some extent understanding, the moods and reactions of other species."[26] Although this capacity is somewhat limited, we are granted with a unique capacity of viewing animals as members of our moral community, a position that has some similarities with environmental stewardship ethics.

The fact that we participate in different communities, many of which include other animals, can help mediate the apparent conflicts between holistic ecological ethics and animal welfare, according to Midgley. All the communities to which we belong have some moral claims on us, even though they are not all the same. We need not, Midgley argues, think about these moral claims as merely competing.

While it is true that we are naturally more inclined toward our own families and species, we are not emotionally or rationally limited in the range of our morality. The mixed community ideal calls for a move beyond abstractions of animals as a whole, or humanity as a whole, and a reconsideration of the existence of actual, concrete animals and human beings living together in a mixed community.

Midgley's work provides a crucial resource for Baird Callicott in his efforts to resolve the conflict between animal and environmental ethics. Callicott originally criticized animal rights theories as both philosophically weak and "utterly unpracticable,"[27] arguing instead for a holistic land ethic that does not prioritize the welfare of individual organisms. More recently, however, he has come to believe that "it would be far wiser to make common cause against a common enemy—the destructive forces at work ravaging the nonhuman world—than to continue squabbling among ourselves."[28]

Callicott seeks "a moral theory that embraces both programs *and* that provides a framework for the adjudication of the very real conflicts between human welfare, animal welfare, and ecological integrity."[29] He uncovers grounds for such a theory in Midgley's concept of the mixed community, which he finds compatible with Leopold's land ethic. Callicott argues that "we are members of nested communities each of which has a different structure and therefore different moral requirements." We are subject to the claims of close relationships, with people and with domestic animals such as pets, and also to the claims of larger wholes, such as those articulated in ecocentric ethics. These varied claims do not cancel each other out, even though they may require that we prioritize and sometimes make hard choices.

Midgley's notion of mixed, moral communities, and Callicott's extension of this idea, are important not only because they help us think about the specific issues raised by nonhuman animals but also because they provide a framework for integrating multiple moral claims—the central challenge of an ethics of sustainability. Callicott and Midgely remind us that different types of moral claims may be equally valid, even though we cannot always fulfill them all. This is true not only of the claims of individual creatures and ecological wholes but also of different types of claims based on social, environmental, and economic criteria.

When it is impossible to give equal priority to all the things we value, ethics can provide resources to evaluate, prioritize, and choose. It can also help us know when a dilemma is truly unavoidable. In order to reach positive resolutions, we must think clearly about the different values that we and other people bring to a problem or situation—meaning we must be clear about what we value, why, and how our different values are related to each other.

ENVIRONMENTAL ETHICS AND THE ETHICS OF SUSTAINABILITY

Earlier we defined environmental ethics as an important dimension of the ethics of sustainability but not the only or determining one. It is important to understand that

BOX 5.4 Distinguishing Sustainability Ethics and Environmental Ethics

Some environmental ethicists use the term "sustainable" as a synonym for "environmental." However, we define the ethics of sustainability as broader than environmental ethics, because the former, by definition, takes into account economic and social as well as ecological aspects.

Some environmental issues do not include these other dimensions, at least not explicitly or substantially. For example, many environmentalists are concerned about the destructive impact of feral and outside cats, which annually kill millions of native songbirds and rodents in the United States, including many members of endangered species. This important ecological problem has relatively few economic or social dimensions.

environmental ethics encompasses a wide range of perspectives, with differing positions on many of the theoretical and practical issues involved in sustainability. Especially important are the distinctions among more and less ecocentric and anthropocentric frameworks, the role of science in various approaches, and the ways some models have integrated social and environmental values.

Identifying Values

One of the most important questions to answer in regard to the relationship between environmental and sustainability ethics is whether one, the other, or both are involved in a given situation. Here, the challenge for the sustainability ethicist is how to identify and address the values that are at stake. This is true of some technology and science issues, which might raise questions about environmental values but not sustainability, or vice versa.

Arguably, some of the questions surrounding wilderness, including the preservation of endangered species and ecological restoration, are primarily environmental, at least in their ethical dimensions—and economic or social considerations come into play primarily as practical rather than philosophical concerns. On the other hand, some uses of technology involve mainly social or economic issues, because the environmental impact of various choices is either negligible or the same in every option. Medical research regarding the use of stem cells falls into this category.

And, of course, some scientific processes entail ethical concerns that are not really about the natural environment or sustainability. This is true for some of the moral issues that arise concerning the treatment of nonhuman animals or humans in medical or scientific experiments, for example. Thus, the question of whether environmental ethics, sustainability ethics, or both are involved must be decided before the relationship between the two can be analyzed.

Emphasizing Human Priorities

Sustainability advocates have adopted a wide range of environmental ethics. In general, however, the framework for thinking about environmental values that is most common, and probably most fitting, within sustainability ethics is fairly anthropocentric.

More human-oriented approaches can accommodate the other values that must also be brought into play. An ethic of sustainability can be defined as an ethic that coherently integrates environmental, social, and economic values without consistently prioritizing any single one. Ecocentric ethics may not meet this requirement, as they prioritize the claims of nonhuman nature, and especially of ecological wholes, necessarily subordinating at least some human values. For example, very few philosophers writing in the tradition of land ethics or Deep Ecology have made social and economic concerns central to their work.

Some environmental philosophies do fit within this definition. Some bioregionalists and agrarians have also developed integrated sustainability ethics, although others within those streams of thought prioritize ecological concerns above social ones. The same can be said of some work in ecofeminist and social ecological perspectives. Pragmatist approaches, which at times emphasize social and economic as well as ecological concerns, may be particularly useful in the context of sustainability.

A good example is the work, discussed earlier, of Ben Minteer, whose environmental civic philosophy is highly pragmatic and anthropocentric, placing as much emphasis on social, political, and economic concerns as on nonhuman nature. Minteer is primarily concerned with protecting nature for human goods, and his approach to environmental sustainability emphasizes creating certain kinds of human communities and institutions. The work of Minteer's fellow pragmatist,

Bryan Norton, also focuses on human goods, and seeks to balance social and economic with ecological values, although he underlines the importance of ecological wholes more strongly than does Minteer.

CONCLUSION

We have seen that the field of environmental ethics focuses on questions regarding nonhuman animals and goods. Note, however, that addressing these questions requires raising profound questions about ourselves and our values. What does it mean to be human? What is the ethical place of humans within the larger context of ecological systems? What rights and responsibilities come with that role? The answers we provide to these questions—explicitly and tacitly—will do much to shape the way that we approach matters of scientific inquiry and technological development.

Leopold understood the cultural importance of these questions. He observed, "An ethic, ecologically, is a limitation on freedom of action in the struggle for existence. An ethic, philosophically, is a differentiation of social from anti-social conduct. These are two definitions of one thing."[30] In other words, ethics evolve in response to a society's needs. Today, these needs include addressing numerous issues specifically concerning the natural systems that support and enrich human life.

We have now completed our series of broadening circles of ethical concern—from the individual, to all human beings, to future generations, and finally to include the Land as a whole. With this broader context for defining community we are now ready to look at the economic leg of sustainability, which offers a wide array of tools for decision making. As you will see, the application of these tools becomes far more complicated with our more inclusive sense of community.

REFERENCES

Abbey, Edward. 1968. *Desert Solitaire*. New York: Ballantine Books.

Berry, Thomas. 1988. *The Dream of the Earth*. San Francisco: Sierra Club Books.

———. 1999. *The Great Work*. New York: Bell Tower.

Berry, Wendell. 1977. *The Unsettling of America: Culture & Agriculture*. San Francisco: Sierra Club Books.

———. 1980. *Home Economics*. New York: Farrar, Strauss & Giroux.

Callicott, J. Baird. 1989a. *In Defense of the Land Ethic: Essays in Environmental Philosophy*. Albany, NY: State University of New York Press.

———. 1989b. "Animal Liberation: A Triangular Affair." In Eugene Hargrove, Ed. *The Animal Rights/Environmental Ethics Debate*, Albany, NY: State University of New York Press, pp. 37–69.

———. 1989c. "Animal Liberation and Environmental Ethics: Back Together Again." In Eugene Hargrove, Ed. *The Animal Rights/ Environmental Ethics Debate*, Albany, NY: State University of New York Press, pp. 249–261.

———. 1994. *Earth's Insights*. Berkeley, CA: University of California Press.

Carson, Rachel. 1998. *Lost Woods: The Discovered Writing of Rachel Carson*. Boston: Beacon Press.

———. [1962] 2002. *Silent Spring*. New York: Mariner Books.

Commoner, Barry. 1971. *The Closing Circle: Nature, Man, and Technology*. New York: Knopf.

Copeland, Warren. 1988. *Economic Justice: The Social Ethics of U.S. Economic Policy*. Nashville: Abingdon Press.

Cronon, William. 1996. *John Muir: Nature Writings*. New York: Library of America.

Gunderson, Lance and C. S. Holling. 2002. *Panarchy: Understanding Transformations of Human and Natural Systems*. Washington, DC: Island Press.

Gustafson, James. 1994. *A Sense of the Divine: The Natural Environment from a Theocentric Perspective*. Cleveland, OH: Pilgrim Press.

Jackson, Wes. 1994. *Becoming Native to this Place*. Lexington, KY: University Press of Kentucky.

Kabilsingh, Chatsumarn. 1987. "How Buddhism Can Help Protect Nature." In Shann Davies, Ed. *Tree of Life: Buddhism and Protection of Nature*, Hong Kong: Buddhist Perception of Nature Project, pp. 7–15.

Katz, E. 1997. *Nature as Subject*. Lanham, MD: Rowman & Littlefield Publishers, Inc.

Kellert, Stephen. 2005. "Japanese Perceptions of Nature." *Conservation Biology* 5: 297–308.

Kempton, Willett, James S. Boster, and Jennifer A. Hartley. 1995. *Environmental Values in American Culture*. Cambridge, MA: MIT Press.

Leopold, Aldo. 1949. *A Sand County Almanac*. Oxford: Oxford University Press.

Merchant, Carolyn. 1983. *The Death of Nature: Women, Ecology, and the Scientific Revolution*. San Francisco: HarperCollins.

Midgley, Mary. 1983. *Animals and Why They Matter*. Athens, GA: University of Georgia Press.

Minteer, Ben. 2006. *The Landscape of Reform: Civic Pragmatism and Environmental Thought in America*. Cambridge, MA: MIT Press.

Muir, John. [1911] 1944. *My First Summer in the Sierra*. Boston: Houghton Mifflin.

Naess, Arne. 1989. *Nature, Community, Lifestyle*. Translated by David Rothenberg. Cambridge: Cambridge University Press.

———. 1973. The Shallow and The Deep, Long-Range Ecology Movements. *Inquiry* 16: 95–100.

Norton, Bryan. 1991. *Toward Unity Among Environmentalists*. Oxford: Oxford University Press.

Peterson, Anna. 2001. *Being Human: Ethics, Environment, and Our Place in the World*. Berkeley, CA: University of California Press.

Plumwood, Val. 1993. *Feminism and the Mastery of Nature*. London: Routledge.

Regan, Tom. 2004. *The Case for Animal Rights*. Berkeley, CA: University of California Press.

Rolston, Holmes. 1988. *Environmental Ethics: Duties to and Values in the Natural World*. Philadelphia: Temple University Press.

Thomashow, Mitchell. 1999. "Toward a Cosmopolitan Bioregionalism." In Michael Vincent McGinnis, Ed. *Bioregionalism*. Berkeley, CA: University of California Press, pp. 124–132.

Tuan, Yi-Fu. 1967. "Attitudes toward Environment: Themes and Approaches." In David Lowenthal, Ed. *Environmental Perception and Behavior*. Chicago: University of Chicago Department of Geography Research Series, no. 109, pp. 4–17.

Watanabe, Masao. 1974. "The Conception of Nature in Japanese Culture." *Science* 183: 279–282.

White, Lynn Jr. 1967. "The Historical Roots of our Ecologic Crisis." *Science* 155: 1203–1207.

Wirzba, Norman. 2004. "Introduction: Why Agrarianism Matters—Even to Urbanites." In Norman Wirzba, Ed. *The Essential Agrarian Reader: The Future of Culture, Community, and the Land*. Lexington, KY: University Press of Kentucky, pp. 1–20.

Worster, Donald. 1994. *Nature's Economy: A History of Ecological Ideas*. 2nd. Ed. Cambridge: Cambridge University Press.

ENDNOTES

1. Aldo Leopold, *A Sand County Almanac* (Oxford: Oxford University Press, 1949).
2. The main critiques are that the land ethic is too holistic and does not allow for intrinsic value or concern for individual entities, including nonhuman animals and perhaps even human beings.
3. Leopold, (1949).
4. Rachel Carson, Lost Woods (Boston: Beacon Press, 1998).
5. Lynn White, Jr., "The Historical Roots of our Ecologic Crisis," *Science* 155 (1967): 1205.
6. Ibid.
7. Willett Kempton, James Boster, and Jennifer Hartley, *Environmental Values in American Culture* (Cambridge, MA: MIT Press, 1995) pp. 90, 92.
8. Stephen Kellert, "Japanese Perceptions of Nature," *Conservation Biology* 5 (2005): 297–308 and Yi-Fu Tuan, "Attitudes toward Environment: Themes and Approaches," In David Lowenthal, Ed. *Environmental Perception and Behavior* (Chicago: University of Chicago Department of Geography Research Series, no. 109, 1967), 4–17.
9. See Masao Watanabe, "The Conception of Nature in Japanese Culture," *Science* 183

(1974): 279–282, or Chatsumarn Kabilsingh, "How Buddhism Can Help Protect Nature," In Shann Davies, Ed. *Tree of Life: Buddhism and Protection of Nature* (Hong Kong: Buddhist Perception of Nature Project, 1987), pp. 7–15.

10. J. Baird Callicott, *Earth's Insights*.
11. Lance Gunderson and C.S. Holling. *Panarchy: Understanding Transformations of Human and Natural Systems* (Washington DC: Island Press, 2002).
12. Donald Worster, *Nature's Economy* (Cambridge: Cambridge University Press, 1994), 114.
13. Edward Abbey, *Desert Solitaire* (New York: Ballantine Books, 1968), p. 191.
14. Leopold, (1949).
15. Kempton et al., *Environmental Values in American Culture*.
16. J. Baird Callicott, *In Defense of the Land Ethic: Essays in Environmental Philosophy* (Albany, NY: State University of New York Press, 1989).
17. Arne Naess, *Nature, Community, Lifestyle*, translated by David Rothenberg (Cambridge: Cambridge University Press, 1989).
18. The term "New Age religions" refers to a number of religions that draw on some major Eastern and Western traditions as well as pagan and Native American religions and cultures.
19. Ben Minteer, *The Landscape of Reform: Civic Pragmatism and Environmental Thought in America* (Cambridge, MA: MIT Press, 2006).
20. Wendell Berry, *The Unsettling of America: Culture & Agriculture* (San Francisco: Sierra Club Books, 1977).
21. Wes Jackson, *Becoming Native to this Place* (Lexington, KY: University Press of Kentucky, 1994).
22. Norman Wirzba, "Introduction: Why Agrarianism Matters—Even to Urbanites," In Norman Wirzba, Ed. *The Essential Agrarian Reader: The Future of Culture, Community, and the Land* (Lexington, KY: University Press of Kentucky, 2004).
23. For example, Paul Taylor's "respect for nature," Thomas Birch's "universal consideration," and Jim Cheney's and Anthony Weston's "etiquette-based epistemology" are all lenses that may be useful to a sustainability framework, but they are beyond the scope of this discussion.
24. Tom Regan, *The Case for Animal Rights* (Berkeley, CA: University of California Press, 2004).
25. Mary Midgley, Animals and Why They Matter (Athens, GA: University of Georgia Press, 1983).
26. Midgley, *Animals and Why They Matter*.
27. J. Baird Callicott, "Animal Liberation: A Triangular Affair," In Eurgene Hargrove, Ed. *The Animal Rights/Environmental Ethics Debate* (Albany, NY: State University of New York Press, 1989).
28. J. Baird Callicott, "Animal Liberation and Environmental Ethics: Back Together Again," In Eugene Hargrove, Ed. *The Animal Rights/ Environmental Ethics Debate* (Albany, NY: State University of New York Press, 1989).
29. Ibid.
30. Leopold (1949).

CHAPTER 6

Economic Dimensions of Sustainability Ethics

It is hard to know exactly when the term "bottom line" burned itself into the American psyche. While used in the 1960s and 1970s, it did not gain steam until the 1980s.[1] A reference to the final line on a ledger where net gain or loss was tallied, the bottom line has become synonymous with what really matters, as in "The bottom line is, if I don't get that paper in by Tuesday, I fail the class."

The privileged importance of the bottom line in business conveys a clear message: it is money that matters. In 1994, however, business consultant John Elkington coined the term "triple bottom line," suggesting that businesses that hope to be successful over the long term must expand their focus. "The idea," explains Elkington, "was that business created—or destroyed—economic, social and environmental value."[2] Potential customers, argues Elkington, will shy away from businesses perceived to focus only on economic value. We will take a closer look in Chapter 11 at Elkington's adoption of the three legs of sustainability into a business model. For now, we will look at the original bottom line, the third leg in our discussion: economic sustainability.

When introducing economic ethics in Chapter 3, we used the case of Western industrial agriculture to illustrate the fact that economic processes develop within the context of the particular social or economic goods a society favors. In other words, how we construct and define "the bottom line" greatly influences the decisions we make. Recall that defining agricultural efficiency as minimizing labor while maximizing productivity resulted in large farms that grow a limited number of crops and are heavily dependent on fossil fuels. We begin this chapter by taking a step back to look at early influences regarding our thinking about economic good, including the rise of neoclassical economics, today's predominant economic theory.

While many characterize neoclassical economics by its general neglect of ecological matters, connections between ecology and economy have garnered much attention throughout the development of modern ecological thought. We will take a closer look at this strand of economic thought that in contemporary times has become its own subfield called ecological economics. With its explicit focus on ecological processes and natural systems, ecological economics provides a set of concepts and ideas that will be useful in placing economics within the context of sustainability.

FROM CLASSICAL ECONOMICS TO ECOLOGICAL ECONOMICS

Modern economics emerged in the latter half of the eighteenth century during a time of great social change and scientific discoveries. It was one of the first examples of transdisciplinary scholarship, in which social science and scientific progress were examined together to gain a better understanding of the functioning of the system of exchanging goods and services. Science brought with it the potential for new technologies and improved quality of life, particularly in a material sense. The result was a conflict between larger social goals and the ability of individuals to gain material security.

The Advent of Modern Economics

The first questions addressed by economics were moral questions regarding the rights of the individual to material gains versus the greater social good. Adam Smith (1723–1790), a moral philosopher, answered this question by suggesting that these two things were quite compatible. He reasoned that if two individuals making a transaction were fully informed of the consequences of their decisions, then both would be better off because both were achieving a desired outcome. By logical extension, a community of people all working toward their own self-interest would make everyone better off, creating a desirable distribution of wealth

and setting an appropriate price for goods. Smith referred to this mechanism of a free market, by which each person acting in his own self interest results in greater good for all, as an "invisible hand," an extension of the Almighty, guiding the economic system for the good of society.

Smith's point is not unreasonable. It speaks to the role of competition. A successful clockmaker strives to make better clocks, but not out of an altruistic goal to create a more punctual world. He simply wants to sell more clocks. Such a goal may not be as noble as altruism, but for Smith, it will do just fine. Smith's world is one where each individual—motivated by self-interest—strives to provide the most economic value he can. The result is not just better clocks, but better everything.

Smith's *The Wealth of Nations* is seen as marking the beginning of classical economics, and this idea of the invisible hand was a key contribution (see Figure 6.1). A second contribution pertains to the idea of value. For Smith—along with the other major classical economists, such as Thomas Malthus (1766–1834), David Ricardo (1772–1823), and John Stuart Mill[3] (1806–1873)—the value of a good generally depended on the effort that went into making that good. While these men differed over exactly how that value might be calculated, they were in agreement on this basic premise. Karl Marx (1818–1883) built on this common theme and further emphasized the importance of labor in determining the value of a good. For this reason, the Labor Theory of Value, which has its origin in the classical economists, is now associated primarily with Marx.

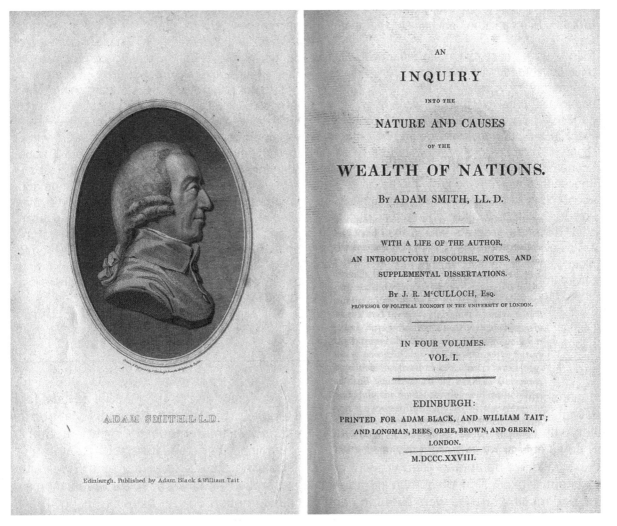

FIGURE 6.1 *Wealth of Nations*, written by the moral philosopher, Adam Smith in 1776, marks the beginning of the classical school of economics.

Ecological Economics and the Classical Economists

While ecological economics is a relatively new subfield, we can find seeds of it even in the writing of classical economists. For example, Malthus was the first to suggest that famine and war were not the result of divine providence but could, instead, be traced to human behavior and thinking. His basic argument was that human population could not continue to increase at an exponential rate because food and other items needed for human survival would quickly prove to

BOX 6.1   Marx and the Communist Experiment

Marx was perhaps the most influential econo-mist concerned with the social consequences of economic policies. While he was not the first economist to believe that the value of economic goods was primarily a function of the labor that went into producing those goods, he took that theory in a direction different than the Classical economists. For Marx, the labor theory of value implied that, being responsible for the value of an economic good, laborers should, in fairness, be able to capture that value when the products are sold. Therefore, Marx viewed profits of nonlabor-ers as evidence that the laborers were being ex-ploited. In addition, Marx attributed social ills and environmental destruction to the atmosphere of greed produced in a capitalist society.

Many have agreed with Marx that a capitalist economic system is fundamentally flawed and encourages personal greed, social inequality, and environmental degradation. These views were central to the experiment with communism in Russia and Eastern Europe. These experiments illustrated rather vividly that abandoning capi-talism and abolishing private property was not necessarily the route to social equality and en-vironmentally responsibility. In the 1990s, when the governments of Russia and Eastern Europe abandoned communism and reopened relation-ships with the countries of western Europe and the Americas, researchers were surprised by the level of environmental degradation that had taken place. Today, most see labor as one of several im-portant inputs in the production of an economic good. As you will see in this chapter, focusing on any one input to the neglect of the others is a recipe for environmental and social ills.

be inadequate to support a large and rapidly growing human population. He suggested even with technological advances, food sup-ply could only grow arithmetically, and there-fore, would not be able to keep up with the exponential expansion of human numbers. The end result would be wars over food and other resources, and the human population would be forced to shrink until it could be supported by available resources.

Malthus' model has never been fully demon-strated on a global basis, but there have been several regional examples where population outstripped the resource base and went through a period of decline. For example, the Great Hunger in Ireland in the 1840s and the civil war in Rwanda in the late 1980s were at least in part due to the inability of local food supplies to meet the needs of local popula-tions. Malthus' model is important from a sustainability perspective because it empha-sizes the finite size of the earth, its limited resources, and the impacts of population and consumption on the planet's health. It also introduced the concept of carrying capacity for the first time. Central to the sustainabil-ity framework, the term **carrying capacity** refers to the maximum population or activity an ecosystem can sustain indefinitely (see Figure 6.2).

David Ricardo introduced another model of economic system behavior that related to the environment. His model was an attempt to justify how landowners received a rent

FIGURE 6.2 Thomas Malthus (1766–1834) predicted a collision course between population growth and resource availability. *(Library of Congress)*

or income from land ownership because of the value of the crops grown on the land. He modeled how the more fertile and valuable land would be farmed first and receive a higher rent because it could produce the most output for the least labor input. Land that was less productive would be farmed later as valuable land was depleted. The less productive land would require far more labor and costs, resulting in less rent for landowners.

The model showed how increasing population would force people to farm in less favorable areas and how previously undisturbed land would eventually be farmed. Moreover, it provided insights into the role that technology, food prices, and population growth plays in land use. Ricardo's work also

foreshadowed the conflict between neoclassical economics, which largely ignored the role of ecological systems in the economic system, and ecological economics in which nature and the environment are central to a healthy economy. More specifically, Ricardo set up the battle between the unlimited economic growth mindset of conventional economic thinkers and the finite planet and resource assumptions built into ecological economics. While Malthus suggested the concept of carrying capacity, Ricardo carried this thinking a step further by suggesting that the next available resources would be of lower quality. The result of their joint work was the labeling of economics as the "dismal science."

Of the classical economists, it is perhaps Mill who most closely foreshadowed the arguments of sustainability. In addition to espousing the importance of social responsibility, Mill was openly critical of the ideal of constant economic growth. In *Principles of Political Economy*, Mill asked, "Towards what ultimate point is society tending by its industrial progress? When the progress ceases, in what condition are we to expect that it will leave mankind?"[4] Mill used these questions to introduce an argument against constant economic growth. For Mill, the ideal economy was one in a stationary state, experiencing no growth. As we shall see, this concept was picked up again much later by ecological economists.

This assertion alone might be enough to endear Mill to the hearts of sustainability proponents, but his reasoning in support of a steady-state economy is even more

remarkable. Mill placed the utmost importance on high-quality natural systems, noting that "solitude in the presence of natural
beauty and grandeur is the cradle of thoughts
and aspirations which are not only good for
the individual, but which society could ill do
without."[5] His expressed dismay at the loss
of natural systems in the name of human
progress is so thorough, it is worth quoting
at length:

> Nor is there much satisfaction in con-
> templating the world with nothing left
> to the spontaneous activity of nature,
> with every rood of land brought into
> cultivation which is capable of grow-
> ing food for human beings; every flow-
> ery waste or natural pasture ploughed
> up; all quadrupeds or birds, which are
> not domesticated for man's use, ex-
> terminated as his rivals for food; every
> hedgerow or superfluous tree rooted
> out; and scarcely a place left where a
> wild shrub or flower could grow without
> being eradicated as a weed in the name
> of improved agriculture.[6]

Indeed, except for the archaic language,
Mills' words might have just as fittingly
come out of the mouths of any number of
contemporary radical environmentalists—
hardly the type of language one would expect in the leading economic text of the early
nineteenth century.

Neoclassical Economics

By the latter half of the nineteenth century,
a new theory had arisen regarding value.
Neoclassical economists emphasized not the
labor or effort that went into making a product, but rather the product's potential utility
to the consumer. Neoclassical economists,
such as W. Stanley Jevons (1835–1882),
applied Bentham's and Mill's ideas of utilitarianism to the study of economics. Recall
from Chapter 3 that the ethical objective in
Utilitarianism is to create the greatest good
for the greatest number of people. Neoclassical economists would put this in terms of
maximizing utility, using "utility" as a general
term representing happiness or satisfaction.

The value of something, then, in the neoclassical view, is based on how much utility it offers a consumer. This shift in emphasis to the
consumers rather than the producer may be
more intuitive to people today. As consumers, the value we place on a product might
have more to do with how badly we want it
rather than how difficult it was to make.

Another neoclassical economist, Vilfredo
Pareto (1848–1923) explored mathematically
how one might achieve maximum utility in
a society. In doing this, he identified what
we now refer to as **Pareto optimality**. Like
Smith, Pareto argued that individuals participate in an economic transaction because
they believe they will be better off for doing
so. If an individual believed that participating
in a particular transaction would decrease
his utility, he would presumably refuse to
go through with it. There may of course be
some cases in which one party increases
his or her utility while the other stays at the
same level of utility. Pareto still considered
such a trade to be positive because it increased one party's utility without decreasing the other's. Pareto optimality in a market

---

BOX 6.2 Jevons' Paradox

Jevons made one of his most important contributions in the context of coal consumption in England. In the eighteenth century, Scottish inventor James Watt developed a coal-fired steam engine that worked much more efficiently than the previous design, performing the same amount of work with less coal. However, England's consumption of coal increased after the introduction of Watt's engine. Jevons explained that the more efficient engine resulted in a drop in price of the materials made using the new steam engine. As those prices dropped, demand for those products increased, which led to more people using furnaces and steam engines to meet those demands. As Jevons explains, "eventually the greater number of furnaces will more than make up for the diminished consumption of each." This explains the rise in the use of coal (see Jevons 1865).

This phenomenon is referred to as Jevons' Paradox or the *rebound effect*, and it remains a concern in the context of energy consumption. Some research indicates that one of the forces driving the increase in the size of the American home has been improvements in heating, cooling, and lighting technologies that permit the operation of larger houses at relatively lower costs. Although Jevons' Paradox and the rebound effect have been applied to energy resources, it is thought that the general effect also governs improvements in the efficient use of resources in general.

---

is achieved when any additional transaction could not increase one party's utility without decreasing another's.

The concept may seem abstract, but it is easy enough to visualize in a small market. Imagine a fruit vendor showing up in a classroom and distributing fruit to all the students. Some students would get oranges, others might get bananas, and so on. The students might decide that they would be happier if they could trade with the other students in the class. The classroom has now become a free market with each student trading fruit. A student with nothing but oranges might try to trade some of those oranges with the student holding nothing but bananas. If the two can cut a deal that makes them both happy, they will do so, and the utility of each student will increase. With some patience, the students will reach a point where no more trades can be made without decreasing the

satisfaction (i.e., the utility) of one of the participants. Therefore, trading will stop. The classroom market has reached Pareto optimality.

Note that at this point, most of the students feel more satisfied than they did with the initial distribution of fruit and, assuming no trickery is involved, everyone is at least as satisfied as when they started. We can see the invisible hand at work. Each student may have simply been selfishly trying to obtain the most desirable combination of fruit available, but their actions within the market resulted in the greater good, the increase of the collective utility of the group.

The concept of Pareto optimality is also called **Pareto efficiency**, and it still provides the foundation for the neoclassical concept of an efficient economy. It is perhaps no surprise that the concept gained popularity.

It is difficult to find fault with a system in which nobody loses and there is no tension between individual welfare and the greater good. Moreover, this desirable outcome happens without outside control as long as the markets are fair. However, people did find fault with Pareto's idea, and exploring this criticism will provide an understanding of critiques of neoclassical economics in general.

Criticisms of Neoclassical Economics

It is worth noting that there are some who argue that a new subfield of economics, such as ecological economics, is not necessary. In this view, the problems raised with the neoclassical model can be resolved by adjusting the neoclassical model. Others claim that fundamental assumptions of this model are significantly flawed. Here we discuss criticism that comes both from within and from outside the neoclassic model.

Most of the Pareto's critics start with a similar claim: that the dynamics described with Pareto efficiency are so rare that they make the concept impractical. For example, some critics pointed out that few real-life changes could be made in a society without hurting at least some people. To be more useful, a theory must provide guidance in situations where there is tension between the good of some individuals and the good of the whole.[7]

Others pointed out that economic transactions can affect people not directly involved with the transaction itself. A.C. Pigou (1877–1959) was the first to bring attention to costs and benefits that lie outside of the market, which he called **externalities**. Since neither the producer nor the consumer of a product is affected by an externality, the external benefit or cost is not taken into account when making decisions. Smoking a cigarette, for example, creates side-stream smoke that can adversely affect the health of people who are not directly involved in the sale or consumption of the cigarette. Since the cost of this adverse health affect is not incurred by either the producer or consumer of the product, it does not affect their decision regarding the transaction. Thus, it is a negative externality. As these health affects became better known, many cities opted to severely restrict where one could smoke in public.

Smoking is an easy target, however. People might debate anti-smoking regulations on the grounds of personal freedoms, but few would seriously argue that smoking in public places is an integral part of our society. What do we do when the process creating the negative externality is considered integral to society? The fact is that every industrial process, from producing a cell phone to driving a car, involves negative externalities such as water pollution and harm to local populations where resources are extracted. Pigou suggested that governments could internalize externalities through implementing a combination of taxes and subsidies. That is, the government could make the price of a product more accurately represent its true cost to society by making socially beneficial products or activities cheaper and socially detrimental ones more expensive. Taxes of this kind are often called **Pigouvian taxes** (see Figure 6.3).

(a)

(b)

FIGURE 6.3 (a) and (b) The concept of Pigouvian taxes can be illustrated by a solar photovoltaic array whose installation was subsidized by taxes paid by operators of fossil fuel power plants for their discharges of air pollutants. The process of mandating that those creating negative impacts or externalities must pay the true cost of the damage to those affected by their activities is also referred to as "internalization." *(Source: a U.S. Environmental Protection Agency, Source: b NASA)*

In a broader sense externalities can impact ecosystems as well, for example, the degradation of forests by acid rain (discussed in Chapter 1). Companies were often ignorant of (or not focused on) the impacts of their discharges, waste, and operations on local communities and ecosystems. Examples are the routine emissions of sulfur dioxide, particulates, and nitrous oxides from coal-burning power plants, chemicals from factories, wastewater treatment plants, metal plating operations, steel mills, paper pulp plants, and a host of other sources.

The problem with externalities is how to compensate those negatively affected by emissions. First, how does one quantify such a cost? Second, how should those affected be compensated? We will look more closely at these questions later in the chapter.

Physical Limitations

So far, the criticism has been aimed at the rather narrow applicability of Pareto's idea. Real-world markets involve complications that are not addressed within Pareto efficiency, but ecological economists argue that even broadening the scope to include the complications of real-world markets is not enough. They assert that economic systems exist within environmental systems, and that viewing situations through the lens of neoclassical economics can cause one to lose sight of the bigger environmental picture.

Consider the work of Harold Hotelling (1895–1973), a mathematical statistician who developed a model that examined and described the conditions governing resource conservation or depletion. He was particularly interested in what he called **exhaustible** or **nonrenewable resources.** Hotelling described a situation where an owner of land containing mineral resources could choose either to mine the resource or to leave it in the ground to be mined in the future. For a rational owner, the decision of when to mine is a function of the bank interest rate (or discount rate) versus the appreciation of the resource. If the perceived appreciation in the value of the resource is greater than the interest rate, the prudent owner would choose to leave the resource in the ground. However, if the interest rate was thought to be greater than the forecasted appreciation rate, the owner would likely mine the resource and put the money in the bank.

In the case of renewable resources, Hotelling's model describes a similar scenario: owners of a renewable resource, such as trees in a forest, would increase the rate of harvest as the interest rate increased. At some point the rate of harvest, driven by increasing interest rates, will exceed the regeneration rate of the forest and result in its decline. From this view, in which the expected interest rate and expected future price of a resource are the primary guides for managing biological resources, high interest rates may lead to depletion and loss of biodiversity, while low interest rates favor a conservation strategy.

According to Hotelling's model, a species that is not generating a flow of services at a rate greater than the rate of interest "should" be depleted. For some, this dynamic does not represent a significant problem because of the concept of **substitutability**, the idea that

one resource can be substituted for another. In this view, famously espoused by the neoclassical economist Julian Simon, whenever a resource is exhausted, people will simply substitute another resource in its place. Simon claimed, based on the dynamics of markets and faith in human ingenuity, that resources are in fact infinitely substitutable.[8] For example, if we run out of oil, we will simply shift more fully to nuclear power or some other energy source not yet discovered.

This idea of technological advance creating the possibility for resource substitutions not yet foreseen is a key aspect of the neoclassical growth model based on the work of Robert Solow and Trevor Swan.[9] This model moves away from the type of steady state economy identified by classical economists like Mill and toward a goal of constant economic growth supported by constant technological advances. This neoclassic ideal of constant economic growth enjoys wide popularity today. Indeed, it reaches so deeply into the public psyche that any decrease in economic growth rates are generally met with severe public criticism of the public officials viewed to be responsible. Current thinkers, however, stress the possibility of—and in fact necessity of—redesigning our economy to function well without growing.

Influences of Ecology

Of course, some historic strands of economic thought included the connections between ecology and economics. Indeed Ernst Haeckel (1834–1919), the man credited with coining the concept of **ecology** in 1866 explained, "By ecology we mean the body of knowledge concerning the economy of nature."[10] Haeckel contrasted this definition with his explanation of economics—the study of the ecology of human beings. From the very beginning, the two fields were closely tied.

We have already seen the role that environmental systems played in the ideas of some of the classical economists and in Pigou's introduction of externality. However, during this same period other thinkers were placing ecological concepts at the center of their investigation into economics. Alfred Lotka (1880–1949) was the first to attempt to integrate ecological and economic systems in quantitative and mathematical terms. He had a broad range of interests– including chemistry, physics, biology, and economics and was particularly interested in the role that energy plays in the dynamics of both ecosystems and economic systems.[11]

Howard T. Odum (1924–2002), a systems ecologist, built upon Lotka's work, continuing to find parallels between the flow if energy through both an ecosystem and an economic system (see Figure 6.4). In Odum's model, all energy is traced back to the sun. In an ecosystem, solar energy is converted to chemical energy through photosynthesis and then transferred throughout a food chain through consumption. Energy powering economic systems can be traced similarly. In this case, the solar energy may have been converted through photosynthesis very long ago (fossil fuels) or more recently (wood and biofuels). Odum used this common currency of energy to bridge ecological and economic discussions.

FIGURE 6.4 Howard T. Odum, a professor emeritus at the University of Florida, founded a branch of ecology known as systems ecology, which modeled systems based on energy flows. Systems ecology can also model the interaction between economic activity and ecological system function and is a useful tool for understanding the interplay of these complex systems. *(Source: Archives of the Center for Environmental Policy, University of Florida)*

Economist Nicholas Georgescu-Roegen (1906–1994) also focused on the primary role of energy in an economy, coining the term bioeconomics to "make us bear in mind continuously the biological origin of the economic process."[12] He focused on the second law of thermodynamics to explain why economic growth would be limited even in technologically advancing societies. Of particular interest to this discussion is Georgescu-Roegen's distinction between a stock and a fund. A stock is a production input that can create flows at any rate. For example, one can burn a thousand barrels of oil in one day or one barrel each day for a thousand days. In either case, the stock itself is changed and can eventually be depleted.

Conversely, a fund can provide an input to an economy without itself being changed. The sun for example, transfers energy to the earth constantly. However, with a fund the rate of the service is limited. One cannot, for example use a thousand days' worth of sunlight at once. Similarly, soil can cycle nutrients, but only at a limited rate. These ideas are central to discussions of renewable and nonrenewable resources and to the concept of ecosystem services. As mentioned in Chapter 1, this term refers generally to the ecological processes that support societies. In Georgescu-Roegen's terminology, a truly sustainable economy must be powered by funds. As we shall see, acknowledging the limited rates of these fund sources plays a large role in the ecological economic model.

THE ECOLOGICAL ECONOMIC MODEL

The world is complex beyond comprehension. All attempts to understand it—whether by a scientist, an economist, or simply an attentive person—are based on models. These models may be formal ones, such as that of neoclassical economics, or informal ones that go largely unexplored even by the people that use them. We might think of these models as sets of tacit assumptions that people use to interpret new information. Consider two friends—one of whom views wilderness as a threatening place fraught with danger, while the other sees it as a fascinating place full of wonders. In an attempt to resolve this difference, the two go hiking whereupon they see a grizzly bear and her cub out foraging for food. In this case, they might both reasonably turn to the other and say, "See, I was right," but one would have seen a menacing monster, while the other would have marveled at the bear's awesome power.

The two friends are using different models to interpret what they see and, thus, focus very different aspects of the bears. As with our discussion of models (or caricatures) of nature from Chapter 5, neither of the friends' models is wrong, but both are incomplete. The first friend's model might cause him to miss out on some truly amazing mysteries of wilderness, while the second friend's model might lead him into unnecessarily dangerous situations. The point here is not to encourage people to develop a model that is perfect. As statistician George Box said, "All models are wrong; some are useful."[13]

Ecological economists accept and adopt many of the analytical tools that comprise neoclassical economics. However, they suggest that the neoclassical model holds some assumptions that decrease its usefulness when applied to contemporary issues regarding resources. So far, we have focused on these criticisms of the neoclassic model. Let us now take a closer look at the assumptions held in the model of ecological economics.

Perhaps the most fundamental assumption of ecological economics is that the economy does not exist solely as an independent, open system. The economy resides in a system, the Earth, which is largely closed, except for solar energy and some incoming matter in the form of meteors and other space debris. Herman Daly, one of the best known contemporary proponents of ecological economics, focuses on the Earth as a materially finite system. Daly's logic looks like this: The Earth, or global system, is finite. Economic systems exist within the global system. Therefore, economic systems are finite. Moreover, the matter and energy that are inputs to the neoclassical model of the economy come from the global ecosystem and even the workforce factor of production is entirely dependent on the health and productivity of ecosystems. Starting from this premise results in a significantly different approach to economic analysis.

Natural Capital and Ecological Services

One way that ecological economists emphasize the biophysical context of economic systems is to include inputs from natural systems into their analysis as capital. The term capital was once limited to a stock of wealth or property that can be owned and used to produce more wealth. Thus, it made sense to discuss, as did classical and Marxian economists, the relative significance of capital and labor as distinct contributions to the value

of products and processes. More recently, however, the term "capital" has broadened significantly so that it can refer to any input into the production of a good or service. Today economists talk about several different types of capital. **Manufactured capital** refers to human-made inputs, such as machinery or infrastructure. **Human capital** refers to the input of workers into production, including labor as well as the knowledge and skills held by individuals. Finally, **natural capital** refers to any stock of natural resources or environmental assets such as oceans, forests, or agricultural lands.[14]

These three types of capital are combined in varying ratios to increase human welfare. In many cases, one type of capital can substitute for another. Machines, for example, can replace people on an assembly line, or vice versa. For some, however, maintaining welfare without natural capital is not a viable option. As ecological economist Robert Costanza asserts, "Zero natural capital implies zero human welfare." In other words, natural capital is not infinitely substitutable. "It is trivial," explains Costanza, "to ask what is the value of the atmosphere to humankind, or what is the value of rocks and soil infrastructure as support systems. Their value is infinite in total."[15]

The limits on the substitutability of natural capital are a second fundamental assumption of ecological economics. Many economists support a form of sustainability called **weak sustainability**. In this form, the goal is to maintain a level of human welfare—the product of manufactured, human, and natural capital. With weak sustainability, the assumption is that all three forms of capital are substitutable. One can make up for a decrease in natural capital by adding more manufactured and human capital to the mix. By contrast, **strong sustainability** requires maintaining a constant level of natural capital specifically, not replacing it with other forms. Strong sustainability proponents like Costanza hold that some forms of natural capital are truly irreplaceable. For example, the ozone layer protecting the Earth from ultraviolet light could be considered critical natural capital.

Similarly, agriculturally productive prime farmland displaced by development and covered with buildings and infrastructure has no real substitutes that are not extremely costly and energy intensive. As Robert Costanza and Herman Daly have noted, "A minimum necessary condition for sustainability is the maintenance of the total natural capital stock at or above the current level. . . .This 'constancy of total natural capital' rule can thus be seen as a prudent minimal condition for assuring sustainability and can only be relaxed when solid evidence is offered that it is safe to do so."[16] (see Figure 6.5).

Discounting the Future

The position of strong sustainability places Costanza and Daly in stark opposition to the logic described by Hotelling for deciding when to exploit a resource. Recall that for Hotelling the important comparison in this decision was between the rate of interest that banks offered (discount rate) and the rate at which the unexploited resource increased in value. Let us see what happens when we follow Hotelling's economically rational logic.

(a)

(b)

FIGURE 6.5 (a) Herman Daly, often called the founder of ecological economics, wrote some of the key early works that defined this discipline, such as *Steady-State Economics* (1991) and *For the Common Good* (written in 1989 with J. Cobb). **(b)** More recently Robert Costanza has been strengthening the case for ecological economics (See Costanza 1991) with his work on the concept of natural capital and valuing nature, often in collaboration with Daly. *(Source (a): Photograph used with permission of Herman Daly, Source (b): Photograph used with permission of Robert Costanza)*

Consider an economic project (e.g., a pine plantation) that would create a $10 million depletion of ecological resources within 10 years with an expected annual return of 10 percent. According to Hotelling, this project would be viable as long as it produced an immediate profit of just under $4 million dollars with no added profit later. While Costanza and Daly may not support such a decision, one can at least understand the motives here. Focusing for the moment just on the dollar figures, one can perhaps understand an individual's preference for $4 million now (which could be invested immediately and earn interest) over $10 million dollars a decade from now. Who knows what might happen during that waiting period?

But sustainability implies a much longer timeframe. Let us look at a different project, one that will create a $10 million depletion of ecological resources within the next century. Using Hotelling's same rubric, this project would be viable as long as it produced an immediate gain of $750. Such calculations present a dismal outlook for those living a century from now. Of course even a century is not a suitably long timeframe in matters of sustainability, but the idea is clear. The problem is that good neoclassical economics, at least relative to short-term profit, often translate into bad ecology.

This preference for present gains over future ones is referred to as **discounting** the future. As John Dryzek observes, "a system may be judged economically rational while simultaneously engaging in the wholesale destruction of nature, or even, ultimately, in the total extinction of the human race. The latter result holds because of the logic of discounting the future."[17] When costs of mitigating pollution, grappling with resource depletion, and responding to the effects of habitat destruction are shifted to future generations, and these costs are discounted by present-day decision makers, then today's economic rationality portends tomorrow's social and ecological disaster.[18]

So good economics today can become bad economics for future generations. It is natural for us to value a bird in the hand more than one in the bush, but when the bird in question is stewing in someone's cooking pot today, future generations who might have collected its eggs must go without. In such situations, the depletion of natural capital (the bird, or perhaps an entire species of birds) leaves future generations without the possibility of living upon the interest that natural capital generates (the eggs). Ecological economists disagree about how to deal with this problem, but there seems to be general agreement that while discounting future value may make sense over the short term, it is not an appropriate practice for long-term economic decisions.

The Economic Value of Natural Systems

Even if we all agree to maintain the current level of natural capital, what does that mean? In 1997 a group led by Costanza attempted a valuation of the global ecosystem and concluded that the value of the services provided by natural systems was about $33 trillion. Half of the value went to nutrient cycling. The open oceans, continental shelves, and estuaries had the highest total value, while the highest per-hectare values went to estuaries, swamps/floodplains, and seagrass/algae beds.[19]

Attaching dollar values in this manner presents a number of problems. The process is most straightforward regarding market products harvested or caught. For example, if a fishery produces X pounds of fish per year, and the fish sells for Y dollars a pound, economists can use these figures, along with the costs of catching the fish, to calculate the value that the marine ecosystem is adding to the market.

Other services are less straightforward, however. In some cases, estimates must be made regarding how much of a service the ecosystem is providing. For example, we may know that wetlands filter water, but studies must be done to produce estimates regarding how much filtering a wetland is actually doing. The estimates become even more difficult when the service is more abstract. A mountain forest may provide a scenic landscape for people to view on their way to work, but how much is that pleasant view worth? A coral reef might be a beautiful place to snorkel, but what is the monetary value of that beauty?

In these cases, economists often calculate how much people would be willing to pay for a service that lies outside of the market. Economists call this figure **willingness to pay**. Several methods exist for calculating willingness to pay. The method used depends largely on the type of service involved. For example, in the case of the wetland filtering water, one might calculate the **imputed willingness to pay**. This is the amount it would cost to build a human-made structure that could perform the service that the wetland currently provides. In the case of the mountain forest, one might calculate an **expressed willingness to pay**. This figure is calculated by surveying the beneficiaries of an ecosystem service about the value of the service to them.

Since the payment is only hypothetical, expressed willingness to pay studies can often produce exaggerated values. **Revealed willingness to pay** produces more conservative values, calculated by looking directly at people's behavior. If a person pays $5,000 to take a dive vacation to a reef, then we can estimate that experiencing the beauty of that reef is worth at least that much money to that individual.[20]

But there are more abstract values still. For example, **existence value** refers to the value one places on simply knowing that an ecosystem or particular species exists. Some people might never plan to see a wolf, and yet feel that the quality of their lives would be diminished if wolves became extinct. Indeed, some argue that it is the abstract values that are the most important. For example, many people attribute an aesthetic or spiritual value to natural areas that they frequent, and in some cases a natural area might play a vital role in the culture or identity of local residents.

Despite the difficulties involved with quantifying these values, ecological economists consider them to be a vital part of economic

---

BOX 6.3 Economic Value—Bees

When considering the economic value of bees most people think first about the value of honey, but in truth, most of the economic value of bees comes from the ecosystem service they provided: pollination of agricultural crops. For example the value of bee pollination in Western Europe has been estimated to be 30–50 times that of the honey and wax harvested from them. In Africa the difference is even greater with the value of pollination sometimes estimated at over 100 times the value of harvested honey and wax. Indeed, one third of the crops eaten by people rely directly or indirectly on bee pollination (see Bradbear 2009). In addition, hay crops (e.g., alfalfa and clover) used to feed animals for meat and dairy products rely heavily on bee pollination. A 2008 study found the value of insect pollination worldwide (mainly from bees) to be worth an estimated $217 billion (see Gallia et al. 2009). This value does not include the importance of bee pollination to biodiversity in natural areas such as forests.

For the most part, the economic value of bee pollination remains outside the market. That is, pollination is an ecosystem service provided by wild bees or a positive externality provided to farms close to apiculture (bee-farming) sites. However, in some cases bee keepers rent their colonies to farmers to provide this service. This practice gives the pollinating services provided by those colonies a direct market value. In many areas, the loss of forests or declines in commercial colonies have resulted in a decrease in this economic service, leaving many farmers in need of pollinators for their crops.

For example in California—the United States' largest producer of agricultural products—the population of pollinators has been steadily decreasing for several years, while farmers' need for pollinators has been increasing. As a result, the price for renting a commercial colony to pollinate one's crops more than doubled between 2004 and 2006, and these prices remain high (see Sumner and Borriss 2006). During some parts of the year beekeepers from as far away as Florida are enlisted to meet California's pollination demands.

---

decisions. They allow for direct comparison between the ecosystems and any proposed change that would decrease the quality of that ecosystem. Government planners must be cognizant maintaining economic opportunities for their constituents. Turning down a proposed development that is likely to be lucrative for the area may be difficult without some hard numbers regarding the value of what is being lost. *The third assumption of ecological economists is that services provided by ecosystems have value, and the difficulty in quantifying that value does*

not make the services themselves any less important. Even rough estimates can make people more aware of the costs involved in development.

Feedback between Ecological and Economic Systems

The fourth assumption of ecological economics is that the ecological system and the economic system are linked causally. In other words, things that happen in the economic system affect the ecological system within which it exists, and vice versa. The depletion of resources, the disposal of waste, the use of energy- and chemical-intensive agriculture, and the production of power all degrade natural capital, which in turn leads to higher costs and reduced profits. In his book, *The Enemy of Nature: The End of Capitalism or the End of the World?*, Joel Kovel describes an ecological crisis resulting from the economy's degradation of its own conditions of production at an ever increasing scale. He notes that, "This degradation will have a contradictory effect on profitability itself . . . either directly, by so fouling the natural ground of production that it breaks down, or indirectly, through the reinternalization of the costs that had been expelled into the environment."[21]

Herman Daly describes this contradiction by contrasting the **Empty World** versus the **Full World model**. In the Empty World, the economy is relatively small and it resides in the global ecosystem with relatively small effects, creating what economists call welfare or quality of life for people. In the Full World, the economy grows and occupies more and more of the global ecosystem until it reaches the physical limits of resources and waste disposal. As a result, production drops off and welfare decreases (see Figure 6.6). One problem posed by ecological economics, then, is how to determine the scale of the economy relative to the global ecosystem such that welfare is maximized.[22]

The size of the economy directly affects the global environment and ecosystems because virtually all the materials and energy resources needed for economic production

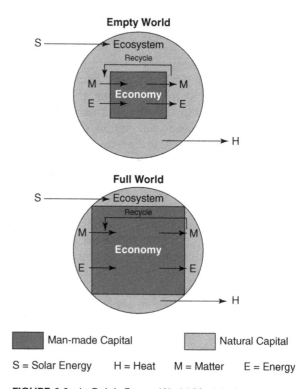

FIGURE 6.6 In Daly's Empty World Model, the economy is small relative to the size of the Earth and the availability of resources and waste assimilative capacity. In the Full World Model the economy has grown such that it dominates the Earth and the physical limits of both resource availability and space for waste disposal are reached. *(Figure is used with permission of Herman Daly)*

have their origins in nature or in geologic structures that underlie and support natural systems. In general, the rate of destruction of natural systems and structures is directly proportional to the scale of the economy—the larger the scale, the greater the mass of materials movement. At some point, the natural systems which support life may be so severely impacted that the delivery of important services such as clean air, potable water, and food may be compromised.

A good index of the scale of human impact on nature is the percentage of photosynthetic production that has been appropriated for human use. The term, **net primary production** (NPP), can be used to help determine the scale of these impacts. Primary producers, such as plants, capture energy from the sun. They metabolize some of that energy. The difference between the total solar energy captured and the energy used by the plants is NPP, which is available for consumers.

According to a 1986 study led by Peter Vitousek, human beings were appropriating about 40 percent of terrestrial NPP and about 25 percent of total NPP, including both terrestrial and aquatic production.[23] Since the appropriation of NPP is likely proportional to population, with one doubling of the then human population of 4.9 billion, almost all the terrestrial NPP would be used by one species, humans.[24] Note that NPP appropriation is proportional to per capita income, with richer countries consuming far more NPP per capita than poorer countries. Therefore, increased wealth is likely to mean even higher proportions of NPP devoted to human beings.

Human beings are also appropriating enormous quantities of the natural flow of water on the planet. In 1996, a research project led by Sandra Postel found that total sustainable potable water available to the earth's land mass was about 110,000 km^3, comprising 70,000 km^3 of evapotranspiration (ET) by plants and 40,000 km^3 of runoff (R). Of the R portion, only 12,500 km^3 is actually available (AR) for human use because of temporal and geographic factors. At the time of the research, it was found that humans were appropriating 26 percent of ET and 54 percent of AR for their own uses, or about 30 percent of all the potable water powered by the natural water cycle. Because water consumption is roughly proportional to population, it is likely that at present 40 percent of ET and 60 percent of AR are being used to meet human needs.[25] In other words, human beings likely use over 40 percent of all available freshwater on earth.

Nonrenewable resources are also key ingredients of the human economy, from fossil fuels such as coal, oil, and natural gas to metals such as iron, copper, and aluminum. As the rich deposits of these resources are depleted, more energy is required to remove more diluted, lower concentrated, and distant deposits. The extraction of iron ore, for example, requires the removal of overburden—the materials, such as soil, that lie above an ore deposit—and the extraction of the rock containing the iron ore. As the rich deposits of iron ore are exploited, the remaining sources have lower concentrations of ore, requiring even more overburden and rock removal. Thus, the combination of economic growth and the exhaustion of high concentration deposits results in an exponential rise in materials movement and natural system destruction.

The phenomenon of mass materials movement to extract nonrenewable resources is sometimes referred to as the **ecological rucksack** of a material, defined as the total mass of materials movement required to obtain a unit mass of the material. For example, the ecological rucksack of aluminum is 85, because 85 kilograms of materials must be extracted and processed to produce 1 kilogram of aluminum. In comparison, the ecological rucksack of recycled aluminum is 3.5, while that of gold extracted from ores is 350,000.[26] This concept is used to provide an index for the ecological impacts associated with various products and materials.

Renewable resources are also inputs to the economy. The desired utilization of these resources to maintain a sustainable economy is to extract them at a rate that is equal to the regeneration rate of the resource, thereby retaining, in Georgescu-Roegen's terms, the resource fund. Sustainable yield forestry, for example, relies on good management practices in which wood is extracted from the forest not only at its regeneration rate, but also in a manner that will not cause damage to the ecosystems of which the forest is a part.

Sir John Hicks, a winner of a Nobel Prize in economics, defined sustainable income, sometimes referred to as **Hicksian Income**, as the maximum amount that can be produced and consumed in the present without compromising the ability to do likewise in the future. More specifically, it is the maximum amount that a person or a nation could consume over a given time period and remain as well off at the end of that period as they were at the beginning.[27] When applied to renewable resources, this could be interpreted as using the surplus or interest of the natural system rather than consuming the principle or core of the natural system itself (see Figure 6.7).

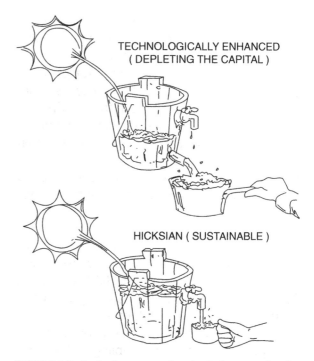

FIGURE 6.7 In the language of ecological economics, for the sustainability paradigm to properly function in an economic sense, society should strive to live off the interest or excess production of nature (Hicksian Income) rather than off of the capital of nature.

There is a temptation not to include the ecological interactions in an economic model, because including them complicates matters significantly and forces people to make hard decisions. The ethical questions would be much simpler in a world in which narrow self-interest aligned itself completely with social welfare or where human impacts on the environment were small enough to neglect. But those assumptions are not useful in our current situation. Economists working toward sustainability must now develop methods and tools for a world in which human behavior has a profound effect on the global environmental system.

BOX 6.4 Estimating Economic Costs: BP Deepwater Horizon Oil Spill

In 1969, after witnessing the devastation from an oil spill off the coast of Santa Barbara, California, Senator Gaylord Nelson proposed that every year a day be set aside to foster environmental awareness and education in the United States. The date was chosen, and the following year the first Earth Day was celebrated on April 22. The result of a blow-out of an offshore oil well being drilled in less than 200 feet of water, the Santa Barbara disaster spewed as much as 100,000 barrels of crude oil into the ocean and onto the beaches of California. At the time, the spill was the largest in U.S. waters. It is credited being one of several key events that stimulated environmental interest, which eventually led to a series of groundbreaking environmental laws in the 1970s.

Flash forward to April 22, 2010. Participants of the 40th Earth Day learned that the Deepwater Horizon oil platform run by BP had just sunk in the Gulf of Mexico off the coast of Louisiana. It had exploded two days earlier as a result of a blowout of its 5,000-foot-deep well. Five million barrels of oil would spew into the Gulf waters before the well was finally capped in mid-July, becoming the largest marine oil spill anywhere in the world.

The ecological damage to marine and coastal life caused by the BP spill proved very difficult to calculate, and may not be known with any certainty for decades. The "cleanup" costs and damage to local economies are more easily determined. Initial estimates of the costs of the BP spill were less than those of the 1989 Exxon Valdez tanker spill in Prince William Sound, Alaska ($3 billion), which was the largest oil spill in U.S. history to date. This premature figure was soon recalculated, with estimated costs rising to $8.2 billion and then to $41.9 billion dollars (see Phillips 2010).

Given that costs of the Exxon Valdez spill were still being negotiated in court as late as 2008, almost two decades after the tanker ran aground off the coast of Alaska, it is likely that the costs of the BP spill will also be the object of lengthy legal battles.

Early negotiations and analyses surrounding the cost of the spill and liability for it, occurring primarily between BP and the federal government, proved controversial. Some believed dollar amounts and liability caps were decided prematurely, before the full extent of social and environmental damages could be well assessed. Accusations were leveled that science, policy, and law were being made to serve corporate interests.

As some of the oldest fisheries in the United States were placed in jeopardy, the coastal cultures and traditions that developed alongside these natural resources were also threatened. The temporary loss of these cultures and traditions cannot easily be measured or reduced to a dollar figure, any more than the degradation of marine and coastal ecosystems can be fully monetized. The psychological damage suffered by millions of people who experienced a devastating blow to their ways of life, places of recreation, and beloved natural environment is impossible to measure with any accuracy. Placing this pain and suffering into dollar figures is very challenging.

In an effort to increase the scientific rigor of economic assessment methodology, cost-benefit analysis (CBA) was performed. However, CBAs of energy production often fail to account for the environmental impact of the rare but real disasters that accompany such industry, and often neglect the fact that much of the real cost

(continued)

(and/or benefit) will be incurred by future generations (see Trumbull 1990). Furthermore, research has shown that CBAs conducted by industry promoters often misrepresent actual costs, while other research questions the underlying value assumptions of CBA. At its best, CBA attempts to represent the greatest consensus regarding dynamic values. At its worst, CBA can be a tool serving special interests that undervalues ecological damage, public goods, and threats to public welfare (see Flyvbjerg, Holm, and Søren Buhl 2002 and Trumbull 1990).

While the Santa Barbara oil spill in 1969 was terrible in its environmental destruction, it also stimulated the birth of the modern environmental movement in the United States. The Deepwater Horizon spill was at least 50 times as large (see Figure 6.8)

The question remains whether there will be significant benefits to offset these tremendous costs, including legislative change, policy innovation, and public education and mobilization.

FIGURE 6.8   The Deepwater Horizon oil spill is the largest in history and is an abject lesson of ecological economics about the true costs of a commodity such as oil. *(Source: NASA)*

TOOLS OF ECOLOGICAL ECONOMICS

Much of the challenge for developing a sustainable economy revolves around internalizing the externalities. Environmental problems such as pollution, loss of biodiversity, and global climate change are largely external to the market. However, there are a number of methods for accounting for these costs and distributing them in the market. This section provides an overview of several of these methods.

The Polluter Pays Principle

We have all seen signs in stores that say, "You break it. You buy it." This type of conventional logic sits at the heart of the **Polluter Pays Principle** (PPP), which says that the costs of pollution should be borne by those who cause it. Its immediate goal is internalizing the environmental externalities of economic activities and ensuring the prices of goods and services fully reflect the costs of production. As an economic principle, PPP reduces pollution by internalizing its social costs if the extra costs to the polluter create a market incentive to reduce pollution. Of course, for a business to remain solvent, the price to consumers is increased to accommodate the internalized costs. Unless the increase is applied to all comparable products, the business which is able to reduce the cost of pollution will be able to sell a cheaper product, which should give it a market advantage. Also, advertisements that convince the consumer the additional cost is the price of cleaning the environment have been known to maintain sales of more expensive products.

The PPP also works as a legal principle. In this sense, the costs of pollution are justly allocated among those specifically causing the pollution. This idea has gained traction in international environmental law. First proposed in a legal context by the Organization for Economic Co-operation and Development (OECD) in 1972, the PPP plays a key role in a number of international treaties and in European Union law.[28]

The PPP can be used to require polluters to pay for abatement costs. For example, the government can set emission standards and require companies to make the necessary investments in technology to meet those standards. This method is often referred to as a **command-and-control approach**. Alternatively, a government can use what is called a **market-based approach**. For example, a government can set up a cap-and-trade system for a pollutant, including Pigouvian taxes and tradable pollution permits. With tradable permits, or cap and trade, the government sets an overall acceptable level for a particular pollutant. Pollution permits are then distributed that in total add up to the overall acceptable level. Companies in an industry are then free to buy and sell these permits. Companies that successfully reduce their emissions may gain extra income by selling their permits to companies that exceed their own permits.

The United States government's use of tradable pollution permits to address the acid rain problems is an oft-cited success story for cap and trade. By setting up a cap-and-trade system on sulfur dioxide (SO_2) the United States was able to reduce those emissions so that by 2002, SO_2 emissions were only 41 percent of 1980 numbers. The health benefits were so substantial that in 2003 the Office of Management and Budget reported that the Acid Rain Program amounted to the largest quantified human health benefits of any program in the previous decade with benefits exceeding costs by a ratio of more than 40:1.[29]

At the international level, the Kyoto Protocol is an example of the application of the PPP. Signatories to the Kyoto Protocol agreed that they have an obligation to reduce their greenhouse gas emissions and must bear the costs of reducing, through prevention and control, their carbon dioxide emissions. Again, the focus in much of the discussion is on a form of cap-and-trade system involving the several types of greenhouse gases.

Extended Producer Responsibility

One concept useful for actualizing the PPP is Extended Producer Responsibility (EPR), which makes manufacturers responsible for the entire lifecycle of the products and packaging they produce—especially for the take-back, recycling, and final disposal of the products. The major impetus for EPR came from northern European countries in the late 1980s and early 1990s as they were facing severe landfill shortages. Rather than forcing municipalities to manage the effects of excess waste from producers and consumers, EPR gives that responsibility to the manufacturers themselves. In this way, EPR shifts the economic burden of managing products that have reached the end of their useful life from local government and taxpayers to product producers and consumers.

There is certainly a justice element to EPR. Arguably, producers (usually brand owners) have the greatest control over product design and marketing and, therefore, have the greatest ability and responsibility to reduce toxicity and waste. In addition, EPR initiatives—such as take-back programs, deposit refund systems, product fees and taxes, and minimum recycled-content laws—can promote major shifts in producers' design goals. EPR initiatives force producers to internalize the environmental costs of their products. When these costs are external, producers are likely to adopt traditional end-of-pipe waste "diversion" programs in which they need not consider the disposal of their products after use.

This latter approach encourages ecologically benign designs for both products and packaging. For example in Germany, EPR is being implemented via government policy, and has reduced packaging waste about 4 percent per year for several years after its implementation in 1991. The European Union has legislated that automobile manufacturers must provide free take-back locations for waste automobiles, referred to as End-of-Life Vehicles or ELVs, and must recycle a minimum of 80 percent of the mass of the vehicle.[30]

Beneficiary Pays Principle

The producer pays principle is a concept for handling the external environmental costs of commercial or industrial processes. In contrast, the **Beneficiary Pays Principle** (BPP) often involves the opportunity cost of not going forward with a development in order to maintain high-quality ecosystems. The basic concept is that each entity that is likely to benefit from the long-term gains contributes to compensate for the forfeit of short-term gains.

For example, in the face of rapid destruction of the Amazonian rainforest in Brazil many have called for Brazil not only to stop, but to reverse that destruction in order to save this rich stock of global biodiversity. However, protecting and restoring the rainforest means that Brazil would not only forgo the extraction of resources and development of agriculture but also have to make a sizable investment in regenerating the already affected ecosystems. Using the BPP, one could argue that because the international community stands to benefit from the restoration of the rainforest—both from the preservation of biodiversity and the sequestration of carbon—Brazil should be compensated for the loss of economic development and the funds invested in the rainforest.

Typically, the contribution of the beneficiary is based on their perceived benefits. For example, in Kenya ranchers are asked by the government to forego production in order to maintain high-quality landscapes. An economic study of the region shows that the opportunity cost of wildlife conservation in protected areas of Kenya, measured in terms of forgone livestock and agricultural production, has been estimated to be around $203 million per year—2.8 percent of total GDP—while revenues from wildlife tourism and forestry contribute only around $42 million per year to the national economy.[31] The authors of the study argue that, given the global nature of the benefits of Kenya's conservation efforts, it is quite appropriate that the international community bear some of the costs of conservation. (Note that these figures do not include several of the more abstract values discussed earlier in this chapter, such as existence value.)

The BPP applies to a wide variety of situations where those foregoing economic opportunities for environmental benefit are compensated by those who gain from the environmental benefit. For example, earlier we discussed the value of a scenic landscape. In this case, willingness-to-pay surveys might be used to assess the benefits that travelers receive from that landscape. Those figures might then be used to set a tax or a toll in order to raise funds that could be put towards compensating local residents for maintaining that scenic landscape.

For example, a hydroelectric utility company benefits from upstream forests retaining sediments since high levels of sediment in the water would increase operating costs for hydroelectric plants. The owners of those forests are unlikely to consider this benefit when making decisions about the forests' value unless they are compensated for the services provided by their forests. In Costa Rica a private hydroelectric company does this, paying farmers upriver an agreed upon rate per hectare for not cutting down their forests.[32] In this case BPP is fairly straightforward since the beneficiaries are easily identified. In larger-scale examples, benefits are widely dispersed making BPP more difficult to implement.

Nonetheless, BPP can be a useful tool for balancing small-scale and broad-scale needs. Whether the goal is maintaining biodiversity, sequestering carbon, or maintaining a landscape, the BPP stems from the recognition that broad-scale gains often involve costs at the local level. We have discussed how environmentalists have been criticized for emphasizing the global, long-term benefits of maintaining highly biodiverse natural areas without recognizing the short-term needs of local populations. The BPP points toward an economic method for sharing the cost of maintaining regionally or even globally important ecosystems.

A related approach, **Product Stewardship**, is gaining in popularity because of its less regulatory nature and its recognition that other parties have a role to play. Product Stewardship means that all parties—designers, suppliers, manufacturers, distributors, retailers, consumers, recyclers, and disposers—involved in producing, selling, or using a product take responsibility for the full environmental and economic impacts of that product. An example of Product Stewardship is a program in Oregon in which the manufacturers of paint sold in Oregon—or a stewardship organization representing manufacturers—are required to set up and run a convenient, statewide system for the collection of unused, postconsumer architectural paint.

Full Cost Accounting, Full Cost Pricing, and Life-Cycle Costing

Of course, implementing any of these tools requires an assessment of the external costs involved with a product or development. The process of assessing and including these costs is often called **Full Cost Accounting (FCA)**.[33] FCA, which includes not only the internalized costs of the externalities produced by production, but also the life-cycle costs of the product or activity, applies to a wide range of accounting systems from businesses to national governments. At a national level, FCA requires a modification to Gross Domestic Product (GDP) as a measure of performance to include other societal and environmental impacts. This adjustment results in what are sometimes referred to as **Alternative Measures of Welfare**, which modify GDP to account for environmental impacts, such as pollution, and social costs of, for example, prisons and people not covered by health insurance.

For enterprise or government accounting systems, the U.S. EPA developed a four-tier system for management to use to account for the environmental costs portion of FCA:[34]

Tier 0. Conventional Capital and Operating Costs

These are the normal costs of a project and include capital expenditures such as buildings, equipment utilities, and supplies plus operating and maintenance expenses such as materials, labor, training, insurance, and permitting.

Tier 1. Hidden Costs

There are a number of environmental costs that may not be accounted for such as monitoring, paperwork, and reporting requirements. These include upfront environmental costs, regulatory or voluntary environmental costs, and back-end environmental costs. Upfront costs are incurred prior to the operation of the process or facility and related to the siting of facilities, qualification of suppliers, evaluation of alternative pollution control equipment, and so forth. Regulatory and voluntary environmental costs include items such as environmental insurance, permitting costs, environmental monitoring and testing, record keeping, voluntary audits, remediation, recycling activities, etc. These costs are often assigned to overhead accounts rather than allocated to departments of products directly. Backend environmental costs are usually also ignored in current decision making as they are not incurred at the present time. Such costs include the future costs of laboratory decommissioning or product take-back requirements.

Tier 2. Contingent Costs

Contingent costs are costs that may or may not be incurred at some point in the future and include penalties, fines, and future liabilities. They can only be estimated in probabilistic terms—their expected value, or the probability of their occurrence. Examples are personal injury claims related to product use, future remediation costs, and fines or penalties.

BOX 6.5 The Gross Domestic Product and Other Measurements of Economic Welfare

For several decades the Gross Domestic Product (GDP) has been the primary indicator for the health of a nation's economy and its citizens' well-being. This product is the total value of all goods and services produced in a year by the residents of a country through both labor and property. Many governments, including that of the United States, use this index to design fiscal policy, businesses use it to develop investment plans, and international NGOs use it as a basis for projects in developing countries. However, many economists have pointed out problems with the GDP as an indicator of economic well-being.

The most common criticism takes aim at the assumption that increased spending translates to increased quality of life. Not all spending is socially desirable. As we saw earlier, the oil spills resulted in billions of added spending, which counts toward the GDP but could hardly be considered contributing to improved quality of life. In addition to including things that should not be included, GDP misses changes that should be included. For example, increased environmental degradation and loss of social cohesion are not accounted for in GDP (see England and Harris [1998] and Costanza et al. [2009]).

Several economists have suggested adjustments to GDP measurements so that they might serve as better indicators for well-being. In 1989 economists Herman Daly and John Cobb, Jr. suggested the Index of Sustainable Economic Welfare (ISEW) (see Daly and Cobb 1989). Using the same consumption data as that used to calculate GDP, the ISEW incorporates deductions to account for income inequality and costs related to mitigation of undesirable developments such as crime and environmental degradation. Since 1990, the United Nations have used the Human Development Index (HDI)—which incorporates GDP as well as life expectancy and adult literacy rate—to assess welfare.

Others prefer to use measures that do not include GDP at all. Subjective well-being has become a subfield of sociology research over the last few decades. The focus here is individuals' self-reported satisfaction with their quality of life. Some object to this kind of research as it depends on respondents personal views and is, therefore, not objective. However, the indices described above all rely upon researchers' views about what constitutes a high quality of life. There is common-sense logic to the idea of finding out about people's well-being by asking them, and the World Database of Happiness in the Netherlands holds volumes of this kind of data (see Veenhoven 2010). International comparisons show interesting results. Beyond a rather low level of wealth, there is very little correlation between wealth and happiness.

Bhutan, a small country east of India has attracted attention of researchers for its focus on subjective well-being. The country has a history of being leery of technology, having only recently opened its doors to cable television and the Internet. Rather than relying on GDP to assess the well-being of its citizens, Bhutan focuses on the goal of Gross National Happiness (GNH). Specific measurements of GNH continue to evolve, but they include both objective measures of income and environmental degradation, as well as subjective responses from Bhutan's citizens. With the multitude of methodologies available for assessing quality of life, researchers agree on two points: (1) no single number can truly capture the complexity involved in assessing a people's well-being, but (2) we can certainly do better than GDP.

Tier 3. Less Tangible Costs

These are the difficult to estimate costs associated with maintaining corporate image and good relationships with investors, employees, and customers. These costs would include the costs of environmental outreach activities (annual community cleanup days or tree planting days for example) and publication of environmental reports, to name a few.

The ultimate goal of FCA is actually what might be called **Full-Cost Pricing**, in which the full social and environmental costs of a product are included in the price paid by the consumer. The consumer is then making a decision based on prices that reflect the full environmental and social costs of the "goods" they purchase.

CONCLUSION

We have covered a wide range of concepts and ideas that will be helpful as we continue to consider an ethical framework for making decisions in the context of sustainability. In Chapter 4, we looked at the role of social justice in the context of extended spatial and temporal scales. In Chapter 5, we extended our ethical perspective yet again, this time to include consideration of nonhuman members of ecological systems, looking at our own roles within these ecological communities. In this chapter, we have reviewed historical failures of economists to adopt this more holistic view, but we have also identified a number of economic tools that may be helpful in constructing an ethical framework for sustainability. The field of ecological economics focuses on including environmental impacts into economic markets. Principles, such as PPP and BPP, provide a foundation for addressing these impacts in ecologically and socially responsible ways.

Each of the three legs of sustainability is important in itself, but truly appreciating their significance requires an understanding of how they relate to each other. Therefore, the integration of social, ecological, and economic concepts into one framework is the focus of the next chapter.

REFERENCES

Barnhart, David K. and Allan A. Metcalf. 1997. *America in So Many Words*. Boston: Houghton Mifflin.

Box, George. 1979. "Robustness in the strategy of scientific model building." In R.L. Launer and G.N. Wilkinson, Eds. *Robustness in Statistics*. New York: Academic Press.

Bradbear, Nicola. 2009. *Non-wood Forest Products 19: Bees and Their Role in Forest Livelihoods*. Rome: Food and Agricultural Organization of the United Nations.

Bugge, H. C. 1996. "The principles of 'polluter-pays' in economics and law." In E. Eide and R. van den Bergh, eds. *Economics of the Environment*. Oslo: Juridisk, 54–73.

Costanza, Robert, Ed. 1991. *Ecological Economics: The Science and Management of Sustainability*. New York: Columbia University Press.

Costanza, Robert, et al. 1997a. "The value of the world's ecosystem services and natural capital." *Nature* 387: 253–260.

Costanza, Robert, John. H. Cumberland, Herman Daly, Robert Goodland, and Richard B. Norgaard. 1997b. *An Introduction to Ecological Economics*. Boca Raton, FL: St. Lucie Press.

Costanza, Robert and Herman E. Daly. 1992. "Natural capital and sustainable development." *Conservation Biology* 6(1): 37–46.

Constanza, Robert, Maureen Hart, Stephen Posner, and John Talberth. 2009. *Beyond GDP: The Need for New Measures of Progress*. Boston, MA: The Frederick S. Pardee Center for the Study of the Longer-Range Future.

Daily, Gretchen C., Ed. 1997. *Nature's Services: Societal Dependence on Natural Ecosystems* Washington, D.C.: Island Press.

Daly, Herman E. and J. Cobb. 1989. *For the Common Good: Redirecting the Economy toward Community, the Environment, and a Sustainable Future*. Boston: Beacon Press.

Daly, Herman E. 1991. *Steady-State Economics: Second Edition with New Essays*. Washington, DC: Island Press.

Daly, Herman E. and John Cobb. 1989. *For the Common Good: Redirecting the Economy Toward Community, the Environment, and a Sustainable Future*. Boston, MA: Beacon Press.

Dryzek, John S. 1987. *Rational Ecology: Environment and Political Economy*. New York: Basil Blackwell.

Elkington, John. Downwave 2 (1992–1998). John Elkington. www.johnelkington.com/time-downwave2.htm

England, Richard W. and Jonathan M. Harris. 1999. Alternatives to gross national product: A critical survey." In Frank Ackerman, David Kiron, Neva Goodwin, Johathan Harris, and Kevin P. Gallager, Eds. *Human Wellbeing and Economic Goals*. Washington, DC: Island Press.

Flyvbjerg, Bent, Mette Skamris Holm, and Søren Buhl. 2002. "Underestimating Public Costs in Public Works Project: Error or Lie?," *Journal of the American Planning Association*, 68(3).

Gallia, Nicola, Jean-Michel Salles, Josef Settele, and Bernard Vaissiere. 2009. "Economic valuation of the vulnerability of world agriculture confronted with pollinator decline." *Ecological Economics* 68(3): 810–821.

Georgescu-Rogen, Nicholas. 1977. "Inequality, limits to growth from a biocentric viewpoint." *Review of Social Economy* XXXV(3): 361–375.

Haeckel, Ernst. 1866. *Generelle Morphologie der Organismen. Allgemeine Grundzüge der organischen Formen-Wissenschaft mechanisch begründet durch die von Charles Darwin reformirte Decendenz-Theorie*. Berlin: Reimer.

Jevons, W. S. 1865. *The Coal Question*. London: Macmillan and Co.

Kovel, Joel. 2002. *The Enemy of Nature: The End of Capitalism or the End of the World*. 2nd ed. London: Zed Books, Limited.

Lotka, Alfred. 1922. "Contribution to the energetics of evolution." *Proc Natl Acad Sci* 8: 147–51.

Mill, J. S. 2004. *Principles of Political Economy*. Amherst, NY: Prometheus Books.

Nash J. R. 2000. "Too much market? Conflict between tradable pollution allowances and the 'polluter pays' principle." *Harvard Environmental Law Review* 24: 465–536.

Norton-Griffiths and Michael and Clive Southey. 1995. The opportunity costs of biodiversity conservation in Kenya. *Ecological Economics* 12(2): 125–139.

Office of Management and Budget. 2003. *Informing Regulatory Decisions: 2003 Report to Congress on the Costs and Benefits of Federal*

Regulations and Unfunded Mandates on State, Local, and Tribal Entities.

Perrot-Maître, D. and P. Davis. 2001. *Case studies of Markets and Innovative Financing Mechanisms for Water Services from Forests.* Forest Trends, Washington, DC.

Phillips, Matt. 2010. "BP Oil Spill: Brief History of The Incredible Rising Cost Estimate Matt Phillips," *Wall Street Journal Blogs, MarketBeat,* June 18.

Postel, Sandra, Gretchen C. Dailey, and Paul Ehrlich. 1996. "Human Appropriation of Renewable Fresh Water." *Science* 271: 785–788.

Simon, J. 1981. *The Ultimate Resource.* Princeton, NJ: Princeton University Press.

Solow, Robert M. 1956. "A Contribution to the Theory of Economic Growth." *Quarterly Journal of Economics* 70(1): 65–94.

Spash, Clive L. 1993 "Economics, Ethics, and Long-Term Environmental Damages." *Environmental Ethics* 15.

Sumner, Daniel A. and Hayley Boriss. 2006. *Bee-conomics and the leap in pollination fees. ARE update,* Univ. California, Giannini Foundation 9(3) Jan/Feb. Available at: www.agecon.ucdavis.edu/uploads/update_articles/v9n3_3.pdf.

Swan, Trevor W. 1956. "Economic Growth and Capital Accumulation." *Economic Record.* 32: 334–61.

Trumbull, William N. 1990. "Who has standing in Cost-Benefit Analysis?" *Journal of Policy Analysis and Management,* Vol. 9, No. 2, 201–218 (1990)

Veenhoven, R., 2010. *World Database of Happiness, Distributional Findings in Nations,* Erasmus University Rotterdam. Available at: http://worlddatabaseofhappiness.eur.nl.

Vitousek, Peter, Paul Ehrlich, Anne H. Ehrlich, and Pamela A. Matson. 1986. "Human Appropriation of the Products of Photosynthesis." *BioScience* 34(6): 363–373.

Vitousek, P. M., J. Lubchenco, H. A. Mooney, and J. Melillo. 1997. "Human domination of Earth's ecosystems," *Science,* 277, pp. 494–499.

ENDNOTES

1. See Barnhart and Metcalf (1997).
2. From Elkington, Accessed 5–14–2010.
3. Recall from Chapter 2 that this is the same individual credited with founding Utilitariansm.
4. See Mill (2004).
5. See Mill (2004).
6. See Mill (2004).
7. Kaldor-Hicks efficiency, named after Nicholas Kaldor (1908–1986) and John Hicks (1904–1989), was suggested to address this problem. In this view a transaction might make an economy more efficient if the utility gained by the winner(s) was more than the utility lost by the loser(s). In theory, the winner(s) would be able to compensate the loser(s) for the loss.
8. See, for example, Simon (1981).
9. It is also called the Solow-Swan growth model. The two men each developed the model independently, both publishing their ideas in 1956: Solow (1956) and Swan (1956).
10. See Haeckel (1866).
11. See Lotka (1922).
12. See Georgescu-Rogen (1977).
13. See Box (1979).
14. For a more thorough discussion of natural capital, see Costanza et al. (1997a). Also, social scientists often refer to "social capital" as a fourth type of capital. We discuss this type in Chapter 9.
15. See Costanza et al. (1997a).
16. See Costanza and Daly (1992).

17. See Dryzek (1987).
18. See Spash (1993).
19. See Costanza et al. (1997a). See also Daily (1997).
20. Some adjustments may be necessary to account for other aspects of the vacation. For example, if 80 percent of the days were spent diving and 20 percent lying on the beach, then one might only attribute 80 percent of the total cost of the trip to the coral reef itself.
21. See Kovel (2002).
22. The Empty World versus Full World models are described by Daly (1999).
23. Human appropriation includes direct use of NPP for food, fuel, fiber, and timber plus reduction in potential because of ecosystem degradation caused by humans.
24. From Vitousek et al. (1986). See also Vitousek et al. (1997).
25. Summarized from Postel et al. (1996).

26. The ecological rucksack was invented by Friedrich Schmidt-Bleek of the Wuppertal Institute in Germany in the mid-1990s.
27. An excellent description of the broader concepts associated with Hicksian Income can be found in Costanza et al. (1997b).
28. See Bugge (1996) and Nash (2000)
29. See Office of Management and Budget (2003).
30. European Union Directive 2000/53/EC spells out the requirements for ELV recovery and recycling. The 80 percent recycling rate increases to 90 percent in 2015.
31. See Norton-Griffiths and Southey (1995).
32. See Perrot-Maitre and Davis (2001).
33. True cost accounting (TCA) is a terminology sometimes used as an alternative to full-cost accounting.
34. The EPA's full-cost accounting process is described at www.epa.gov/waste/conserve/tools/fca/index.htm.

CHAPTER 7

Integrating the Three Legs of Sustainability

The term *sustainable development* has been criticized by some as an oxymoron—two opposing concepts wrapped up into one term. This criticism is based partly on a limited view of development as growth, whereas the Brundtland Commission used the term "development" to signify improvements in the quality of life. As individuals, we expect to stop physically growing in our teens or early twenties, but we hope to continue developing throughout our lives. While one might be able to sustain improvements in quality of life, it would be practically impossible to sustain growth. But the criticism has deeper roots as well. Some argue that the goals of the three legs of sustainability are inherently opposed to each other, reflecting different ethical principles as well as different practical priorities. In this chapter, we attempt to integrate the three sets of concepts we have discussed so far.

People grappling with matters of sustainability rarely have perspectives that equally incorporate all three legs. As ecologist C. S. Holling suggests, those focusing on the ecological leg often underestimate the importance of an economic system that fosters human enterprise.

The practical emphasis here is often on regulations designed to maintain high-quality ecological systems. People who emphasize the economic leg tend to ignore the variability of ecosystems or act as if that variability can be replaced with human-built systems designed for stability. In this view, the policy goals generally revolve around getting the price right. Finally, those focused on the social leg may fail to acknowledge the limits of community empowerment. From this perspective, stakeholder ownership becomes the primary concern, with the positive benefits of markets and ecological limitations neglected.[1]

Holling acknowledges that each of these viewpoints stems from strong theoretical approaches, including those of community activism and social organization (social), ecology and evolution (environmental), and free-market models (economic). While all of these models are applicable in a limited sense, Holling suggests that they are incomplete: "We lack an integrated theory that can serve as a foundation for sustainable futures, a theory that recognizes the synergies and constraints among nature, economic activities, and people."

Such a view must acknowledge the importance of broad stakeholder participation in making socially responsible decisions, but must also acknowledge the limits of those decision makers. It must include the complex dynamics of ecosystems without oversimplifying them as infinitely bountiful or hopelessly fragile. Also, it must recognize the importance of innovation and enterprise without forgetting the costs when people focus solely on immediate payoffs. An ethic of sustainability is more than an exercise in piling various ethical responsibilities one on top of another. It requires a model that can incorporate the aspects covered over the last three chapters into a single vision, giving weight to the sometimes competing ethical principles involved. To address this need, we will explore the concepts relevant to the study of complex adaptive systems (CASs), including scale, complexity, and resilience. As you will see, these concepts provide useful tools for understanding the connections between social, ecological, and economic processes.

We begin exploring what such an integrative model might look like with a discussion of the **precautionary principle**, a concept that most consider to be a necessary foundation stone for any ethic of sustainability. Drawing on concepts from all three legs, this principle is meant to help define our moral responsibilities to present and future generations, stimulate scientific inquiry into the effects of our actions, and cultivate the political abilities to control these effects while at the same time acknowledging our limitations. Thus, the precautionary principle provides a useful context for putting together the various concepts of the last three chapters.

THE PRECAUTIONARY PRINCIPLE

At its most basic level, the precautionary principle asserts that when the effects of an action are uncertain and potentially harmful, one should err on the side of caution. While this principle is often considered an integral part of the ethics of sustainability, prudence, the virtue that sits at the core of the precautionary principle, far predates the rise of sustainability as a global ethic in the 1980s.

Words of wisdom handed down through the generations testify to the widespread endorsement of the ancient virtue of prudence. We have long heard that "a stitch in time saves nine." Our grandparents shared with us the counsel "better safe than sorry," and Benjamin Franklin cautioned that "An ounce of prevention is worth a pound of cure." The latter aphorism may actually date back as far as the first century BCE, when Cicero, the ancient Roman orator and statesman, wrote that "Precaution is better than cure."[2] Prudential thought and action, Cicero believed, were the hallmark of good government and the most important public virtue (see Figure 7.1).

To wait until a crisis is upon one before responding is to act imprudently. In many cases, it is to act too late. Things broken cannot always be fixed. Prudence is the virtue of avoiding crises whenever possible and adequately preparing for them whenever necessary—that is to say, prudence requires acting with the future in mind so as to preempt the need for reparation or regret. Elder statesmen of both conservative and liberal leanings have long endorsed our obligation to prepare

FIGURE 7.1 Marcus Tullius Cicero (106–43 BCE): The Roman orator Cicero may have been one of the first politicians to express the logic of a precautionary principle. *(Source: Wiki Commons)*

for and care for the future. Precaution is the chief means to fulfill that obligation and prevent the need for painful cures.

A Legal Context

Implicit endorsements of principles that promote precaution as a means of safeguarding prospects and opportunities for future generations may be found in many legal documents that predate the actual formulation of the precautionary principle. The environmental laws codified in the United States in the early 1970s, for instance, such as the National Environmental Policy Act (NEPA) and the Endangered Species Act embody a precautionary approach. NEPA requires that projects receiving federal funding first undergo an environmental impact study that

demonstrates that there are no safer alternatives. The act mandates:

> the continuing responsibility of the Federal Government to use all practicable means, consistent with other essential considerations of national policy, to improve and coordinate Federal plans, functions, programs, and resources to the end that the Nation may . . . fulfill the responsibilities of each generation as trustee of the environment for succeeding generations.[3]

Safeguarding the future was the central value of early environmental legislation, as embodied in NEPA.

The actual term *precautionary* can be traced back to the German word *Vorsorge*, which means *care for the future*. The first national legislation explicitly articulating a precautionary principle, a *Vorsorgeprinzip*, was enacted in the Federal Republic of Germany in the mid-1970s.[4] Targeted at the protection of clean air and the preservation of forests, policies invoking a *Vorsorgeprinzip* outlined the need not only to ward off imminent hazards and repair damage but also to protect environmental resources from *anticipated* hazards and damages.

Importantly, such hazards and damages, although anticipated as much as possible, were not certainties. They did not have to be scientifically *proven* as *inevitable* consequences of (intended) actions. This issue of the burden of proof lies at the heart of the principle. Note that the precautionary principle entailed taking preventative action to protect natural resources even before scientific research had fully established a clear, causal link between potentially harmful practices and environmental damage.[5]

The "Earth Summit," which brought representatives from 172 national governments and over 100 heads of state to Rio de Janeiro, Brazil, in 1992, produced the first truly international agreement that explicitly articulated and endorsed a precautionary principle. Principle 15 of the Rio Declaration states that "In order to protect the environment, the precautionary approach shall be widely applied by States according to their capabilities. Where there are threats of serious or irreversible damage, lack of full scientific certainty shall not be used as a reason for postponing cost-effective measures to prevent environmental degradation."[6] The Rio Declaration gave precautionary thinking and action its first truly global forum.

In the United States, later that decade, the President's Council on Sustainable Development expressed support for the precautionary principle, stipulating that "even in the face of scientific uncertainty, society should take reasonable actions to avert risks where the potential harm to human health or the environment is thought to be serious or irreparable."[7] The principle took center stage in 1998 when scientists, lawyers, environmentalists, and philosophers gathered at the Wingspread Conference to develop a formal definition. The Wingspread definition has become one of the most frequently cited and employed: "When an activity raises threats of harm to human health or the environment, precautionary measures should be taken even if some cause and effect relationships are not fully established scientifically. In this context

the proponent of an activity, rather than the public, should bear the burden of proof."[8]

In this and many other definitions of the precautionary principle, there are two main clauses. First, regulation of an intended action aimed at preventing harm to the welfare of current and future generations should not be precluded due to incomplete (scientific) knowledge regarding how those actions may cause the anticipated harm. In other words, a reasonable suspicion regarding potential harm from an activity can be enough to warrant regulation. Second, the proponents of an activity, rather than those who might be harmed by the unintended consequences of an activity, are required to demonstrate that the level of risk associated with it is acceptable. Effectively, the precautionary principle shifts the burden of proof. No longer do the potential victims have to demonstrate that an activity is unsafe. Instead, the proponents of a potentially dangerous activity have to demonstrate, beyond all reasonable doubt, that the activity is harmless.

Third, there is the assumption of proportionality, that is, the greater the potential for harm, the more precaution should be taken. In the case of climate change, for instance, the wide range of enormous negative consequences, from higher average global temperatures and rising sea levels, to more violent hurricanes and a reduced ability to grow food, mandate strong and consistent action on the part of national and international bodies, and as soon as possible. In contrast, nanoparticles, which can be toxic if combined with certain chemicals or biochemicals, pose a significant but far smaller risk when compared to the vast scale and long duration of the effects of climate change.

The precautionary principle has also been cited and advocated by international nongovernmental organizations, such as Oxfam, and international governmental organizations, such as the World Bank. For example, with the dangers of climate change specifically in mind, the World Bank stipulates that "When confronted with risks which could be menacing and irreversible, uncertainty argues strongly in favor of prudent action and against complacency."[9] Many non-legally-binding national and international declarations and resolutions reference the precautionary principle as well. These agreements, resting on voluntary compliance, encourage but do not enforce specific actions.[10]

In turn, the precautionary principle has also been advocated and implemented voluntarily by scores of corporations, including H&M, an international clothing retailer, and Dell, the computer manufacturer. Such corporations employ the precautionary principle in their efforts to screen hazardous chemicals from their products.[11] Walmart, the world's largest retailer, also explicitly embraces "the spirit of the Precautionary Principle." The suspicion that an ingredient in a product it sells may harm the environment or human health will prompt a search for alternatives.[12] But while the popularity of the precautionary principle seems clear, one might reasonably ask, "Can it be effectively implemented?"

Precaution in Practice

Skeptics claim that the precautionary principle has been so popular precisely because it remains vague. It allows institutions and organizations to give voice to their environmental values without binding them to any particular set of actions. None of the expressions of the principle covered here spells out what level of risk is tolerable or acceptable. Moreover, nothing is said about who should bear the risk or how should it be mitigated.

For instance, the careful reader will have noted that Principle 15 of the Rio Declaration states that the precautionary approach should be "widely applied by States according to their capabilities." The clause allows states to implement the precautionary approach "widely," which is to say, selectively rather than universally. In turn, the implementation of the approach depends upon their "capabilities." The determination of whether a state has capabilities—the economic capacity, technical know-how, or political will—to implement and enforce a precautionary approach is for government officials themselves to decide in each instance.

Certainly, this clause allows national governments a great deal of wiggle room in their efforts to employ precautionary standards.[13] Some have argued that it renders the declaration toothless. The same might be said about any number of the other international declarations and agreements that cite the precautionary principle but do not spell out specific procedures or parameters for its implementation. Indeed, most of these international agreements are not designed to provide specific procedures or address protocols, which is precisely why so many nations can agree to them. They represent a first step toward international recognition of the importance of precaution and these types of agreements are often followed by more specific treaties. On the other hand, they continue to be subject to criticism that their contents (in this case the precautionary principle) are unenforceable.

In this respect, the precautionary principle is like many other ethical principles: it is a general code of conduct outlining the ideals that are meant to guide action. It is not a specific policy statement providing enforceable rules for specific cases. As the World Commission on the Ethics of Scientific Knowledge and Technology observed, the precautionary principle "is not a decision algorithm and thus cannot guarantee consistency between cases. Just as in legal court cases, each case [that applies the precautionary principle] will be somewhat different, having its own facts, uncertainties, circumstances, and decision-makers, and the element of judgment cannot be eliminated."[14]

What, then, does it mean to have a precautionary orientation? To act with precaution is to exercise one's best judgment so as to avoid unnecessary risk. One might say that precaution is a form of risk management.

Precaution as Risk Management

Some criticize the precautionary principle for leading to paralysis.[15] Faced with risks on all sides, those invoking precaution as their principle would find themselves unable to act at all. Risk is an inevitable part of life. It cannot be wholly avoided, only limited. The precautionary principle does not ask us to do the impossible by avoiding risk altogether. Rather, it asks us to manage risks prudently.

To be sure, certain risks—which we may deem unnecessary or too grave—can be avoided altogether. One may personally avoid the risk of being caught in an avalanche, for instance, by staying miles away from snowy slopes. In avoiding or limiting certain risks, however, we inevitably increase others. Staying away from snowy slopes may require plying one's way through city traffic, with all of its attendant risks. Likewise, medications taken to prevent certain illnesses we wish to avoid may cause other maladies, and some cures prove worse than the disease. By providing inexpensive, effective refrigeration, chlorofluorocarbons (CFCs) reduced the risk of botulism and other illnesses caused by the consumption of bacterially contaminated food. However, CFCs also depleted stratospheric ozone and, thus, increased risks for cataracts and skin cancer.

In short, risk management involves tradeoffs. This is true of the risks we manage in our personal lives, as well as those we manage collectively, as members of societies and states. Every activity, or lack of activity, incurs some risks. The only way to know whether a certain level of risk is acceptable given the benefits it provides is to compare it to the level of risk associated with other actions that secure similar benefits, or to the risks associated with the absence of any action aimed at securing such benefits.

Choosing city travel rather than mountain roads is a personal choice in which each individual can decide which combination of risks and benefits are preferable. Many of the risks that we experience in our daily lives, however, are not voluntarily assumed. They are collective risks that we bear—whether we want to or not—as members of societies and nations. No modern state could exist without imposing some involuntary risks upon its members. A state that provides the infrastructure for mechanized travel and allows fast-moving, polluting vehicles on its roads effectively imposes involuntary risks to the health and safety of most if not all its members, whether they are drivers, passengers, bicyclists, pedestrians, or urban dwellers.

The imposition of involuntary risks is also associated with food production, healthcare provision, and virtually every other facet of modern life. These risks may be mitigated, but they cannot be wholly avoided. Involuntary risks confront us the moment we sit down to breakfast or set our foot out the door. And we do not only suffer these risks as potential victims—we also co-produce them.

We are all implicated in creating and heightening environmental and other risks by our participation in social and economic life. We increase risks to pedestrians and cyclists every time we drive our cars. We potentially increase risks to current and future generations every time we create, produce, or deliver a technological product or service. Managing these risks properly requires not only being aware of them but also evaluating them comparatively.

Cost-Benefit Analysis

The effort to measure comparative risk may be seen as part of a more encompassing exercise called **cost-benefit analysis (CBA)**. CBA typically weighs the economic costs of proposed actions (or restrictions of action, such as regulations) against the economically quantified benefits that such actions (or

absence of regulations) produce. While the focus here is typically economic, one might also include noneconomic costs in the calculations, such as risks to human health specifically or environmental health in general.

Indeed, risks are often measured in terms of the economic costs of repairing damage done by the offending action. Maintaining public health in the face of pollution-induced disease, for instance, might be measured in terms of the costs of medical care to treat these diseases and the cost of productive workdays lost to sickness and early death. For this reason, cost-benefit analysis is sometimes called **"risk-cost-benefit analysis" (RCBA)**. RCBA is defined as an assessment that "incorporates notions of probability and uncertainty as a basis for estimating technology and environment-related risks and for determining their values as costs."[16]

With its focus on economic values, CBA can lead to the same kind of short-sided logic discussed in the previous chapter, but in the context of the precautionary principle, CBA can shift to a discussion about wise spending. For example, money or resources allocated to treat disease or to compensate bereaved families and businesses does not produce the same level of human welfare as would be obtained by preventing disease in the first place. Similarly, funds spent on replacing services that had previously been provided by a mangrove forest might be better spent on preserving the mangrove ecosystem.

But while CBA may be useful in some instances, it has distinct limitations. Some "goods" are simply not for sale: we cannot legally sell our votes in an election, and we cannot legally sell anyone into slavery. Certainly, we would not want the federal government to do a CBA before determining whether it was economically too costly or risky to protect our right to free speech or our other civil rights. These goods, we might say, are priceless.

Even if one accepts the process of economic valuation, CBA is likely to favor the more concrete values over the abstract ones. Recall from Chapter 6 the difficulties involved in placing quantitative values on many aspects of natural systems. The result of those difficulties is that the calculated values of abstract services lose their persuasive power.

Consider the protection of endangered species. The preservation of native species in the United States is not particularly expensive, with annual federal allocations approximating the cost of constructing a few miles of urban interstate highway or building a few military aircraft.[17] Still, these costs are real and measurable, and there are other costs to protecting endangered species that are borne by landowners and developers. Again, these costs are real and relatively easy to quantify.

What of the benefits of preserving endangered species? There may be many economic benefits to the recreation and tourism industries, but these may be difficult to assess accurately. It is not clear, for instance, that fewer people would travel to national parks if there were no grizzly bears or wolves inhabiting them. Indeed, given the fear that these carnivores may induce in potential park visitors, their absence may actually increase tourism. Even more challenging will be the calculation of a price to represent the moral, aesthetic, and spiritual benefits to preserving endangered species. Measuring such benefits across many generations becomes especially problematic.

Yet the economic costs of enforcing the Endangered Species Act is quite easily calculated, and these dollar costs are fully borne by the current generation each year. Since moral, aesthetic, and spiritual benefits are difficult to quantify, such soft variables may get ignored in favor of the easily assessed economic costs of preservation. The same sort of problem occurs whenever industries place a new product on the market. While the cost to a corporation of not selling the product is relatively easy to calculate and project, the health and environmental costs associated with the product—say a new drug or a new piece of machinery—may be much more difficult to determine.

The problem is further complicated because CBA does not generally focus on who bears the costs and who receives the benefits. As the World Commission on the Ethics of Scientific Knowledge and Technology observed, cost-benefit analysis may support risky activity "as long as the sum of the benefits outweighs the sum of the costs, even if a small group of people get the benefits and a whole community suffers the costs. Thus aggregation of costs and benefits may obscure ethical issues of fairness and equity."[18]

Including Stakeholders

Given these difficulties, some sustainability advocates object to the use of cost-benefit analysis. They feel that CBA privileges technological and economic development by business corporations or other elites while undervaluing the risks and deprivations suffered by the general public and future generations.

Notwithstanding such concerns, engaging the best science in conversation with ethical values in a comparative and inclusive analysis of risks, costs, and benefits is preferred. Neglecting such exercises may keep abstract

---

BOX 7.1   Technology Tribunals

Technology tribunals are citizen-based, decision-making forums concerned with whether and how a particular technology should be utilized or further developed. Such public meetings facilitate the exchange of information and improve lines of communication. Focused on dialogue between citizens—or between policy makers, experts, and citizens—these deliberative and decision-making experiences allow diverse forms of knowledge to be shared in pursuit of consensus and common visions.

Participatory and integrative political processes are prominent in many countries. They are part of a broad-based effort to develop and promote *deliberative democracy*, a form of political decision making in which policy and laws arise through the participation of citizens. Within the United States, a tradition of citizen participation in New England style "town hall" meetings is well established. The "21st Century Town Meeting" developed by AmericaSpeaks (www.americaspeaks. org) is a contemporary example. In such forums, facilitated discussion and deliberation among small groups of citizens is paired with the technological means for collecting and disseminating information and ideas between groups, conducting instant polling, and sharing decisions. AmericaSpeaks has developed citizen forums on issues such as climate change, urban planning, and a 21st Century Summit.

In Denmark, citizen-based forums have played a key role in policy formation, such as the public

rejection of nuclear power in 1984. The Danish Board of Technology was established in 1986 in response to such concerns. It continues today to organize and empower citizens as an active part of the process of discerning appropriate technological innovation and diffusion, including issues such as gene technology, sustainable transportation systems, and water supply (Anderson and Jæger 1999).

Wedding these traditions, the Loka Institute (www.loka.org) advocates Danish-style citizen panels in the United States and other countries, and promotes practical methods for improving citizen participation in federal policy making for new technologies. It has been especially active in regard to large technological issues such as human genome, nuclear, and space research (Cordes, Crutcher, and Worthington 2003). In 2003, the Loka Institute was involved in ensuring that *the 21st Century Nanotechnology Research and Development Act* enacted by the U.S. Congress included a clause providing for "public input and outreach to be integrated into the program by the convening of regular and ongoing public discussions, through mechanisms such as citizens' panels, consensus conferences, and educational events" (http://thomas.loc.gov/cgi-bin/query/z?c108:S.189).

Deliberative, democratic forums are an important means of improving the quality of life for all citizens by enhancing the public exploration of the social, ethical, economic, and environmental impacts of technological innovations and the development of sustainable solutions.

costs from gaining *any* voice and thus maintain the values of the status quo.[19]

Inevitably, however, to engage in CBA comparatively and inclusively presents the challenge of pitting the often ambiguous benefits of environmental protection and social welfare against an arsenal of figures detailing the economic costs of regulating or prohibiting economic and technological development. The primary means to combat these problems remains the involvement of a wide array of stakeholders. One possible means to address this challenge is to establish "technology tribunals," where citizen juries, informed by scientific data and ethical discourse, evaluate the risks, costs, and benefits of such matters as the production and use of synthetic chemicals or the deployment of new industrial or technological processes. We will discuss the key aspects of stakeholder participation in more detail in Chapter 10.

Including Science

One way of refining CBA calculations is through the use of science, and whether citizen tribunals, government agencies, or corporate departments are involved in CBA, the best science should play a prominent role. However, scientists and nonscientists alike can have an exaggerated confidence in the ability of science to introduce certainty to the discussion. As we have seen, issues involving technology and sustainability take place in the uncontrolled, multivariable, highly interactive conditions of the social and biological world. Certainty is a scarce resource in this world.

For example, many pesticides, though relatively benign to nontarget species when applied in isolation, may be a thousand times more disruptive of hormone and reproductive systems of nontarget species when organisms are exposed to two or more of them over time—as often occurs in the natural environment.[20] Similar "synergistic" effects are evident in the realms of climate change, where positive feedback loops and interactions between the causes and effects of global warming make predictions particularly difficult. Indeed, the web of life is so complex that no amount of scientific investigation can fully reveal the intricacies of its patterns or the long-term consequences of severing any particular strand or introducing new relationships.

Even the most advanced scientific models of environmental systems acknowledge the role of unpredictability, the role of surprise. The key for decision makers is to act within this context of surprise, to build technological and social systems that are resilient in the face of unpredicted changes. Risk assessment, if pursued from a precautionary approach, underscores the limits of scientific predictions and heeds the fact that these predictions become increasingly speculative the further they extend into the future.

With such uncertainties in mind, and aware of the inevitable need for the assessment of costs, benefits, and risks, economist Richard Norgaard argues that practicing sustainability does not entail exact prediction or firm control of the indefinite future. Such a level of knowledge and power is beyond our reach, even with the best science and technology.

If we refuse to act in the absence of certainty, our only choice would be passivity, which bears its own set of costs and benefits. Therefore, a precautionary approach—grounded in a thorough understanding of the dynamic interdependencies of the web of life—links sustainability not to inaction, but to prudent engagement.[21]

To practice sustainability is to exercise caution while strenuously pursuing the best scientific knowledge and the most diverse stakeholder perspectives—including the imagined perspectives of future generations. As one commentator observed regarding the generationally deferred costs and risks associated with climate change, "If we are to err, then let us, conscious of our responsibility to future generations, err on the side of caution."[22]

Compensation for Risks

To adopt a sustainability framework is not to stop progress, petrify human experience, or turn the planet into a museum. Human ingenuity is an important feature of the good life that needs to be sustained and evolutionary change is the fulcrum of life on the planet. The precautionary principle, in this respect, accepts risk as an inherent part of life and an intrinsic part of all discovery and creative processes. At times, the risks inherent to fulfilling human lives will be largely borne by current generations. At times, future generations will bear some of the risks, just as they will share in the benefits of our current activities and achievements.

However, the precautionary principle does not allow us to burden future generations with risks we ourselves would be unwilling to assume. It also requires that we devote resources to the discovery of means to mitigate any risks we find ourselves imposing on future generations. If, for instance, fossil fuels are burned notwithstanding the risks to future generations of climate change, or nuclear energy is produced notwithstanding the risks to future generations of radioactive contamination, then there is an accompanying duty to devote resources to the discovery and development of alternative energy sources that will impose fewer risks on future generations for the energy we enjoy today.[23]

Inevitably, some of the risks we take will have untoward consequences. The precautionary principle suggests that the proponents of such risks remain responsible for any compensation or remediation for these damaging effects. One proposed means of institutionalizing such compensation are financial instruments called **assurance bonds**. The value of an assurance bond is based on the best scientific estimates of potential environmental or social damages that might be incurred by a proposed activity.[24] Corporations involved in the development of new technologies would post these interest-accruing bonds to insure that future generations were not saddled with the risks and costs associated with unintended consequences.

Were such a bond-posting system employed, economic and technological development would not be paralyzed by the uncertainties associated with risk assessment. Still, given that money would have to be put on the table, we would have greater assurance that a rigorous risk assessment was conducted. As long as there were no problems, the bonds and the interest would return to the developer of the product after a predetermined time. If problems arose, however, those who benefited financially from the development and marketing of a product, not its victims, would become responsible for the costs of reparation. In this vein, insurance companies today are beginning to take the carbon footprint of corporations into their calculations of the cost of insuring them. The higher premiums paid by large carbon emitters is the equivalent of an assurance bond.

BOX 7.2 Unacceptable Risks—Genetically Engineered Human Beings

Are there cases where no assurance bond or any other form of compensation could be large enough to allow the taking of certain risks? As we previously observed, there are goods that are priceless or sacred to us. Presumably, risking these goods, even if compensation were offered for their damage were it to occur, might be deemed illegitimate. Consider the case of genetic engineering.

One day soon we may be able to engage in genetic engineering that makes people healthier, stronger or smarter. The prospect of such genetic engineering raises the specter of Frankenstein-like monsters being created through experiments gone horribly awry. As was the case with the invention of nuclear weapons, however, the most frightening prospect may not be failed experiments. The greatest danger from genetic engineering may not be that it goes wrong, but that it succeeds beyond all expectation (Wachbroit 1997). What could be wrong with healthier, stronger, and smarter people? Expanding one's time horizon illustrates the problem.

As Bill McKibben (2003) observes in his book, *Enough*, the germline manipulation of human fetuses will likely set off a biological arms race that rivals in its danger the arm race set off in the Cold War by the invention of the atomic bomb. Faced with the prospect of their children's friends and fellow students having enhanced IQs, many parents who otherwise would prefer not to manipulate their children's DNA will feel they have little choice but to do so. To abstain from such manipulation would relegate one's child to an uphill climb in school, to overwhelming competition in the marketplace, and potentially to second-class status in society.

To make the problem worse, the techniques for genetic enhancements will likely quickly improve. So the child equipped with a state-of-the-art upgrade today may well find herself outdone by next year's model, which promises an additional 20 or 30 points of IQ. McKibben writes:

> The vision of one's child as a nearly useless copy of Windows 95 should make parents fight like hell to make sure we never get started down this path. But the vision gets lost easily in the gushing excitement about "improving" the opportunities for our kids. (2003, 34–35)

McKibben concludes that the only time to stop such technology is before it gets started, before the genie of human genetic engineering gets out of the bottle. Keeping such technological genies in the bottle is only possible through the cultivation of a precautionary approach. Prevention is the only option because there may be no cure. Some risks, McKibben suggests, are simply too big to take.

Of course, to determine the size of an assurance bond, one has to determine the level of risk. Risk refers to an undesirable future state of damage that has some probability of occurring. To determine the level of risk, one multiplies the magnitude of the damage by its probability. A high probability of insignificant damage (e.g., the risk of getting sore muscles after a long hike) constitutes a small risk. A very low probability of great damage (e.g., the risk of getting struck by lightning on a sunny day) also constitutes a small risk. Large risks are products of relatively high probabilities coupled with relatively high damage, and if the damage is high enough (e.g., the collapse of civilization owing to climate change), even middle-range probabilities can produce a sufficiently high risk to warrant precautionary action or dictate the posting of a sizable assurance bond.

The March of Progress

Human beings are a curious, adventurous species. Many believe that there is no way to slow down, much less stop the economic growth and technological development that allows us to pursue greater comfort, wealth, and power. While there are numerous critiques of the idea that ongoing technological development is inevitable, the difficulties of restricting technological developments in accordance with the precautionary principle are considerable. In the absence of a clear understanding of risks and in the face of our curiosity, our desire to grow evermore powerful, and the prospect of economic gain, skeptics argue that most technological innovations will proceed apace.

Many scientists, in particular, believe that it is desirable and even necessary to pursue innovation regardless of the costs. In the words of J. Robert Oppenheimer, the original director of the Manhattan Project, which produced the first atom bomb: "When you see something that is technically sweet you go ahead and do it and you argue about what to do about it only after you have had your technical success. That is the way it was with the atomic bomb"[25] There are endless numbers of technically "sweet" opportunities available to us today, such as genetic engineering, and in all likelihood such opportunities will increase at an exponential rate. The problem with these new technologies is that once they have been invented—as was the case with nuclear weapons—they cannot be uninvented.

How, then, do we decide which risks are unacceptable and beyond compensation? We might add this challenging question to a raft of others that this chapter has prompted. How are we to balance the pursuit of current needs and wants with our concern for the welfare of future generations? To what extent should we sacrifice goods so that future generations might thrive? Should we deprive our children of certain benefits if this appears a necessary means to ensure the welfare of our great-grandchildren? These are not easy questions to answer, and science, while providing us much valuable data about costs, benefits, and risks, cannot answer them for us. Only ethical deliberation sets us on the right course.

Even ethical deliberation does not in itself provide answers, however; in most situations, we cannot simply reason our way to solutions. Rather, ethical inquiry and deliberation help stimulate the development of the values, perspectives, and processes necessary for the crafting of answers. The meaning we gain and the moral satisfaction we obtain from caring for future generations, local or distant neighbors, our family and friends, and other species cannot be derived from logic or reason. In many cases, rational argument is but one piece—often not the most important—of ethical concern and action. Emotions, relationships, imagination, and other nonrational (though not at all irrational) factors all help make up our ethical priorities. Reason and logic can help us see the consequences of our actions, and they can help us be consistent in the pursuit of our values, but no rational calculus can generate these values in the first place nor, in the end, can it make us care.

IRRECONCILABLE DIFFERENCES

Grappling with the precautionary principle provides a sense, then, of the ways we might begin to bring together the various aspects of sustainability; of how a sense of fairness and justice, along with an understanding and appreciation of our supporting environmental systems, can be brought to bear on decisions; and of how economic tools might help to clarify our thinking. However, it also shows where those tools will fail without the fundamental extension of ethical concern beyond restrictive boundaries of geography, time, and species. Indeed, one could argue that the key ingredient in this sustainability stew of values is the development of more extensive relationships of caring out of formerly unseen or unappreciated connections.

The argument for more extensive relationships of caring would likely have made ecologist Garrett Hardin scoff. For Hardin the sense that we are all in this together, and that we can best proceed by linking social, ecological, and economic concerns is not only misleading, it is dangerous. Writing his most prominent articles before the term sustainability rose to popularity, Hardin's arguments still act like a splash of cold water on the ideals of sustainability. For Hardin, the modern predicament is largely one of survival, and in such situations, the extension of ethical connections rarely plays a prominent role. In this section, we explore Hardin's ideas in order to test the feasibility of our goal for this chapter: integrating the legs of sustainability.

Lifeboat Ethics

In Chapter 4, we discussed Adlai Stevenson's call for us all, as crew members on Spaceship Earth, to unite in maintaining the global environmental systems that make our lives on that ship possible. Stevenson acknowledged the difficulty of achieving this global sense of alliance with current global inequities—a population "half fortunate, half miserable"—but his speech helped to popularize the Spaceship Earth metaphor of unification. In 1974, Garrett Hardin wrote a famous article critical of this image.[26]

In this article, Hardin agreed with Stevenson that life on Spaceship Earth is inequitable, although he notes more accurately than Stevenson that it is not half the population that is poor and despairing, but a significant majority. Given this reality, Hardin proposed that we give up the spaceship metaphor and adopt instead the image of a lifeboat. A small number of people, residents of the rich nations of the world, find themselves safe and secure in the lifeboat; their needs are largely being met. The vast majority of people, residents of poor nations, find themselves bobbing treacherously on the open seas without the resources to survive, let alone thrive.

To invite the needy masses into the small boat would be disastrous, Hardin claims. As more and more waterlogged people boarded the craft, it would eventually exceed its carrying capacity. Soon enough, the lifeboat would sink, and all its occupants would share a single, inglorious fate. Sharing resources in such a situation—the essence of social justice—might be seen as the only ethical thing to do. However, given the limits of the physical system, Hardin concluded, the results are certain: "The boat is swamped, and everyone drowns. Complete justice, complete catastrophe." Having the best intentions and attempting to meet everyone's needs may be fine prescriptions for an ethical theory, Hardin maintained, but such well-intentioned morality proves problematic, if not disastrous, in practice. Taking care of oneself, one's family, and one's nation is at odds with efforts to satisfy the needs and safeguard the opportunities of global neighbors.

Tragedy of the Commons

Hardin disputed the notion that extending ethical bonds produces desirable results in a world of scarce resources. Nice guys finish last, Hardin observed, and selfishness will always beat out good intentions. However,

Hardin was not suggesting that unrestrained individual selfishness is the best recipe for protecting the global environment. In an earlier and even more widely cited article entitled "The Tragedy of the Commons," Hardin used another metaphor to explain why individual selfishness produced environmental catastrophe.[27]

The "commons" Hardin described were pastures in England where people grazed their sheep. A typical livestock owner, Hardin argued, would take maximum advantage of the free forage by grazing all of his animals on the commons. Of course, his likeminded and equally self-interested neighbors, being economically rational people, would act similarly. As relatively few herders and relatively few sheep exploited a relatively large commons, no real problems would arise. However, lack of self-restraint practiced by increasing numbers of self-interested herders placing more and more sheep on a limited acreage would quickly produce a pasture eroded by overgrazing. The formerly lush, green commons, like the swamped lifeboat, would be rendered useless. All the sheep, and eventually all the herders, would starve.

Hardin's point was that the tragedy of the commons is inevitable when the commons—understood broadly as publicly available natural resources—is open to exploitation by individuals in the absence of a central authority to regulate their actions. With no one to control overexploitation, Hardin insists, the commons will be depleted to the point of collapse—then everyone loses. In writing "The Tragedy of the Commons," Hardin was concerned not only with the overuse and erosion of public lands, but with the depletion of all natural resources in an overpopulated world. His conclusion was that "Ruin is the destination toward which all men rush, each pursuing his own best interest in a society that believes in the freedom of the commons. Freedom in a commons brings ruin to all."[28] The only viable solution to environmental destruction in an overpopulated world of scarce resources, Hardin maintained, was to coercively impose restraint.

Hardin's Challenge

Hardin was dubious that all three legs of the stool of sustainability truly support one another. Strengthening the economic and environmental legs, he believed, necessitates ignoring the leg of social justice. He made two major claims that advocates of sustainability must confront. First, he claimed that in an overpopulated world of scarce resources, the attempt to meet the needs of the poor and disadvantaged will prove environmentally disastrous. The predictable result is that the carrying capacity of the commons—the planet as a whole—will be exceeded, with dire consequences for all.

Second, he claimed that a sovereign authority is required to protect natural resources, that individuals trying to meet their own needs in the absence of a recognized authority will destroy the commons. Because people are fundamentally self-serving and shortsighted, a sense of social justice or voluntary cooperation will not produce acceptable results. Let us examine each of these claims in turn.

POVERTY REDUCTION VERSUS ENVIRONMENTAL PRESERVATION

Will meeting the needs of the disadvantaged prove environmentally disastrous as Hardin asserted? Some scholars dispute Hardin's lifeboat metaphor itself, suggesting that an emergency situation with little time for planning does not accurately represent the current challenge regarding sustainability and falsely constrains the range of possible responses to that challenge. Still, we might concede to Hardin that there are indeed conflicting approaches to sustainability, depending on the focus of one's concern as primarily social or primarily ecological.

For example, when environmental justice advocates assert that the goals of social justice and environmental protection are compatible, they are usually speaking from a distinctive ethical perspective, one which tends to be more anthropocentric than ecocentric. Their environmental values, in other words, center upon the protection of natural resources and places that support the quality of life for particular human communities. From this perspective, the focus is usually on urban problems. Moreover, the concern here is not generally for the intrinsic value of nature (nature for nature's sake) but rather for the instrumental value of nature (ecological services to human beings).

As a result, environmental justice approaches sometimes conflict with more ecocentric ethics, especially in regard to wilderness protection. In a number of cases in the United States and elsewhere, indigenous people have challenged policies and restrictions regarding their access to protected wilderness areas, either for permanent homes or for hunting or fishing, citing values of environmental justice as well as native sovereignty. Sometimes Native communities have come into conflict with environmentalists seeking to preserve "pristine" wilderness areas, free of any human intervention or use. Increasingly, however, these types of conflicts do not necessarily involve the stark either/or type of decision that Hardin presents. In many cases people, who are motivated to work toward sustainability for a wide range of reasons, are working together to address multiple legs of sustainability simultaneously. In this section, we explore these types of efforts.

Linking Social and Environmental Goals

Several philosophical models shed light on managing these types of conflicts between various approaches to sustainability. One, discussed in Chapter 5, is based on Midgley's notion of mixed or nested communities. Applying this model to perceived conflicts within sustainability, we might aim to protect the health of families and neighbors, while also recognizing the claims of nonhuman animals and places, which are also threatened by many of the same hazards. Many toxic chemicals, for example, ranging from deliberately applied pesticides to discarded PCBs, are dangerous to human beings and nonhuman animals, as well as destructive to soil and water. It may well be possible to protect the interests of all these constituencies or nested communities—for example, through systematic cleanup—without having to choose between competing values.

The environmental ethics associated with a bioregionalist perspective can also offer helpful tools for thinking about environmental justice. The local focus of bioregional (and agrarian) thought encompasses social and natural goods. What is good for nature in a given place, in other words, is often good for humans, both in terms of community values and in terms of economic security. Small-scale, diversified farms, for example, using environmentally sound methods and serving a local economy, can both protect local watersheds and strengthen the justice and economic security of the human community. As Wendell Berry argues, "nature and human culture, wildness and domesticity, are not opposed but are interdependent."[29] The key to strengthening both natural and human values is to maintain a proper scale, thereby avoiding the destructive consequences of mass production, homogenization, and what Berry calls the "monocultures" of industrial civilization, which suppresses both cultural and natural diversity and democratic processes.

We can see that both of these frameworks—nested communities and bioregionalism—present a marriage of social, ecological, and economic goals. We can see a similar link between ecological, social, and economic goals in physicist and economic ethicist Vandana Shiva's arguments. She observes, "Giving people rights and access to resources so that they can regain their security and generate sustainable livelihoods is the only solution to environmental destruction and the population growth that accompanies it."[30] It is with this same conviction that the Brundtland Commission determined, decades earlier, that "inequality is the planet's main 'environmental' problem."[31] Here, Shiva and the Brundtland Commission insist that social justice is not at odds with protecting the global commons. Indeed, social justice is the only thing that can save it.

Finding Synergistic Solutions

The idea of solutions that address several problems simultaneously may seem too good to be true. Most of us have been trained to address large problems by first splitting them into smaller, easily solvable problems. By this method, we might list the problems in a particular region—for example, poverty, loss of biodiversity, decrease in ecosystem services. We might then proceed by addressing these problems or by dividing them up further until they appear more manageable.

However, this approach to sustainability has tended to exacerbate rather than resolve the original problems. Wendell Berry sarcastically praises the "genius" of American farm experts for exactly this type of thinking: "they can take a solution and divide it neatly into two problems."[32] Berry's point gives us a sense of Holling's holistic view mentioned in the opening of this chapter. By understanding the various challenges as aspects of a complex system, we can better view their relationship to each other. As in the fishery example in Box 7.3, addressing sustainability challenges in concert often has a practical payoff.

Indeed, empirical research gives weight to the connections between ecological quality and economic and social well-being.

Countries with more equal income distribution and more egalitarian political rights generally do a better job protecting their environments. A similar relationship occurs domestically, when one compares economic equality and environmental health in the 50 U.S. states. Environmental caretaking and economic equity appear to go hand in hand. The conclusion reached by many scholars is that "social justice and environmental sustainability are inextricably linked, and that the achievement of the latter without greater commitment to the former will be exceptionally difficult."[33] In an ecologically and technologically shrinking world, an expanding sense of social solidarity provides a crucial foundation for sustainability.

The stubborn fact is that great wealth and great poverty are both environmentally disastrous—the former owing to the massive consumption and waste that it encourages, the latter owing to the environmental degradation that results from poverty. Developing countries currently account for well over 95 percent of world population growth. Stemming this tide will entail more than sharing words of concern for environmental protection. It will entail sharing the knowledge, technology, and resources that allow for the development of sustainable livelihoods. Research has consistently shown that education and economic opportunities, particularly for women, are one of the surest and fastest means to lowering reproduction rates and moving toward more sustainable societies.[34]

All this is to say that in theory, and in practice, the protection of the environment may

BOX 7.3 Public Participation in Marine Protected Area

The quality and production of many marine systems and fisheries around the globe are currently much lower than historic levels. In many cases, new technologies have made fishers much more effective at catching fish. The change sounds beneficial, but this increased effectiveness combined with economic pressures has resulted in depletion of many fish stocks. Fish that were once abundant have become much less common. As a result, the human communities that depend on these fish for subsistence and economic opportunities are struggling to maintain their quality of life. Longer hours must be spent to catch fewer fish. From a social and economic perspective, these communities are unable to support themselves, and the failure of the resource often creates a loss of social cohesion. From an ecological perspective, the continued attempts to eke out a living from the degraded ecosystem only results in further degrading the fishery.

Marine protected areas (MPAs) are a popular management tool in coastal and marine systems. The basic idea is to exclude some or all human activity in an area in order to allow the marine ecosystem to restore itself without the obstacle of human-based stresses. While relieving an ecosystem from fishing pressure can in the long-term help increase the quality of that system, it also represents a short-term loss of income for the people that become excluded from that area. For this reason, local communities often resist MPAs, arguing that they are unable to manage another blow to their already diminished incomes.

In some communities, however, MPAs have been used as a tool to address—rather than exacerbate—economic and social problems in local communities. For example, faced with severely depleted fish stocks in 2002, several communities in the Fiji Islands opted to institute community-managed MPAs with support from the national government and the University of the South Pacific's Institute of Applied Science. The goal was not only to increase the level of sustainable fish catch but also to decrease poverty. In the years that followed, yields of both fish and shellfish increased significantly, but the social and economic impacts of the MPAs were even more encouraging. A 2008 study showed that household income and luxury items (e.g., bicycles, radios) had increased since the MPAs were instituted. In other words, the MPA ultimately resulted in a richer resource, which in turn led to social and economic benefits for local communities.

Moreover, the focus on community management created an atmosphere of social participation within the communities. In a survey of individuals within these communities 83 percent of respondents felt that the community had become more united and 84 percent felt that women had a stronger voice in the community (Leisher et al. 2008). These types of improvements are not simply a matter of having more resources. The challenge of managing their resources sustainably became a unifying goal for the community. In meeting those challenges together, community members developed skills and relationships that did not exist previously and, as a result, will be better prepared to address future challenges. The details regarding the importance of community relationships will be discussed in Chapters 9 and 10.

be helped, not hindered, when the impoverished and disadvantaged are aided in their efforts to gain education and economic opportunity.[35] This is by no means a universal conviction even among those who label themselves environmentalists, but it is intrinsic to the sustainability framework.[36] To embrace sustainability is to accept that economic security—the ability to earn one's livelihood—is a universal pursuit, a universal right. People will always seek economic security as a means of survival, and given the chance, most will pursue economic prosperity. Given this reality, people will continue to destroy the environment if that is the only way for them to survive economically. The sustainability framework insists that the only way to protect the environment is to help the disadvantaged develop environmentally benign livelihoods.

The anthropologist and conservationist Richard Leakey put the point succinctly when he said: "To care about the environment requires at least one square meal a day."[37] This linking of economic security and ecological concern is widespread in environmentalist movements in developing countries. Consider international efforts to preserve primates. Today, one of the chief threats to primates is the destruction of native habitat as subsistence farmers slash and burn forests to grow crops for export, such as tobacco (Malawi), palm oil (Indonesia), or soybeans (Brazil). Equally devastating in some countries is the hunting of "bushmeat" by impoverished people. Preserving chimpanzees and gorillas and orangutans is a wonderful idea, but to those families that might starve in the absence of a meal of bushmeat or crops

cultivated in former forests, saving wildlife seems a privilege they can ill afford. Similarly, the reintroduction of wolves to the western United States has significant ecological benefits, but even here such programs are more successful when they include incentives and technical assistance for ranchers who must adjust to having large predators in the region.

In Africa, Indonesia, India, Brazil, and elsewhere, early efforts by Western environmentalists to preserve wildlife and wilderness areas by cordoning off habitat without thought to the economic needs of local residents were met with limited success and great resentment. Typically, such efforts were viewed as catering to the needs of Western tourists.[38] In contrast, community-based natural resource management efforts that tie wilderness preservation to the development of sustainable local economies have been more promising.[39] Of course, some conflicts still exist, such as problems with poaching and deforestation, but these become more manageable when efforts are made to work with local communities and return the profits from managing wildlife back to the inhabitants.

The Role of Technology

The connection between environmental protection and the need for economic development is not limited to the preservation of biological diversity. Zero-emission and low-emission automobiles are now widely available, but their cost may be prohibitive for those who live below the poverty line. Well-constructed, well-insulated housing or even new refrigerators that conserve energy are also often beyond the economic reach of the poorest sectors of society. While the poor consume far fewer resources than the wealthy per capita, poverty often means that one cannot afford to be energy efficient. In such cases, economic development and sustainability go hand in hand.

In the developing world, a similar relationship exists between poverty and the inefficient use of other natural resources. Although kerosene lamps use 50 times more energy per watt produced than electric light bulbs, many urban slum dwellers and the rural poor still use kerosene lamps, contributing more to greenhouse gas emissions and also suffering from the smoke and unhealthy emissions. Solar cookers use reflected rays from the sun to cook food and, where necessary, pasteurize water, yet relatively few people have such cookers (see Figure 7.2). Indeed, about 80 percent of the world's people still collect and burn vast amounts of wood and charcoal for cooking. In many areas, bushes and trees are cut for firewood faster than they can be replenished, leading to the erosion of mountainsides and savannas and desertification. In these cases, increased conservation of natural resources and improved human welfare would be made possible through the provision of appropriate technology and sustainable economic development.

The development and deployment of appropriate technology and the creation of sustainable local economies will not happen sufficiently or quickly enough if the disadvantaged of the world are left to their own resources. In large part, that is because the disadvantaged are already integrated

FIGURE 7.2 Solar cookers have been a cost-effective way to pasteurize water in rural areas, decreasing the occurrence of waterborne diseases. *(Photograph Courtesy of Zahana.org and GlobalGiving.org)*

into—and are further pushed into unsustainable livelihoods as a result of—a global economy. The opportunity is available to the wealthier countries of the world, those that consume most of the planet's natural capital and produce most of its toxic pollution, to help foster sustainable economies across the globe.

MANAGING THE GLOBAL COMMONS

Now we can see the error in Hardin's suggestion that meeting the needs of the poor will prove environmentally disastrous. Such a view applies an unnecessarily narrow logic to contemporary challenges and fails to acknowledge a number of links between environmental quality and social needs. In fact, history suggests that just the opposite is true. Contrary to Hardin's argument, *failing* to meet the needs of the poor has often proved environmentally disastrous.

But what about Hardin's second challenge? In the "Tragedy of the Commons" and "Lifeboat Ethics," Hardin claimed that the commons cannot be preserved in the absence of a coercive authority. At first glance, this position appears to leave only two options. To be sustained, the commons must either be divided up into parcels of private property (each managed by a sovereign owner) or protected by a sovereign world government. Both options present their own problems.

World government is unlikely to develop any time soon. (The United Nations, Hardin maintained, is a "toothless tiger" incapable of doing the job.) If it did develop, the threat of global tyranny would be ever-present. In turn, the presence of a central world government by no means guarantees ecological well-being. Many nations with strong central governments—such as the former Soviet Union—had abysmal domestic records of environmental protection.[40] There is no reason to assume that centralized authority on a global scale would be more ecologically benign than the centralized authority of many of the world's nations with the poorest environmental records.

Likewise, the option of privatizing the commons, effectively parceling it up into packages of real estate owned and protected by individuals, is often neither workable nor effective at ensuring its protection. Some commons, the open seas or the atmosphere, cannot effectively be divided up and privatized. Further, the historical "enclosing" of common lands has not deterred their depletion, erosion, and destruction.[41] Private property is often abused and destroyed for quick profit.

Thus, centralized authority is no guarantee that the global commons will be preserved, and the privatization of property does not ensure that its natural resources will not be depleted or its ecological health maintained. Thus, given the constraints suggested by Hardin the situation indeed looks bleak. But let us take a closer look at Hardin's assertion. Is a coercive, centralized authority really required to preserve the global commons?

The Need for a Central Authority

Within a group of friends or colleagues, there may be no need to coercively enforce laws forbidding thievery. A sense of care and common morality—the ethics of reciprocity—is sufficient. Within larger groups of individuals, such as nation-states, however, it is not hard to understand Hardin's logic. In these cases, laws that forbid thievery and guarantee honest transactions appear necessary. These laws might be followed willingly by most people most of the time out of a sense of moral rectitude or cooperative engagement. Still, the presence of a police force and judicial system to enforce the law appears necessary to ensure that stealing does not become an irresistible temptation.

Anarchists disagree. They believe that order can be maintained within large organizations of people without any coercive authority or central government. Anarchism has a long and vibrant history, and its theory is much debated. Occasionally—and usually in very short-lived experiments—it has been put into practice. Embracing the sustainability framework does not entail the endorsement of anarchism. Within nation-states, advocates of sustainability are almost universally supportive of laws that uphold human rights, civil rights, and honest practices while forbidding transgressions such as thievery and bribery. Governments with coercive powers are understood to be the necessary means of enforcing such laws.

In this respect, the sustainability framework does not dispute the claim that centralized authority may be useful, and is often required, to achieve many goods, including protection of the environment. A great deal of environmental preservation occurs in the absence of centralized authority, however.

Moving beyond the Tragedy of the Commons

Hardin called for "mutual coercion, mutually agreed upon."[42] Many scholars have responded to Hardin's ideas by describing how such coercion can exist without a central authority. While we might concede that a group of purely selfish and myopic individuals using an open-access resource are likely to collapse the resource as Hardin suggests, there are a number of factors that can lead to a much different result. First, consider the people involved. While many people do act in narrowly selfish ways, broader motivations also hold some influence. For example, social norms often play a large role in people's behavior.

We will explain the concept of social norms in more detail in later chapters, but a brief example here will help to illustrate a potentially powerful force for avoiding the tragedy of the commons. A social norm is simply an

expectation that individuals have of one another (and themselves) that they use to distinguish between appropriate and inappropriate behavior. Consider the practice of standing in line. Many people are indoctrinated into this custom at a young age. In countless situations (school cafeteria, bank, deli, movie theater, and so on) when the number of people waiting for a service is greater than the number that can immediately be served, we form a line. Equally as important, when we come upon such a line and we desire that same service, we willingly take up a position at the end of that line.

This is by no means the only option. So what motivates one to take position at the back of the pack? It is not an expression of selfish preference. Most would prefer to be served immediately rather than wait for everyone else ahead in line to be served first. Nor is there a central authority forcing us to the end of the line (with the possible exception of school cafeteria monitors). Rather, we accept our position at the end of the line because that is the social norm. There may be some instances where we could successfully push our way to the front of the line, but we recognize that the process as a whole will work more efficiently if all opt to wait their turn. In the end, our sense of fairness along with the threat of rebuke from others standing in line is enough to push us away from the narrowly selfish act.[43]

Standing in line is a rather ordinary example, but most societies have developed norms of cooperation, many of which apply to the use of natural resources. For example, traditional taboos regarding fishing and hunting often have the effect of helping communities to avoid overexploiting a resource. However, in many cases evolved norms are not enough to promote the cooperation necessary to sustainably manage a resource. In these cases, the norms must be supplemented by a set of clear, enforceable rules.

In some cases, these rules can be developed and enforced through the collective efforts of the users of the resource. For example, farmers in Nepal successfully developed a set of rules to manage collective irrigation systems as a group, and this system was often more successful than strategies applied as a result

---

BOX 7.4   Managing the Commons

Examples of commons management are everywhere. Forest commons harbor and conserve many of the planet's most important natural processes and resources, including countless plant and animal species, carbon storage, hydrological recycling, and the provision of timber, and other products. Research shows that while forest commons in Asia, Africa, and Latin America often require further protection by governmental (national) institutions, those forested lands are best conserved and protected when they are maintained by the local communities that have traditionally inhabited and utilized them (Chhatre and Agrawal 2009). For example, the Communal Areas Management Programme for Indigenous Resources project in Zimbabwe was initiated to place more power regarding wildlife management in the hands of local communities. In some areas, the program has had success not only in increasing revenues from the forest but also in decreasing poaching and shifting attitudes towards conservation (Arnold 1998).

Such "natural" commons find their complement in so-called "cultural commons." Language might be considered a cultural commons. It is an important cultural resource that is neither privately owned nor controlled by a government. Rather, it is an open access resource that is freely accessible,

publically shared, and collectively maintained and transformed.

An increasing number of cultural commons today are "virtual." Among the most prominent of the virtual commons are Internet resources such as Wikipedia, the free, online encyclopedia, the Public Library of Science (PLoS), and various sites that publish scientific papers as open access intellectual resources, such as BioMed Central, PhysMath Central, and Chemistry Central. The data and knowledge provided on these websites is freely given by contributors and freely accessible to the general public. Some of these websites, such as Wikipedia, are wholly maintained by volunteers.

Like natural commons, virtual commons have guidelines or regulations for the management and dissemination of their resources. These may be formally instituted through the Creative Commons Attribution License (CCAL), one of several Creative Commons Licensing (CCL) methods for cultural commons (Creative Commons 2010). With CCL's in place, the general public may freely utilize, copy, and distribute the submitted works, often with minimal restrictions, such as giving the author the appropriate acknowledgment.

Natural and cultural commons are one means to facilitate the equitable sharing of resources. When well managed, they prove to be models of sustainable practice.

of outside influence.[44] Sometimes outside assistance in developing and implementing rules is necessary, but even in these cases, there are numerous systems of governance that resource users can adopt in order to avoid the tragedy of the commons, and empirical studies suggest that including resource users in the development and implementation of the rules can improve compliance and increase chances of success.[45]

Indeed, there is a long history of communally managed resources, often called **common pool resources** such as pastureland, water sources, forests, and fisheries. As Nobel prize winner Elinor Ostrom[46] has demonstrated, these commons have been sustained across the generations through the cooperative engagement of local stakeholders, and this has been achieved in the absence of central, sovereign authorities.[47] Providing information about the resource and feedback about declining stocks or quality, creating a community where compliance with rules is demanded and monitored, addressing conflicts that arise between users with power differentials, and creating opportunities to explore options and adapt to change are some of the essential attributes of successful commons management.[48] We will discuss this process more in Chapters 9 and 10.

International Multilateral Agreements

Scores of **multilateral environmental agreements** between and among countries have also served to protect the global commons in the absence of a centralized authority, but through the organizing efforts of international agencies such as UNEP and UNESCO. The Montreal Protocol, which protects the stratospheric commons and its protective layer of ozone, is a good example. Likewise, the Convention on International Trade in Endangered Species of Wild Fauna and Flora (CITES), which monitors and regulates trade in endangered species, has achieved a significant level of protection to more than 30,000 different species of plants and animals without a world government to enforce it. The Antarctic Treaty, adopted in 1961 by twelve signatories and now including 46 nation-states, safeguards our southernmost continent, which like the world's oceans and atmosphere, is a true commons belonging to no nation and shared by all. The treaty protects Antarctica from militarization, nuclear testing, and waste disposal while promoting peaceful, international scientific cooperation.

Consider efforts to address the transboundary movement and disposal of hazardous waste. Highly industrialized countries produce most of the hundreds of millions of tons of hazardous waste generated each year. Significant portions of this waste crosses national borders, with most of it moving from industrialized to developing nations. The Basel Convention, which came into force in 1992 and now has 172 signatories, controls the trafficking of many forms of hazardous waste across national borders. The convention upholds the "Legal Principles for Environmental Protection and Sustainable Development" adopted by the World Commission on Environment and Development.

A "nondiscrimination" principle maintains that nations "shall apply as a minimum at least the same standards for environmental conduct and impacts regarding transboundary natural resources and environmental interferences as are applied domestically."[49] In effect, the Basel Convention applies the golden rule to the international relations of toxic waste disposal, and it has proven quite effective. Along with many other multilateral treaties and agreements, the Basel Convention was created and maintained in the absence of a central, sovereign world government.

Non-Governmental Organizations

The efforts of nongovernmental organizations (NGOs) to protect the global commons are also noteworthy. The most prominent of these groups, such as Conservation International, the World Wide Fund for Nature, the Nature Conservancy, and the International Union for Conservation of Nature (which brings together government agencies and NGOs), span the globe and boast millions of members. While some of these groups are funded by foundation grants and government contracts, thousands of small, local NGOs (e.g., Save Our River) are supported only by the work of their members to improve their communities, their environments, and their quality of life.[50]

No centralized authority coerces these groups to do the work they do or forces members of the general public to join, donate money, time, or effort to furthering their missions. Yet these organizations foster tens of thousands of initiatives that further sustainability around the world. Not infrequently, their efforts eventually stimulate domestic or international governmental action. For example, CITES was originally drafted at a 1963 meeting of members of the International Union for Conservation of Nature, an international NGO, before being adopted over the following decades by 175 sovereign states.[51]

Earth Share, a conglomerate of NGOs formed in the late 1980s, created a motto to capture the sensibility of its constituents. NGO members voluntarily contribute money, time, and effort to the protection of the global commons. In the 1990s, the Earth Share motto simply read: "It's a Connected World. Do Your Share." Doing your share in an interdependent world is more than a moral imperative: it is a practical necessity if sustainability is to be furthered.

NGOs dedicated to environmental conservation have historically appealed to the welfare of endangered animals and to the welfare of future generations. Increasingly—and markedly so in the last two decades—they have also linked their conservation efforts to the pursuit of social justice. The World Wide Fund for Nature (WWF), for example, works to protect wildlife in biologically rich but economically poor countries. Their early efforts met with mixed success and often alienated local peoples. In the late 1980s, WWF's perspective and strategy changed: the organization shifted from a narrow focus on protecting charismatic megafauna—species such as lions, rhinoceroses, tigers, and elephants—to the preservation of biodiversity and the promotion of sustainability through local economic development and community empowerment.[52] The idea was to make habitat protection a paying proposition for local residents.

Likewise, The Nature Conservancy shifted its strategic orientation in the 1980s. Earlier efforts were oriented to the purchase of large swaths of ecologically rich land, with the subsequent task that of policing these preserves against poachers or other environmentally destructive practices. Now efforts to preserve landscapes are often tied to the sustainable economic development of local populations.[53] The protection of biodiversity is grounded in "**community-based conservation**."[54] As one Nature Conservancy official stated," conservation works place by place . . . in every ecosystem we're working in, we need long-term community support or we will fail."[55]

An example of a successful NGO that focuses its efforts on community-based solutions is Engineers without Borders. This organization supports development programs in communities around the world by helping to design and implement sustainable engineering projects. With more than 400 projects in 47 countries, Engineers without Borders-USA (there are dozens other affiliates in other countries) primarily focuses on low-cost, sustainable water and energy projects. In each case, meeting the basic needs of local residents and developing community leadership and ownership of projects is central to the mission of the organization. For Engineers without Borders, sustainability begins at home, in self-responsible communities that develop the tools and resources to meet their own needs.

The Role of Government

While governmental authorities and the laws they promulgate and enforce will always be necessary to protect public goods, including environmental resources, a centralized, coercive force is no guarantee of environmental protection. The dual role of government is to protect and empower its citizens. Thus, government has the responsibility to protect citizens from the law-breaking of other citizens, from the power of business corporations and other organized groups, and importantly, from the unconstitutional and excessive intrusions of government itself. Additionally, government has the responsibility to empower citizens to sustain themselves and their world as individuals and through the nongovernmental organizations they form. By way of this empowerment, through the customary and cooperative engagement of local stakeholders and the efforts of transnational nongovernmental organizations, the domestic and global commons often gains much-needed protection.

The key point here is that while Hardin's arguments help to highlight the challenges that must be addressed when integrating the three legs of sustainability, neither of his challenges represent insurmountable barriers to sustainability. In the first case, we have seen that social, environmental, and economic goals are not necessarily at odds with one another. In fact, achieving lasting success within one leg of sustainability often requires addressing needs in the other two.

In the second case, we can amend Hardin's tale of inevitable tragedy. Hardin called for "mutual coercion, mutually agreed upon" in order to avoid the tragedy of the commons. This goal can be achieved at times, as Hardin suggested, through a central authority.

As you have seen, however, it can also be achieved through the cooperative engagement of stakeholders, including communal management and multilateral treaties. Having addressed these challenges, we can now take a closer look at the integrative perspective that C. S. Holling referred to at the beginning of the chapter.

TRANSCENDING THE THREE-LEGGED STOOL MODEL

Mastery of a model requires understanding its limitations. We have used the three-legged stool as a model to structure our discussion of sustainability. One key aspect of this model is that each leg is necessary to achieve sustainability. Take any one leg away and the stool falls down. On the other hand, however, all three legs do not need to be equal for the stool to be stable. One can be slightly shorter or longer than the others and the stool will not wobble.

While this image helps to convey the need for all three legs, the danger in viewing sustainability with this model is overemphasizing the separation between each leg. As we saw from Holling's words at the beginning of this chapter, there is a tendency to approach matters of sustainability as essentially about one of the three legs, with some deference required to the other two. However, seeing matters as essentially social, essentially ecological, or essentially economic misses the point.

Having separated our discussion into three parts for the sake of analysis and explanation, we have seen in this chapter that sustainability issues are inextricably linked. We are now ready to understand the challenge of sustainability as taking place not in sets of social, ecological, and economic systems, but as what Holling (and many others) refers to as social-ecological systems.[56] One important consequence of this shift in terminology is that it discourages viewing current challenges in terms of competing legs of sustainability. The holistic concept of social-ecological systems helps us avoid the problems and often false conflicts that arise when one attempts to address social, environmental, and economic problems in isolation. In this section, we take a closer look at the concept of social-ecological systems and explore how it can inform an integrated approach to the ethics of sustainability.

Integrating the Three Legs

We have discussed interconnectivity in several contexts at this point and need not dwell long on the topic here. However, it is worth noting the shift in perspective that the concept of social-ecological systems encourages. For example, the issue of the displacement of wilderness areas by agricultural development need not be couched in terms of the needs or rights of human beings versus those of nonhuman animals or whole ecosystems. Rather, we can view the situation as a social-ecological system with a number closely connected issues and stakeholders. In this way, one can avoid the mistake of viewing social and ecological welfare in dualistic terms.

Such a view does not imply the adoption of a weak sustainability position, in which human and manufactured capital can simply replace natural capital. To the contrary, aspects generally considered natural capital, such as biodiversity or the ability to provide ecosystem services, remain an integral part of the functioning of the entire system. While there may be conflicting value claims made, these conflicts do not necessarily cut across the three legs as we have discussed them. For example, value claims of indigenous peoples may conflict with those of farmers and ranchers. We can view these conflicts within the context of the social-ecological system within which both communities reside.

The story of the six blind men and the elephant makes an appropriate analogy here. In the story, each blind man touches a part of the elephant in order to discern what the elephant looks like, and each gets a different picture, depending on where he touched the animal. The one who touches the trunk pictures a snake, the one who touches the stomach pictures a wall, and so on. One benefit of framing the ethics of sustainability in terms of social-ecological systems is that it encourages one to view the whole elephant, rather than just a part.

In this way, we might think of the concept of social-ecological systems as a contemporary, scientifically-based interpretation of Aldo Leopold's concept of "the land." Recall that Leopold used the concept to draw attention to a broader scale of consideration that included ecological processes as well as social ones. Viewing the land ethic in terms of social-ecological systems can provide some insight into retaining the "integrity" of the land. Social-ecological systems are examples of **complex adaptive systems**. In order to understand how this perspective can inform our integrative framework for sustainability ethics, we must first gain an understanding of complex adaptive systems.

Complex Adaptive Systems

Complex adaptive systems (CASs), which provide the basis for the "nature evolving" caricature from Chapter 5, are characterized by a particular set of structural and behavioral attributes. They are composed of multiple, interconnected elements. As a result of these connections CASs exhibit emergent, nonlinear behavior. We can see this behavior in something as simple as a pile of sand. Imagine building a pile of sand by adding one grain at a time. As each grain is added to the pile, the system (i.e., the pile of sand) will change. In most cases, that change will involve becoming slightly bigger with basically the same shape as before. Occasionally, however, the added grain will cause a mini-avalanche in the pile, significantly changing the shape of the pile.

This first change is linear. The incremental addition of one grain of sand causes an incremental change in the shape of the sand pile. In the second case, however, the behavior of the system is both emergent and nonlinear. It is nonlinear because an incremental change of one grain caused a disproportionate effect in the shape of the pile. It is emergent because it depends on the existing relationship between the grains of sand and cannot be predicted from the characteristics of the individual grains. In other words, the avalanche-causing grain of sand is identical to the one added just before it; the difference that resulted in one grain causing incremental change and one grain causing nonlinear change is in the organization of the sand pile.

The adaptive aspect of CASs refers to their ability to change their structure and response to outside stimuli. A car is a system with many connected parts, but it is not adaptive because the parts of the car always respond in fully determined ways. The connections do not change, so the response of the car to turning the steering wheel, pressing the brake, and so on does not change—a consistency that everyone in or near a car depends upon. In CASs, the connections themselves can change depending on the situation. On an individual level, we might think of this change as the process of making new cognitive connections that affect our decisions and behavior (i.e., learning). On a broader scale, we might talk about connections in terms of relationships between individuals and how those change over time. The idea may seem foreign, but examples of CASs abound, including a person or family, a city or nation, a business or stock market, and the entire global system. All ecosystems are CASs, as are all social systems.

Notice the range in scale represented by these examples, including everything from the individual (and indeed smaller) to the entire planet. The social-ecological systems that form the context of our lives can be viewed as nested sets of CASs existing at a broad range of scales. Let us look more closely at how this multi-scale concept can inform our integrated framework for sustainability ethics.

Integrating Behavior at Different Scales

Recall from Chapter 3 that the first step in developing a system of ethics is shifting from narrowly defined self-interest to considering the welfare of other community members. In Chapter 4, we explored how to define community in a world of global interconnections. Within the framework of social-ecological systems, we can look at this shift in terms of scale—from the CAS operating at the individual scale (our own self-interest) to the CAS at the broader scale (e.g., our local community). In other words, a system of ethics acknowledges that decisions made at the individual scale affect and are affected by the broader-scale system.

As we have seen, however, our decisions affect far more than our local communities. From this view, the past few chapters can be seen as an exploration into our role as active members of a multitude of social-ecological systems operating at a wide range of scales. Indeed the future focus of sustainability forces us to assess our behavior at scales far vaster than we are accustomed to considering. Decisions made on the individual scale regarding what kind of job to pursue, what kind of technology to develop or support, and even what kind of products to buy must now be weighed in the context of global processes operating on the scale of decades, centuries, or even millennia.

In order to make these connections across vast temporal and spatial scales, we might focus on those traits that are common to all CASs. For example, CASs are characterized by constant change. Lance Gunderson and C. S. Holling describe the development of these systems as a series of cycles, which include long periods of relatively slow and incremental change (which they call growth and development), as well as short periods of rapid and radical shifts from the status quo (which they call release and reorganization) (see Figure 7.3).[57] We can see a representation of these stages in our sand pile. The many grains of sand that do not cause an avalanche collectively represent the period of growth and development. Note that while these grains do not cause an avalanche, they do make one more likely. The grains that do cause an avalanche represent the period of release and reorganization.

Florida's sand pine forests provide a suitable ecological example. As these forests grow, nutrients are taken up by the trees and stored in branches and pine needles. Over time, an understory of oaks, pines, and other plants builds up. During thunderstorms common in Florida summers, lightning ignites this fuel, and under extremely dry and windy conditions the wildfire may also consume the mature sand pines in a blazing inferno. Some nutrients from the burned vegetation are released back into the soil for use by other plants. The fire also kills the tops of oak shrubs and trees and other understory plants. Importantly, its heat opens sand pine cones, which allows the seeds to disburse. This process sustains the forest in the long term even though it will take years for the young seedlings to create a new pine overstory. The fires and the subsequent new growth can be seen as intermittent periods of release and reorganization.

(a)

(b)

FIGURE 7.3 (a) and (b)   Fire in Pine Forest: In sand pine scrub ecosystems, intermittent fires, which represent a period of release in terms of CASs, play an important ecological role. *(Photographs Courtesy of David Godwin, P Clausa Imaging).*

In an economic context, these periods of rapid change are referred to as "creative destruction," a term coined by economist Joseph Schumpeter (1883–1950). In this case, an industry goes through a relatively long period of growth. Then, a competing entrepreneur introduces an innovative idea that disrupts the industry, forcing large, entrenched companies to make major changes or face being outcompeted by more nimble, upstart companies. For example, in the 1980s Michael Dell, while a student at the University of Texas at Austin, began selling computers out of his dorm room, using component parts from other companies. By effectively outsourcing the production of the component parts, Dell was able to decrease overhead costs and respond quickly to consumer preferences. As a result, the Dell Computer Corporation grew quickly, forcing larger computer manufacturers to adopt a global assembly-line structure in order to remain competitive.

We can see this pattern of long periods of stability and growth with intermittent periods of release and reorganization across a wide range of scales. These periods of rapid change can produce both positive and negative effects. The key aspect, however, is that whatever these effects turn out to be, they cannot be predicted before the changes occur. As Holling describes, during these periods of rapid change "several alternate futures become suddenly perceived and unpredictability explodes."[58] This unpredictability arises because during these times, even slight differences in conditions can result in drastic differences later. In other words, not only can we not predict the time and place of the next lightning strike in a forest or the next innovation in an industry; we cannot predict the impacts of that change on the next growth phase of the system.

This explosion of uncertainty comes in part from how these cycles can align across scales, allowing individual or small-scale collapses to bring about larger-scale ones. Rosa Parks' refusal to give up her bus seat to a white passenger in 1955 is a good example. She was not the first African-American to refuse to relinquish her seat in opposition to instituted segregation. However, her example helped motivate others, generated discussion, and ultimately sparked the Montgomery Bus Boycott, which gave the civil rights movement one of its largest victories. Her act occurred at a time when city and indeed national systems were ripe for release and reorganization.[59] Acts such as Parks' rarely spark such dramatic change. However, under the right circumstances, they can have dramatic effects and impacts—real and symbolic—that eventually make a large difference.

In another example, the floating wood, cardboard, and oil regularly burned on the Cuyahoga River as it came through Cleveland in the latter half of the nineteenth and first half of the twentieth century. One fire in 1952 lasted for three days and burned buildings, causing over 1.5 million dollars of damage. Only one of these fires caught the nation's attention, however—the one in 1969. It lasted for 30 minutes and was extinguished before a photograph could be taken. Yet the growing sentiment to protect the environment enabled that fire to become another powerful symbol of environmental neglect across the nation that helped to spur the United States' environmental movement.

In each of these examples, the conditions at the broad scale enabled small scale events to have broad impacts. Note also the role that mass media plays in these cross-scale linkages. Broad-scale impacts require broad-scale information exchange. In the examples here, that was largely achieved through newspapers, television, and radio, but as you will see later in this chapter (for example, Box 7.6), the Internet offers new opportunities for communicating with large audiences. These new pathways for communication will continue to play important roles in enabling people to understand small-scale events within a broader context.

Resilience in Social-Ecological Systems

In light of the constant change and inherent unpredictability of complex adaptive systems, Holling suggests that any definition of sustainability that involves maintaining a static set of ideal social, ecological, and economic conditions is bound to fail. For Holling, the key is to maintain the social-ecological system's ability to respond to change.[60] This ability is referred to as **resilience**. More specifically, we can define resilience as "the capacity of a system to absorb disturbance and reorganize while undergoing change so as to retain essentially the same function."[61] We might look at "function" here in terms of maintaining the broadest spectrum of life on this planet. Or more anthropocentrically, we might define it as high-quality ecosystem services, viable economic opportunities, and just distribution of benefits, costs, and risks inherent in those opportunities.

For many, a view of sustainability that embraces change may seem counterintuitive. When we hear of an impending large-scale change, our usual response is focused on avoiding it, maintaining the current conditions. But such a response can be misguided. As the Rosa Parks example illustrates, some changes are desirable, bringing about what many feel is an improvement over the former system, and even when the change is undesirable, it is often very difficult to avoid. Holling and other proponents of resilience have made careers out of identifying examples where efforts to avoid a collapse only succeeded in making the eventual collapse worse than it would have been originally.[62]

We can return to wildfires for an example of this. For most of the twentieth century, wildfire management in the United States was focused on suppressing fires to enable newly planted trees to grow, flourish, and replace the forests that were harvested in the late 1800s. Little attention was paid to the ecological role of fire in those ecosystems. Under this type of management, the forests did not experience the periods of release and reorganization in the form of fires. As a result, the dried forest debris, which was usually burned in relatively frequent fires, began to build up and denser vegetation developed in the understory (i.e., groundcover and shrubs that grow beneath the canopy of the taller trees).

In other words, more debris and a denser understory meant that more fuel was available when a fire did occur. Consequently, the resulting fires were much more intense and burned over larger areas. While that change may not be problematic, the fact that many of these forests contain human communities creates significant challenges for maintaining forest health and protecting human lives and structures. Current wildfire management now acknowledges the ecological role that fire plays and includes prescribed burns (i.e., planned periods of release) as a tool for management.

By allowing relatively minor collapses in the form of prescribed burns, forest managers are able to maintain a high level of resilience. The forests are able to undergo the periods of change without undergoing a shift to a completely different ecosystem. We can see the same logic in a political context in the form of term limits for politicians. For example, a president of the United States is allowed to serve only two terms. Some might question the wisdom of forcing someone who has been successful for eight years out of office, but this requisite change of power can be seen as a legislated period of rapid change. While some may point to particular cases in which the country might have been better served by allowing politicians to serve past term limits, in the long run the planned release in the form of a change of leadership enhances the resilience of the system.

Resilience and the Precautionary Principle

This goal of maintaining the resilience of a social-ecological system can provide new insight into the precautionary principle. From this perspective the precautionary principle is not simply a matter of always expecting and preparing for the worst, nor is it a prescription for passiveness in the face of potential dangers. Rather, it is a call to actively prepare for as yet unforeseen changes. Preparing for surprise may seem paradoxical. How does one prepare for something that, by definition, is unknown? In the systems language, preparation for surprise is strengthening the system's resilience.

One way to improve resilience is to maintain a high number of potential responses to change. This can be achieved by maintaining a high level of diversity. In a financial context, investors talk about maintaining a diversified portfolio. That way if one investment or set of investments fails, the others are likely to make up for the loss. There is a cost to this investment strategy. Placing all of one's resources into one investment that does well will produce a larger short-term return, but most investment analysts recommend the more diversified portfolio as having the biggest long-term payoff.

In terms of social-ecological systems, diversity can take a number of different forms. While a diverse investment portfolio might be applicable to a single person or household, a diversity of industries represents a parallel benefit at the level of a political community. A nation that is narrowly focused on one service or industry is overly susceptible to large changes within that industry.

The biological diversity of a social-ecological system is also important. Biological diversity can be measured on many different scales, including genetic diversity within a species, a diversity of species, and even a diversity of available habitats. The particular aspects of biological diversity that are important to a system may vary depending on the context. In any case, biological diversity will no doubt play a large role in a social-ecological system's resilience.

Social-economic systems also require political and social diversity. This means a diversity of people and perspectives playing a role in decision-making processes and a diversity of formal and informal institutions, including various levels of government along with groups of concerned citizens (e.g., NGOs, local community groups). Because social-ecological systems involve a multitude of interconnected CASs working at a wide range of spatial and temporal scale, no single perspective can be used to capture them completely. Therefore, the goal of developing an integrative framework for sustainability ethics does not imply deciding which perspective trumps the others, but rather appreciating how the various perspectives collectively provide a more encompassing picture of the issues at hand than any one of them could alone.

Resilience and Technology

From a resilience perspective, ethical analysis of technology must include an assessment of the likely impacts of the technology on the resilience of the social-ecological systems involved. Let us return to some of the examples we have covered so far to see how such an analysis works. We have discussed criticisms of our current system of industrial agriculture, which has created a fossil-fuel-based model in order to maximize production while minimizing the input of human labor. One result of this focus has been the replacement of small farms with an assortment of products by very large farms producing a limited number of crops.

In terms of resilience, this shift has resulted in a decrease in both social and ecological

diversity. In the small farm system, each farm acted as a separate experiment in which each farm owner could make choices about which crops to grow and how best to grow them. The point here is not that each farmer individually made wiser choices than are currently being made, but rather that on a regional level the small farms created a patchwork of approaches to food production (see Figure 7.4).[63]

One result of this kind of patchy agricultural landscape is that individual farm owners might have different responses to external disturbances to the social-ecological system. In other words, a diversity of farm owners operating in slightly (or perhaps significantly) different ways represents a variety of options available to respond to changing conditions in the social-ecological system. We might think of this as the agricultural equivalent of a diversified investment portfolio.

FIGURE 7.4 Small-scale farms are often more labor intensive than large-scale ones, but they are also more adaptable and able to manage more diverse crops.

In a biological context, one result of this variety is an increased level of biological diversity in the form of a variety of crops. On the scale of the individual farm, crop diversity represents the farm owner's diversified portfolio, and small farms' focus on human labor made the cost of this diversity relatively small. On a landscape level, crop preferences depend in part on farm owner preferences, so a diversity of farm owner preferences would tend to create a higher diversity of crops. This diversity means that pest populations are not able to balloon as easily because they do not have large expanses of their favorite food.

Where large farms all plant corn, in contrast, pesticide applications keep insects and disease at bay. The mechanized focus of industrial farms favors not only particular types of vegetables and fruits, but particular varieties as well. Those varieties that facilitate increased efficiency in harvesting and shipping tend to dominate the landscape. As a result, most consumers think of agricultural products like tomatoes and potatoes as rather limited categories including only a handful of varieties.[64] Many do not think of *banana* as having any varieties at all. The Cavendish banana—the one that dominates the commercial market—has come to represent a class of fruits that includes, by some counts, over a thousand varieties.

In short, the industrial agricultural system has been able to use fossil fuels to maximize the production of a limited number of crops. As a result of this increased production, Malthus's prediction of starvation because of populations increasing beyond the capacity of agricultural productivity has not come to pass. However, this increased production has come at the cost of lost social and ecological diversity at local and regional scales. Dependence on fossil fuels, a decrease in the number of participants within the industry, and an overreliance on a relatively small number of crops have resulted in low resilience in our dominant agricultural system.

In some cases, even technological goals promoted to address sustainability challenges can decrease resilience. We discussed earlier in this chapter the impending shift away from fossil fuels. Many see recent developments resulting in the improved fuel efficiency of cars as steps toward this goal. However, even the most ardent supporters of the fossil fuel industry acknowledge that fossil fuels are a limited resource—a stock resource to use Georgescu-Roegen's terminology from Chapter 6. While opinions may vary as to when this source will run out, no one denies the certainty of that event. Therefore, our fossil fuel-based economy will eventually have to shift to a different energy source.

In light of this impending change, increased efficiency in fossil fuel use cannot be seen as a solution to the problem. It is a response that postpones the inevitable period of change but does not prepare the social-ecological system for that change. In other words, there is a stark difference between using less fossil fuel per mile and using no fossil fuel per mile, and developments that achieve the former goal do not necessarily bring us closer to that latter. To the contrary, inasmuch as they encourage complacency regarding the shift away from fossil fuels, such increases in efficiency may work simply to make that shift more difficult.

BOX 7.5 Hard Tomatoes

In his text on the diffusion of innovation, Everett Rogers provides an example of unintended consequences from technological advances. He explains that prior to 1962, about 4,000 farmers in California—employing approximately 50,000 people—produced tomatoes. In that year, a mechanized harvester was introduced, greatly decreasing labor needs for harvesting tomatoes. Another change was in the tomato itself—the harvester required a harder tomato that could endure rough handling by the machine.

Within a decade, 99.9 percent of the tomatoes in California were being harvested mechanically. The decrease in labor needs meant a decrease in jobs for many farming communities. In addition, tomato growing shifted to areas of the state better suited for growing the harder tomatoes.

In addition, the cost of the machines meant that only large farms could afford to use them, giving them a competitive advantage over small farms. In light of these changes, critics of the mechanized harvester argued that "corporate agriculture's preoccupation with scientific and business efficiency has produced a radical restructuring of rural America" (Hightower 1972, p. 10).

The mechanized tomato harvester was developed by an agricultural engineer as a solution to an engineering problem. Therefore, the social and ecological implications of the solution may not have been fully considered, to say nothing of the taste of the harder tomato. This pattern of events has been repeated often with other crops as well and no doubt new agricultural innovations will continue. In assessing these innovations, we would do well to view them as more than engineering problems.

Conflicting Values

We have seen that couching challenges of sustainability in terms of the resilience of social-ecological systems can help us to focus on the connections that cross boundaries of the three-legged stool model. Moreover, the concept of resilience can facilitate the type of understanding required to consider a wide range of scales—that is, to think globally and act locally. This is not to say that the challenge of achieving sustainability comes without hard decisions involving conflicting values. When we acknowledge the validity of different moral claims, it is not always possible or even desirable to treat every claim the same. Thus, in a sustainability ethic that includes environmental, social, and economic values

across multiple scales, there are times and circumstances when one particular kind of value might be most important. The question is how to determine what is called for in a particular situation.

Here the work of economic ethicist Warren Copeland[65] is helpful. Copeland argues that we can value different qualities, such as equality, individual liberty, and social solidarity, while also emphasizing one of these values over others in a particular setting. It is not necessary to pick a single value over all others, and in fact philosophies that have only one foundational concern often become irrelevant in complex, changing settings. Copeland advocates first identifying the values of primary concern, then carefully analyzing the particular problem or situation to evaluate how these values are being enacted, or not, and how they might be better fulfilled. In any given situation, it is likely that one value is more fully developed than others, which means that principles of balance and compensation should be invoked. In concrete political terms, Copeland argues, we should advocate for whatever is most missing.

This sheds some light on efforts to balance and integrate diverse values in the ethics of sustainability. In analyzing a particular problem—involving, for example, a laboratory experiment, the construction of a building, or a public policy—we should first identify the values that are most important. Making the values at play—including shared values—explicit can help to facilitate discussion as to what extent each of these is being enacted and how it might be more fully implemented. This approach will not satisfy many environmental advocates, who want to prioritize the claims of nonhuman nature consistently. However, it is certainly possible to argue, in many situations, that ecological concerns receive much less effective attention than social and economic ones and, thus, according to Copeland's guidelines, should receive more attention in order to achieve better balance.

It is also important to note that some philosophers assert that their philosophical frameworks do take into account all important moral factors. Deep Ecologists, for example, would interpret economic, political, and social issues in light of their understanding of ecological interdependence, which makes all human problems by definition natural ones as well. Ecological interdependence is not only the primary value here but also the first and most important explanatory factor for other problems. Thus, there is no need to "balance" social, economic, and environmental concerns, since attending to ecological problems in the proper way will inevitably resolve other, secondary issues.

This single-minded approach is far from unique to Deep Ecologists. There are philosophers and activists who place their faith in the explanatory power of economic, racial, gender, or other dynamics and subordinate all other concerns to these. We do not need to decide or even debate these issues here, but merely to point out that for the ethics of sustainability, no single variable will suffice. Sustainability is not a single goal, and it cannot be understood in light of a single issue or achieved by attending to only one kind of problem. Much of the value of the resilience perspective comes from its focus on the need for multiple perspectives at a wide variety of scales. In the final section of this chapter, we explore concepts that address the need to incorporate these multiple perspectives.

THE DISTRIBUTION OF POWER IN DECISION MAKING

America's "father of conservation," Gifford Pinchot, spearheaded the creation of the U.S. Forest Service and was its first chief from 1905–1910. The agency was in charge of managing public lands newly established as national forests. It found itself battling the "boomers" and "land grabbers" of the day, men who plundered western lands for mineral wealth and timber. What Pinchot said about conservation at the turn of the century applies well to contemporary sustainability. Pinchot wrote:

> The central thing for which Conservation stands is to make this country the best possible place to live in, both for us and for our descendants. It stands against the waste of natural resources which cannot be renewed, such as coal and iron; it stands for the perpetuation of the resources which can be renewed, such as the food-producing soils and the forests; and most of all its stands for an equal opportunity for every American citizen to get his fair share of benefit from these resources, both now and hereafter. [66]

Conservation, Pinchot maintained, was a moral duty. It entailed the "application of common sense to the common problems for the common good," producing a "wise use of the earth," with the goal of attaining "the greatest good of the greatest number for the longest time."

Gifford Pinchot argued that conservation was an inherently democratic movement. The same might be said about sustainability—for two reasons. First, as recent empirical studies have demonstrated, democratic forms of deliberation and interaction tend to promote a future focus, an expanding sense of community, and holistic thinking, all of which dovetail nicely with sustainability values.[67] Second, the social justice facet of sustainability requires not only the equitable distribution of social benefits and risks but also the equitable sharing of power.

As the World Commission on Environment and Development observed, "the pursuit of sustainable development requires . . . a political system that secures effective citizen participation in decision making." [68] Of course, democracy is no panacea. To the extent democracy is tied to a hyper-individualistic consumer culture or to nationalistic commitments, it may thwart long-term, global sustainability. However, if we define democracy as the equitable distribution of political power such that citizens (or stakeholders of businesses, universities, or civic groups) become widely and meaningfully involved in the processes of deliberating and securing the common good, then democracy is indeed an inherent feature of sustainability. Governance, which is grounded in democratic principles and practices such as civil rights, the rule of law, open elections, and transparency, sustains environmental caretaking and social justice. [69]

The Principle of Transparency

In any democratic system, power is primarily held by representative bodies whose members are elected to office. In such systems, the principle of **transparency** is a crucial means of ensuring responsible governance. Transparency refers to the openness of decision-making processes to examination by the general public. Open parliamentary debate and open legislative (roll call) votes are key features of transparency in government, allowing the public to hear arguments in favor and against each piece of legislation and to know which elected representatives voted for or against it.

Transparency in governance goes beyond what happens on the floor of the legislature. It includes the public's right to know how legislators were influenced in their decision-making processes prior to debating and voting in the chambers of government, as well as the roles that businesses and NGOs play in lobbying legislators. Of course, legislators may be influenced by myriad people and events. There is no practicable way of keeping track of all these potential influences, or determining which of them proved particularly salient. However, many governments require their elected officials to keep formal logs of meetings. Perhaps more important, elected officials are often required to keep records of their meetings with professional lobbyists, and to disclose the names of donors to their (re)election campaign funds. The assumption here is that money often speaks with a particularly loud voice. Making the influence of professional lobbyists and campaign contributors public information is one of the more effective means of bringing transparency to government.

Transparency in governance aids citizens in their own decision-making processes. Citizens have a responsibility to elect the best candidates to office. Determining which candidate will make the best representative requires information. Knowing what candidates campaigning for reelection said in legislative session, how they voted, and whom they met with and received money from are crucial pieces of data to inform the discerning voter.

Transparency in Industry

Likewise, transparency in business corporations is a crucial means for consumers concerned with sustainability to inform their own decision-making processes. In this case, the data do not help the public decide between competing candidates in open and free elections. Rather, they help the public decide between competing products or investments in an open and free market. The idea is that consumers have a right to know if the products they buy have social and environmental impacts on their local communities and on the planet. Several strategies have been deployed to increase transparency through the adoption of **Corporate Social Responsibility**. However, if the public does not trust a corporation, no amount of transparency will help it communicate its products' advantages. In this case, outside certification systems have been developed to offer a credible guarantee of the information the corporation has provided.

In the late 1970s, a step was taken toward such transparency in business with the creation in Germany of the "Blue Angel" environmental label. The Blue Angel organization gave their seal of approval to those products that had minimal environmental impact. Effectively, consumers could now see deeper into products and businesses. A decade later, the "Green Seal" program was initiated in the United States.[70] To earn the Green Seal, a product must meet certain environmental standards set out by the organization that tests the products, employing scientific methods. Since the mid-1990s, a conglomeration of 25 organizations, including Green Seal, formed the Global Ecolabelling Network (GEN) to promote and improve environmental performance monitoring and labeling across the globe, allowing consumers to distinguish brands by their environmental impacts.

Ecolabeling is not the only means to improve a company's effort to achieve transparency. A number of organizations evaluate and rate products in the marketplace, employing social and environmental criteria and provide this information to the public on websites. Effectively, they provide the sustainability equivalent of *Consumer Reports*. These evaluation and rating organizations, such as Goodguide,[71] rank products and companies based on their health risks, environmental performance, and social impact. Although no labels actually appear on the products they evaluate, greater trust is gained through the information they provide, allowing sustainability-oriented consumers to make better-informed choices. Shoppers today appreciate the federally mandated labeling that displays the ingredients as well as fat, protein, sodium, and caloric content of packaged foods. Ecolabeling and rating services attempt to provide similar transparency regarding the environmental and social impacts of many of the other things we buy.

The origins of environmental transparency stem not from the assessment of the environmental impact of purchased goods, but rather from the assessment of risks. As you saw in Chapter 4, Rachel Carson's investigation of the effects of chemicals on local ecologies stimulated "Right to Know" legislation that created greater transparency in the production and release of toxic chemicals. This information allowed workers and residents to become more informed about the safety of their workplaces and neighborhoods. By

extending our "right to know" from the category of toxic chemicals to a broad range of social and environmental impacts of goods in the marketplace, ecolabeling and environmental rating services provide consumers with the means to evaluate the sustainability of their purchases.

In an economically interdependent world, where consumers enter a global marketplace, transparency is crucial. The purchaser of a steak or hamburger in New York may not realize that the cattle that produced his meat were nourished with feed exported from soybean plantations in Brazil, plantations that have destroyed millions of acres of rainforest. The consumer of doughnuts in Los Angeles may not realize that her product contains palm oil from plantations in Malaysia and Indonesia that have leveled rainforests in these tropical lands, destroying vital habitat for millions of species and contributing to global warming. Likewise, consumers of wheat, corn and soybeans grown across the MidWest may not realize their contribution to the growing Dead Zone in the Gulf of Mexico because of fertilizer-laden sediment and pesticides that are regularly washed down the Mississippi River.

In all of these cases, products designed to satisfy the needs and wants of distant consumers have had the effect of decreasing biodiversity, contributing to climate change, or undermining the sustainable livelihoods of local subsistence hunters, gatherers, small farmers, and fishermen. All of these processes contribute to a decrease in the resilience of social-ecological systems at several scales. The chief threat to global sustainability, with this in mind, is not only or even primarily the very visible overuse of resources by the growing populations of developing countries, but the ever increasing demand for resources by nonlocal consumers, primarily from developed countries.[72] Providing these consumers with usable information about the products they buy is crucial to the development of a sustainable global marketplace.

Transparency and Technology

Francis Bacon, the seventeenth-century polymath, famously said that "Knowledge is power." The principle of transparency is one of the central features of the more encompassing ethical obligation of sharing power. Transparency in business affairs entails sharing knowledge of the components or ingredients of products and services, and the social and environmental costs and risks associated with their production, distribution, use, and disposal. This puts more power in the hands of consumers, workers, and residents who can make environmentally and socially informed decisions about what they purchase, where they work, and where they live.

Knowledge is power. More data and information do not always translate into more knowledge, however. For example, many consumers do not understand the health or environmental implications of the various ingredients listed on their packaged foods. To complicate matters, much of today's technology—whether provided through agricultural services, medical and pharmaceutical services, media services, industrial and construction services, or military services—remains several steps removed from the consumer. The consumer of services may never become aware of the technology employed to conduct tests on her blood, the pesticides used in growing her food, the resources involved in making the films and Internet websites she enjoys, the machines and components that produce her appliances, or the craft and weaponry developed to outfit the armed forces mandated to protect her. Yet all of this technology has social and environmental impacts. More often than not, the technology is so sophisticated that consumers would not be able to evaluate the data describing it even if it were made available.

Certainly government has a role to play in assessing the social and environmental impact and risks of technology. There are, in turn, various NGOs, many of which serve as "watchdog" groups, which have taken on this task. The Union of Concerned Scientists, for instance, with over 250,000 members, is a leading science-based NGO working in the sustainability field. Its founding statement, issued in 1969, contained these words:

> The vastly increased importance and complexity of technology has, in effect, increased the ignorance of the public and its elected representatives. . . . Only the scientific community can provide a comprehensive and searching evaluation of the capabilities and implications of advanced military technologies. Only the scientific community can estimate the long-term global impact of an industrialized society on our environment. Only the scientific community can attempt to forecast the technology

that will surely emerge from the current revolution in the fundamentals of biology. The scientific community . . . must engage effectively in planning for the future of mankind, a future free of deprivation and fear. . . . Far-reaching political decisions involving substantial applications of technology are made with virtually no popular participation. It is our belief that a strengthening of the democratic process would lead to a more humane exploitation of scientific and technical knowledge, and to a reduction of the very real threats to the survival of mankind.[73]

Today the Union of Concerned Scientists focuses on making transparent the benefits and risks of technological developments, government policy, demographic change, and consumer patterns related to energy production, transportation, security, agriculture, wildlife conservation, and climate change. Arguably, those who have benefited from higher levels of expertise, such as scientists and technical professions, have a heightened responsibility to assess, evaluate, and disseminate the social and environmental impacts and risks posed by technology.

The Value of Autonomy

The principle of transparency is grounded in the assumption that all who potentially bear the risks associated with the development and use of technological innovations and processes, products, and services have a right to be informed of these risks and involved in evaluating their acceptance or rejection. Arguably, government agencies mandated with

evaluating such risks should include or seek counsel from representative bodies involving multiple stakeholders—independent scientists and business representatives, as well as consumer and citizen advocacy groups. If the monitoring agencies find that the risk involved is too high, products should not be allowed to be sold. When the risk involved is within acceptable limits, the product may be made available for purchase. In such cases, transparency still demands that the level and nature of the risk be made patent, so that individual consumers may exercise their autonomy in deciding for themselves if this is a risk they are willing to bear.

What happens in cases where risks are not restricted to those consumers who purchase the new technology, product, or service? When, if ever, is it legitimate for an individual or agency to foist risks on a wide range of consumers or citizens without their awareness or consent, effectively stripping away their right to choose for themselves? In Box 7.2, we touched on this concern regarding the issue of the genetic engineering of humans. The autonomy of parents to refuse the technology was limited in such cases by what might be considered market forces, but this autonomy was not wholly denied. There are many examples, however, where the autonomy of stakeholders to refuse new technology and products, and the risks associated with them, is denied.

Consider the case of genetically modified crops. The United States currently produces more than half of all the genetically modified crops in the world, with soybeans and corn engineered to be resistant to herbicides

BOX 7.6   Technology and Transparency

Technology now offers numerous ways to increase transparency. In 2007 after a disputed general election in Kenya, ethnic violence broke out all over the countryside. Approximately 1,500 people were killed, but at the time incidents of violence were underreported because the Kenyan government put a ban on live-media reporting. In response, Kenyan blogger Ory Okolloh, who was then living in South Africa, began posting reports of violence sent to her from NGO's and contacts within the government. She posted contact information on her website and called for readers to report the violence they were witnessing.

Soon she was overrun with reports, so she asked if there were any programmers among her readers who could develop software to help her manage all the information coming in. A few of her readers were Kenyan programmers living abroad. Within days, they developed a website called Ushahidi, Swahili for "testimony," which allows reports of violence sent through emails or text messages to be recorded and posted on a Google map. Powered by this user-friendly software, Ushahidi allows people in remote areas to send reports using computers or cell phones.

The problem was not that nobody knew about the violence, but that those who were witnessing violence knew only about what was happening in their immediate area. The solution was crowd-sourcing information. People from all around Kenya could photograph or describe the violence on their cell phones. Those reports could be verified with the help of international press, NGOs, or government employees and then compiled in a way that allowed people to see the bigger picture. Not only did the site help to document the events both for the international community and for Kenyans themselves, but it also became a tool to coordinate efforts to respond to the needs of Kenyan's affected by the violence.

After its success in Kenya, the software developers continue to design "tools for democratizing information, increasing transparency and lowering the barriers for individuals to share their stories" (www.ushahidi.com). These tools have been used in numerous other situations, including tracking political campaigns in Columbia and Brazil, as well as from Haiti after the 2010 earthquake and from around the Gulf of Mexico following the BP oil spill.

These applications may indicate a larger trend. It is not difficult to envision other applications in which transparency would be enhanced by compiling widely diffused information in a useful way. Customer reviews offered by online retail sites provide an example. When purchasing a product online, an individual often has access to information provided by, in some cases, thousands of previous customers. This feature has primarily been used to assure potential customers that the retailers are responsible and will stand by the products or services they provide, but there is also the possibility of using these types of tools to compile information about the social and environmental impacts that specific corporations and manufacturers have around the globe.

composing the largest portion of this total. Up to 75 percent of all processed foods in the United States contain a genetically modified ingredient.[74] There is significant scientific research indicating that genetically modified organisms (GMOs) are safe to eat. However, concerns remain about possible allergens and other safety issues for consumers.

In addition, since many of the plants that are engineered are modified to be more resistant to herbicides or pesticides, it is possible that GMOs will have the effect of increasing the use of these chemicals, which will have unanticipated and undesirable environmental effects. For example, there are concerns that gene transfers may occur between GMOs and weeds, making the latter more resistant to biocides. Gene transfers may also affect other organisms. For example, monarch butterflies appear to be harmed by the pollen from genetically modified corn that incorporates Bt, a soil bacterium that produces a protein that is toxic to the European corn borer. Finally, genetically modified crops may prove too expensive for many farmers in developing countries, potentially undermining their pursuit of sustainable livelihoods. Often farmers are not allowed to save viable seed from GMO crops, but must purchase new seed every year.[75]

In short, there are comparative risks associated with GMOs. In the face of such risks, is it possible for consumers and farmers to refuse GMOs? Can they exercise their autonomy by effectively opting out of this technology?

First, it is important to recognize that in the United States (unlike many European countries), food that contains GMOs is not required to have any special labeling. This violates the principle of transparency. Yet there is more at stake. Genetically modified crops may cross-pollinate with regular crops. If and when this occurs, farmers of non-genetically-modified crops and consumers who wish to eat only non-genetically-modified foods have no effective way of ensuring that what they produce or consume is indeed free of GMOs.

In the same vein, people who try to limit their own use of fossil fuel still have to bear the effects of climate change. People who may choose not to benefit from nanotechnology will still face the risks of "grey goo" if self-replicating nanobots get out of control. In these cases, and many more, the ethics of sustainability confronts us with the obligation not only to ensure transparency, but to safeguard, to the greatest extent possible, the rights of individuals and groups to opt out of technologies whose costs and risks they are unwilling to bear.

From a resilience perspective, technological developments with such broad influence effectively eliminate the possibility of making choices at individual or even regional scales. The pursuit of sustainability does not require that we eliminate risks, but that we maintain the ability to respond to unforeseen changes at a wide range of scales. This requires, to the greatest extent possible, that individuals retain the autonomy to determine, in the light of information made available through transparent processes, which risks they choose to bear.

CONCLUSION

Two millennia before Garret Hardin penned "The Tragedy of the Commons," Aristotle wrote in *The Politics:* "That which is common to the greatest number has the least care bestowed upon it. Everyone thinks chiefly of his own, hardly at all of the common interest."[76] Protecting a commons—including the global commons stretching into the distant future—will never be easy. Shortsightedness and self-interest make sustaining of public goods a hefty challenge.

Can we forego the effort to pursue social justice, reject ecological imperatives, and simply deny the reality of a global community? Kofi Annan, Secretary-General of the United Nations, addressed the World Summit on Sustainable Development in Johannesburg, South Africa, in 2002 with these words:

> A path to prosperity that ravages the environment and leaves a majority of humankind behind in squalor will soon prove to be a dead-end road for everyone.... Unsustainable practices are woven deeply into the fabric of modern life. Some say we should rip up that fabric... I say we can and must weave in new strands of knowledge and cooperation.[77]

Annan insists that sustainability and social justice are not quixotic ideals. They are not even possibilities among other options. Rather, they are necessities for survival. Knowledge and cooperation are the means to their pursuit.

At times, knowledge and cooperation may produce new national and international treaties, protocols, agreements, policies, and laws that promote sustainable development through legally and politically enforceable means. At times, knowledge and cooperation may produce new businesses and products that foster sustainable development by employing the market to deliver green technology. At times, knowledge and cooperation may produce voluntary associations of NGOs working to foster sustainable livelihoods. At times, knowledge and cooperation may produce new relationships and efforts to realize sustainable development through institutions of democratic decision-making, power-sharing, education, and self-governance.

In this chapter, we began integrating the dimensions of sustainability ethics by exploring the precautionary principle and how it can inform ethical decisions in social, ecological, and economic contexts. We then investigated Hardin's claims regarding the inherent conflict between social and ecological goals, and we found that while the challenge of sustainability is not without conflict, attempting to isolate problems as purely social, purely ecological, or purely economic is not a helpful strategy. We discussed the concept of social-ecological resilience as a tool for integrating various perspectives across a wide range of scales, emphasizing the role that transparency and autonomy must play in maintaining a range of responses to unforeseen changes.

Although the resilience perspective is a useful tool for integration, like the three-legged stool model, it is only a tool. We closed the first section of this chapter with the observation that care and concern do not stem from logical roots. The resilience perspective can help us to understand the consequences of our actions within a web of complex adaptive systems, but it cannot make us care. And regardless of the framework we use, the extension of care will be an essential aspect of making the difficult decisions that the pursuit of sustainability presents.

Slavery was once considered, at least by those in power, to be a natural and unavoidable institution. It had been practiced since the dawn of civilization in ancient Sumer, Assyria, Egypt, and Greece and was assumed to be an indispensable means of economic survival and the inevitable product of human nature. Slavery was a part of life in Britain since prehistory, from before the time of the Roman invasion. As its empire grew in the 1700s, Britain had established the largest slave trade of any country in the world. Then, quite abruptly in the early 1800s, Britain outlawed slavery throughout its dominion, owing in large part to efforts of abolitionists, who viewed slavery as inherently immoral and unjust and who argued their position effectively, both through nongovernmental organizations and other forums.

While those who opposed the end of slavery argued that it would signal the end of British economic might and global power, history turned out quite differently. Within decades of the outlawing of slavery, Britain's industrial revolution came into full force, providing an engine for its growth and the development of the largest empire the world has ever known. The British Empire, of course, was not a model of perfect justice. Still, its fullest economic development was realized not by abiding age-old injustices, but in the wake of visionary efforts to end a moral outrage. The sustainability movement might look to the end of slavery as a demonstration of the power of ethical resolve over ancient prejudice. It might argue, with the abolitionist movement as its exemplar, that the pursuit of sustainability within the context of a global community will not be the harbinger of decline but the catalyst of greater prosperity.

REFERENCES

Agyeman, Julian. 2005. *Sustainable Communities and the Challenge of Environmental Justice.* New York: New York University Press.

Agyeman, Julian, Robert Bullard, and Bob Evans. 2003. "Towards Just Sustainabilities: Perspectives and Possibilities." In Julian Agyeman, Robert Bullard, and Bob Evans, Eds. *Just Sustainabilities: Development in an Unequal World.* Cambridge, MA: MIT Press.

Anderson, Ida-Elisabeth and Birgit Jæger. 1999. "Danish Participatory Models." *Science and Public Policy* 26 (5): 331–340.

Aristotle. 1996. *The Politics and The Constitution of Athens.* Cambridge, UK: Cambridge University Press.

Arnold, JEM. 1998. *Managing Forests as a Common Property.* Rome, Italy: Food and Agricultural Organization.

Athanasiou, Tom. 1996. *Divided Planet: The Ecology of Rich and Poor.* Boston: Little, Brown.

Barry, John. 1996. "Sustainability, Political Judgment and Citizenship: Connecting Green Politics and Democracy." In Brian Doherty and Marius de Geus, Eds. *Democracy and Green Political Thought.* London: Routledge.

Benedick, Richard Elliot. 1993. "Equity and Ethics in a Global Climate Convention." In Theodore Goldfarb, Ed. *Taking Sides: Clashing Views on Controversial Environmental Issues*, 5th ed., Guilford, CT: Dushkin Publishing, pp. 306–314.

Berry, Wendell. 1987. *Home Economics.* San Francisco: North Point Press.

————. 1996. *The Unsettling of America: Culture and Agriculture.* Washington, DC: Sierra Club Books.

Bhalla, Surjit S. 2002. *Imagine There's No Country: Poverty, Inequality, and Growth in the Era of Globalization.* Washington, DC: Institute for International Economics.

Bodansky, Daniel, Ed. 2002. *Evolution and Status of the Precautionary Principle in International Law.* The Hague: Kluwer International Law.

Bornstein, David. 2004. *How to Change the World: Social Entrepreneurs and the Power of New Ideas.* New York: Oxford University Press.

Brown, Lester R. 2009. *Plan B 4.0: Mobilizing to Save Civilization.* New York: W.W. Norton.

Bullard, Robert, Ed. 1994. *Unequal Protection: Environmental Justice and Communities of Color.* New York: Random House.

Burger, Joanna, Elinor Ostrom, Richard Norgaard, David Policansky, and Bernard Goldstein. 2001. *Protecting the Commons.* Washington, DC: Island Press.

Chhatre, Ashwini and Arun Agrawal. 2009. "Trade-offs and Synergies Between Carbon Storage and Livelihood Benefits from Forest Commons." *Proceedings of the National Academy of Sciences.* 106(42):17667–17670.

Colborn, Theo, Diane Dumanoski, and John Peterson Myers. 1996. *Our Stolen Future.* New York: Dutton Books.

Copeland, Warren. 1988. *Economic Justice.* Nashville: Abingdon Press.

Cordes, Collen, Evan Crutcher, and Rick Worthington. 2003. *Citizen Panels and Technological Decisions.* Loka Institute.

Costanza, Robert. "Three General Policies to Achieve Sustainability." In A. Jansson, M. Hammer, C. Folke and R. Costanza, Eds. *Investing in Natural Capital: The Ecological Economics Approach to Sustainability.* Washington, DC: Island Press, pp. 392–407.

Cox, Susan Jane Buck. 1985. "No Tragedy on the Commons." *Environmental Ethics* 7: 49–61.

Creative Commons. "History." 12 July 2010. http://creativecommons.org/about/history/.

Daly, H. E. and J. B. Cobb, Jr. 1994. *For the Common Good: Redirecting the Economy toward Community, the Environment, and a Sustainable Future.* 2nd ed. Boston: Beacon Press.

Deslarzes, Luc P. 1993. "Strategic Elements of the WWF Environmental Education Programme for the 1990s." In Hartmut Schneider, Ed. *Environmental Education: An Approach to Sustainable Development.* Paris: Organization for Economic Co-operation and Development.

Diamond, Jared. 2005. *Collapse: How Societies Choose to Fail or Succeed.* New York: Viking Press.

Dietz, Thomas, Elinor Ostrom, and Paul Stern. 2003. "The struggle to govern the commons." *Science* 302(5632): 1907–1912.

Feeny, David, Fikret Berkes, Bonnie J. McCay, and James M. Acheson. 1990. "The Tragedy of the Commons: Twenty-two Years Later." *Human Ecology* 18: 1–19.

Food and Agricultural Organization of the United Nations (FAO). 1996. *The State of the World's Plant Genetic Resources for Food and Agriculture.* http://apps3.fao.org/wiews/docs/swrfull.pdf.

Freestone, David, and Ellen Hey. 1996. *The Precautionary Principle and International Law: The Challenge of Implementation.* The Hague: Kluwer Law International.

Glover, Jonathan. 2000. *Humanity: A Moral History of the Twentieth Century.* New Haven: Yale University Press.

Guha, Ramachandra. 1994. "Radical Environmentalism: A Third-World Critique." In Carolyn Merchant, Ed. *Ecology: Key Concepts in Critical Theory.* Atlantic Highlands, NJ: Humanities Press.

Gundersen, Adolf G. 1995. *The Environmental Promise of Democratic Deliberation.* Madison, WI: University of Wisconsin Press.

Gunderson, L. and C. S. Holling. 2002. *Panarchy: Understanding Transformations in Human and Natural Systems.* Washington, DC: Island Press.

Gunderson, L., C. S. Holling, and S. S. Light, Eds. 1995. *Barriers and Bridges to the Renewal of Ecosystems and Institutions.* New York: Columbia University Press.

H&M. Environment. H&M. www.hm.com/gb/corporateresponsibility/environment_environment.nhtml.

Hardin, Garrett. 1977. *The Limits of Altruism: An Ecologist's View of Survival.* Bloomington, IN: Indiana University Press.

———. 2007. "Living on a Lifeboat." In Thomas Mappes and Jane Zembaty, Eds. *Social Ethics.* New York: McGraw-Hill. Originally published in Bioscience (1974), pp. 443–449.

———. 1993. *Living Within Limits: Ecology, Economics, and Population Taboos.* New York: Oxford University Press.

———. 1968. "The Tragedy of the Commons." *Science* 162: 1243–1248.

Hawken, Paul. 2007. *Blessed Unrest: How the Largest Movement in the World Came into Being and Why No One Saw It Coming.* New York: Viking.

Hawken, Paul, Amory Lovins, and Hunter L. Lovins. 2000. *Natural Capitalism.* New York: Little, Brown and Company.

Heilbroner, Robert L. 1981. "What has Posterity Ever Done for Me?" In Ernest Partridge, Ed.

Responsibilities to Future Generations. Buffalo, NY: Prometheus Books, pp. 191–202.

Hightower, Jim. 1972. "Hard tomatoes, hard times: Failure of the land grant college complex." *Humanities, Social Sciences and Law* 10(1): 10–22.

Holling, C. S. 2000. "Theories for sustainable futures." *Conservation Ecology* 4(2).

———. 2008. "Forward: The backloop of sustainability." In F Berkes, J. Colding, and C. Folked, Ed. *Navigating Social-Ecological Systems: Building Resilience for Complexity and Change.* Cambridge: Cambridge University Press.

Investor Environmental Health Network. Corporate Policies and Case Studies. Investor Environmental Health Network. www.iehn.org/tools.corporate.sampling.php.

Kaplinsky, Raphael. 2005. *Globalization, Poverty, and Inequality.* Cambridge: Policy Press.

Leisher, Craig, Pieter van Beukering, and Lea M. Scherl. 2008. "Nature's Investment Bank: How Do Marine Protected Areas Contribute to Poverty Reduction." The Nature Conservancy. www.nature.org/initiatives/protectedareas/files/mpa_report.pdf.

MacNeill, Jim, Pieter Winsemius, and Taizo Yakushiji. 1991. *Beyond Interdependence: The Meshing of the World's Economy and the Earth's Ecology.* New York: Oxford University Press.

Martinez-Alier, J. 1991. "Environmental Policy and Distributional Conflicts." In Robert Constanza, Ed. *Ecological Economics.* New York: Columbia University Press.

May, J. M. and J. Wisse, trans. 2001. *Cicero on the Ideal Orator (De Oratore).* Oxford: Oxford University Press.

Mayhew, A. 1985. "Dangers in Using the Idea of Property Rights: Modern Property Rights Theory and the Neoclassical Trap." *Journal of Economic Issues* 19: 959–966.

McKibben, Bill. 2003. *Enough: Staying Human in an Engineered Age*. New York: Henry Holt.

National Wildlife Federation Newsletter. 1994. August-September.

Nature Conservancy. 1994. May/June.

———. 1996. July/August.

———. 1997. March/April.

Norberg, J., J. Wilson, B. Walker, and E. Ostrom. 2008. "Diversity and resilience of social-ecological systems" In. Norberg and G.S. Cumming, Eds. *Complexity Theory for a Sustainable Future*J. New York: Columbia University Press.

Norgaard, Richard B. 1994. *Development Betrayed: The End of Progress and a Coevolutionary Revisioning of the Future*. London: Routledge.

O'Riordan, T. and J. Cameron. 1996. *Interpreting the Precautionary Principle*. London: Earthscan Publishers.

Ostrom, Elinor. 1990. *Governing the Commons: The Evolution of Institutions for Collective Action*. Cambridge: Cambridge University Press.

Ostrom, Elinor, James Walker, and Roy Gardner,. 1994. *Rules, Games, and Common-Pool Resources*. Ann Arbor, MI: University of Michigan Press.

Ostrom, Elinor, Joanna Burger, Christopher Field, Richard Norgaard, and David Policansky. 1999. "Revisiting the commons: Local lessons, global challenges. *Science* 284(5412): 278–282.

Pinchot, Gifford. 1910. *The Fight for Conservation*. New York: Doubleday, Page and Company.

The President's Council on Sustainable Development. 1999. "Towards a Sustainable America: Advancing Prosperity, Opportunity, and a Healthy Environment for the 21st Century." Accessed at http://clinton4.nara.gov/PCSD/Publications/index.html.

Qaim, Matin. 2005. "Agricultural Biotechnology Adoption in Developing Countries." *American Journal of Agricultural Economics* 87: 1317–1324.

Sawhill, John. 1998. "President's Report." *Nature Conservancy*. January/February.

Schmidheiny, Stephen. 1992. *Changing Course: A Global Business Perspective on Development and the Environment*. Cambridge: MIT Press.

Schumacher, E. F. 1973. *Small Is Beautiful: Economics as If People Mattered*. New York: Harper and Row.

Segger, Marie-Claire Cordonier and C. G. Weeramantry, eds. 2005. *Sustainable Justice*. The Netherlands: Martinus Nijhoff.

Shaffer, Mark. 1992. *Beyond the Endangered Species Act: Conservation in the 21st Century*. Washington, DC: The Wilderness Society.

Shiva, Vandana. 2005. *Earth Democracy: Justice, Sustainability, and Peace*. Cambridge: South End Press.

Shrader-Frechette, Kristin. 2002. *Environmental Justice: Creating Equality, Reclaiming Democracy*. Oxford: Oxford University Press.

———. 1985. *Science Policy, Ethics, and Economic Methodology: Some Problems of Technology Assessment and Environmental-Impact Analysis*. Boston: D. Reidel Publishing.

Shiva, Vandana. 2005. *Earth Democracy: Justice, Sustainability, and Peace*. Cambridge: South End Press.

Sunstein, Cass. 2005. *Laws of Fear: Beyond the Precautionary Principle*. Cambridge: Cambridge University Press.

Trouwborst, Arie. 2002. *Evolution and Status of the Precautionary Principle in International Law.* The Hague: Kluwer Law International.

UNEP. 1992. "Rio Declaration on Environment and Development." Accessed at www.unep.org/Documents.multilingual/Default.asp?DocumentID=78&ArticleID=1163.

Union of Concerned Scientists. 2009. "Founding Statement (1969) of the Union of Concerned Scientists." *Catalyst* Spring.

Wachbroit, Robert. 1997. "Genetic Encores: The Ethics of Human Cloning. "In *Report From the Institute of Philosophy and Public Policy.* College Park: University of Maryland.

Weeks, W. William. 1997. *Beyond the Ark: Tools for an Ecosystem Approach to Conservation.* Washington, D.C.: Island Press.

Wenz, Peter. 2007. "Does Environmentalism Promote Injustice for the Poor?" In Ronald Sandler and Phaedra Pezzulo. *Environmental Justice and Environmentalism: The Social Justice Challenge to the Environmental Movement.* Cambridge: MIT Press.

Wingspread Statement. 1998. Accessed at: www.sehn.org/wing.html.

World Commission on Environment and Development. 1987. *Our Common Future.* Oxford: Oxford University Press.

———. 2005. *The Precautionary Principle.* Paris: UNESCO.

World Wildlife Fund. 1994. "1993 Annual Report." *Focus* 16: 1–2.

Yoder, Robert. 1994. *Locally Managed Irrigation Systems: Essential Tasks and Implications for Assistance, Management Transfer and Turnover Programs.* Colombo: International Water Management Institute.

ENDNOTES

1. Holling (2000).
2. May and Wisse (2001).
3. The text of the NEPA can be found at: http://ceq.hss.doe.gov/nepa/regs/nepa/nepaeqia.htm.
4. Trouwborst (2002).
5. For a history of the precautionary principle, see Bodansky (2002). See also the 1987 London Declaration regarding the protection of the North Sea, which can be accessed at www.seas-at-risk.org/1mages/1987%20London%20Declaration.pdf.
6. UNEP (1992).
7. The President's Council on Sustainable Development (1999).
8. Wingspread Statement (1998).
9. Quoted in MacNeill et al. (1991).
10. For a comprehensive account of the principle's implementation up to 2002, see Bodansky (2002).
11. From H&M.
12. From Investor Environmental Health Network.
13. See Freestone and Hey (1996).
14. World Commission on the Ethics of Scientific Knowledge and Technology (2005).
15. Sunstein (2005).
16. Shrader-Frechette (1985).
17. Shaffer (1992).
18. World Commission on the Ethics of Scientific Knowledge and Technology (2005).
19. Shrader-Frechette (1985).
20. See Colborn et al. (1996).
21. Norgaard (1994).
22. Benedick (1993).
23. For a discussion of the "proactionary principle," see www.maxmore.com/proactionary.htm.
24. Costanza (1994).
25. Glover (2000).
26. Hardin (2007).

27. Hardin (1968).
28. Hardin (1968).
29. Berry (1987).
30. Shiva (2005).
31. World Commission on Environment and Development (1987).
32. Berry (1996).
33. Agyeman et al. (2003).
34. See Brown (2009).
35. Wenz (2007).
36. Agyeman (2005).
37. Quoted in Schmidheiny (1992).
38. Guha (1994).
39. See Deslarzes (1993), p. 116; See also Weeks (1997).
40. Cox (1985); Feeny et al. (1990); Ostrom (1990).
41. Martinez-Alier (1991); Mayhew (1985).
42. Hardin (1968).
43. Of course, this sense of fairness may play a lesser role when, for example, someone yells "fire" in a crowded building.
44. See Ostrom et al. (1999); Yoder (1994).
45. Ostrom et al. (1999); Dietz et al. (2003).
46. Although Ostrom is a political scientist, she was awarded the Nobel Memorial Prize in Economic Sciences with Oliver E Williamson. She is the first woman to win a Nobel in this category. See also, Ostrom (1990) and Ostrom et al. (1994).
47. See Ostrom (1990); Burger et al. (2001).
48. Dietz et al. (2003).
49. World Commission on Environment and Development (1987).
50. Hawken (2007).
51. Bornstein (2004).
52. Quoted in Deslarzes (1993); World Wildlife Fund (1994).
53. Nature Conservancy (1994), p. 5; Nature Conservancy (1997), p. 14. See also Weeks (1997).
54. Sawhill (1998).
55. Nature Conservancy (1996).
56. This term is not intended to downplay the importance of economic issues. The term "social-ecological system" was intended to integrate human systems (which include both social and economic systems) into the larger context of environmental systems. In other words, the "social" part of the term refers to those issues within the social and the economic legs of sustainability.
57. Gunderson and Holling (2002).
58. Holling (2008).
59. Part of the context for change occurred as a result of careful planning and organization by civil rights organizations, and in particular the NAACP (National Association for the Advancement of Colored People). At the time of her action, Parks served as secretary of the Montgomery branch of the NAACP.
60. Holling (2000).
61. Norberg et al. (2008).
62. See, for example, Gunderson et al. (1995).
63. This is not to say that a variety of farmers guarantees diverse methods. The Dust Bowl of the 1930s is an example where farming methods were adopted regionally that did not acknowledge local soil and climate conditions, creating a regional crisis.
64. According to a 1996 FAO report, The State of the World's Plant Genetic Resources for Food and Agriculture, 86 percent of the apple varieties documented as in use in the United States between 1804 and 1904 have been lost, as well as 95 percent of the cabbage, 91 percent of the field maize, and 81 percent of the tomato varieties.
65. Copeland (1988).
66. Pinchot (1910).
67. Gundersen (1995). See also Barry (1996).
68. World Commission on Environment and Development (1987), p. 65.
69. See the Sustainable Governance Indicators developed by the Organization for Economic Co-operation and Development, accessed at www.sgi-network.org/.

70. See www.greenseal.org/.
71. See www.goodguide.com.
72. See Shiva (2005).
73. Union of Concerned Scientists (2009).
74. See the U.S. Department of Agriculture website on biotechnology at www.ers.usda.gov/briefing/biotechnology/.
75. For a good overview of the controversies surrounding GMOs, see www.csa.com/discoveryguides/gmfood/overview.php. See also Qaim (2005).
76. Aristotle (1996). p. 33.
77. Quoted in Segger and Weeramantry (2005).

CHAPTER 8

Improving Our Thinking about Sustainability

As the first chapters suggest, we are at a turning point. The modern, conventional models of economic development and business have catapulted many nations out of agricultural subsistence and into the luxury of industrial production and consumption. However, new agricultural and industrial processes take advantage of available resources with little regard for ecosystem limits of extraction and nutrient cycling or human rights. While we have generated an incredible variety of technologies to facilitate our life on earth, we do not have a very strong record of distinguishing "good" technology from "bad."

No one sets out to make a bad decision, of course. The tobacco industry enabled many small landowners in the Appalachian foothills to scratch out a living and build themselves and their stockholders a fortune by creating a highly desirable product. The Aswan Dam held the promise of better control of Nile floodwaters for irrigation during drought. In hindsight, both cigarettes and large-scale dams have created unforeseen problems that suggest that they were not ideal decisions, at least not in the long term. We might chalk these examples up to lessons learned—

mistakes made out of ignorance or oversight. However, the litany of disasters and current problems suggests that we do not have a good system of vetting proposed products or taking into account both the factors that must be considered and the level of uncertainty that hides unknown consequences.

While each example of new technology or development might provide a specific lesson (e.g., smoking decreases public health and large dams alter ecosystem processes), the more general lesson we want to emphasize focuses on the decision process itself. In Chapters 8, 9, and 10, we explore the process of decision making, identifying tendencies that lead to poor decisions and ways in which we might increase our ability—as individuals and as a society—to make better and more ethical decisions with respect to sustainability.

In this chapter, we begin this discussion by looking at the how people perceive and process information. There is no doubt that information is essential to good decisions about sustainability. There is evidence that we have trouble sharing and understanding the information. It may be important to conquer that hurdle before we attempt to share and understand ethical perspectives. Both challenges affect tendencies that often lead us to make ill-advised choices. The second half of this chapter focuses on ways that people can improve their ability to think critically about social and ecological systems and ultimately learn to make more ethical decisions.

OBSTACLES TO MAKING GOOD DECISIONS

We make so many decisions every day that we probably do not recognize most of them as decisions. What we wear, what we eat, which route to take to work, which supplies we order for a job, what projects we tackle first, whether we speak at a meeting, and whom we hire are some examples of decisions we make in our personal and professional worlds. Common, daily decisions are often made without a great deal of attention or introspection; they are often governed by habit, personality, or previous experience. Big, special, or new decisions, however, usually require thought; in such cases, the process of decision making is more obvious. Both types of decisions use basically the same process and using an example of each will illustrate how we make decisions. For simplicity's sake, consider the steps of buying cereal and the process of buying a car.

Rational Decision Making

For many of us, buying cereal requires little thought or attention, which enables us to focus on the more important aspects of our

FIGURE 8.1 The variety of breakfast cereals typically available in a supermarket allows customers to consider numerous variables in making their selection.

grocery list. We either purchase the same tried-and-true cereal (see Figure 8.1) or we venture into the unknown following the promise of an advertisement or a friend's recommendation. In either case, we unconsciously list the characteristics we desire and match them to the set of cereals that conform to our expectations. If several cereals match our need for nutrition, sweetness, or crunch, for example, we begin to consider which variables are more important to us. Is the banana flavor more appealing than blueberry? Is one shape more likely to get soggy than another? All things being equal, we tend to pick the cheapest box, or the most familiar one, and move on to peanut butter. And it all happens in a blink of an eye.

Economists refer to this basic process as **rational decision making**, or **rationality**, and use it frequently to model decisions. The theory suggests that people make choices that maximize their interests. They do this by assembling all the information about the choices, prioritizing and weighing the characteristics, and selecting the choice that scores the highest on the important features. The process can work well if the assumptions are met—if the decision maker has all the information needed about all the relevant features and if the best option can be calculated. If someone only cares about three factors in cereal, perhaps vitamin B content, whole wheat, and price per ounce, it can be a straightforward process to collect the relevant information and make a decision. Cereal boxes and grocery shelves in the United States provide this information, since many people want to know. And since everyone does not share the same priorities for ideal cereal, a variety of combinations are strategically offered to aim to please everyone.

But what happens when we make a more complicated decision, and particularly one with consequences for sustainability? For most people, a car is a significant enough purchase that it deserves careful consideration, and our transportation choices clearly have economic (quality, service, price, new or used), environmental (fuel, hybrid or traditional engine, emissions), and societal (U.S.-based industry, labor unions) dimensions. Choosing to share a car, rent a car, or use public transportation should also be considered, of course. For those who settle on owning a personal vehicle, it takes a bit of time to read up on the current models, compare loan packages, consider mileage and fuel options, and recall the characteristics they desire or dislike about automobiles.

First, they collect information. Then, they compare options and contemplate whether they want headroom in the backseat or a trunk that is easy to load. They think about whether they can find biodiesel fuel and how often each model needs repair. They must also look at their bank account and think about the risk associated with buying a used vehicle. They then prioritize the options they care about based on what matters most. If several options are basically the same, they pick "the best," which is probably the cheapest, and they happily drive away.

However, they likely have not made a completely rational decision. The assumption of perfect information, for example, is rarely met. They do not know when the brakes will need to be replaced or the muffler will fall off. They may not have read the consumer ratings to know how the car compares to others. As critics of rationality point out, if we do not have all of the information, we must not be making a thoroughly rational decision. This lack of information represents our first obstacle to making rational decisions. The fact that we still make a decision suggests there are other strategies at work.

Proponents of rationality say that we calculate the probability of unknown things happening. How likely are the brakes to fail in the first 50,000 miles, and how much would it cost to replace them if we followed the manufacturer's recommendations? If a consulting firm were bidding for the design of a new project, they would certainly aim to predict every possible scenario and cost out all conceivable problems. The more complex the decision, the more factors that are included. They would use a computer model and reams of historic information to improve the accuracy of their prediction. The mathematical study of rational decision making involves calculating probabilities and determining when people are successful rational actors.[1] However, most people do not make a dissertation out of each decision, nor, as will be explained below, are they capable of doing so.

The field of engineering, for example, has generated a number of theories and shelves of reference books about decision making in complex situations. Many of these theories fall under the general term "multiple criteria decision making," referring to decisions made in situations that have a variety of objectives, variables, constraints, alternatives, stakeholders, and perspectives.[2] Each of these elements generates criteria that can be considered part of the decision-making process. Since people have limitations in their mental processing, computers are programmed to reduce the problem, identify probabilities, and help the decision maker think systematically about the situation.

In order to add additional variables into the equation or to compare dissimilar components (such as mileage efficiency and comfort), we have to translate them into a common measure, usually money, and decide which variables are most important. As we move to consider the other aspects of sustainability, more variables are added. Some comparisons are easier than others: What does better gas mileage cost—both in terms of the initial investment of a more efficient engine and in the increased savings of purchasing less gas for every 1,000 miles driven? Which is better in the long run, a new car that is more efficient or an older, cheaper car? And as you saw in Chapter 6, some of the advantages of the more efficient vehicle (e.g., less emissions) are difficult to translate into a dollar value. Also, what if you cannot get both a quieter ride and a smaller trunk? At some point, we make a selection and convince ourselves that it is just a car and does not deserve such agony. In other words, at some point, we decide that we have enough information to make a decision and we proceed with our best guess.

Limits of Rationality

The lack of available information represents perhaps the clearest barrier to rational decision making. Grocery shelves rarely reveal where the food was grown, for example. Unless we have a third-party certification system, consumers may not know if the workers were really paid a fair wage as they created sneakers or bicycle seats. These infrastructure limitations on what information is available to us are significant barriers to rationality. Making rational sustainability decisions ought to include having information about the resources and labor practices that were used to create the product.

Some available information may be misleading. Hand driers mounted in public restrooms proclaim this to be a pollution-free device, suggesting that we should be happy to save the trees that would have produced paper toweling. Yet electricity usually is not generated without environmental and social costs, and most of us know that. The label on the drier, however, makes it easier to avoid thinking about the reality of mountain-top removal, environmental justice, dammed rivers, acid rain, or nuclear waste repositories.

We can see that accurate, readily available information relevant to sustainability would help us make rational choices. Indeed, many believe that making rational decisions merely requires having the appropriate information available. Such a view, however, overlooks well-documented biases at play when people process information. The psychologist Herbert Simon was one of the first to suggest that, at the individual level, people do not make decisions according to the ideal rational model mentioned above because they do not have the necessary information or information-processing capacities.[3] Furthermore, he suggested, they do not really need the rational best choice most of the time when a good choice is quite sufficient; they "satisfice." Interestingly, however, they think they are making rational decisions and considering all options. The difference between our perception and the reality constitutes a bias in thinking.

First, human perception is selective rather than comprehensive. People are limited in the amount of information they can take in at one time. Therefore, perception is an active process, involving both filtering and interpreting stimuli received from sensory organs. As a result, we tend to selectively recognize and process the available information that meets our expectations. We see what we expect to find, which is why having a mental picture of what you seek is a good strategy for recovering lost items. However, it also means we will not see what we are not looking for. It is what Albert Einstein meant when he said, "It is quite wrong to try founding a theory on observable magnitudes alone. In reality the very opposite happens. It is the theory which decides what we can observe."[4]

Furthermore, working memory is limited. Psychologists suggest we have the capacity to handle 5 to 7 units of different information at the same time before we start forgetting some of them.[5] People can work with larger amounts of information, of course, if similar items are chunked together. Phone numbers, for example, are 10 digits, but the area code is usually remembered as a single unit. That leaves 7 random digits to remember. Our information storage capacity, however, is not limited by working memory and has huge capacity. The limitation is with how much information we can work with at once.

In addition to these perceptual challenges with information, our attitudes about a topic may predispose us to avoid or ignore information that challenges our existing ideas. Despite concern about health care, for example, some voters are not able to consider proposals made by those who sit on the other side of the political fence. Finally, we may not recognize when the circumstances are not familiar and we need to pay closer attention.[6] As the example in Box 8.1 illustrates, even top scientists are not immune to this kind of bias.

As experts have realized, people do not take the time or have the mental horsepower to calculate the probabilities of all the options, weighted by all the preferences, as in the car

---

BOX 8.1   Failure to Detect Ozone Depletion

Even when we build the monitoring systems to give us important feedback, we have to learn to pay close attention to potentially important changes. For example, two papers published in 1974 predicted the erosion of the ozone layer as a function of chlorine atoms that could be traced to chlorofluorocarbons (CFCs). The papers triggered additional research on atmospheric chemistry, defensive postures by industry, and international monitoring programs. In 1984, British scientists reported a 40 percent decrease in ozone over Antarctica. Although they had seen a steady decrease for 10 years, they did not publish their findings earlier because their computer models predicted a decline of only a few percent in ozone. Their data did not conform to their expectations, so they had assumed there was an error.

The British scientists published their findings only when they found confirming reports from a monitoring station about 1,000 miles from theirs. NASA scientists were perplexed by the publication, however, since their Nimbus 7 satellite had never reported an ozone hole, and it had been taking measurements since 1978. After checking, they discovered that the computers were programmed to reject very low readings, since they were likely to indicate instrument error. Incorporating the rejected data into the analysis resulted in findings that paralleled the British results and mapped an enormous hole the size of the continental United States (Meadows et al. 1992).

As this example demonstrates, in the midst of a decision we ought to take the time to ask about our data, our assumptions, and our assumptions about the data. Unfortunately, it is more typical to be under pressure for a speedy decision or to rely upon information that is easily accepted and expected. Sometimes it is the unexpected results that provide the deepest insights.

---

purchase above. Instead, they use **bounded rationality**, a term coined to acknowledge the effect our cognitive limitations have on decision making.[7] Faced with the impossibility of acquiring and processing all necessary information to make a rational decision, people tend to simplify decisions based on intuition and cognitive shortcuts that psychologists call **heuristics**—rules of thumb that people use to approximate rational behavior.

Cognitive Heuristics

The work of Daniel Kahneman and Amos Tversky—two psychologists who developed a series of insightful experiments to test decision-making processes—helps clarify the heuristics that affect our decision-making capacity.[8] They suggested that "people rely on a limited number of heuristic principles, which reduce complex tasks of assessing probabilities and predicting values to simpler judgmental operations. In general, these heuristics are quite useful, but sometimes they lead to severe and systematic errors."[9] Several of their heuristics offer insights into decision making around issues of sustainability.

Availability Heuristic
Several of Kahneman and Tversky's experiments revolve around our ability to use information stored in memory. Information is available when it is easily recalled, and when an event

from the past is easy to remember, we tend to consider its occurrence in the future more likely. For example, when faced with a question about the future likelihood or frequency of an event, people tend to favor the choice that is easiest to imagine or recall.[10] The more familiar we are with one option (or the more recently it occurred), the more available this information is in our brain, and the more likely we are to believe it will happen again.

This shortcut works well in cases when frequently occurring events keep happening. It causes us to err, however, when the easier to recall information is actually rarer. If we regularly drive by a home with solar panels visible on the roof, we may believe they are common, just because we see that roof every day. Similarly, we might believe that jets crash more frequently than they do because of the extensive media coverage on this relatively rare events.

This availability heuristic has a variety of applications. When television ads showed Meryl Streep explaining the health risk of apple products to babies (because apples are typically sprayed with Alar to delay ripening) and later giving testimony to Congress, there was an immediate drop in apple juice consumption. Uniroyal, the maker of Alar, removed the chemical from the U.S. market. This publicity campaign succeeded even though EPA studies and reports failed to affect the manufacturer's production of the chemical.[11] Meryl Streep is not a chemical expert, but her celebrity status makes her memorable to many viewers. The availability of that information made the decision to boycott apple juice easy for parents to make.

When information is provided in vivid, imaginable terms, people can build a picture in their minds that will help them recall that information more easily. Vivid information, then, is more available and, therefore, used in decision making more frequently. In terms of making rational decisions that move us toward sustainability, if the information is not readily available in our memory or if the data are described unimaginably (as in descriptions of water-borne chemicals in parts per million), we will have a more difficult time remembering, retrieving, and using that information appropriately. As Nisbett and Ross summarize:

> The problem with the use of the vividness criterion is simply stated: The vividness of information is correlated only modestly, at best, with its evidential value. By accident or by the design of the communicator, vivid information is often misleading, particularly when duller but more probative information is cast aside in its favor.[12]

This bias helps to explain the difficulty in implementing the precautionary principle. We remember and respond to catastrophes (e.g., an oil spill) far more actively than to more probative reports regarding practices that decrease system resilience and make such catastrophes more likely. In other words, we tend to pay attention to issues only after they have caused a serious problem, when they are most vivid.

Anchoring and Overconfidence
Tversky and Kahneman also demonstrated that people tend to anchor their beliefs on

an initial fact and do not adjust their perceptions enough to reflect additional data. In one study, they asked respondents to estimate the answer to a factual question and then to provide a range that should include the correct answer. Despite an opportunity to create a very large range, half of the respondents chose upper and lower estimates that did not include the true value. The ranges were anchored by their initial guess, and that first impression made it cognitively difficult to consider other possibilities.

This anchoring heuristic can be a substantial component of the difficulties adversaries have in modifying their initial position during a negotiation. Once advocates have established their position and justified it with the factors they consider important, it may be hard for them to change their minds. As a result of this heuristic, people tend to be more confident of their ideas than they should be. First impressions or ideas tend to create an anchor that affects future ideas. Perhaps this is one reason why people do not readily continue to make progress toward energy efficiency and stop after an initial justifiably significant activity.

Problems with Probability

Our ability to use logic and probability fails us when we see patterns inappropriately. A coin, for example, has a 50 percent chance of landing either heads or tails every time it is thrown. After a coin lands headsup nine times in a row, however, most people will bet that the 10th toss will be tails. The fact that we think we "are due for tails" is an example of this heuristic. If we expect a random behavior and see a pattern, we think it is more

likely than the logical 50/50 chance that the next occurrence will break the pattern.

This heuristic may be at work when people think a wildfire will not occur in the same vicinity twice. Indeed, if all the fuel has been burned by the first fire, the chances of another are slim. However, given enough time for vegetation to return, or if the area was not completely burned by the first fire, the conditions that led to one fire may favor a second, but people are not likely to see it that way. Neither will residents of a floodplain community expect to experience two 100-year floods in the same decade. Even though we are all exposed to chance events, human beings have not learned how to use knowledge about probability effectively.

Uncertainty

The certainty (or uncertainty) heuristic suggests that people avoid probabilities and uncertainty where possible and tend to select situations that offer certain results. Not only do people lean toward information that promises certainty, but there are strong cognitive preferences and desires for certainty.[13] Since recognizing uncertainty makes people uncomfortable, they may deny it to reduce anxiety. While some psychologists suggest this tendency comes from a desire to have control in uncertain situations, others believe people desire opportunities to participate in meaningful ways to affect the situation.[14] Both explanations would lead people to avoid circumstances where their input would be hopeless because uncertainty is great. They would probably rather spend their energy working on issues where they stand a better chance of being successful. The public's confusion about climate change projections demonstrates how difficult it is for people to use information that includes elements of uncertainty.

Unfortunately, most predictions regarding future impacts of good and bad technology involve some element of uncertainty, and this alone makes it difficult to understand and communicate with decision makers and the public. As a consequence, naysayers who wish to derail the technology employ exaggerations and fear tactics to draw attention to the possibility of calamity or focus on the lack of certainty to help drive the public's attention elsewhere. Although the fear strategy and debates attract media, research suggests people rarely act on threatening messages unless adequate strategies for reducing risk are also provided.[15]

The recent responses to climate change projections and solutions demonstrate how all of these biases overlap and interfere with communicating information, understanding issues, and making good decisions. Over the decades, many models have been created and many reports have been issued; there is a great deal of information available, but it is not all consistent. These inconsistencies often arise from exploring slightly different aspects of the problem, starting with different assumptions, and using different data sources. This is to be expected as problems increase in scale, but it does not help non-experts gain an understanding of an issue that will help them make decisions. As a result, they always feel confused, uncertain, and incapable of participating in solving the problem.

Not only does uncertainty plague the issue of climate change, but so too do the facts that predictions are based on probabilities, initial ideas are hard to change, and great uncertainty makes it very difficult to provide concrete, vivid information that people can grab and remember, despite the melting glaciers. Perhaps one of the best ways that people can begin to "see" climate change is the phenological information that has recently become more available. Cherry trees in Japan are blooming earlier. Bird ranges are changing. Thus, the lack of information; the confusion associated with the information; the inability to recall available information; the challenges of changing impressions, having originally heard one story and now the facts are different; the problems of relying on people understanding probabilities; and the uncertainty about projecting climate change into the future all conspire to make it difficult for people to make good decisions that take climate change into account. Our poor ability to cope with this scenario is amplified by the problems of looking into the future and the complexity of the issue.

Discounting the Future

Of course, our biases go beyond the processing of information. In Chapter 6, we discussed the practice in neoclassical economics of discounting the future value of resources. We found that with this practice, even economically rational decisions can lead to ecological hardships for future generations. It is not only in economic affairs that human beings discount the future, however. To be sure, businesses chiefly concerned with the bottom line in a competitive global marketplace are often focused on short-term profits at the cost of

BOX 8.2   Rachel Carson and the Need for Expanded Time Horizons

We face a special danger today: the economic, personal, and political discounting of the future may be increasing at precisely the time that technological innovations suggest the need for expanded time horizons. One of the first people to sound the alarm of this incongruity was Rachel Carson, whose book *Silent Spring* almost single-handedly jump-started the modern environmental movement. The message of *Silent Spring*, published in 1962, was as straightforward as it was disconcerting. Common pesticides of the day, such as DDT (dichloro-diphenyl-trichloroethane), did not just kill pests; they also had the unintended and unexpected effect of decimating entire populations of other animals, including many birds. Absent its birds, Carson predicted American neighborhoods would face a silent spring, free not only of pesky bugs but also of avian singers.

Carson explained in great detail how the age-old attempt to gain "control of nature" through the use of pesticides was self-defeating because it failed to comprehend the intricate relationships that constitute "the whole fabric of life" (Carson 1962). Carson insisted that pesticides should really be called *bio*cides because they often prove lethal not only to the targeted insects or weeds but also to many other forms of life or biota. Manufacturing and applying them indiscriminately was shortsighted; the pests might be abated in the near term, but many would adapt and return in force. In the meantime, ecosystems would be disrupted, other species would decline, and human health would suffer.

Only recently, Carson observed, has humankind gained the power significantly to alter the planet through technological means. That power is growing exponentially, as are its repercussions on the natural world. Carson insisted that we had a responsibility to future generations to pass on a diverse and life-supporting planet. In a chapter of *Silent Spring* entitled "The Obligation to Endure," Carson explains, "Future generations are unlikely to condone our lack of prudent concern for the integrity of the natural world that supports all life" (Carson 1962, page 13). The *obligation to endure* created a right to know what was being done to undermine the fabric of life. Ultimately, Carson's efforts stimulated "Right to Know" legislation that allows people to learn what toxic chemicals are being produced and released in their counties and neighborhoods.

Rachel Carson was predominantly concerned with the effects of pesticides and other industrial chemicals. "The most alarming assault upon the environment," she wrote, "is the contamination of air, earth, rivers, and sea with dangerous and even lethal materials" (Carson 1962, page 6). If we expand our understanding of "dangerous and even lethal materials" to include greenhouse gases, Carson's groundbreaking cry for caution and foresight, now a half-century old, is equally valid today. It well describes the ways we are fundamentally altering the climate and other life-support systems of the planet.

long-term sustainability. One might concede some level of this myopia in the business world, taking solace in the hope that longer-term thinking predominates in other realms of life. In the area of personal health, however, we know that individuals often let the short-term pleasures of comfort (watching television rather than exercising) and eating (too many fats and sugars and not enough fresh vegetables) jeopardize their long-term health.

We can see a similar bias in politicians. Although one might expect them to have extended local, regional, national, or global interests at heart, they are often equally myopic. Just as today's corporations may focus on quarterly earnings as they confront their self-interested shareholders, so politicians encountering electoral pressures may forgo long-term concerns and perspectives. The temporal horizon of politicians, who face re-election in two to four years, is often as short as the campaign sound bites they produce.

Box 8.2 points out the particular importance of an extended time horizon for the general public in light of technological advances, such as chemical insecticides. Most of the insecticides that concerned Carson, if applied to a field or lawn when *Silent Spring* was published in 1962, would have dissipated within their environments to relatively innocuous levels today (though they may have started lethal chain reactions). Today's greenhouse gas emissions, in contrast, may have their greatest effects—in terms of melting glaciers and icecaps, changing climate patterns and weather systems, and disrupting ecosystems—50, 100, or 500 years down the road.

In other words, the stakes have been raised, and much of the necessary change will come as a bottom-up process. Businesses will not extend their time horizon unless their potential customers extend their own time horizons. Likewise, politicians are unlikely to look past the next election cycle unless they feel pressure from their constituents to do so. Box 8.2 discusses Right to Know legislation sparked by Rachel Carson. This type of legislation indeed marks an important

advance for private citizens. However, the right to know about the social and ecological effects of a new product has little value if it is not met with a corresponding desire to know on the part of the public. Incorporating the ethical obligations toward future generations discussed in previous chapters will require overcoming the common tendency to restrict ourselves to a short-term focus.

Complexity

In Chapter 7, we developed our integrative ethical framework by viewing contemporary challenges of sustainability in the context of social-ecological systems, a term that encompasses social, ecological, and economic aspects of sustainability and emphasizes the complexity of these systems. While many may not be familiar with the concept of complex adaptive systems, most people recognize the mental overload that occurs when dealing with complex problems involving a large number of variables. Reaching the limit of our working memory can lead people to confusion and avoidance behaviors. People often throw up their hands when faced with the multitude of variables that play a role in matters such as global climate change or international trade.

Even when the variables are limited, the behavior of complex adaptive systems can be puzzling. In one study by Erling Moxnes, participants were asked to work with a computer simulation of a fishery.[16] In order to avoid complications introduced by tragedy of the commons, each participant had sole access to a virgin cod fishery, and in order to avoid a short-term bias, participants were rewarded for the success of their simulated fishery on an infinite time horizon. That is, they were rewarded immediately based on their success in creating a sustainable fishery. Participants could vary their fishing fleet by managing investment into more ships or keeping ships at dock. Each simulated year, they would receive information about their catch and make decisions for the following year.

Although most of these participants were fishers, resource managers, or researchers, they overwhelmingly tended to overinvest in their fleet. On average, participants opted for a fleet size almost two times larger than would have been sustainable. As a result, the simulated fisheries deteriorated. Catch levels dropped dramatically, leaving participants in the same situation that describes many fisheries around the globe: too many boats chasing too few fish.

Note that even without the complications of a common resource or the temptation of short-term gains, people still acted in a way that caused the fishery to collapse. The failure resulted from the participants' inability to recognize the fishery as a complex adaptive system. In the context of the present discussion, the most interesting aspect of this study is the participants' responses to their poor results. Each time Moxnes performed the experiment—even in different contexts—when participants were faced with results that did not fit their expectations, they often abandoned their original strategies and began guessing wildly or became irritable, blaming the results on a computer glitch rather than on their own decisions. The

inability to understand the dynamic aspects of complex adaptive systems can often result in failure and frustration even when one has the best of intentions.

In addition to the difficulty of dealing with large numbers of variables and understanding how environmental systems behave over time, the wide array of perspectives, values, and attitudes that people bring to an issue can make it even more confusing. Experts can help us understand issues by simplifying the system, creating models, and packaging information in a way that people can understand. Nonetheless, no one person has complete understanding of a system. Addressing complex problems must be a group effort, requiring people who may think and feel quite differently about an issue to work together. Therefore, communicating effectively with one another becomes and added challenge.

How Barriers to Rationality Affect Decisions

This brief summary of cognitive biases and limits to rationality illustrates some of the ways that people make predictable mistakes when retrieving information and making decisions in the context of uncertainty (see Table 8.1). In experiments, even when people are given plenty of time for calculations and rewards for correct answers, they do not do significantly better.

Our mental shortcuts often override rational thinking, which may lead us to make poor decisions. It is easy to see that skipping over some information and attaching greater

TABLE 8.1 Summary of Limits to Rationality

1. Information	May not exist	Selective perception prevents us from seeing it	May be overwhelmed by competing attitudes	Preconceptions and assumptions about data may prevent learning
2. Heuristics	Availability: Information retrievability limits information usefulness	Anchoring & Overconfidence: First guesses, no matter how wrong, confine future perceptions	Probability: We don't intuitively think in probabilities	Uncertainty: We prefer to avoid situations of uncertainty
3. Complexity	Working memory is limited to 5 to 7 chunks	Sustainability issues require information and expertise in a number of areas, and a systems perspective	Inability to perceive causal loops, nonlinearity, and systems behavior over time	Confusion and frustration can prevent perception and understanding

importance to other information could result in poor decisions. Similarly, avoiding situations that are confusing or uncertain and believing that we know more than we do will also make it difficult, if not impossible, to accept new ideas and behaviors.

For example, recent projections suggest that the use of home-grown biomass (i.e., wood and agricultural products) as an energy source can play a key role in reducing the use of fossil fuels. However, some worry that using biomass for energy will result in loss of forests, increased pollution, and higher energy prices. The positive projections can lead those who stand to profit from agricultural or woody biomass to ignore concerns about land use, price controls, invasive exotics, and air quality. Similarly, those who have concerns about environmental and social consequences are likely to shun the reassurances that this is indeed an excellent source of energy because the message comes from the

very industries that would profit the most. A lack of trust, missing information, and the biases we have for ignoring what we don't want to hear, sticking to original estimates, and misrepresenting probabilities all intersect to create anything but rational conversations about biomass energy.

While most of these heuristics and biases had important benefits for functioning efficiently at one point in time, they evolved in a very different environment than we live in today. In a simpler world, past experience and the stories of neighbors were excellent guides to solving problems. Even very small communities likely had the knowledge and resources to address those problems independently. However, in today's world, where new technologies and complex situations are generated in less than one generation, neighbors and past experiences are rarely helpful for making decisions. The heuristics that helped us find food, build shelters, and care for children put us at a disadvantage when wrestling with disposing of toxic material or enabling developing nations to provide health care and education to all their residents. An example of how we deal with risk may make these limitations more clear.

Many sustainability questions that involve new technologies include some level of risk. If we are not completely certain about the future impacts and outcomes of genetically modified organisms or the toxicology of pesticides, there are risks in using them. Those risks could involve ecosystem or human health, with some individuals at greater risk than others (usually workers, infants, and the elderly). In these cases, questions of risk tend to involve two if not all three areas of sustainability. Such questions represent particularly difficult challenges because of the cognitive heuristics and problems mentioned above.

Our discomfort with uncertainty is the first hurdle; we might rather ignore than talk about risk. Our intuitively bad approach to probability means that we have to think hard about how to weigh risks and what they mean. How the media convey information, what memories are recalled, and how the issue is framed makes a great deal of difference to how the people respond to warnings and engage in discussions. In addition, we have a tendency to be overconfident of our knowledge and to exaggerate the true frequency of relatively rare risks. Given these hurdles, people will likely not be using all the information that is available when they approach a question of risk. Experts are regularly frustrated by the public's overreaction to some

minimal risks, such as that of a nuclear plant meltdown, and their apparent lack of concern over greater risks, such as lightning strikes or radon contamination.[17] It is clear from the limits to rationality, however, that the public is not given information in a way that helps them overcome the biases that we all have.

Box 8.3 illustrates the difficulty involved in legislatively managing the risk involved in food additives. Therefore, the responsibility of managing that risk is passed onto the consumer. Although people should not assume their food supply is safe, without the ability to monitor and regulate the industry, it is difficult for the public to know which chemicals are problematic and which foods contain them. People are involuntarily exposed to pesticides and other food additives when they consume mass-produced food. The growth of the organic food movement may be in reaction to this uncertainty—at least some people now have a strategy to make some synthetic chemical additive consumption voluntary.

These challenges to rationality make it more important to carefully communicate information about risk, probability, and uncertainty to the public. Yet on issues where the risk is involuntary (as with the public food supply) and the issue can generate great sympathy for the less fortunate (e.g., infants), there are emotional overtones and powerful media messages that exacerbate attempts to employ rationality. Applying the ethical principles discussed in earlier chapters can provide another way to approach difficult decisions that play health against economic and environmental welfare.

BOX 8.3 Importance of How an Issue Is Framed: Regulating Chemical Additives in Food

How Congress chose to regulate chemical additives in food provides a window to the world of risk communication, decision making, and sustainability. (See Meadows [1996] and Jacobson [1972]). With the growth of the chemical industry after World War II, the Delaney Amendment was added to the Food, Drugs and Cosmetics Act of 1938 in 1958 to protect consumers from food additives "found to induce cancer in man, or, after tests, found to induce cancer in animals." One can see several assumptions behind this simple, straightforward clause: (1) a substance that causes cancer in animals will be dangerous to people, (2) there is a linear or constant relationship between a cancer-inducing substance and cancer, such that if it causes cancer at a very large level in a short-term experimental test on animals, it will cause cancer at a very small level over a lifetime in a human, and (3) the government will be able to test every food additive for the potential to cause cancer.

Congress took the moral high ground with a precautionary approach and created a zero tolerance for chemical additives. Dangerous chemicals do not belong in food. One can imagine that the food industry was not pleased, but how could anyone suggest we should allow dangerous chemicals in food?

While this clause was meant to protect human health, it also had environmental implications and disrupted the agricultural industry. The Federal Insecticide, Rodenticide, and Fungicide Act (FIFRA) of 1947 permits the use of pesticides on food crops. The Department of Agriculture (and later the EPA) was designated under FIFRA to set levels of allowable pesticide residue in produce. Since some pesticides could cause cancer,

the two bills were in conflict. To resolve this dilemma, Congress decreed that pesticides are not food additives so they would not fall under the Delaney amendment. Interestingly, the nascent organic farming movement was probably not strong enough to help question the necessity of pesticides. Had the issue been approached through a sustainability lens, however, different elements might have received greater consideration.

When raw foods are processed, however, they are concentrated. It is possible for the pesticide residue to appear in larger quantities in ketchup or apple juice, for example, than was permitted in tomatoes or apples. Despite pressure from agricultural lobbyists, Congress decided this scenario fell under the intent of the Delaney amendment and said that pesticides that caused cancer were not permitted in processed foods. Because of the increasing sensitivity of laboratory testing equipment and the inability of any test to prove zero concentration levels, the FDA set a limit for pesticide residue in processed foods of causing one cancer in one million people.

Over years of debate it became obvious that the intent of a precautionary regulation may not be appropriate after the development and distribution of a product. Precaution is best applied in the decision-making mode. Although the point where more people care about agricultural practices is when additives are present in food, the chemicals were already developed and legally used for reducing pest problems long before the food was processed. Preventing pesticides from going into production or being used might be a better course for regulation. Real change might not be possible until economically equivalent options are available, such as an alternative pesticide or organic strategies.

(continued)

The Delaney amendment was quietly retired when Congress passed the Food Quality Protection Act of 1996. Its disappearance marked a victory for the industry that cannot supply huge quantities of food without leaving chemicals in it. Its history marks the idealistic attempt to protect human health from the hazards of chemicals and the difficult nature of decisions about toxicity and technology. It has become possible to detect tiny amounts of chemicals in food, but we do not have adequate knowledge of the risk of ingesting that chemical. This is a problem of inadequate knowledge, as well as a problem of understanding probability, complexity, and uncertainty.

STRATEGIES FOR ADDRESSING LIMITS TO RATIONALITY

The process of applying the ethical considerations from earlier chapters to decision making requires addressing these limits to rationality. For example, holding steadfastly to our own anchored beliefs makes us less likely to consider diverse perspectives. Skewed interpretations of probability will likely result in skewed analyses of risks involved with a technological change or development. Even the integrative framework of complex adaptive systems discussed in Chapter 7 can become overwhelming without the cognitive tools necessary to understand complexity.

The most fundamental step in addressing our limits to rationality on a personal level is acknowledging them. If we know that human perception is selective, then we can actively seek information useful for making decisions that promote sustainability. If we know that we are more prone to remember vivid information, we may be more careful when viewing a news story geared more for sensation than education. Likewise, we may be more proactive about exploring issues beyond news headlines.

If we understand our tendency to anchor our beliefs on initial facts, we can make a point to receive subsequent information with an open mind. By increasing our understanding of the behavior of complex adaptive systems, we can begin to look for variables that might be hidden, and manage risk and uncertainty more sensibly. In this section, we discuss how to improve decision-making skills in the context of sustainability.

Becoming Environmentally Informed

Solid information about the environmental, social, economic, and ethical dimensions of sustainability can help build a foundation for effective action. Knowledge alone is not enough to create a more sustainable society, but it is an essential step. In academic literature on sustainability, more information is readily available about sustainability's environmental dimensions than about its social and economic aspects, especially in relation to consumption and other daily activities.[18] Resources from economics, business, and related fields can be vital to help integrate the social, economic, and environmental dimensions of sustainability in personal as well as professional settings.

Understanding the environmental dimensions of sustainability in our lives can begin with information about the environmental impact of ordinary activities. This impact can be measured, at least in part, by calculations of one's **ecological footprint**. This calculation provides a measure of the environmental impact of a person's daily activities, including energy expenditure in the home, transportation, and the impact of food consumption, among other factors. The "footprint" refers to the approximate area of land that a person uses through resource extraction, waste absorption, pollution, and other forms of environmental consumption.

Various organizations have produced calculators, which individuals can use by entering information about their food, home energy use, and transportation, for example. Some footprint calculators include additional items, such as the sources of energy used in a community (e.g., coal, wind, nuclear). Macro-structural factors of this sort clearly lie beyond the control of individuals, but they affect the environmental impact of individuals' everyday actions. Using the information an individual enters into the calculator, the ecological footprint program will indicate how much that person uses of the earth's land, water, and resources. Most footprint calculators indicate how many planets would be needed if everyone consumed at the same level as the individual entering the information.[19] Ecological footprint calculators vary in the amount of detail and the specific questions they ask, and thus results for the same person will vary depending on the particular indicators used.

While the ecological footprint has become a widely used estimate of human impact on the Earth's land, water, and other natural resources, there is at least one variation, the carbon footprint, which measures the amount of greenhouse gas emissions produced by daily activities. The great advantage of the footprint model is that it quickly provides a vivid and easily comprehensible snapshot of personal ecological impact. Most calculators also permit users to see how their footprint would change were they to modify certain factors, for example by eliminating meat from their diets or switching from a private car to public transportation. However, the footprint model has received criticisms for failing to account for differences among social groups within nations, as well as for simplifying the complex processes by which humans use and degrade nature.

Similar criticisms are made of Paul Ehrlich's IPAT equation, discussed in Chapter 2. Recall that according to this equation ecological impact (I) is the product of population (P), affluence (A), and technology (T). IPAT was valuable as one of the first efforts to think systematically about the ways that technology, social factors (especially wealth), and population combine to affect ecological processes and natural resources. This attempt at integration makes IPAT an important piece of the history of sustainable decision making. However, the formula has been criticized for a variety of shortcomings, including that it is overgeneral in its application and addresses only limited impacts on limited resources. Certainly the equation is not especially helpful for individuals, households, or even businesses that hope to implement more sustainable decisions and practices.

Still, the IPAT equation does highlight a fact that is vital for thinking about sustainability: environmental impact is tied to wealth, for both individuals and societies. Per capita resource usage tends to increase as affluence grows. This is true because greater wealth usually leads to more use of private cars (and to larger cars, driven more often), more meat consumption, larger homes, more garbage production, and so forth. Thus, residents of wealthier nations generally consume more and have larger footprints than those in poorer nations. Even within the same country, more affluent residents generally consume more than poorer ones.

However, the link between affluence and environmental impact is not always straightforward. Technology represents an important dimension. For example, some wealthier nations use fewer resources than others, reflecting factors such as greater energy efficiency in housing, greater use of alternative energy, better public transportation, and lower consumption of meat and highly processed foods, among others. For them, T may be in the denominator of the equation. For example, most European nations have much lower per capita resource consumption than the United States. This is true even for some nations that have better quality of life indicators (such as life expectancy, infant mortality, and education) than the United States. In addition, resource consumption and ecological footprints of some developing nations, notably China and India, have expanded very rapidly in recent years. Thus, the equation helps us look for relationships, seek information, and become more informed.

Becoming Socially and Economically Informed

As an integral measure of social, economic, and environmental factors, sustainability cannot simply be measured by environmental impact. Unfortunately, measures of social and economic impacts are not as widely available as are the ecological footprint calculators. While there are not measures or calculators, there are marketing programs that provide some indication of social goods and costs, such as those reflecting the use of **Fair Trade** practices, which certify that a product has been made without exploitative labor practices. Union labels also generally reflect a higher degree of employee compensation and benefit and, thus, of social goods.

These indicators, however, are partial and are available on a limited array of goods. It is impossible, at present, to calculate the overall social impact of a product or activity in a way akin to the ecological footprint. Because definitions and priorities are so varied, it is also difficult for people to agree on how to measure economic goods such as efficiency, productivity, or durability. The distortion of market mechanisms by factors such as advertising and government subsidies means that the law of supply and demand does not consistently weed out poor quality products or inefficient production processes. The calculation of sustainability's economic and social dimensions, in other words, is much more difficult than the calculation of ecological impact— which itself is complicated enough.

Nonetheless, people seeking sustainability in their work or their personal lives must try to weigh ecological, social, and economic factors in relation to each other. This entails questions that are difficult to answer at collective levels, such as whether greater use of natural resources corresponds with higher levels of social goods such as education, employment, or life expectancy. If so, can resources be used more efficiently without reducing important social goods? Which benefits are essential and which might be reduced or eliminated? Will people be willing (and able) to pay more for some environmental or social goods? These questions are still challenging but perhaps more manageable for individuals and families. Clearly science and technology play an important role in answering these questions, as does public policy and corporate responsibility. However, individual choices can also have a significant impact on the ability of a community or entire nation to achieve greater sustainability.

Systems Thinking

As we have seen, overcoming many of the obstacles discussed above, at least in the short term, can be achieved by being aware and conscious of our shortcomings as we make decisions. This is not the case, however, when it comes to understanding complex adaptive systems (CASs). When making a decision, we can choose to pay more attention to information that is vital, if not vivid. We cannot, however, improve our understanding of CASs simply by choosing to do so. Attaining a greater understanding of how CASs behave requires a new set of critical thinking skills.[20]

For most of us, critical thinking is a familiar topic. Most states, as well as the National Academy of Sciences, include critical thinking (or critical analysis) as a core aspect of their educational standards, and many teachers at primary, secondary, and tertiary levels of education take this goal seriously. The distinction from simply memorizing information is important. Critical thinking is not simply a matter of obtaining information, but of interpreting, processing, and evaluating that information in a way that is useful. The problem is that when it comes to understanding CASs, most of us lack the necessary concepts to process information in a way that will allow us to make good decisions. The term systems thinking refers to our ability to think critically about CASs. In this section, we will look at a number of concepts that can improve our systems thinking skills.

Synthesis

In Chapter 7, we described the conventional approach to difficult problems—dividing them into smaller, more manageable components and considering each component separately. The pervasiveness of this approach is no surprise. Indeed, our education system has divided the world into separate subjects (e.g., language arts, mathematics, and physical science) and departments (e.g., religion, political science, and economics), and therefore, our training and expertise are similarly fragmented. As you learned in Chapter 7, however, very few decisions can be made in isolation. Most issues cross disciplinary boundaries, and by definition, decisions about sustainability must include the previously disparate worlds of economics and development, the environment, and social justice. Therefore, by creating our integrated framework for sustainability ethics in Chapter 7, we have already taken the first step to becoming systems thinkers by acknowledging the inadequacy of addressing sustainability purely in terms of its component parts.

Scale

Our integrative framework provides a second key aspect to becoming a systems thinker. Recall that we discussed the ethical responsibility of understanding our individual actions (small scale) in terms of their effect globally and in the distant future (large scale). This concept of scale is important for understanding CASs. It will always be necessary to define boundaries of some sort, as considering the entire world is not helpful, but where we place those boundaries can have a large impact on our understanding of the system. One strategy to decide whether the boundaries are appropriately placed might be to consider whether all the key stakeholders will be included in the decision.

If we consider the development of a strain of genetically modified rice that provides additional vitamin A, for example, the development company will focus on the genetic possibilities, the cost, the licensing agreements, and potential for recovering their research investment. The new technology would be at the center of the model, with inputs such as research capital and outputs such as healthier people and profit. In their world, the system is their company. Developing and selling more products create more profits for the company.

A broader view of the system might encourage us to consider other dimensions of the problem, wonder about the farmers, and ask if anything will change in the way they grow rice if they use the modified seed. If the health of the rice consumers were at the center of that system instead of the rice, we might ask ourselves what created the Vitamin A deficiency in the first place. Does providing new rice hide other problems that will continue to affect this population? While the genetic engineers might claim it is not their job to consider all the components that would be included in the expanded system, one could suggest that the decisions to make, market, or use golden rice cannot be made ethically without the broader perspective. Making ethical decisions about sustainability, rather than about product success, demands that we consider a system at a scale that includes societal welfare and ecosystem resilience along with economic development.

Stocks and Flows

Recall from Chapter 6 Georgescu-Roegen's distinction between stock resources (e.g., coal) and fund resources (e.g., solar energy). In systems thinking, we make a similar distinction between stocks and flows. Understanding systems in terms of stocks and flows can help to explain what might otherwise appear to be puzzling behavior of CASs. Global climate change offers a good example. Even if we were to immediately reduce greenhouse gas emissions to zero, the temperature of the earth would continue to increase for several decades because of the existing levels of greenhouse gases. Given the intensity of debate revolving around proposals for much less drastic reductions in emissions, one can imagine the furor that would result if reductions were put in place and the temperature continued to rise. Skeptics might argue that the reductions are not meeting their intended goal, but such an argument rests on a misunderstanding of the stocks and flows affecting climate.

To understand the error in that logic it might help to consider a more familiar system. Most people understand that the sun's intensity is highest at noon. We are often warned that this is a particularly important time for sunscreen. However, the hottest time of the day is typically around 2 p.m. To understand why the hottest time of the day does not coincide with the most intense solar rays, we need to look at temperature as an indication of the stock of heat at the earth's surface. The sun's rays represent an energy flow into this stock, while the radiation of heat off of the earth represents flow out of this stock. Changes to the level of a stock depend on the relationship between the inflow and the outflow. Looking at Figure 8.2, you can see that while the intensity of incoming solar energy starts decreasing immediately after noon, the inflow of energy does not come down below the level of outflow until the middle of the afternoon. At that point the stock of heat (i.e., the temperature) begins to decrease.

Now, we can apply these same concepts to global climate change. In this case we need to consider a minimum of two stocks. The first is atmospheric greenhouse gases. Greenhouse gas emissions represent the inflow to this stock, while the reduction of greenhouse gases from weathering and other processes

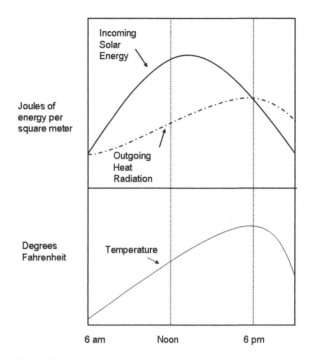

FIGURE 8.2 While the sun's rays on the earth's surface are typically strongest at noon, the hottest time of the day occurs later. The delay can be explained by understanding stocks and flows.

represents the outflow. Figure 8.3a provides a conceptual picture of these flows. Outflow of greenhouse gases is approximated as constant and shown as the solid horizontal line. Note that at Time 1, greenhouse gas emissions are reduced to near zero. After Time 1, the outflow is greater than the inflow. Therefore, there is a net reduction in the stock of atmospheric greenhouse gases. We can see this reduction in Figure 8.3b.

To accurately describe the behavior of the system, we need to consider all stocks that affect that behavior. In this case, that means including a second stock—that of heat. Just

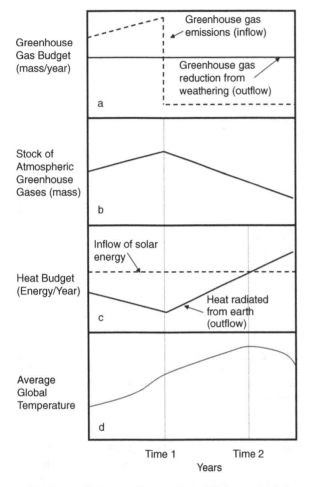

FIGURE 8.3 Understanding stocks and flows can be helpful in understanding time delays regarding global climate change.

heat. You can see this process in Figure 8.3c. Here, the inflow of energy from the sun is approximated as constant and shown as a dotted horizontal line. Note that the rate of outflow begins increasing at Time 1, when the stock of atmospheric greenhouse gases begins to decrease. However, from Time 1 to Time 2, the rate of outflow of heat is still less than the inflow of solar energy. Therefore, the temperature in Figure 8.3d (which indicates a stock of heat energy) does not start decreasing until Time 2.[21]

Failure to appreciate this type of time delay in CASs has contributed to complacency regarding global climate change. Many people adopt a wait-and-see attitude, with the assumption that if climate change begins to cause major problems, we will take drastic measures then to deal with it.[22] However, this example shows that even drastic changes regarding emissions will not produce immediate affects. Remember that the lag between Time 1 (the institution of radical reductions in greenhouse gases) and Time 2 (first signs of temperature decrease) will be measured in decades. With and understanding of stocks and flows, one can view these delays as part of a longer process.

Feedback Loops

As we learned in Chapter 7, much of the unpredictable behavior of CASs are the result of feedback loops within the system. While understanding these loops will not necessarily allow us to predict specific behavior of a system, it will allow us to understand the patterns of behavior that we see. Recall from Chapter 5 the Nature Balanced and Nature Anarchic caricatures. In the Nature

as in the daily temperature example, the inflow to this stock is energy from the sun, while the outflow is heat energy radiating off the earth. Greenhouse gases help to trap heat within the earth's atmosphere. Reducing the stock of those gases in the atmosphere increases the rate at which heat radiates off the earth. That is, it increases the outflow of

Balanced view, ecosystems (examples of CASs) exist at an equilibrium state. Any change to conditions is responded to by stabilizing forces that return the system to that equilibrium.

Consider the process of driving. Even on a straight road, one does not simply let the wheel go and trust the car to follow a completely linear path. Rather, driving requires constant adjustments. We can consider these adjustments a balancing feedback loop. When the car goes too far left, we correct by turning slightly to the right. When it goes too far right, we correct again, each time maintaining the car's position on the road. The road, in this example, is analogous to the equilibrium state in the Nature Balanced view. Now we can understand the Nature Balance world as one characterized by balancing feedback loops.

Conversely, the Nature Anarchic world is characterized by reinforcing feedback loops. While balancing feedback loops work to decrease change and return to an equilibrium state, reinforcing feedback loops reinforce change. That is, small changes become amplified into large changes. Exponential population growth of an organism (e.g., bacteria, plants, humans) provides a good example. Given adequate resources, larger populations are capable of higher increases in population. For example, one bacteria cell is capable of becoming two cells in the next generation—a gain of one cell. Ten cells, however, can become twenty cells in the next generation—a gain of ten cells. Figure 8.4 shows a graph of the growth of a bacteria cell.

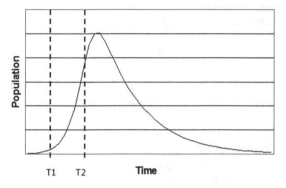

FIGURE 8.4 Reinforcing feedback loops can lead to unexpectedly rapid growth.

Notice how the growth of the population appears relatively moderate up until T1 but then takes a sharp rise between T1 and T2. It is this relatively short period of rapid change that often catches us off guard. If a population of water lilies will cover a pond in 30 days by doubling their population every day, it will take 27 days to cover 12.5 percent of the pond. That does not seem to be much of a threat, but three days later the pond will be completely covered with lilies. While that may be good if you want to grow lilies for economic benefit, it is bad if you want to swim or maintain any other organisms in the system.

Of course, there are always limits to growth. A truism of systems thinking is that every reinforcing feedback loop is bounded by a balancing feedback loop at a broader scale. In our bacteria example, the growth is sustained by a resource (for bacteria, this is usually a stock of food). At T2, that resource has been all but used up, resulting in a decline in the population after T2. This general pattern

BOX 8.4   Vicious and Virtuous Cycles

While vicious cycles tend to warrant the most attention, positive feedback loops have also been used to effect beneficial change. In the Indian state of Rajasthan, managing water has always been a challenge. The region receives little rain, and what it does receive comes primarily during the three-month monsoon season. Until the 1940s, local residents had successfully managed their water using *johads*, small dams made of mud and rocks to collect rainwater. In addition to providing a more stable water supply, the johads also helped recharge groundwater by allowing water to percolate into the aquifer below.

In the 1940s commercial logging resulted in a loss of forests and the subsequent erosion of soil from the mountainsides filled up the *johads*. Without the recharging effect of the johads, the groundwater continued to decrease, causing further loss of forests. Deep wells were dug to satisfy short-term demands for water, but these wells only further decreased available groundwater, exacerbating the problem in the long term. As these wells went dry, women had to spend large parts of their day traveling long distances to retrieve water.

In 1985 Rajendra Singh, a volunteer from an NGO called Tarun Bharat Sangh, arrived intent on opening on clinic to tend to local residents' medical needs. However, he quickly learned that the most immediate need of local residents was a stable water supply. Instead of building a clinic, Singh and his colleagues dug out a *johad* that had been filled with eroded soil. As a result, during the next monsoon season, the *johad* again performed the dual service of providing a water supply for residents as well as recharging the groundwater. Local residents saw this success and dug out another *johad* for the following year with still more success.

This success bred more success. By 1996, there were nine johads and the water level in the aquifer had risen significantly. The village even began reforesting the hillside, aware of the forests' importance in avoiding soil erosion and providing resources. Other villages, seeing this success, followed suit with their own programs to rebuild *johads*. As of 2005, there were 5,000 *johads* in 750 villages with hundreds of previously dry wells flowing once again. The experience has created a new era of environmental consciousness within the region. Residents now have a better appreciation of the value of their local resources and have successfully fought legal and economic battles to keep commercial forestry, fishing, and mining interests from degrading their local resources. (See Marten et al. [2005] for more information.)

is applicable far beyond bacteria. It can be seen with any population that sustains its growth with nonrenewable resources.

Indeed, reinforcing feedback loops sit at the heart of many sustainability issues. For example, we discussed earlier the relationship between poverty and environmental degradation. That relationship can be expressed in terms of a reinforcing feedback loop in which environmental degradation causes an increase in poverty, and that increased poverty results in greater environmental degradation. This pattern of events is so prevalent that we have a term for them: vicious cycles. However, as Box 8.4 illustrates, reinforcing loops are not inherently bad. If we learn to recognize the presence of balancing and reinforcing loops, we will be able to identify the leverage points in a system that will allow small changes that we make to reverberate through the system and effect larger changes.

Resilience

Applying the systems thinking concepts above can help us to understand decisions in the context of resilience. Recall from Chapter 7 that resilience refers to a CAS's ability to respond to change. People often blame external events for dramatic changes in stocks, such as the impact of Hurricane Katrina on the dikes in New Orleans or the 2009 earthquake in Haiti. It is painfully obvious that without the hurricane or earthquake, New Orleans and Haiti would not have suffered the disaster. In each case, the trigger is not the sole cause of the problem, however. A systems perspective would suggest that internal aspects of each system already contained the seeds for the disasters, creating systems more likely to fail.

Building a city below sea level in a hurricane zone and not strengthening the dikes created a system that was prone to failure. From a systems perspective, the original design of New Orleans is as much to blame for the disaster as the trigger of the hurricane. The same can be said of Haiti's earthquake. Less than two months after Haiti's 7.0 magnitude earthquake, which caused an estimated 200,000 deaths, Chile experienced an 8.4 magnitude quake, causing an estimated 1,000 deaths. Some of this difference in loss of life can be attributed to the proximity of the earthquakes to population centers. Still, much of the destruction in Haiti from the earthquake has been attributed to high poverty, high corruption, poor construction practices, and limited experience with earthquakes. In short, Haiti's social and economic systems were much less resilient than Chile's.

The lack of resilience in the physical infrastructure of New Orleans and Haiti are easy enough to see. Using systems concepts can help us identify less obvious issues regarding resilience. Stocks affecting resilience might be physical (e.g., food supply) or more abstract (e.g., trust between stakeholders). The rate at which stocks change is dependent largely upon the causal loops affecting them. One can gain a better understanding of how this works by becoming familiar with **system archetypes**—common patterns of causal loops identified to describe common patterns of behavior observed in a number of contexts including sustainability. For example, the tragedy of the commons can be seen as multiple reinforcing feedback loops at the small scale (i.e., decisions to add grazers) bounded by a balancing loop at the collective scale (i.e., the reduction of capacity of the land).[23]

Understanding a system helps us ask different questions about a decision, helps us anticipate consequences differently, and will likely enable us to make decisions that increase their sustainability. By helping us identify common pitfalls and strategies for avoiding them, systems thinking can also help us make better decisions. A full explanation of systems concepts is beyond the scope of this text, but we close this chapter with a number of ways in which one might apply the information in this chapter toward improving one's decision-making skills.

BOX 8.5   Another Look at the Delaney Amendment

History tells us that the Delaney amendment, however noble, was not realistic or functional. What would good food safety regulations look like and how should we make these decisions? If we use the suggestions above, we could fashion a hypothetical set of process and considerations to illustrate these concepts.

If food safety is the goal, the system of study must include agriculture, food preservation and processing, as well as marketing and distribution. Considering sustainability will encourage the addition of human and environmental health experts to the system. A set of meetings will be necessary for them to learn how to talk to each other and to better understand issues, the responsibility, and the power they have. It may be useful to begin the process by focusing on an additive that is less complicated.

If recommendations are focusing on one piece of the system, such as artificial sweeteners, it is important to consider the consequences of removing them from the U.S. market to those who might be most affected (diabetics and dieting people). The feedback loops that affect this stock are one way to explore these consequences.

The process of approving new additives might be different from that of screening existing additives. New chemicals that bring an acknowledged risk may be rejected on the basis of precaution. How often should a chemical be reviewed? What types and levels of feedback should trigger additional investigation? What type of test result would enable the manufacture to agree to remove the chemicals from the market? As the number of additives skyrockets, a government lab cannot be expected to perform all the approval tests, and the maker might not have the best interest of the consumers at heart. Who should provide this service? Who should pay for that research? Who will increase their revenue as a result of approving the additive? An adaptive collaborative management strategy could be designed with the input from the chemical manufacturers, the human health experts, the social justice advocates, and the environmental community to establish a system of trigger points that could launch additional tests for the chemicals which, based on a historic review of similar chemicals, are most likely to generate problems.

What are the ultimate goals of this group, and can agreement on a vision help remove the differences they will stumble over as they protect their interests? What is their duty toward the most vulnerable populations? Perhaps the group could agree to establish different food quality limits for items most typically consumed by infants and the elderly or employ the use of warning labels for foods that are a greater risk to pregnant women. To what extent should known mutagens that could change the genetic makeup of future generations be regulated differently than additives that are toxic to pesticide applicators?

Do we have the technological ability to know the consequences of these food additives? How do we balance uncertainty, risk, and the promise of a new product? If epidemiology tests on mice are not generalizable to people, and we are not comfortable testing additives on people, does precaution win, or do we establish agreements that will enable companies to remove additives if they fail to pass a future test? Can we ever know the impact of a single chemical given the combination of additives we consume regularly? Recognizing the difficulty that we have in understanding probability and uncertainty should help our hypothetical team develop better analogies to explain the test results to each other, the media, and the public.

CONCLUSION

From this brief introduction to processing and interpreting information, we can point out ways to improve our decision-making skills in the context of complex social-ecological systems.

1. Include an awareness of our cognitive limitations and biases in the critical thinking process. We have only covered a small fraction of the errors in judgment people make as a result of cognitive heuristics. While deliberating on every decision *ad infinitum* is not feasible, we can improve the quality of our decisions by making a conscious effort not to fall into the types of traps explained above. If we have the responsibility of conveying information to others, we can improve decisions by respective cognitive biases such that help people perceive and understand the material. How the information is shared is just as important as what the information is.

2. Define a system with boundaries big enough to include all aspects of the sustainability framework.[24] Many of the most important stocks in the context of sustainability lie outside the conventional scope of people's decision-making process. Assessing the impacts of technological developments requires looking at direct and indirect effects. Our economic system has ignored environmental externalities for decades, and most people now agree that practice has made it difficult to understand and pay for the effects of pollution.

Remember that scale is both spatial and temporal. The definition of sustainable development asks us to consider the impacts into the future. If our system boundaries only include the present, our deliberations will be based on false assumptions and a lack of information. Life-cycle analysis (see Chapter 6) is a tool that quantifies and considers the inputs and outputs for each product. Doing so enables us to make choices in products and production systems to reduce extractive impacts and waste generation.

3. Identify the important stocks in the system and the significant flows in and out of those stocks. In many cases, technology increases the rate at which we can increase and decrease important stocks, including both physical stocks (e.g., natural resources) and more abstract ones (e.g., public awareness). Look for changes that may affect the level of stocks without immediately affecting the behavior of the system. The level of important stocks often has a large effect on the resilience of a system. Also look for how stocks might affect the timing of a system's response to change.

4. Identify both balancing and reinforcing feedback loops. The stabilizing influence of balancing feedback loops can be valuable, but these loops have limits. Too often policies try to enforce growth in a system that is hitting its limits or create stability at a level that is not sustainable. Shipping food to refugees helps bridge a gap in an emergency situation and is not usually thought of as a bad policy because of humanitarian principles. Increasing agricultural efficiency may be a better long-term strategy, however, as it helps a nation generate its own food, if this can be done within environmental limits.

Reinforcing feedback loops can result in unpredictable behavior, but as we have seen, understanding these loops can help us to spark significant positive change.

5. Look for strategies to increase information flows such as identifying indicators of positive and negative change patterns. Delays in providing information can slow the system's response to changes, which can cause negative consequences. Make sure all of the concerned parties are getting feedback information so that they can adjust their behavior, too. Technology should be used to make feedback more visible, rather than hide the signals that the system might be sending.

6. Rather than blaming an event for a calamity, look at the system. In how many other ways was the system affected, in addition to the trigger? National debates often turn on this question—does our foreign policy reduce or increase terrorism? The answer is probably buried in the intertwined feedback loops and flows of weapons, goodwill, money, drugs, and products that link our global economy.

The BP oil spill discussed in Chapter 6 was not merely a technical failure. It was the result of several years of decisions characterized by overconfidence in technological capability and lack of precautions. In other words, careless management directives and poor government regulation resulted decreased the resilience of the drilling operation. Thus, a more complete analysis of the situation requires broadening the scale from a specific event to the pattern of decisions made over a period of time. It may be tempting to stop there in the analysis, and simply

demand justice be done and those parties directly responsible for the poor decisions held accountable. This may be true, but the analysis would not be complete without acknowledging the role that the United States' demand for inexpensive oil played in creating those careless management directives and poor regulation.

This is not an exhaustive list of measures we can take to improve individual decision making, but establishing these habits will provide a world of insights into sustainability that was not previously apparent.

REFERENCES

Braun, W. 2002. *The System Archtypes*. www.u .uniklu.ac.at/gossimit/pap/sd/wb_sysarch.pdf.

Brower, Michael, and Warren Leon. 1999. *The Consumer's Guide to Effective Environmental Choices*. New York: Three Rivers Press.

Carson, Rachel. 1962. *Silent Spring*. Boston: Houghton Mifflin.

Center for Media and Democracy. 1997. "One Bad Apple? Facts and Myths Behind the 'Alar Scare,'" PR Watch, 4(2). Accessed on October 18, 2009 from www.prwatch.org/prissues/1997Q2/alar .html.

Gardner, G. T. and P. C. Stern. 1996. *Environmental problems and human behavior*. Boston: Allyn and Bacon.

Hogarth, R. M. 1980. *Judgement and Choice: The Psychology of Decision*. New York: Wiley Publishing.

Hrab, N. 2004. "An apple a day." Hrab Op-Ed at American Spectator Online, Jan 18, 2004.

Accessed on October 9, 2009 from http://cei.org/gencon/019,03821.cfm.

Jacobson, Michael. 1972. *Eater's Digest: The Consumer's Fact-Book of Food Additives*. Doubleday & Co.

Jacobson, Susan K., Mallory D. McDuff, and Martha C. Monroe. 2006. *Conservation Education and Outreach Techniques*. Oxford: Oxford University Press.

Kaplan, R. and S. Kaplan. 1982. *Cognition and Environment: Functioning in an Uncertain World*. New York: Praeger.

Kaplan, S. 2000. "Human nature and environmentally responsible behavior." *Journal of Social Issues*. 56 (3): 491–508.

Karl, T. R. and K. E. Trenberth. 2003. "Modern global climate change." *Science* 302: 1719–1723.

Mandler, G. 1975a. "Memory storage and retrieval: some limits on the research of attention and consciousness," In P. M. Rabbitt and S. Dornic, Eds. *Attention and Performance*, Vol.V. London: Academic.

———. 1975b. "Consciousness: respectable, useful, and probably necessary," In R. L. Solso, Ed. *Information processing and cognitive psychology*. Hillsdale, NJ: Erlbaum.

Marten, Gerald, Steve Brooks, and Amanda Suutari. 2005. "Environmental tipping points: A new slant on strategic environmentalism." *World Watch Magazine* 6(10): 10–14.

Meadows, Donella. 1991. *The Global Citizen*. Washington, DC: Island Press.

———. 1996. "Farewell to the Delaney Amendment," *The Global Citizen*, September 26 1996, Accessible at www.pcdf.org/meadows/.

———. 2008. *Thinking in Systems*. White River Junction, VT: Chelsea Green.

Meadows, Donella, Dennis Meadows, and Jorgen Randers. 1992. *Beyond the Limits*. Post Mills, VT: Chelsea Green.

Mollaghasemi, M. and J. Pet-Edwards. 1997. *Making Multiple-Objective Decisions*. Washington: IEEE.

Moxnes, E. 2000. "Not only the tragedy of the commons: misperceptions of feedback and policy for sustainable development." *System Dynamics Review* 16(4): 325–348.

Nisbett, R. and L. Ross. 1980. *Human inferences: Strategies and shortcoming of social judgment*. Englewood Cliffs, NJ: Prentice Hall.

Peterson, C. R. and L. R. Beach. 1967. "Man as an intuitive statistician, *Psychological Bulletin* 68: 29–46.

Simon, Herbert. 1955. "A behavioral model of rational choice," *The Quarterly Journal of Economics*. 69:1: 99–118.

———. 1956. "Rational choice and the structure of the environment." *Psychological Review* 63(2): 129–138.

———. 1972. "Theories of bounded rationality." In C. B. McGuire and R. Radner, Eds. *Decision and Organization*, 161–176. Amsterdam: North-Holland Pub. Accessed in the Herbert Simon Collection, of Carnegie Mellon University, Article Reprint #361, http://diva.library.cmu.edu/webapp/simon/item.jsp?q=/box00065/fld05032/bdl0001/doc0001/.

Slovic, P., B. Fischhoff and S. Lichtenstein. 1977. *Annual Reviews of Psychology*. 28: 1–39. Accessed on April 13, 2009 from www.annualreviews.org/aronline.

Slovic, P. 1987. "Perception of risk." *Science* 236: 280–285.

Sterman, J. D. and L. B. Sweeney. 2002. "Cloudy skies: Assessing public understanding of global warming." *System Dynamics Review* 18(2): 207–240.

Tversky, A. and D. Kahneman. 1974. "Judgment under uncertainty: Heuristics and biases." *Science*. 185: 1124–1131.

————. 1981. "The framing of decisions and the psychology of choice," *Science* 211: 453–458.

ENDNOTES

1. Peterson and Beach (1967).
2. For example, see Mollaghasemi and Pet-Edwards (1997).
3. A variety of discussions of the limits of rationality exist, particularly in Hogarth (1980), Kaplan and Kaplan (1982), and Gardner and Stern (1996). More of Simon's original contributions can be found in Simon (1955 and 1956).
4. Nisbett and Ross (1980, page 65).
5. Kaplan and Kaplan (1982), citing Mandler (1975a and 1975b).
6. Nisbett and Ross (1980).
7. Simon (1972).
8. Slovic et al. (1977). Kahneman was awarded a Nobel Prize in economics for his work challenging rationality in 2002. He could only share the prize with his partner in spirit, unfortunately, as Tversky died in 1996 and the award is not given posthumously.
9. Tversky and Kahneman (1974).
10. Tversky and Kahneman (1974).
11. Hrab (2004) and Center for Media and Democracy (1997).
12. Nisbett and Ross (1980, page 60).
13. Gardner and Stern (1996), Kaplan and Kaplan (1982), and Tversky and Kahneman (1981).
14. Kaplan (2000).
15. Jacobson et al. (2006).
16. Moxnes (2000).
17. Slovic (1987).
18. Brower and Leon (1999).
19. Examples of calculators can be found at www.myfootprint.org/, www.footprintnetwork.org/en/index.php/GFN/page/calculators/, and www.ecologicalfootprint.org/Global%20Footprint%20Calculator/GFPCalc.html, among others.
20. Donella Meadows has been one of the leaders of several efforts to understand systems and one of the few to make systems accessible to the general public. Her biweekly syndicated column, The Global Citizen, was picked up by newspapers across the country, and used to explain systems thinking in the context of the national debt, current political debates, or gardening (Meadows (1991) and www.pcdf.org/meadows/). Meadows (2008) provides an excellent introduction to systems language and the applications of a systems perspective.
21. Note that there are a number of other factors that could influence the energy budget of the earth. This example is used here to illustrate the concept of stocks and flows. For a more thorough discussion regarding global climate change, see Karl and Trenberth (2003).
22. For a more thorough discussion on the relationship between misunderstanding this time delay and complacency regarding climate change, see Sterman and Sweeney (2002).
23. For a more thorough discussion of system archetypes, see Braun (2002).
24. For a more in-depth discussion of how to apply this and other systems concepts to decision making, see Meadows (2008).

CHAPTER 9

The Process of Changing Behavior

Chapter 8 focused on how our thinking challenges the decision-making process and how we might improve the way we think about decisions with which we are faced. While this is certainly a fundamental step in making better decisions, simply promoting clearer thinking about sustainability issues will not bring about the changes required to become a more sustainable society. People's behavior regarding an issue depends on much more than how they think about that issue. In this chapter, we will explore a number of other factors that play a role in implementing changes and the obstacles they present in the context of shifting toward more sustainable behavior. We begin by looking specifically at one commonly used theory of behavior change that can be applied to both the individual scale and the social scale. By understanding this process and the range of factors involved, we will be better able to promote more sustainable behavior both in ourselves and in others. This chapter closes with some suggestions for how to do that.

THEORY OF PLANNED BEHAVIOR

What determines whether individuals accept and put into practice a new idea? Psychologists

have wrestled with this question for decades. One critical element of adopting a new practice is information. People need to know what, how, and sometimes why before they will be motivated to make a change. Information enables people to form beliefs about the potential behavior and the consequences of that action. However, even people who are well informed and believe the behavior is the right course of action often fail to make adjustments necessary, as demonstrated by the number of people who begin to smoke cigarettes while well aware of the negative health effects. Therefore, factors besides information and beliefs must play a role in behavior.

There are a number of models for predicting people's behavior. One of the most useful is Martin Fishbein's and Icek Ajzen's **Theory of Planned Behavior**.[1] According to this theory, there are three important factors that help determine our intention to try something different: **attitudes**, **subjective norms**, and **perceived control**. A fourth factor, **actual control**, also plays an important role. Taken together, these four elements do a fairly good job of predicting whether people will adopt or change a behavior (see Figure 9.1). Let us look at them in turn.

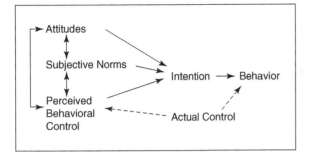

FIGURE 9.1 The influences in the Theory of Planned Behavior interrelate to affect intention, which leads to behavior. *(Adapted from Ajzen 1985)*

Attitudes

An attitude predisposes someone toward or away from an action. Attitudes are based on beliefs (which are formed from experience or information) and a positive or negative emotional response to that belief. Generally, a behavior includes several attitudes. For example, an individual could acknowledge the negative health consequences of eating high-fat and high-sugar foods, but hold a stronger positive attitude about the perceived benefits of eating fast, convenient, prepackaged food. The attitude component of the Theory of Planned Behavior refers to the sum of attitudes about the expected consequences of the behavior in question.

In some cases, deeply held ethical values probably give some attitudes greater weight than others. For example, when an ecosystem has become overpopulated with a particular species, such as whitetail deer, it is common practice for managers to cull the population to avoid widespread damage to the ecosystem. Residents who place a value on the individual rights of animals will probably believe this is

not an appropriate solution while those who value ecosystem health (biocentrism) might believe it is. In this way underlying values contribute to attitudes which help determine willingness to support certain decisions or behave in one way.

With most behaviors, however, several conflicting attitudes may influence a single individual's decision. The combination of attitudes an individual holds regarding such things as health, status, job security, or family well-being may not all support the same behavior. In these cases, people either tolerate the dissonance between conflicting attitudes or convince themselves that some factors are not very important. Personal preferences and desires, as they relate to this behavior, are factored into this element. So something as basic as buying food for dinner might involve numerous conflicting attitudes, including one's sense of taste, whether children will eat it, the relative value, its origin, whether it was produced with environmentally-friendly practices, and so forth. Of course, just as beliefs alone are not predictive of behavior, neither are beliefs and attitudes.

Subjective Norms

Most people care about what other people think. Even the most rebellious among us adhere to some set of social norms. Some of these amount to etiquette (e.g., closing one's mouth while chewing, raising one's hand in class), while others may revolve around matters of style (e.g., clothing choice and hairstyle). This social influence is not awarded to everyone. We do not necessarily care about what *everyone* else thinks, but each of us can probably identify at least a few people whose opinions we care about. In the preceding example, if friends frown upon eating hamburgers, the individual is less likely to stop for one.

The norms that affect one's behavior are subjective in part because they depend upon whose opinion a person values. They are a combination of what important others think about the behavior and the degree to which the individual cares about that social pressure. These dynamics apply in a wide array of contexts, including sustainability. If people perceive a norm of environmentally and socially responsible behavior among a group whose opinion they respect, they will be more likely to adopt that behavior. This component of the model is functioning when people pay attention to whether their neighbors have placed their container of recyclables on the curb each week, and recognize that their neighbors will expect them to do the same. Valuing their neighbors' approval, they feel an obligation to remember their recyclables. Activating this norm may be most helpful with behaviors that are more effective when adopted by a group.

Perceived Control

The best information, the most positive attitudes, and the most supportive subjective norm will still not change behavior if people believe they are not able to perform the behavior—hence the importance of perceived control. If an individual does not have the confidence in his or her ability to perform the action, or believes that performing the behavior will never actually amount to much, the lack of perceived control will prevent the behavior from occurring. This factor includes a variety of potential barriers to behavior change, such as the perceived lack of time, lack of skill, and lack of opportunity. Some, for example, may express a willingness to purchase fair-trade chocolate, but point out that such a product is not carried at their local store. However, other convenient opportunities may exist to purchase the product (e.g., the Internet or a specialty store). Also, grocery store managers are often quite responsive toward suggestions made by frequent customers. If they think a product will sell, then they are generally willing to order it.

In this example, increasing perceived control may involve identifying possible strategies to reduce perceived barriers. An increase in perceived control could also be the result of training to build skills, of a practice session to acknowledge that the requisite capacity does indeed exist, or working toward changing the availability or opportunities. When students collect water quality data, analyze their findings, and report their results to the community leadership, they are gaining a variety of skills that often empower them to believe they can help resolve environmental problems. Their self-efficacy helps increase perceived control.

Of course, there are plenty of instances where the perceived lack of control is quite accurate. When the physical infrastructure is a very real barrier, the theory identifies this as actual control. For example, it is difficult to stop driving single-passenger vehicles when roads are not safe to walk or bicycle on, public transportation is inadequate, or regional planning has placed living, shopping, and working places far from each other. If these are real and intractable barriers to alternate transportation choices, individuals are not likely to change behavior despite knowing, caring, believing others want them to, and believing they can do so. Actual control can influence our perception of control, or once we have an intention, it can influence our inability to act.

Understanding Planned Behavior

The theory suggests that the first three factors predict intention, and as long as there is no significant time lag and the opportunity exists, intention predicts behavior. We can return to the purchasing of food to see how these factors combine to affect behavior. Regarding attitudes, many people lack knowledge about where to buy more sustainably produced foods or even what foods are more sustainable. Thus, their beliefs about foods do not include information about how those foods were produced or the potential consequences of consumption. Even if they do know which foods are produced in more environmentally and socially responsible ways, personal preferences in the form of attitudes can have a significant influence. People often prefer food that is familiar and find it difficult to make changes, especially when the kinds of changes that are associated with a more sustainable diet—eating less meat and more seasonal foods—requires learning different recipes and expanding one's tastes.

Subjective norms also play a significant role in food purchases. Families often have strong traditions about special meals and gatherings. Knowing that grandma will feel bad if the oyster stuffing and turkey are rejected at Thanksgiving may cause a newly minted vegetarian to cave in. If grandma was a gardener and even ate the weeds in her salad, however, she might be excited to discover a grandchild's interest in organic, seasonal foods and support that behavior. For some behaviors, this factor plays a minimal role, but for others, people most certainly care about what important others think about potential behavior changes.

Finally, perceived and actual control often become important factors in terms of people's available time, money, skill, and opportunity. One may have to travel farther to purchase sustainably produced products and those products may cost more than the conventionally (and unsustainably) produced alternatives. Knowing what to do with weird, locally grown vegetables and wondering if one can produce edible entrees can be a barrier. Even if people understand the external costs of products (see Chapter 6), they may feel like their personal financial situation precludes the purchase of more expensive products.

It is possible to make a similar analysis of obstacles for many other aspects of our lives— how we get ourselves to and from work, wash and dry our laundry, heat and cool our homes, and so forth. In each case, the factors of beliefs and attitudes about consequences, the perceived social pressure from important others, and the real and perceived ability to adopt the behavior help predict whether someone intends to take the plunge. This is not to say that other factors do not exist. Researchers have explored factures such as

---

BOX 9.1   Unexpected Barriers to Recycling

Sometimes the information necessary for changing behavior is not about fundamental aspects of the social-ecological system. In a study in Ann Arbor, Michigan, researchers were trying to identify why some residents used the curbside recycling while others did not. Surveys uncovered no significant differences in knowledge about the benefits of recycling or in attitudes regarding its importance. Finally, they found what was missing. Those who were not recycling reported being unfamiliar with how to do it. Flyers explaining which materials were recyclable and in which bins those materials belonged proved to be what was needed. In this case, a lack of procedural information regarding the desired activity proved to be the barrier (De Young 1988–1989).

---

values, sense of place, and responsibility, for example, and developed additional theories to explain behaviors.

The strength of the Theory of Planned Behavior is that it is specific to a particular behavior. A generic sense of environmental values or sustainability ethic, therefore, is not a factor itself, but probably influences one's attitudes regarding a behavior. Another theory[2] uses values and world view as the basis for beliefs and sense of responsibility, all of which dictate a personal norm for environmental behaviors. This is a more generic model. It has less predictive power, but may help tease out the more global constructs that are at work when people consider a variety of positions and opportunities.

Nevertheless, predicting sustainable behaviors is not an easy task. Different behaviors will require more of one factor than another. Different people with different values and experiences will require their own mix of factors. There is no "one size fits all" for encouraging sustainable behaviors.

A variety of strategies can help make people more likely to act on beliefs, know how their neighbors feel, and believe that they can successfully take actions. Some strategies work by motivating behavior. External motives, such as money or status are incentives that can help drive behavior. Of course, if the reward is so great that it becomes the only reason people adopt a behavior, it is not very durable in the face of resource constraints.[3] Small rewards, such as prizes for stream cleanup competitions may be more appropriate. Internal motives, such as satisfaction and frugality, are considered to be valuable components of environmentally responsible actions and can be emphasized in persuasive testimonials about how great it feels to do the right thing.[4] Finally, working with others to make a difference is a significant motivator that can help drive parents to mount campaigns to raise funds, build schools, and improve community safety.[5]

OBSTACLES TO SUSTAINABLE BEHAVIOR

Whether people intend to take action is a function of how strongly people consider the importance of each of these elements (attitude, subjective norm, and perceived control), assuming of course that the action is possible. A number of factors contribute to how communities and individuals weigh their importance.

Political Obstacles to Sustainable Behavior

Political structures, including government at local and larger levels, influence the ways people can enact more sustainable practices in their everyday lives. This is evident in the impact of tax subsidies in areas such as agriculture, transportation, and energy use, which can influence individuals to behave in more (or less) sustainable ways. Legislation is typically enforced with regulations that create disincentives (such as fines or fees) and sometimes incentives (such as cost-share funds for the installation of new manure pits or constructed wetlands).

Government also affects behavior through enabling people to become engaged in planning decisions. The types of participatory processes that people have access to are critical to building trust in leadership that affects whether even those who never intended to become engaged believe the outcome is fair and equitable. Chapter 10 addresses the importance of multi-stakeholder processes.

Lack of Social Capital

The importance of subjective norms suggests that interpersonal networks can do a great deal to facilitate and support sustainable practices if strong enough and if they are clearly oriented toward sustainability. Many programs suggest that people form such supports groups (Transition Towns,

Sustainability Street, Slow Food). Beyond subjective norms, however, these networks can serve other roles. If such networks are not in place—if people feel isolated or powerless—then it is much harder for people to act in a positive way. The same is true, of course, if strong networks exist but reinforce unsustainable practices and values. This has been the topic of much debate in recent years, especially around the concept of **social capital**. As defined by political scientist Robert Putnam, social capital refers to "connections among individuals—social networks and the norms of reciprocity and trustworthiness that arise from them."[6]

Social capital, like natural, human, and manufactured capital, can include both private and public goods. Strong connections to other people improve an individual's quality of life. Similarly, a network of strong connections within a community can increase that community's resilience by improving the ability of residents to form a coordinated response to new community needs as they arise. For this reason, social capital is also vital for robust democratic politics. Healthy public institutions—which are crucial for the achievement of greater environmental, social, and economic sustainability—require widespread participation in the networks of civic engagement that embody social capital.[7]

Putnam argues that social capital "has eroded steadily and sometimes dramatically over the past two generations."[8] Other evidence supports his claim, including a 2006 study, which concluded that not only have informal and formal networks declined, as Putnam notes, but close personal ties have also diminished in recent years. Declines in social networks and increases in social isolation are important for efforts to achieve greater sustainability for several reasons. First, organizations and movement for sustainability, as for other kinds of social change, cannot succeed without both informal and formal social capital—the connections among participants that keep the organization together and effective. In this way social capital can significantly increase community involvement in local sustainability initiatives.[9]

Additionally, declining social networks make democratic processes less effective, so that sustainability advocates will not be able to change laws, policies, and institutions. For example, public apathy and low voter turnout can result in unpopular political outcomes. Third, and perhaps most important, people who are socially isolated and lack deep and meaningful connections with others are less likely to act on their values—because they lack peer pressure, moral support, good examples, and social structures that facilitate environmentally and socially responsible behavior.[10]

Accepting Unsustainable Outcomes

One problem that arises from a personal lack of social connections is the sense that one faces the daunting challenge of sustainability alone and is, therefore, doomed to fail. While proper collective action can lead to more positive outcomes, there is a temptation on the part of individual stakeholders to become overwhelmed in the face of the challenges involved in creating a more sustainable society. This response may parallel the tragedy of the commons that Hardin described.

Another way to describe this challenge might be the "drop in the bucket" excuse. When faced with the short-term costs (e.g., time, money, effort) of adopting more sustainable habits, many people wonder about the significance of their individual actions. Global climate change provides the context for a common question made in these types of arguments: What difference will my riding public transit make if everyone else is still driving gas guzzlers? Their answer may be to accept unsustainable behavior as inevitable and continue with irresponsible practices. This argument may hold some truth: a single individual's change in behavior is unlikely to cause significant changes in global, complex problems.

But then, this logic also applies to other social goals. What difference does one teacher make in the goal of improving the United States' educational system? Does one judge really have a significant impact on the development fair and just legal system? We do not accept these attitudes in other contexts, and we need not accept them in the context of sustainability. From a deontological perspective, we do them because they are the right thing to do. From a consequentialist perspective, our actions do combine to make a real difference. For example, a recent analysis suggests that even in the context of a challenge like global climate change, individuals' actions can make a difference. By making 17 relatively easy changes to their behavior (e.g., changing air filters and drying clothes outdoors), Americans could decrease the United States' national carbon output by 626 million metric tons, slightly more than France's annual carbon output.[11]

Indeed, sustainability is a collective, social goal. Like other social goals, it is influenced by individual choices but not solely determined by the individual. People who aim to act on the ethics of sustainability find that there is no easy way to understand the impact or significance of specific individual choices in larger contexts. This is true in part because of the complex relationship among the different scales at which sustainable decisions and actions take place. These different levels are interrelated and influence each other, although they do so in unequal ways.

The uncertainty inherent in such complex systems often provides the context for interplay between deontological and consequentialist ethics (see Chapter 3). Guided by a consequentialist ethic, which focuses on the results of actions, an individual may choose to ride a bus in an effort to contribute in a measurable, albeit small, way to larger efforts to decrease greenhouse gas emissions. A person guided by a deontological (rule-based) ethic might ride the bus based on a belief that decreasing one's contribution to global climate change is the right thing to do regardless of consequences. For such an individual, personal conviction may by itself be enough to motivate sustainable behavior. In practice, however, most people incorporate some aspect of both deontological and consequentialist ethics into their decisions. When principles and calculations of consequences fall short in the face of the overwhelming problems we face, our personal loyalties and connections to others can reinforce our good intentions.

Individualization

Some people may avoid fatalism in the face of overwhelming problems, but instead go too far in the other extreme—toward **individualization**. At first glance, individualization may seem like a positive trend. No one wants to be just another cog in a wheel. They want to be appreciated as unique individuals ready to make their own special mark on the world. We do not want to deter people from such aspirations. However, the problem arises when the individual scale becomes the only scale we see. In this sense, individualization refers to the tendency to think of social problems, including environmental harm, as essentially individual in both their causes and potential solution.[12] Some tend to believe that small scale actions—such as planting a tree or riding a bike—can make enough difference to "save the world."[13]

While energizing individuals to take action is generally a good thing, there are situations where the actions might actually be futile or misguided. When we individualize responsibility for environmental problems, we ignore the ways that large-scale patterns and institutions, including economic systems and the nature and exercise of political power affect individual behavior.[14] We think that the decision about, for example, whether or not to drive to work alone reflects only private factors, such as personal preferences, family lifestyle, and economic circumstances. Further analysis, however, quickly reveals that such decisions are also heavily influenced by structural factors such as the availability of public transportation, the safety and accessibility of pedestrian and bicycle routes, and

---

BOX 9.2   Addressing Obesity at Multiple Scales

Obesity is an example of an issue that has both individual and community infrastructure elements and thus provides an interesting glimpse into how more sustainable practices might benefit individual health, community well-being, and environmental quality. More frequent use of our own two feet as a transportation option is certainly better for our health and the environment than using a fossil fuel-propelled vehicle, for example. Yet the ability of an individual to safely walk from home to a store is partially determined by community transportation plans. Individuals are clearly able to adjust the amount of food they eat, but if restaurants do not offer dieters' options, people cannot choose appropriate meals. Weight reduction in general is also a function of social norms; many of us care about whether our friends approve of dieting or exercising, and attitudes about body image are very much a socially constructed. Technology has helped generate weight gain in the United States with the production of high-fat, high-sugar foods in addition to addictive and sedentary electronic activity, as well as solutions such as pills and surgery.

The town of Albert Lea, Minnesota, is collectively using all of these avenues to move toward better health through improved diet and more exercise. As one of the first communities in the Blue Zone Vitality Project, they worked with university experts and other consultants to increase options and make it easier for people to choose health. School menus and grocery labels were revised to feature more healthy options. Restaurants and households were encouraged to invest in smaller dinnerware to give the appearance of a full plate. Designated parents meet students at collection points and walk up to a mile in the "walking school bus" program. The town created new sidewalks and paved a 5-mile loop around a lake in town. Two-thirds of the community's restaurants agreed to make changes in their menus, such as offering salad as an option to French fries. The business community is subsidizing wellness programs for employees, and some are offering fruit during the monthly "doughnut day." Motivational speakers provide strategies for making life improvements.

Even in a personal and individually controlled behavior such as eating and exercising, behavior change is easier when addressed in a group. Engaging in a behavior with a group not only provides support and feedback but can build momentum to help reduce infrastructure barriers and create appropriate choices in places where community leaders are not steering change. In Albert Lea, the success is impressive. Businesses report less absenteeism and reduced health-care costs. Residents comment on the importance of new friends in walking groups. In just 10 months, the program participants have increased their life expectancy by 3.1 years. No doubt the town's social cohesiveness and the support individuals have from one another help make these infrastructural changes and personal changes possible. Both reinforce each other in a virtuous feedback loop (Brink 2010).

---

the location of businesses and other public and private facilities.

The failure to take seriously the larger social forces that shape individuals' decisions often leads to wrong diagnoses of causes and ineffective efforts at solutions. We may think that educating people about the consequences of a particular action is all that is necessary to achieve lasting change, but we have already seen the influence that social and institutional factors can have on a person's motives, intentions, and behavior. Further, and perhaps more important, even when individual behavior does change, the scale may not be adequate to address the major environmental (or social or economic) problems that we face. Thus, in addition to changed individual behaviors, such as using public transportation or eating locally, environmental and social problems require changes in regional and national policies and institutions.

Such changes might include increased miles per gallon standards for vehicles, greater funding for public transportation, and an end to the subsidies that encourage environmentally damaging agricultural production or having more than two children, among many others. This is not to say that individual behavioral changes are not necessary and important. Indeed, they are. However, our personal practices may not matter unless we understand them in larger contexts, and only with very small problems are individual actions alone enough to solve a problem.

There are no purely individual solutions to social problems such as racial and gender inequality or homelessness, nor to economic problems, including the banking, housing, and employment crises that appeared in 2008. While individual practices can contribute to these problems and to their solutions, individuals as individuals can neither cause them nor solve them. This is true for all the social, economic, and environmental dimensions of sustainability, which are collective goals that can be achieved only by collective efforts. Such efforts must include large-scale changes in public policy, infrastructure, land use, and economic institutions, among other factors. If we think about these problems as merely personal issues, we fail to understand their causes and potential solutions.

Distancing

Our final perspective that can be a barrier to sustainable behavior takes us back to the discussion that closed Chapter 4 regarding the ways in which our decisions can affect people very far away in space and time. When a process creates costs that are not felt by the producer or the consumer, economists call it a negative externality. When consumers fail to take those costs into account in their purchasing decisions, social scientists call it **distancing**.[15]

Distancing can result from consumers' lack of information, but also their lack of interest in the ecological (and social and economic) effects of production and consumption. Often, people distance themselves from the problems caused by production and consumption processes because they are (or perceive themselves to be) "upstream" from the effects of their actions. The classic example of this phenomenon is the factory that dumps pollutants into a river flowing away from it, so that only the water downstream is contaminated. This perspective is accounted for in the Theory of Planned Behavior in the beliefs about the consequence of the behavior. When individuals believe their actions have no important consequences, there is no cause for concern or change.

It is also possible to be metaphorically and temporally upstream, insofar as the harmful

BOX 9.3 Community Supported Agriculture

For people who want to live according to an ethic of sustainability, addressing the problem of distancing can be challenging. One effort to reduce the social, economic, and environmental harm that can be caused by "distanced" consumption is the movement to buy food and other products locally. "Buy Local" advocates argue that buying locally produced goods, direct from the producers or through farmers' markets or locally owned businesses, increases accountability, fairness, and environmental stewardship. While these movements consist of many diverse elements, their centerpieces are farmers' markets and community-supported agriculture (CSA).

The CSA movement aims to close the gap between consumers and farmers by connecting them in a direct relationship that is social, environmental, and economic. Members buy annual or seasonal shares that entitle them to a weekly bag or box of seasonal produce and sometimes also herbs, flowers, eggs, or dairy products. More than 100,000 CSA members currently buy shares from over 1,000 farms in North America, most of which produce organic or otherwise sustainably produced products. CSAs eliminate the middlemen required for conventional marketing and thus make it possible for farmers to receive better returns. Because members share risks and production costs, farmers are less vulnerable to economic and natural crises. Finally, CSAs link consumers directly to local food producers which increases their knowledge of the local "foodshed."

Still, buying locally is far from a complete solution to the environmental, social, or economic challenges of sustainability. It is important to note, for example, that when people in the U.S. and other wealthy nations buy more locally produced goods, the markets for fair-trade, organic, and similar products produced in the Global South may diminish. Also, proponents of industrial agriculture are quick to point out that large grocery chains provide more affordable food for the majority of the population that meets all government regulations for quality. In some cases, it also has a smaller carbon footprint than the locally grown food. For example, apples from NZ beat apples from the UK, even in the UK.

Many of the consumers and farmers who participate in CSAs are also involved in farmers markets, an old institution that has found new life in recent years as increasing numbers of people want to buy locally produced food directly from producers. The number of farmers markets has increased rapidly throughout the U.S. in small towns and large urban areas, with 4,385 markets operating weekly in 2008, according to the U.S. Department of Agriculture (USDA).[16] That figure has grown 6.8 percent since 2006 and more than doubled since 1994. Further, the USDA probably under-reports the actual number of markets around the country, many of which are not officially registered.

As farmers markets and CSAs have grown, so also have infrastructure and movements to support these and other local food programs. A number of certification and marketing programs promote locally grown and harvested food and help consumers find farmers, markets, and stores.[17] Related movements include those that assist people who want to grow their own food, either in traditional backyard gardens or with "edible landscapes" that incorporate fruit and nut trees, berries, herbs, and vegetables as both landscape elements and sources of food. A number of private and public schools have also begun vegetable and herb gardens that educate children

(continued)

about food and gardening, beautifying campuses, offering opportunities for exercise, and providing food for school lunches. The "100 Mile Diet"[18] encourages people to eat food grown and produced near their homes, and nonchain restaurants are beginning to feature locally produced foods. An umbrella term for these various movements, "**locavore**," was selected by the *Oxford American Dictionary* as the word of the year for 2007, reflecting the increasing popularity as well as scholarly significance of localist movements. (For more information, see Kingsolver, Kingsolver and Hopp [2008], Nabhan [2001], and Pollan [2007].)

effects of one's actions are felt much later, beyond the life span of the actor. When people distance themselves, temporally and spatially, they are unlikely to act with the care required, for example, by environmental justice or precautionary principles. More generally, when people distance themselves from the damaging environmental or social effects of their consumption, they do not think about the likely consequences of their actions.

The danger of distancing, as Thomas Princen summarizes, is that "When critical resource decisions are made by those who will not or cannot incur the costs of their decisions, accountability will be low and what gets counted is likely to be financial capital, not social and natural capital."[19] When people with power do not experience the negative effects of their choices, or adequately consider those to do, they are unlikely to make changes that would reduce these effects, which are usually felt by people without power and by the natural world.

Distancing has been discussed primarily in relation to environmental problems, but the concept can also be helpful in reflections on the social and economic elements of sustainability. It is possible, in other words, to distance ourselves from the negative social and economic results of our actions just as it is from their ecological consequences. Our consumption and purchasing decisions may support industries that use unfair labor practices or that damage local communities, for example, by shifting production and jobs to nations with fewer regulations and lower wages. However, few consumers feel their effects, other than those who work for the business or live in the company town. Most of us live upstream from the negative effects of our decisions to buy the cheapest possible product or shop at the most convenient store. Box 9.3 describes how community supported agriculture has presented an alternative to distancing with food production.

While we should not think about individual actions in isolation, individual and personal practices are important and necessary in order to support institutional changes in the marketplace and workplace, in community and civic organizations, and in local and national government. They can also be valuable in a host of other less tangible ways, including setting examples, mobilizing consumers, showing possibilities, and creating community. They are critical if new and better technologies are to succeed. Seeking sustainability is always a multifaceted and challenging task. It involves thinking about environmental, social, and economic components of each decision and option. It requires thinking about different geographic scales, from the local to the global. It entails thinking about individual actions as well as their systemic and structural contexts. Perhaps most of all, understanding and seeking sustainability demands that we think about the relations among these various dimensions, scales, and levels.

HOW CHANGE HAPPENS

We have now explored several factors that influence our decisions, including knowledge and understanding, attitudes, subjective norms, and perceived control. We have looked at a number of barriers to sustainable behavior within the context of these factors. In this section, we take a closer look at the process of behavior change both at the level of the individual and the community.

The Five Phases of Individual Change

Social theorist Everett Rogers describes five successive steps an individual goes through when changing behavior: knowledge, persuasion, decision, implementation, and confirmation.[20] While Rogers' theory is not the only way to understand change, it provides a helpful starting point for discussion of this process. Let us look at each of these steps in turn, paying particular attention to how the factors described previously play a role in the process.

Phase 1: Knowledge
Rogers argues that people must first become aware of the potential action, behavior, technology, or idea. It helps if people understand the problems that this innovation addresses. While presenting information about problems can be depressing, linking that with information about the solution can be powerful. As we learned in Chapter 8, people are selective in the things to which they attend. In addition to paying more attention to vivid and easily processed information, people attend to things they care about and often miss information that appears to be irrelevant. Therefore, it is important to understand what the audience cares about in order to increase awareness and concern in a meaningful and relevant way. Both are important precursors to knowledge. In addition to awareness, however, facts and figures, pros and cons, and detailed information about the behavior and how to perform it are needed.

Phase 2: Persuasion
Once people are informed, according to Rogers, the next step is for them to form a positive or negative attitude about the innovation. Interest can be piqued by presenting the innovation in a relevant and meaningful context, of course. Providing culturally sensitive information, showing examples of how others who are similar to the target audience have used the product, and helping people believe this could be good for them helps enhance this phase.

Because it is helpful to understand how the action is performed, what the behavior looks like, and how others feel about having participated, the most valuable information may come from personal contacts, friends, and workshops, not from mass media. Even a presentation that helps participants realize a problem and develop their own reason for change is an effective form of persuasion— especially if participants believe they came up with the idea themselves. If individuals take the time to thoroughly evaluate the consequences and outcomes of each aspect of the innovation (understanding the information and how they feel about it), a great deal of effort can be spent in phases 1 and 2.

Phase 3: Decision

Rogers's third phase occurs after people perceive the change to be good or bad, when they decide whether they wish to adopt or reject the change. In some cases emphasizing the possibility of reversing a change may encourage people to try the new behavior. For example, farmers are often given free samples of seeds to plant in one field to test for a year prior to agreeing to a complete conversion of the farm. Simply adding, "You can always quit the group if you don't think the project is working," might enable more people to join. A testrun is extremely important for innovations that carry a risk of catastrophic failure. If a pilot test is impractical (such as a space walk or plane landing), simulations are typically created to enable potential users to develop needed skills and "experience" the intended outcome.

In other cases, "trial-by-others" can be sufficient to help push the adoption decision. Extension agents use demonstration areas to show homeowners how native plants can be maintained without synthetic fertilizer and pesticides, and ranchers can see what a silvo-pasture[21] will look like. Of course, a decision to adopt the new behavior is based not only on information and attitudes but also on the perceived ability to perform the behavior. Not having access to the requisite equipment for participating in a webinar or funds to attend a conference will limit one's ability to engage in professional development, regardless of the strength of the decision.

Phase 4: Implementation

At this stage, according to Rogers, an individual engages in the new behavior. The process is no longer just something they think about, but a real activity. Because this is the first time the person is conducting the action, he or she may have questions or need support. Procedural information is critical at this stage to prevent frustration and backsliding. This is also the stage where individuals may determine that a slightly different strategy will work better. In this phase, a person may modify the activity to fit his or her specific needs. This process is referred to as reinvention. As good ideas spread across a community, it is often necessary that adopters understand that adaptation is possible and even welcomed.

Phase 5: Confirmation

While the implementation-reinvention stage represents the end of the process for some innovations, Rogers contends, others may require a fifth stage in which the individual seeks additional information to confirm the decision is right. Supportive messages help to firmly establish the change, particularly messages that provide feedback about how the change is being adopted by others or how the environment is changing. Large thermometers that track donations to charity help reinforce decisions to give and prompt those who have not yet opened their wallets. For the former, this is a confirming "feel-good" message, and for the latter it is a persuading reminder.

Different people will move through these phases at different rates, and with some innovations, phases may be skipped. In terms of adopting a new technology, it is easy to see that a prospective consumer must first be aware of the opportunity and convinced that it would be useful. If they are deciding to make a purchase, they may check with a friend who has the item before making the plunge, and if they do not return it, that would be the end of the process. In terms of making a commitment to engage in a habitual behavior, all five phases might be visited.

Diffusion of Innovation

Although the Theory of Planned Behavior suggests that attitudes about the behavior, approval of important others, and a belief that people have the ability to do the action play a role in decisions to change behavior, some individuals are more likely to adopt new ideas quickly and others will take a much longer period of time to believe the change is worth making. This variation among individuals, according to Everett Rogers, occurs in every collection of people—from the day shift factory workers to county employees, teachers in an elementary school, or members of a church. His theory of the **Diffusion of Innovation** suggests that each social system is made up of five types of people.[22] Note that "innovation" here can refer to adoption of a new technology or a different behavior. While each individual follows the path of five

phases mentioned above, they each do so at a different rate. The variation in rate is described in the five types of people that follow.

Those who are at the forefront of creating a new idea or who do not need much time to decide at all are called **innovators**. The presentation of an idea may be all it takes for them to snap their fingers and say, "I'm on it; let's go." They are accustomed to wild new ideas; they are not afraid to try untested waters. They tend to have enough financial and social capital that these new ventures do not entail substantial personal risk. While Rogers believes every community or group has some innovators, there are not very many around, and they may not interact well with "regular" folks. They can, however, help experimenters understand how a new technology might function, but innovators are often not too good at helping others understand their infatuation with the new idea.

When an innovation is marketed to an audience, it tends to go through media channels that attempt to reach that audience. Some people are more able to access to these channels than others. Among farmers, those who live closer to big cities and use the Internet may be the ones to receive new information first. For engineers, it may be those who are active members of their professional association. Trade magazines, radio, Internet, conferences, and organizational newsletters are examples of these media channels. **Early adopters** are those people who get this information and are able to take advantage of it. They are often well-respected and well-integrated members of their community or association. They can be trendsetters. If they try a new idea and like it, others are more likely to follow in their footsteps. These are the people most of us first saw driving a hybrid vehicle. (The innovators were driving an earlier model, but not in places we frequent, such as Aspen, Colorado or Hilton Head, South Carolina.)

The **early majority** follow the early adopters. They interact with early adopters and others in their network but are less likely to be in leadership positions. They require someone else to set the example before they make their decision, but they will adopt a new behavior slightly ahead of the vast majority. Because urban dwellers are more likely to see more hybrids on the road than rural dwellers, the early majority in a city will adopt hybrid cars faster than their small town brethren. Some policies (e.g., cash for clunkers) may be designed to attract the early majority, especially when political and economic factors are considerations in decisions to make a change.

The **late majority** tend to be skeptical of change. They are more likely to respond to peer pressure—they need an overwhelming response before they feel comfortable adopting the change. In their case, more adopters may not be the only criteria pushing them toward change. They may need more evidence as well. They may be waiting for the price of gas to stay high or for service reports on hybrid batteries. They are still driving their gas-efficient small car but are paying attention and saving their pennies for a switch someday to a hybrid.

The last to adopt any innovation are the **laggards**. They are traditional, suspicious,

and resistant to change. These characteristics also protect them from risk; those who survive at the margin cannot afford to try something new. They are not even contemplating something as different as a hybrid vehicle. There is no reason to change a good thing, and gasoline-powered transportation is completely dependable. The laggards, of course, are also the people for whom the existing infrastructure most greatly hampers. People who can't afford a new technology (refrigerator or hybrid car) will continue to use their more wasteful tools and be at the mercy of high electricity costs or a poor public transit system. They may simply lack the capacity to step out of their constraints.

This theory has been applied in a large number of contexts around the world and appears to have reasonable explanatory power when looking at the success or failure of an innovation. Of course, what defines an early adopter in an African village may be different than in a Chicago suburb, but the fact that there are some people who are regarded as having leadership qualities remains. The model is widely used by public health and extension agents where organizations and agencies attempt to encourage adoption of vaccines or nutritional foods. Of course, bad technologies and innovations can be disseminated in exactly the same way. If they are marketed to encourage early adopters to accept them, they may succeed.

Applying Diffusion of Innovation

These labels apply to people in specific contexts. They are not universally appropriate in every context. An urban minister, for example, may be an early adopter when he encourages his flock to retrofit a nearby homeless shelter to conserve energy and also a laggard when he refuses to own a cell phone because it distracts him from work. The Amish are typically labeled laggards because of their rejection of electricity and automobile ownership, but are at the forefront of wise, economical farming practices in Ohio's rolling hills where tractors are less efficient than horses. As problems are discovered with technology such as synthetic pesticides, the laggards who rejected the Green Revolution have become recognized as the innovators of organic farming.

Rogers' categories can be helpful when analyzing how innovations spread through a community and determining how to accelerate the process for desirable innovations. By knowing something about the determinants that motivate people to consider new actions and the characteristics of the people who are likely to lead such efforts, we can be more effective at suggesting new strategies to our colleagues, targeting people to champion a new activity, or realizing why an apparently good idea never took off. In addition, matching appropriate messages and media channels to subsets of an audience can provide the information they need to consider and adopt a change more readily.

When a new technology is available, for example, the mass media is the best way to increase awareness and help people understand what problem it might solve. When it comes to actually deciding to invest, however, hearing about how it works from a friend or

seeing evidence for oneself is the best way to commit to a new practice and adopt the technology. Thus, an advertisement with nine of out ten doctors might help you consider a new cold remedy, but it is probably your best friend who will get you to buy it.

The diffusion of technology is often described as following an S-curve pattern in which initial progress in the development of the technology is slow and then once a critical mass is reached, the technology flourishes until it matures and has saturated the market, eventually to be replaced by an even newer and better approach (see Figure 9.2). The S-curve is actually a map of these five groups choosing a new idea. In each case, Rogers estimates that the innovators are about 2.5 percent of any community; early adopters total 13.5 percent; early and late majority each contain 34 percent; and the laggards complete the total at 16 percent. They form a normal bell curve (see Figure 9.3). When this bell shape is converted to the number of adopters over time, it is the familiar S-curve.

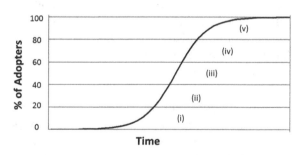

FIGURE 9.2 The shape of the S-curve results from the addition over time of the various groups identified by Rogers: (i) Innovators, (ii) Early Adopters, (iii) Early majority, (iv) Late majority, (v) Laggards. Adoption by the early and late majorities represent the steepest portion of the curve. *(Adapted from Rogers 1995)*

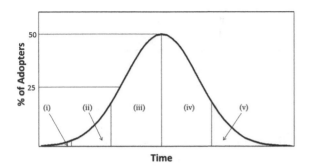

FIGURE 9.3 The normal bell curve shows the various categories of adopters identified by Rogers: (i) Innovators, (ii) Early Adopters, (iii) Early majority, (iv) Late majority, (v) Laggards.*(Adapted from Rogers 1995)*

FIGURE 9.4 Parking areas in the Netherlands are clearly used for bikes, not cars, establishing a cultural norm that makes it more acceptable to travel on two wheels. *(Photograph by Jon Monroe)*

Of course, not all new good ideas are popularized and successfully diffused. The diffusion curve depends on whether the "right" people are supportive. Bicycle riding has long been the mode of transportation for students and the homeless; until people who are perceived as community leaders start riding regularly (see Figure 9.4), the majority will stick to their cars—hybrids and clunkers alike. People to whom others look for advice and leadership are called **opinion leaders**. They may hold this influential position because of their job (rabbi or mayor) or their personality (the newspaper gossip columnist). If the cultural norm leads people to disregard a new idea because it is trivial or backward, an opinion leader could draw new attention to the concept.[23]

Opinion leaders can be found in each of the five categories and can help to sway others in their category toward their point of view. Jim Dearing, one of Rogers' students, claims that Rogers was disappointed that his theory was most commonly used to target early adopters—those people who could kick-start the adoption process, and not the opinion leaders of the late majority and laggards—those people who could help the less fortunate gain the advantages of an innovation sooner.[24] Since many of the predictors of adoption are characteristics that are difficult to affect, like exposure to information, formal education, socioeconomic status, travel, and social networks, Rogers felt it should be our duty to use these theories to overcome the barriers that constrain whole demographic groups. In this way, diffusion theory can be used to promote sustainability innovations with those who would otherwise be the last to gain the advantage, as do ethical decisions that favor the less fortunate.

The power of the theory of innovation is its ability to explain how individuals can make decisions on their own and in the context of their community. Rogers brought to light the power of a social group or community in helping to bring about change. This theory is

---

BOX 9.4   Speed of Diffusion—Cell Phones and Fax Machines

Some innovations (e.g., cell phones) sweep through a community with a steep slope, while others take a long time to become popular. Fax machines, for example, were invented in 1843 and took 144 years to sell one million per year.[25] Cell phones, in contrast, sold 13 million in the first 10 years of existence in the United States (Rogers 1995). While both technologies accelerate communication and enhance sustainability by increasing access and requiring fewer resources, a fax was only useful once they were common, whereas cell phones could be functional when calling a land lines. Fax machines were limited to use in offices, whereas cell phones could be seen in public as people walked to work or waited in restaurants.

The differences in these innovations led to a faster adoption rate for cell phones because, in part, the early and late majorities were able to see the early adopters use their phones and realize the advantages for themselves. Given these data, we could hypothesize that visible innovations will be more likely to quickly be adopted than hidden ones (such as solar panels vs. in-ground heat pumps). It also shows that innovations that can be used in concert with existing technology will be more easily adopted than those that require their own unique system.

---

one of many often used to understand social mobilization and large movements for collective social change.

STRATEGIES FOR EFFECTING CHANGE

The elements from the Theory of Planned Behavior and the stages of adopting a new behavior are similar and complementary. Beliefs are formed during the knowledge stage, and attitudes are shaped in the persuasion phase. How important others feel about adopting the new idea or product (subjective norm) may be important information that can be provided in the decision stage. Perceived control, or believing that the user can indeed manage the innovation and it will be successful, is exactly the outcome of the implementation phase, and feedback from this may be helpful if a confirmation is sought.

While these theories can be useful in the context of changing our own behavior, they can also be used to help convince colleagues and supervisors to consider a new idea, to work together on a project, and to approve a new and more sustainable practice. In this section, we identify a number of ways to promote more sustainable behavior using the concepts and theories discussed in Chapter 8 and in this chapter. They can be applied to a variety of situations to help move people toward new technology and change.

Small Wins

Given how people respond to overwhelmingly complex and uncertain problems, Karl Weick suggests that it is psychologically more appealing and infinitely more practical to define tasks as small, winnable challenges rather than huge, intractable problems. Rather than changing how a culture views homosexuality, for example, the Task Force on Gay Liberation took on the more readily achievable task of changing the way the Library of Congress classified books on homosexuality. Prior to 1972, these books were assigned numbers alongside books on sexual crimes and perversions. The new classification moved the books to the shelf with varieties of sexual life.[25]

Similarly, the first administrator of the U.S. Environmental Protection Agency (EPA), William Ruckelshaus, launched the new agency with five major lawsuits against big cities over water pollution. He did not choose the most important or the most visible task; he chose the most winnable challenge, from which he generated additional success. Even if the win is predictable, the resulting success empowers people to continue to another challenge.

Reasonable Person Model

Rather than looking at ways to change the problem, we might also consider how the environment and information stymie or support the people involved in making a decision. From their years of work on human preference and cognitive capacity, Rachel and Stephen Kaplan have developed such a model to suggest the situations and environments that help foster reasonableness.[26] Situations in which people are not reasonable include those where they are confused, overwhelmed, hopeless, and often helpless. The great variety of circumstances that can contribute to these situations have in common that information plays a central role. The Reasonable Person Model (RPM) thus concerns situations where the information is insufficient or excessive, or not understandable. Furthermore, reasonableness may be undermined if one lacks the skills to take actions, does not know what can be done, or is prevented from opportunities to make a difference.

People do not enjoy being in these situations, so they resist, remove themselves, or react angrily. As a result, they can defend their position without listening to other perspectives, they can ignore controversy or avoid confrontation, or they can simply abdicate responsibility and let someone else solve the problem. If making more sustainable decisions involves engaging more people and more varieties of expertise, then finding ways to appropriately engage them in a process that uses and respects their contributions is essential. There are three basic interdependent elements to promoting situations and creating environments in which people can become more reasonable (see Figure 9.5).

Building Shared Understanding

People need to understand the problem or situation. They need to have a model in their heads that matches reality. If a group of people work to solve a problem, then they must have a common understanding of the situation. If experts are explaining a new technology to decision makers, they both should have a similar mental conception of what the advantages, disadvantages, and relevance of the innovation. Since knowledge is a necessary ingredient to decision making, shared knowledge enables communication which builds understanding.

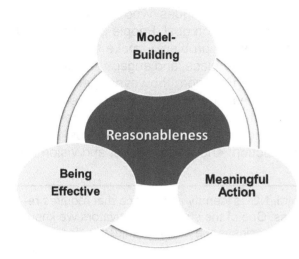

FIGURE 9.5 The Reasonable Person Model's three interacting components identify ways in which environments can provide information to encourage supportive and appropriate behaviors. *(Figure by Rachel Kaplan © 2011)*

Enabling people to have a shared understanding is more complicated than passing out a brochure, however, as it depends greatly on what they already know and care about. People have to be motivated to explore the information, make sense of it, and see what possibilities it creates for them. Detailed imagery helps to convey information if people do not have a high degree of familiarity with the problem, in part because its vividness enables us to remember and retrieve information. Misconceptions and other basic differences in how people perceive the issue must be acknowledged and addressed so that there is the possibility of useful, meaningful, successful communication. Common experiences could help immensely, especially if people discuss what they perceive to help overcome differences. In sum, helpful information and the motivation to use it

enable people to build a mental model and make sense of the world. Greater understanding should lead to the ability to compare alternatives, analyze information, and predict outcomes.

Enhancing Confidence and Clarity

People must feel competent to be part of a decision-making process. This requires having some idea of how these decisions have been made in other circumstances, as well as feeling that they have a grasp of the problem itself (which is part of having a shared understanding, of course). The requisite degree of ability, capacity, agency, efficacy, or perceived control (to use a variety of similar terms) may depend on reducing the complexity of the decision (see "Small Wins," earlier in this chapter) and on practicing the skills needed to explore other facets of the issue. Imagery, success stories, and case studies can be quite empowering and can help overcome the notions of hopelessness and despair.[27] Conducting simulations or trials can build confidence and give people insights into their abilities.

Another facet of this component is providing an environment that enables people to function effectively. Cluttered, crowded, busy spaces can overwhelm newcomers as much as trying to decipher all the information about climate change. When people are overwhelmed with tasks, worried about unrelated problems, or under stress, they do not respond well. Managing information is an essential component of achieving clarity about the problems at hand. Simplified, clear instructions to tasks can help achieve that. So can environments that help people restore their ability to focus attention; even a window with views of trees can enhance mental clarity.

Providing Opportunities to Engage

In some circumstances, asking someone to help enables them to join. Providing a doable task and inviting assistance could change people from grouchy, complaining onlookers to helpful colleagues who are working toward a common goal. People generally want to help solve problems, make their community a better place, and engage in solutions.[28] Their participation, however, generally requires that the scale of the problem is appropriate for their actions and that they have the knowledge, skills, and abilities to take this action. Knowledge, skills, and vision can

---

BOX 9.5   Motivational Practices of NGOs

NGOs provide a valuable example of these concepts in practice. Whether oriented toward sustainability or the pursuit of other goods, NGOs manage to attract and motivate their members in three primary ways (Gamson (1992). First, they develop and promote a sense of agency, making more feasible the ability for concerted action to alter the situation at hand. While it may often seem impossible to make much of a difference to the preservation of the global commons as an individual, joining together with other like-minded people allows a greater sense of empowerment and efficacy.

Second, these groups foster a sense of collective identity or teamwork. At base, *homo sapiens* are social animals. Today, as in prehistoric times, we primarily live, work, and thrive in communities; we have an instinct for solidarity. Friends demonstrate that they will "do anything" for friends. Athletes belonging to sports associations, and the fans that support them demonstrate their loyalty and willingness to "give it their all" for the benefit of their teams. Citizens and soldiers do the same for their countries, often sacrificing life itself for the collective good. In the same fashion, NGOs give their constituents a sense of membership and identity. In this way, the success of the group also becomes the member's personal victory.

Third, NGOs identify an injustice that requires redress. One of the strongest motivators we know as a species is the sense of injustice. Indeed, it often proves stronger than the pursuit of self-interest. Economists and social scientists have demonstrated this fact—already well known to historians—through empirical research.

In an experiment called the "Ultimatum Game," players interact to decide how to divide a sum of money. The first participant chooses how to split the sum, while the second participant either accepts or rejects the proposal. If the second player rejects the proposal, neither player receives any money. If the second player accepts the proposal, the money is divided up according to the agreement. In many instances, the first player will propose a 50/50 split, presumably out of a sense of fairness. What is remarkable is that proposals that are too lop-sided typically will be rejected. If the first player proposes a 70/30 split, or an even more lop-sided distribution, the second player will often choose to go home with nothing rather than suffer the perceived injustice of gaining a small portion of the total sum. People naturally attempt to redress injustice, even if doing so will incur a personal cost. In the same fashion, NGOs that identify and work to redress perceived social or environmental injustice translate this natural sense of moral indignation in their members into collective action (Finger, 1994).

come from shared understanding and confidence. Examples, case studies, simulations, and practice opportunities help here as well. Providing a chance for individuals to express their ideas to decision makers can be empowering, although the contexts for such public involvement are often intimidating for people who recognize the limits of their expertise and are reluctant to speak in public. The RPM thus emphasizes the importance of communicating that people are being heard and respected.[29] Without the sense that one's actions matter, actions are not meaningful. Strategies to enable participation can also help overcome the frustrations of hopelessness and helplessness which often combine to derail decision making.

With the ability to understand and communicate their perspectives, a sense of clarity about how to play a role, and with the confidence and hopefulness to engage in meaningful actions, we would thus expect people to act reasonably. Organizers, leaders, managers, and coordinators can create the environments or platforms to provide and promote the opportunities and strategies that help create this reasonableness. It might even help foster reasonableness in those who are in leadership positions themselves.

Moving People toward Change

In this section, we cover a quick list of techniques useful in moving people toward change. Again, this list is not exhaustive, but it should provide some helpful ideas for promoting positive changes in the workplace and in recreational settings, as individuals and groups make decisions about adopting new technologies and behaviors.

- Provide information about the advantages and disadvantages in all three realms of sustainability, with emphasis on the realm that the audience cares the most about. In the private sector, this might be the profit, although the public relations arm of the company might be interested in community service. In the public sector the environment and social dimensions may become the major effort, but balancing the budget will not be far behind.

- Offer stories, case studies, or examples of others who have done similar work. If the technology is controversial, examples where decisions were made against the change may be just as helpful as those of adoptions. Demonstrations and models can be helpful to enable people to see the difference the decision might make.

- If perceived control is a barrier to adoption, organize training sessions to build skills or provide tools and equipment for people to borrow, them. Then allow participants to practice these new skills in a safe environment and with guidance before they need to perform for real or on their own.

- Identify the opinion leaders of the audience you are reaching and meet with them before your presentation. Allow them to ask questions and help you refine your approach. If they approve, ask them to say so in front of others.

- Remind people that options to move toward sustainability will ultimately serve everyone's best interests.

- Critique the innovation and determine if it is likely to be adopted easily, or if it can be modified to make it more adoptable. If the innovation is used in public, if it is visible, if it can be borrowed and tested, or if it fits in well with the current culture, it is more likely to be successfully adopted.

- Explore the barriers to adopting a new behavior or technology in detail. For whom is the lack of alternatives a barrier? Who needs procedural information? Where could a change in infrastructure make a significant difference? Persuading audiences with information, even carefully crafted with subjective norms, may not help everyone engage with or sustain the innovation.

- Identify the early adopters in your office and make sure they are likely to try the new idea, that they like the new idea, and that they are happy to share their success with their networks.

A recent survey of US Forest Service employees about their environmental behaviors at the workplace reinforces many of these ideas. Respondents revealed that a commitment from the leadership was important for employees, and those who perceived their leaders were strongly supportive of certain practices were three times more likely to perform the action than those who believed their supervisor was not supportive. Support in the form of social norms and expectations from coworkers and the public were also important for those who conducted and maintained environmental actions. These respondents had positive attitudes toward the behaviors, knew about and how to perform the actions, and reported that supportive policies and procedures were important to the successful implementation of the environmental actions. They reported that workplace reminders and incentives influenced their behaviors and recommended that rewards be used to engage others.[30]

CONCLUSION

You have learned in this chapter that decision making—at the individual and collective scale—is a multistage process involving a number of aspects. A common mistake made by those attempting to effect behavior change is to focus only on one or two of these aspects. The result of such efforts is often the accomplishment of the narrow goal (e.g., better attitudes, heightened awareness, more available options, or more bus routes) without the desired change in behavior. In order to be effective, efforts to change behavior—including our own and that of others—will require a combination of strategies that accounts for all of the various influences discussed in this chapter.

One useful way of approaching behavior change is in terms of barriers and bridges. After the desired behavior is identified, explore the situation in terms of the influences we have discussed. What are the barriers keeping people (or ourselves) from exhibiting the desired behavior? Is it lack of understanding about the issue? Is it a lack of practical knowledge about how to go about the new behavior? Is there a perceived norm that opposes change? Once you have identified the barriers to the desired behavior, you can begin making efforts to remove those barriers and create bridges to more ecologically and socially responsible behavior.[31]

REFERENCES

Ajzen, Icek. 1985. "From intentions to actions: A theory of planned behavior." In J. Kuhl and J. Beckman, Eds. *Action-control: From cognition to behavior.* Heidelberg, Germany: Springer, pp. 11–39.

Bardwell, Lisa. 1991. Success stories: Imagery by example. *Journal of Environmental Education* 23: 5–10.

Bellah, Robert, Richard Madsen, William M. Sullivan, and Ann Swidler, 1985. *Habits of the Heart: Individualism and Commitment in American Life.* Berkeley: University of California Press.

Brink, Sarah. 2010. "A Town's Health Makeover: How one Minnesota community is going after a longer and fitter life span," *US News and World Report,* 147(7): 24–27.

De Young, Raymond. 1988–1989. "Exploring the difference between recyclers and non-recyclers: The role of information." *Journal of Environmental Systems* 18(4): 341–351.

———. 1993. "Changing behavior and making it stick: The conceptualization and management of conservation behavior." *Environment and Behavior* 25: 485–505.

———. 2000. "Expanding and evaluating motives for environmentally responsible behavior." *Journal of Social Issues.* 56 (3): 509–526.

De Young, Raymond and Martha Monroe. 1996. "Some fundamentals of engaging stories," *Environmental Education Research* 2(2): 171–187.

Dearing, J. 2005. "Accelerating the diffusion of effective techniques." Presentation at the International Conference on Transfer of Forest Science Knowledge and Technology. May 10–13, 2005. Troutdale, Oregon.

Dietz, Thomas, Gerald Gardner, Jonathan Gilligan, Paul Stern, and Michael Vandenbergh. 2009. "Household actions can provide behavioral wedge to rapidly reduce US carbon emissions." *Proceedings of the National Academy of Sciences of the United States of America* 106(44): 18452–18456.

Finger, Matthias. 1994. "From Knowledge to Action? Exploring the Relationships Between Environmental Experiences, Learning, and Behavior." *Journal of Social Issues* 50.

Gamson, William A. 1992. *Talking Politics.* Cambridge: Cambridge University Press.

Kaplan, Stephen. 2000. "Human nature and environmentally responsible behavior." *Journal of Social Issues.* 56 (3): 491–508.

Kaplan, Rachel and Stephen Kaplan. 2008. "Bringing out the best in people: A psychological perspective," *Conservation Biology,* 22(4): 826–829.

———. 2009. "Creating a larger role for environmental psychology: The Reasonable Person Model as an integrative framework," *Journal of Environmental Psychology,* 29(3): 329–339.

Katz, Elihu and Paul Felix Lazarsfeld. 1955. *Personal Influence: The Part Played by People in the Flow of Mass Communications.* New York: The Free Press.

Kingsolver, Barbara, Camille Kingsolver, and Steven Hopp. 2008. *Animal, Vegetable, Mineral: A Year of Food Life.* New York: Harper Perennial.

Maniates, Michael. 2002. "Individualization: Plant a Tree, Buy a Bike, Save the World?" In T. Princen, M. Maniates, and K. Conca, Eds. *Confronting Consumption.* Cambridge, MA: MIT Press.

McKenzie-Mohr Associates and LURA Consulting. 2001. "Turn it off: Reducing vehicle engine idling." Final Report. Available from Community-Based Social Marketing Web site: www.cbsm.com/Reports/Idlingsummary.pdf.

McKenzie-Mohr, Doug and William Smith.1999. *Fostering Sustainable Behavior: An Introduction to Community-Based Social Marketing*. Gabriola Island, BC: New Society Publishers.

Monroe, Martha and Stephen Kaplan.1988. "When words speak louder than actions: Environmental problem solving in the classroom." *Journal of Environmental Education* 19(3): 38–41.

Monroe, Martha C., Annie Oxarart, Lauren McDonell, and Richard Plate. 2009. "Using Community Forums to Enhance Public Engagement in Environmental Decisions," *Journal of Education for Sustainable Development* 3(2): 171–182.

Nabhan, Gary Paul. 2001. *Coming Home to Eat: The Pleasures and Politics of Local Food*. New York: W.W. Norton & Company.

Pollan, Michael. 2007. *The Omnivore's Dilemma: A Natural History of Four Meals*. New York: Penguin.

Princen, Thomas, Michael Maniates, and Ken Conca, eds. 2002. *Confronting Consumption*. Cambridge, MA: MIT Press.

Princen, Thomas. 2002. "Distancing: Consumption and the Severing of Feedback." In T. Princen, M. Maniates, and K. Conca, Eds. *Confronting Consumption*. Cambridge, MA: MIT Press.

Putnam, Robert D. 2000. *Bowling Alone: The Collapse and Revival of American Community*. New York: Simon & Schuster.

Rogers, Everett. 1995. *Diffusion of Innovation*, 4th ed. New York: The Free Press.

Selman, Paul. 2001. "Social Capital, Sustainability and Environmental Planning." *Planning Theory & Practice* 2 (1): 13–30.

Stern, Paul C. 2000. "Toward a coherent theory of environmentally significant behavior." *Journal of Social Issues*. 56 (3): 407–424.

Weick, Karl E. 1984. "Small wins: Redefining the scale of social problems."*American Psychologist* 39(1): 40–49.

Winter, Patricia L. 2008. *Pacific Southwest Research Station and Region 5 Sustainable Operations Report*. PSA-MISC-8-083. USDA, FS, PSRS. 84 pp. Available at: www.fs.fed.us/psw/publications/documents/psc_misc8083.pdf.

ENDNOTES

1. Ajzen (1985).
2. The Value-Belief-Norm theory is another inclusive theory about why some people exhibit environmentally responsible behaviors. See Stern (2000) for more information.
3. McKenzie-Mohr and Smith (1999).
4. De Young (1993).
5. Kaplan (2000).
6. Putnam (2000, page 19).
7. The authors would like to acknowledge the work of Sam Snyder on this section.
8. Putnam (2000, page 287).
9. Selman (2001).
10. See, for example, Putnam (2000) and Bellah et al. (1985).
11. Dietz et al. (2009).
12. Princen et al. (2002).
13. Maniates (2002).
14. Maniates (2002).
15. Princen (2002).
16. The USDA announcement can be found here: www.ams.usda.gov/AMSv1.0/getfile?dDocName=STELPRDC5072472&acct=frmrdirmkt.

17. A good example is "Buy Local Florida" (www .buylocalflorida.net/).
18. Found at http://100milediet.org/
19. Princen (2002, page 29).
20. Rogers (1995).
21. An agroforestry technique that enables landowners to harvest timber and cattle from the same property. It has both economic and environmental benefits, and when it helps small landowners retain family property, is a social value as well.
22. Rogers (1995).
23. The term opinion leader was described in Katz and Lazarsfeld (1955). The book reports on Lazarsfeld's Decatur study and suggests that mass communication shapes public opinion because key individuals read newspapers (or listen to the radio) and discuss these ideas with others. This two-step process of communication relies upon opinion leaders to select, filter, and interpret information which they share with their personal networks.
24. Dearing (2005).
25. Weick (1984).
26. Kaplan and Kaplan (2008, 2009).
27. Bardwell (1991); Monroe and Kaplan (1988); De Young and Monroe (1996).
28. Kaplan (2000); De Young (2000).
29. Monroe et al. (2009).
30. Winter (2008).
31. For a practical but more in-depth discussion on changing behavior, see McKenzie-Mohr and Smith (1999), and for an insightful evaluation of a program to reduce automobile idling, see McKenzie-Mohr Associates and LURA Consulting (2001).

CHAPTER 10

Creating Change with Groups

So far we have focused on behavior change within individuals or as it spreads from individual to individual across communities. However, many ideas about sustainability will be born in groups. The disparate dimensions of economics, the environment, and equity often require expertise from several people. If they all are not working together from the initial conception, new ideas or technologies may require selection or modification by representatives from the missing dimensions. In addition, as discussed in the previous chapter, changes that enable our communities to move toward sustainability are more likely to involve collective action at the level of organizations, institutions, and municipalities, as people consider the ethical dimensions of sustainability as it relates to equity among future and less advantaged populations, environment, and economic development. In this chapter, we explore the process of decision making and social change in relation to social groups.

ADVANTAGES OF GROUP DECISION MAKING

In a conventional top-down management model, one or perhaps a few people make decisions, and anyone involved is expected to adhere to those decisions. If we define efficiency in terms of the amount of time and effort it takes to come to a decision, then this top-down model typically scores highly. However, defining efficiency in this way does not take into account the time and effort of implementing that decision or of dealing with the issues that arise from the decision. In other words, we can see the same pattern that we have criticized in several chapters now, emphasizing the short-term gains while neglecting future costs. The perceived efficiency of this model has made it dominant in management, whether it is management of a natural resource, a business, or a household. However, the long-term problems that result from this model have resulted in a more inclusive model that embraces a wider variety of perspectives.

Of course including the relevant perspectives represents no small challenge. **Stakeholders** are individuals or groups that affect or are affected by an issue or process, and as a result of the breadth of most issues regarding sustainability, a wide variety of stakeholders are usually included, often with quite different perspectives. The activity of diverse groups of stakeholders working together is called a **multi-stakeholder process** (MSP) and it can be a slow and at times frustrating process. However, this more inclusive model of management offers a number of advantages over the top-down model. In this section, we discuss three of the most commonly cited advantages.

Additional Insights

An MSP typically expands the information and ideas being discussed because it includes multiple perspectives. The insight a particular individual can provide depends largely on that individual's relationship with the issue at hand. New insights often come to light by including individuals who have previously been excluded from the decision-making process. For example, factory workers, with their hands-on experience, may suggest improvements that did not occur to managers, and women often have a different perception of safety issues concerning public transportation than men.

Similarly, daily users of a resource (e.g., fishers or farmers) will likely have information about that resource that may be otherwise unavailable to resource managers. An individual who has been living and working for decades within a particular ecosystem (e.g., forest, wetland) will likely have insight into that system that is not readily apparent to a scientist who has only been studying a system for only a handful of years. Similarly, a community that has been living and working within a particular ecosystem for centuries will likely have developed a set of practices and beliefs regarding that system. In the past, researchers often ignored such sources of

information. The conventional view was that while these traditional beliefs were based largely on superstition, science could provide accurate information necessary to manage the resource properly.

Within the last few decades resource managers and scholars have come to recognize the arrogance of those who dismiss the knowledge of local communities as worthless. Robert Johannes' describes this arrogance:

> Imagine people [e.g., scholars] who confidently assume they can best describe and manage the natural resources of an unfamiliar region alone—ignoring local hunters who know every cave and waterhole and the movements and behavior of a host of local animals—overlooking the farmers who know the local soils, microclimates, pests and seasonal environmental changes—disregarding the native fisherman who know the local current and the movement and behavior of marine life in their waters.[1]

Johannes was one of the leading proponents for acknowledging the value of local information, referred to as **traditional ecological knowledge** (TEK), as a source of insights for addressing contemporary issues regarding sustainability.

In some cases, the insights may be a sense of the historical conditions of the ecosystem prior to when scientists began to study it, such as permafrost conditions in the Arctic. In other cases, local peoples point out ecological relationships and processes previously unseen by Western scientists. More recently, scientists have begun to turn toward TEK for insights into how best to manage a resource. In Box 10.1 you can see how traditional fishing technology of the Cree in Canada helps to promote ecological resilience in the fishery. There are, in fact, numerous examples in which traditional management practices have offered valuable insights for contemporary resource managers.[2]

BOX 10.1 Traditional Ecological Knowledge— Cree Fishing Technology as a Tool for Sustainable Fishing

The challenge of fishery management is largely to promote sustainable fishing—that is, to promote fishing practices that do not decrease the fish populations' ability to reproduce. Some fishing practices are so effective that they result in too many fish being taken in a short time. For example, a small mesh can be an effective tool for catching most of the fish that pass through a particular area. The problem with this method is that many juvenile fish are caught before they have had a chance to reproduce, causing the population in subsequent years to decrease quickly.

A second highly efficient fishing method is to capitalize on the spawning habits of fish. Many fish form large aggregations for spawning. Depending on the species, these aggregations may form nightly, monthly, or seasonally, but a specific population of fish will often return to the same place again and again. Fishers can use this information to focus their efforts on the times and places of the spawning aggregations to greatly increase their catch. Again, this practice can result in a level of catch beyond what the fish population can support.

Because of the problems often caused by these practices, fishery managers often prohibit targeting spawning aggregations as well as the use of nets with small mesh (usually designating a minimum size mesh that allows juvenile fish to pass through the nets). However, in northern Quebec members of the Cree—one of the largest Native American groups living in Canada—seem to defy this conventional management wisdom (Berkes 1998). They target spawning aggregations and use small mesh in order to increase their fishing efficiency, yet the fish populations in the area show all the signs of a sustainable fishery.

Over many generations, the Cree developed fishing technology and practices that apply concepts that have only recently become more popular in the context of modern management. The idea is to spread the impact of fishers so that no one population or age group becomes overwhelmed. To that end, the Cree use fishing nets with varied mesh sizes. Rather than heavily impacting the adult fish, the Cree spread the impact among small (i.e., young) and large fish. Similarly, the Cree do not fish the same area year after year. They use a method called "pulse fishing," focusing intensely on a particular area and then not fishing it at all for a period of time, allowing the fish population time to recover. While the Cree developed these techniques many generations ago outside the context of modern science, research in fish ecology and biology has only recently produced a scientific picture of why these techniques have been so effective.

The challenge of sustainability is not unique to modern society. TEK represents a set of responses to that challenge that developed independent of modern science. These responses may vary in their effectiveness and in the degree to which they apply to a contemporary context, but in many cases—as the Cree example illustrates—they can provide useful insights for addressing today's challenges.

Note that the goal here is to supplement, rather than displace, the perspectives of conventional decision makers (e.g., managers, scientists). Most proponents of TEK are careful not to idealize traditional beliefs and practices, just as they are careful to acknowledge to new and valuable insights contributed through scientific inquiry. There are indeed limits to traditional or local knowledge. Leaving the fate of spotted owl to the local population who worked for the timber industry probably would not have created the broader economic base that the communities have today. And some indigenous knowledge was more useful and appropriate when smaller bands of nomads roamed their territory. Similarly, a company would likely not want to make decisions based solely on the perspective if its factory workers. The point is to recognize the limits of any one perspective. In light of these limits, we can see that including multiple perspectives can produce a richer view of the issue at hand.

New Discoveries

The term **synergy** refers to the idea in systems thinking that a whole is more than the sum of its parts. In business, the term is often used to emphasize the value of teamwork. Consider the task of folding a king-sized sheet. One person can do it, and it may take about two minutes, but when there is a second person available to help, something extraordinary happens. One might expect that doubling the manpower would cut the time in half. This is generally how we think about work. If one person takes 20 minutes to perform X units of work, then two people can do that same about of work in 10 minutes

(assuming equal capabilities of the people). By this logic, our sheet folders would likely take one minute to complete their task, but anyone with any sheet folding experience at all knows that this will not be the case. In all probability the two will have the sheet folded in less than 30 seconds—that is, in less than half the predicted time.

When synergy is involved, one cannot predict the results simply by adding the individual inputs. The sheet-folding team working together could work more than twice as fast than either of them could individually. The same concept applies when groups work through a decision (see Figure 10.1). If the various stakeholders are each approaching

FIGURE 10.1 Community groups include diverse members working together to address contemporary challenges. *(Photograph by Larry Korhnak)*

the issue with an open mind, then the benefit can be more than simply the exchange of different insights individually offered by participants. It can include the development of new insights that result from the discussion itself. The group can come up with new ways to address the issue that had not occurred to any of the individual participants. This synergistic creativity of groups can be a powerful tool in addressing sustainability issues.

Increased Buy-In

A decision regarding a regulation or a policy is only effective if the stakeholders involved pay attention to it. One way to encourage stakeholders to abide by a policy is to attach a penalty to breaking the established rule. An employee going against company policy may risk loss of a promotion or even face termination, depending on the violation. Natural resource managers often fine businesses or individuals found to be in violation of their policies. Enforcing an unpopular policy through the use of penalties can be a costly endeavor, as it requires personnel and other resources devoted to catching the rulebreakers. The task of enforcement becomes much easier if the policy itself has public support. Stakeholders who understand the reason for a policy are more likely to follow it without the threat of punishment. Stakeholders who helped create the policy may even advocate for people to follow it.

In any issue involving widely different perspectives, there is a good chance that no stakeholder will receive everything he or she had hoped for going into the process.

Compromises are generally made, with each stakeholder willing to make some adjustments provided that he or she sees other stakeholders making similar accommodations. When stakeholders are not involved in the decision process or communicating with other stakeholders, they may have difficulty understanding such compromises in the context of the larger picture. Allowing the stakeholders to experience firsthand through MSP the complexity of the issue and the range of stakeholders can help them to view policy changes from a broader perspective.

Additionally, the process of developing a policy can play as significant a role in stakeholder acceptance as the policy itself. When people feel ostracized from the development of a policy and feel that their needs have not been adequately addressed, they are unlikely to abide by that policy. Conversely, when they feel that they have played a significant role in the formation of the policy, they are much more likely to support it because they have developed a sense of ownership of the policy.

Recall from Chapter 3 the discussion of procedural justice. This term applies not only to the outcome but also to the process by which the outcome was reached. Satisfaction with the process can result in supporting a policy or change even when the change itself is not desired. Consider presidential elections. If the candidate we vote for loses, we may criticize the outcome, but few would suggest rejecting the outcome altogether (i.e., rebellion). As long as we have confidence in the fairness of the voting process, we accept—perhaps grudgingly at times—the outcome.

TYPES OF COLLABORATIVE PROCESSES

Input from stakeholders can be collected through a variety of models. One common way of assessing stakeholder perspectives is simply to hold an open meeting, where the general public is invited to come and share their views about an issue or policy. This method is popular because it requires a relatively small amount of resources and time. However, because of the number of participants at such meetings, the structure looks more like a sequence of short speeches rather than a discussion. In most cases, the will of the public is not revealed, but rather the interests of those with the most to gain or lose. Decision makers may indeed obtain better insight into some stakeholders' perspectives, but these meetings are unlikely to result in new ideas or in significant changes regarding the stakeholders' sense of ownership of the policy. In addition, these meetings are often scheduled after the decision has been made, and few participants ever believe their comments are duly considered.

In some cases, key representatives of stakeholders are asked to sit on a citizen advisory board or stakeholder panel. These groups are set up by a managing agency or company specifically to gain the perspective of key stakeholders before making a decision, selecting a marketing plan, or launching a new product. Stakeholders usually play an advisory role. That is, they do not necessarily have any actual power in the final decision, but they can provide input on the issues they are formed to consider. They can request outside assistance or expertise, they can form joint task forces, or even collect data themselves. The limits of their role should be agreed upon before the group first convenes.

There is a tradeoff here when considering how much power a group of stakeholders should be given. In some cases, a company or managing agency may feel that it does not have the time or resources to support a long-term MSP. In this case, placing stakeholders in a purely advisory role may be desirable, as it allows the company or managing agency to end discussion without having to reach any sort of consensus within the group of stakeholders. However, limiting the power of the stakeholders also limits the advantages of collaborative processes described previously, as stakeholders may be less committed to a process in which they have no real influence. People usually want to be wanted. Appreciating volunteers is essential to keeping them, and listening to their recommendations is one way to keep stakeholders engaged and happy. Conversely, collaborative processes that give stakeholders significant power in the decision-making process risk becoming mired in stakeholder disputes. In the following section, we discuss how one might avoid this occurrence and get the most advantage out of the multi-stakeholder process.

There are costs to these multi-stakeholder processes, too. They involve time. Urgent issues may not allow a time-intensive problem-solving process. The more people that are involved, the more time the process is likely to require. Having the appropriate number of stakeholders to create good representation may create challenges for the communication and decision-making process.

MAKING THE MULTI-STAKEHOLDER PROCESS WORK

Because of the benefits, a growing number of industries and agencies have adopted a collaborative approach to better explore problems, understand issues, and jointly recommend actions. These stakeholders usually represent as many viewpoints as possible, and are likely to include economic, justice, and environmental interests. There are a number of processes and characteristics that must be involved in order for these groups to be successful. In this section, we look at some of the most important ones.

Social Learning

In a general sense, **social learning** is the process of interacting with and learning from others. In the context of sustainability, social learning is the process of sharing and reflecting on experiences and ideas between people and groups as they collectively strive to resolve conflicts and implement more sustainable practices.[3] Although educators have been aware of the value of learning from others for years (e.g., vicarious learning, cooperative learning, group learning), business leaders and natural resources managers have recently begun to use this term to draw attention to the importance of facilitating group interaction that brings together different perspectives.

Some experts consider social learning to occur only when people who hold diverse views interact and everyone learns something from each other. In these cases, the groups are designed to build trust among individuals and are facilitated to enable people to realize that their ideas are changing. A continuous process of questioning the assumptions that each person brings and reflecting on the similarities and differences among them helps to create social learning.

By definition, leaders of sustainability initiatives should carefully consider social learning as well. For many individuals, the chance to share their ideas about a concept is the best way for them to learn.[4] While many educational approaches rely primarily on simply providing information to individuals, giving individuals the opportunity to discuss the ideas with others can alter the way they understand that information. Interestingly, whether the group discussion occurs before or after the individual receives information can influence how he or she perceives new ideas about change. For example, a recent study at Columbia University suggests that doing one's homework, which in this case involved reading about a controversial investment in wind energy, before a group meeting tends to result in people bringing a strong sense of their own perspective to the group discussion. If the first time they hear of the controversy, however, is in a group discussion where someone expresses a different perspective from their own, people were more likely to consider those opposing ideas than if they formed their own opinion first.[5]

We might view the participants' behavior in the context of the Chapter 8 discussion on anchoring. Introducing a controversy in a group setting resulted in the people being less

BOX 10.2   MSP—New Zealand Land Care Trust and Kristianstad, Sweden

Systems thinking is often a key facet of MSPs because it encourages to stakeholders to develop a broader perspective and better understanding of the social-ecological system involved. Examples of these collaborative initiatives with a systems perspective span the globe.

The New Zealand Land Care Trust (www.landcare.org.nz/) is an organization that uses community involvement to create sustainable land management practices. Working with over 150 local land care groups, they organize landowners—often farmers with a vested interest in economic survival—around common problems and help provide a platform for seeking information, developing research projects, and exploring solutions. Groups bring in experts who can help provide information or design experiments that will result in necessary and relevant new knowledge. Building trust among those with conflicting views is an essential part of their activities and comes with the territory of increasing biodiversity and water quality in an agricultural region. These conflicts make the work of developing a common understanding and agreement for creating informed decisions all the more essential.

On the other side of the planet, in southeastern Sweden, the people of Kristianstad came to realize that centuries of farming, channeling water, dredging canals, and fertilizer use had significantly altered the shallow lakes and wetlands near their city. They hoped that international recognition for their local wetland would bring about important changes, but after 10 years were disappointed with the continuing decline in environmental quality. Their frustration fueled a new process that enabled agency staff and citizen groups to work together to map the region, explore possible solutions to restore the wetlands, and report their results to the public.

They worked with local farmers to understand that different grazers (cows and horses) create different surfaces (tussocks and smooth) on the flooded meadows that attract different species of birds. Restoring traditional forms of agriculture to the wetlands was a vital step in maintaining the ecosystem but also led to conflict. Cranes, for example, damage crops but attract bird watchers. Through a stakeholder work group the farmers agreed to sacrifice some of their land to the cranes in exchange for compensation for their loss (Walker and Salt 2006). Bringing together various stakeholders enabled this coalition to engage in discussions, share responsibility, explore possibilities, and establish consensus on decisions that reflect economic, environmental, and social goals.

anchored to a single perspective and more open to others'. If developing consensus is the goal, therefore, introducing new ideas in a group setting may be more successful than asking people to prepare for a meeting by themselves. If creating a discussion of divergent opinions is the goal, assigned reading may be more likely to achieve it.

Participant openness to new ideas is necessary for social learning to occur. The process is not about entering into contentious issues with a firm position and using persuasive techniques to sell a particular solution. Rather, the participants explore the issue together from multiple perspectives. This distinction is vital. For example, the synergistic development of ideas discussed previously will likely not occur at all without openness among stakeholders to other stakeholders' perspectives.

A diversity of members within the group ensures that multiple perspectives will be heard (assuming that the group is functional, that all members are respected, and that each member is encouraged to speak). However, there will always be important perspectives that are not represented directly within the group, including those of future and distant citizens. Participant openness, then, applies both to other group members and to unrepresented perspectives.

Building Shared Understanding

From citizen advisory boards to lengthy collaborative deliberations, social learning processes enable groups of experts and the public to share perspectives, learn together, build trust, and recommend solutions that are likely to be sustainable.[6] But these goals are impossible to achieve without clear communication between stakeholders, and since stakeholders often do not share the same expertise or perceptions, communication itself can become a real challenge. Poor communication can be the result of purposeful omissions or unavoidable confusion because of assumptions that stem from different experiences. This is common when scientists and policy makers work with the public, but it is also a concern when working with colleagues in other departments or supervisors. Knowing how to listen for misconceptions and identify a source of confusion can help immensely.

Developing a shared understanding of the problem and the consequences of any solution is a key step toward implementing new ideas that carry the promise of sustainability. Recall from Chapter 9 that shared understanding features prominently in the Reasonable Person Model as a basic requirement for engaging people in solving problems. Of course, it is also one outcome of social learning. As a result, a closer look at the problems associated with the simple step of communicating ideas within a varied group may be useful. Following are three specific situations that can arise in stakeholder groups and workplace teams.

1. When pieces of truth do not convey the whole truth.

   When team members assemble, they bring not only different perceptions of the problem but also different assumptions and experiences that can be so tightly woven into their ideas that it is difficult to recognize where opinions differ from facts. It is easy to see these communication challenges between opposing advocacy groups who traditionally call each other derogatory names, but more subtle variations of the same problem can be found everywhere. Advocacy groups tend to carefully select bits of facts that support their perspective. Over time, it is easy to rely on the message as representing the whole truth, when in fact it is just a part of the truth. That message will be utterly and unavoidably true from the originator's perspective, and equally and totally false from the other.

For example, environmentalists have long sounded an alarm that landfills are reaching their limits and we should reduce, reuse, and recycle rather than burying our waste. A plastics industry representative was heard to respond by saying such statements are bold lies: we are not nor will be in danger of running out of landfill space. It is easy to see how such a war of words can escalate into mudslinging. What both sides omitted from their "truth" is location, cost, and justice. Cities in New Jersey may not have many local landfill sites, while those in Nevada have sites in abundance. If East Coast residents paid enough, they could find a landowner willing to bury their garbage, at least for a while. What does this mean for people in New Jersey (and their environment) who do not have the discretionary income to ship their garbage across the continent? Will the wealthy residents of Nevada also be accepting waste from the East, or only those in need of cash?

Complete information is needed to convey the ideas that all parties would find truthful. Such an exchange may allow a one-dimensional environmental issue to become a three-dimensional sustainability concern, as in the previous example. This degree of thoroughness may be seen as unnecessary, however, by those who agree with the original statement, by journalists who want short sound bites, and by editors who want to polarize the issue. As a result, interest groups on all sides trumpet their limited views and feel justified in accusing their opponents of lying. The public, caught in the whirlwind of confusion, stops trying to make sense of the controversy and lets someone else decide what to do. The intentional and the accidental omission of facts make it difficult for people to resolve and understand conflicting opinions. It also keeps issues one-dimensional when the full complement of concerns would be useful to work toward a practical and sustainable resolution.

The fact of the matter is that seeing an issue through different lenses is a very difficult task. It is obvious, for example, that climate change is thawing Arctic ice, which will most certainly alter the habitat of some populations of polar bears at some point in time. The image of gaunt, starving polar bears has become global climate change's canary in the coal mine. It is an image that has galvanized the public into considering their actions. That is useful to help communicate the importance of an issue that has few immediate consequences. However, wildlife biologists note that where polar bear populations are at an all time high (based on recent records), in the normal course of dynamic population changes, more bears are likely to starve from competition for food now than ever before.[7] Bear populations will most assuredly fall in the near future, but not solely as a consequence of climate change.

It may be difficult to discern what percentage of bears starve because of increased competition among bears or larger habitat changes. Those who wish to see change in American habits of consumption and energy use are not likely to even ask this question or try to challenge the popular conception that polar bears will starve because of climate change. It is not an intentional omission, but more likely a perspective that does not have a place in their world view. Since an emotional portrayal of polar bears helps raise awareness, this species provides an effective avenue to attract attention. The danger, of course, is that the environmental advocates will lose credibility if a different version of bear population decline is accepted.

Similarly, the forest industry has often claimed that forests are in better shape than they have been because there are more trees in North American now than in 1920. This is no doubt true, and it does represent a success in forestry that today's forests are vibrant and productive. However, it hides the fact that the forests in 1919 had been cut and harvested for decades, or even centuries (see Figure 10.2).

FIGURE 10.2 Comparisons to forests of the early twentieth century can be misleading since many forests of that time were already heavily impacted, as shown in this historic photograph from New Hampshire. *(Source: New Hampshire Historical Society)*

This additional information takes the wind out of the forestry advocates' sails and challenges the very notion that they have a success story to talk about.

Successfully incorporating opposing advocates into stakeholder groups will require exposing these kinds of assumptions and omissions and challenging long-held dogmas about their positions. Staunch advocates may not easily abandon their beliefs, slogans and public images, but creating a process that enables them to do so is vital. The goal is not simply to debate an issue but to discuss it in an open and honest way so that everyone can achieve a new and more complete understanding.

2. When new information does not make any sense.

When people cannot accept the information, it may be because the explanations they have built from their experiences and observations are rooted in fundamentally different ways of understanding the world (often called naïve conceptions or misconceptions in children). Their different mental model can make it nearly impossible to have a productive conversation. If an explanation does not make sense, the listener is likely to proclaim the information is false or biased and the speaker does not know of what they speak.

For example, experts in the conversion of wood to energy are quick to point out that the wood-fired power plants emit so few air pollutants that they rarely need emission controls to pass air quality standards. Audience members who are prone to skepticism will not accept this as a fact, particularly if they have experienced campfire smoke or a wildfire. Their first hand experience with stinging eyes, massive amounts of smoke and ash, and choking coughs from burning wood suggest to them this expert must be crazy. Furthermore, this must be another trick for the energy companies to make a fast buck off the environment. Mistrust creates the perception of bias and destroys the opportunity for learning.

A more careful presenter might acknowledge the accuracy of the audience's experience with campfire smoke and explain that the smoke they have seen comes from using a variety of fuel sizes at various moisture levels and the relatively uneven temperatures in a campfire. In other words, she starts her explanation with what the audience knows and believes. She would then explain that incomplete combustion from damp wood and big chunks mixed in with twigs and leaves creates tiny particles of unburned wood and gases that rise with the hot air. In a power plant the wood would be chipped to a regulation size, dried, and burned at extremely high temperatures in a controlled environment. The boiler is able to burn the fuel evenly and completely, which reduces the amount of particulates in the smoke.

She might also be careful to explain that wood has fewer air emission problems than coal. When wood is compared to a zero-emission energy source, it is not so clean, but in comparison to a fuel we currently use, it brings some measurable benefits to air quality. The simple sound-bite promise of a cleaner fuel has now turned into a rather detailed explanation to help build understanding and change recalcitrant mental models.

Misunderstandings in communication are often the result of basic undetected differences in how people explain their world. These explanations arise from a lifetime of experiences and observations. The misunderstandings are common and require listening skills and time to engage people in a conversation to explore these differences. Questions such as "what makes you say that?" or "where have you seen that?" might open the door to improved understanding. Groups working on issues of sustainability will, by definition, bring a variety of experiences and expertise to the discussion. Misunderstandings are likely to be the norm. It will be essential to build a sense of trust and a practice of questioning assumptions to enable communication that explores and understands differences in perception, experience, and understanding.

3. When new information involves risk.

Communication about proposals that involve risk tends to lead to extreme degrees of mistrust, misunderstanding, and downright outrage. These communication challenges between experts and the public have led to a number of studies that reveal basic differences in mental models. The difference: engineers and other experts tend to calculate risk based on the probability of human fatalities.

This makes nuclear power dramatically safer than coal power, since the United States averages 33 coal mine fatalities each year.[8] However, the public includes in their calculations of risk a number of other factors, such as the degree of disagreement in the scientific community, the possibility of catastrophic problems, the risks to future generations, the controllability and voluntary nature of the risk, and the degree to which the risk is observable, known, and immediate.[9] These different definitions for the same concept cause a breakdown in communication.

There are some patterns in risk perception, however. A number of variables cluster around "dread" and make these risks appear worse to the public than experts think they are. Such risks tend to be uncontrollable, globally catastrophic, fatal, not equitable, not easily reduced, and involuntary. They also tend to increase in intensity, representing even higher risks to future generations. Nuclear power fits this scenario. The opposite set of variables tends to be perceived as less dangerous. Caffeine, tobacco, and skateboards, for example, are controllable, voluntary, nonfatal risks that are not likely to lead to catastrophic or inequitable problems since they are individually chosen. The public also perceives a second factor in risk, defined by variables such as unobservable and unknown effects, delayed effects, and uncertainties. This explains why chemical additives or electrical fields might be perceived to have great risk, while fireworks and automobiles appear to be more benign.

Note that several of the challenges to decision making arise in this discussion of risk: considering future generations, uncertainty and unknown effects, probability, and system delays. These challenges make the need and role of ethics in sustainability decisions all the more critical. Approaching such challenges with an understanding of the ethical principles that could affect a decision will help engage people in deliberations around these key elements of the issue.

These patterns of risk perception make it impossible for experts to credibly speak to the public unless they understand and base their discussion on the factors the public considers important. The patterns suggest that while experts might equate the annual risk of a nuclear accident to the risk involved in riding an extra three miles in an automobile (because both result in the same risk of fatality), such comparisons are meaningless to the public because the public assesses the risk from these two activities in completely different ways. The added factors that they consider make nuclear power plants much riskier than automobile travel. These patterns suggest that both experts and the public have important perspectives to contribute to discussions about the acceptable risks of a new technology.

These types of communication challenges surface regularly in the many groups and gatherings where different perspectives should be included to enhance learning,

BOX 10.3   MSP—Frankfurt Airport Expansion

The conflict around the expansion of the Frankfurt airport in Germany represents an impressive case of a successful MSP (Meister and Gohl 2009). Neglecting to balance economic growth with the negative impacts on residents and the environment resulted in public outcry when a third runway was proposed in 1984. The protest movement ended when snipers killed two policemen in 1987 at a mass rally. When a fourth runway was proposed in 1998 the state government initiated a mediation process with 21 stakeholders who were asked to balance economic growth with environmental and public health concerns. After two years of deliberation, they recommended the new runway be built if the airport eliminated night flights, took steps to reduce noise, and implemented a Regional Dialogue Forum (RFD) to continue to build understanding and explore solutions.

Shortly after the mediation process's recommendations were received, the RFD was established with four different objectives: to build understanding, to conduct research, to provide counsel on formal procedures, and to protect the mediation process. The Forum established a leadership group of 34 stakeholders which held hearings to explore issues and the need for further research. They established five subgroups which had open membership. Over the course of the Forum these subgroups held over 200 sessions and attracted over 130 additional interested participants. Close to 2000 students took part in a mediation simulation program, the media were regularly invited to report on developments, and open meetings were held for the public to share what the teams were learning.

The night flight ban, flight routes, and approach and departure procedures, for example, were highly technical components. Discussing these problems required answers to legal questions, additional research to document noise levels, and significant negotiation among stakeholders on what would be monitored. Alterations in German legislation and European agreements that govern international transportation, commerce, and public access to information changed the questions and possible outcomes that the Forum explored.

Interestingly, such important aspects of the operations of an international airport had never been considered with the social and environmental costs of doing business. An elaborate process of research was established: the Forum and project team invited researchable questions, a team of experts formulated the call for proposals and reviewed submissions, and the Forum selected a winning proposal and asked the runner-up to serve as a monitor of the quality of the research conducted. The results and recommendations were considered and approved by the project team, quality safeguard team, and Forum before their release to the public. The process helped build faith in the data, reduce the notion of unsubstantiated claims by opposition groups, and created a framework that was cited and referenced in future negotiations.

understanding, problem solving, and decision making as people consider sustainability. Merely wanting to solve the problem will not remove communication challenges, but it will likely provide the requisite vision that will help people be patient with each other, ask questions when they become confused, and work harder to communicate. The information and perspectives that each individual brings to the meeting are important to uncover as their perspectives are the lenses through which all new information is perceived.

Communication challenges can be avoided when people trust each other enough to interrupt to say, "Wait, I don't understand." Such levels of comfort are rare in stakeholder groups that meet only twice a year, unless they are carefully facilitated and opportunities are created for questions to be asked. Speakers may find it helpful to engage the group in discussions and to facilitate the development of their understanding by walking through questions, observations, and realizations. When a group represents a great many different types of expertise, however, this too is a challenge because everyone starts with a different set of experiences and assumptions. An audience assessment is one way to learn about the various perceptions that a group brings and may help a presenter think about how to share new information with analogies that will resonate with subgroups of the audience.

The example of the Frankfurt Airport expansion in Box 10.3 illustrates how a participatory process, while time-consuming, can greatly change the public response and result in a satisfying outcome. The process of deliberative and social learning helped convert a divisive conflict into an opportunity for a win-win negotiation. As the process began to reach closure in 2007, even the most critical opponents wished to see a similar process continue to provide a forum for exploration and understanding. The MSP was deemed by stakeholders to be a good

strategy for creating solutions that everyone could live with.

Before closing this section on building shared mental models, it is worth pointing out a potential danger in this process. While social learning is an important aspect of successful MSPs, there is a danger in decreasing independent thinking and creativity. In a process referred to as groupthink, the pressure to reach consensus and the desire to avoid conflict can lead to the development of consensus without full consideration of the risks of a particular action or the alternatives to that action.[10] If a majority of participants (or even a minority of particularly vocal participants) appear to be in agreement regarding a particular course of action, other members may be inclined to suppress their doubts and go along with the group. In order to avoid this, the facilitator and group members must be careful that their shared mental model is not so rigid as to preclude adjustment based on other viewpoints and ideas. As you will see, there are a number of potential obstacles that a skilled facilitator must avoid.

Trust

We have mentioned trust several times in the above discussion. In order to appreciate the importance of trust, we might look more closely at the desired outcomes of an MSP. Most consider the set of decisions or policy changes to be the desired outcome. Indeed, this is true, and since addressing the issue or policy is the reason for developing the group, this is often the most visible outcome. However, often the most important outcome from the process is the institution of formal and informal connections established between stakeholders. In other words, the relationships between stakeholders that are forged and fostered during the process often play a more significant role in the resilience of the social-ecological system.

When stakeholders first enter the process, their level of trust in other stakeholders and in the group as a whole may be quite low. Stakeholders do not often begin with the attitude of openness described previously. Trust both in other stakeholders and in the process itself must be built up through the process. This underscores the importance of having a skilled facilitator who can develop a group and take it from a condition of very low resilience—where even minor problems can cause the entire process to dissolve—to a highly resilient group that is capable of continued decision making in the face of unforeseen changes.

The first step in developing this trust is determining the group's members. Care must be taken to ensure that all stakeholders are represented in the group and that each member is an opinion leader within the stakeholder group they represent. Failure to include some stakeholders will not only represent a loss of potentially different and valuable perspectives but could result in producing enemies of the process who may undermine potential gains. In addition, if the members are expected to represent others, they must be legitimate representatives who will carry information between the group and their constituents and help convince both sides of the value of the others' perspectives.

Sometimes the hardest part about including all stakeholders is not identifying them but convincing them to be a part of the MSP. Barriers to attending meetings must be addressed. Something as seemingly simple as the time and place of the meetings may significantly affect attendance. If there is a history of exclusion, some stakeholders may make be wary about the implications of attending. Also, in some cases stakeholders may see their chances of influencing the outcome to be better if they do not attend but plan to use the legal system to delay progress, for example.

Of course, merely being at the table does not mean all members speak, are heard, or are included in deliberations as equals. If the issue involves a looming lawsuit, for example, some representatives will not wish to reveal all their interests and considerations. Also, if the issue involves passionate pleas or traditional knowledge, these justifications may not be given the same weight as scientific data. Clearly, the selection of members should be given considerable thought for a healthy mix of personalities who can help create an atmosphere that welcomes different opinions and who can listen respectfully.

Although much is implied about the importance of democratic participation and the empowerment of all participants, there is often a power imbalance in multi-stakeholder groups. For example, the industry or agency in question may hold the ultimate decision-making power if the MSP is created with only the ability to make a recommendation. Some stakeholder groups may represent thousands of citizens, giving them the perception of greater power. Several interest groups may subscribe to the same perceptions or mind sets, making their common position stronger. Facilitators must take these types of details into account to provide room for all members to voice opinions, watch interactions to nip destructive comments early, and help integrate information into shared understanding. Good facilitators have the skills to recognize which

ground rules will be most useful (see Figure 10.3), how to engage more people in discussion, when to move forward with a decision, and how to help the group think critically about their deliberations.[11]

To begin building trust, a facilitator may choose to focus early meetings on aspects of the issue about which there is broad agreement. In contentious issues, people

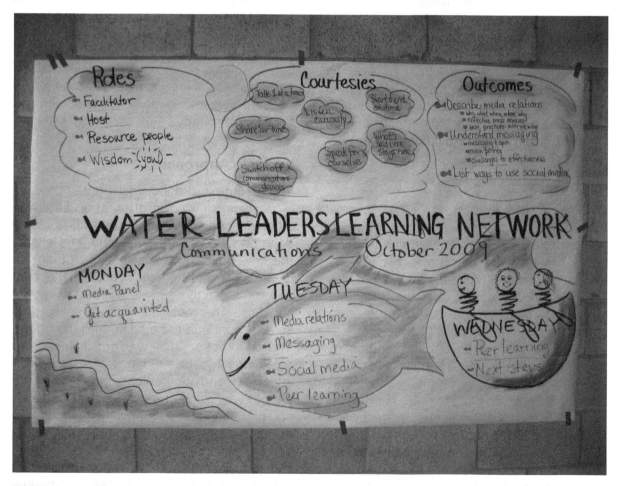

FIGURE 10.3 Agendas, ground rules, and expectations of a meeting can help participants stay focused and achieve their intended outcomes. *(Photograph from Charlotte Young, ENVision)*

tend to focus on the differences in positions and may not realize the degree to which positions overlap. A facilitator might also choose to keep early discussion general, again in order to foster early agreement. Often even strongly opposed positions can find agreement in general terms. For example, in the proposal of a new wood-burning power plant, some stakeholders may see the proposed facility as a way to address the challenge of greenhouse emissions in a way that promotes social and economic goals. Others may see it as a step toward high-priced power and the loss of local forests. These differences would have to be sorted out, but likely all stakeholders could agree on a common goal of producing affordable power for the local community in an ecologically sound way that does not decrease the quality of life for local community members.

MSP is a slow process in part because it takes time to hear the many perspectives represented in the group, but also because trust is a slow-growing stock. Groups that are early in the process have inherently low resilience because trust that may take months to build can be destroyed in an instant by a single breach. The slow rate of progress may be a point of frustration for some members or outside critics. Some facilitators choose to have the group create a document outlining general goals for the group. These goals may be expressed in quite broad terms in order to achieve universal support within the group. Nonetheless, they can instill a sense of solidarity and direction among group members and facilitate the further formation of trust.

The key point here is that the formation of a functional group that fosters understanding and communication among stakeholders can be more important than any single policy or recommendation the group makes. Often, these are long-term groups that convene for years to identify needs, sponsor joint fact-finding and research, listen to every perspective that comes forward, establish strategies to make decisions that respect all parties, and make recommendations. They build skills in perspective-taking and communication as well as build understanding in environmental science, monitoring, economic costs and benefits, legal procedures and political pressure, and social justice. Their members may become valuable leaders in other contexts for the community.

Iterative Approach

In the context of policy making, the process of decision making is often seen as linear. One is faced with a crisis, makes a policy decision to deal with that issue, and enacts the new policy. This new policy is then followed until another crisis arises. The tacit assumption in this approach is that the policy chosen is the most appropriate policy now and will continue to be so far into the future. This assumption is flawed for at least two reasons. First, given that we usually have imperfect and incomplete information and are not very good at making decisions about complex, uncertain, and risky situations, the policy chosen at any one time might not be the best policy available for the circumstances. Second, we have seen that social-ecological systems are constantly changing. The policy that may work best today may not be as applicable in a year or even months, depending on the rate of change of the system.

The linear approach to policy making has resulted in a number of widely publicized failures regarding natural resource management, including fishery management policies that have resulted in collapsed fisheries around the world and pest control policies that have resulted in chronic outbreaks of pests despite high use of pesticides.[12] The term **adaptive management** was coined in the context of ecosystem management but has been used increasingly in other contexts. It represents an alternative to this linear approach.[13] Within an adaptive management framework an ecosystem manager would favor small, purposeful management actions and engage in continual monitoring and analysis of their impacts. By reviewing monitoring data at regular intervals, managers can assess the appropriateness of their original plan and make changes as necessary.

Adaptive management enables managers to acknowledge that the system may be more complex than they understand and that the circumstances that dictated a particular course of action may have changed. Perhaps more importantly, it allows them to explore and learn as they proceed with a course of action and to respond to impacts to the very components of the system that may be most challenging to measure and predict—global changes, social justice, economic developments, and other ethical dimensions. When this strategy is applied to MSP, it is called **Adaptive Collaborative Management** (ACM), a term that signifies the importance of continued assessment and learning as well as the inclusion of multiple stakeholders in the process.[14]

From the perspective of ACM, we can better understand why the institution of the group itself is often more important than any single policy that comes from it. The details of any policy will go through a series of changes, to account for either new information or new circumstances. At times, changes in circumstances beyond the group's control (e.g., regional economic crisis) can present stark challenges not only to policy but to the decision-making group itself. In these instances, the resilience of the multi-stakeholder group can be the difference between a coordinated response and the dissolution of stakeholder connections and the inability to create or implement new policy.

While each MSP is different, they tend to include four phases: initiation, adaptive planning, collaborative action, and reflexive monitoring.[15] The initiation phase involves the establishment of the group, the development of appropriate expectations and common purpose, an orientation to the situation, and the development of a leadership group. In cases where the group already exists but is facing a different challenge, this stage still involves the initial analysis. The adaptive planning phase enables the group to build trust as they learn about each other's interests and perspectives. This phase often involves future visioning exercises or scenario planning. Such an exercise may reveal where significant disagreement occurs or where serious gaps in knowledge exist.

BOX 10.4   Applying These Ideas—An International Process to Assess GMOs

The concepts of social learning, multi-stakeholder process, and the development of learning organizations to improve understanding and solve problems that encompass technology, the environment, society, development, and ethics can be illustrated in the following case. Rapid advances in genetic engineering have created opportunities for technology to address a wide range of agricultural challenges with genetically modified organisms (GMO). Nutrient-rich rice, corn that has greater resistance to pests, and fish that mature faster are among the new GMOs that have been created by inserting genes from one organism into another. The advantages of GMOs could greatly enhance our ability to feed, clothe, and heal people around the world.

Because the GMOs are new and involve complicated technology, few people are well versed in their advantages and disadvantages. There is substantial uncertainty about the potential consequences of planting a new organism in open fields, for example, where pollinators may spread designer genes to wild cousins or across international borders to nations which have refused to allow these crops. There is controversy about the traditional practice of saving seeds for next year's planting if the seeds themselves are licensed genetic material. The science is difficult to understand, the advocates on both sides use compelling tactics, and nations are faced with important challenges as they consider whether to allow each GMO into their agricultural systems.

In 2000, the nations who signed the Convention on Biological Diversity authored the Cartagena Protocol on Biosafety—an agreement designed to use the precautionary approach to help protect people and the environment from the uncertainties associated with widespread use of GMOs. As of October 2007, 143 nations had signed on the protocol. The suggested process of assessing a potential GMO should include scientific information and expertise to explore the proposed benefits and possible interactions that could arise with the environment and society, an opportunity for those who will be most affected by a decision to contribute to the decision, and a process to guide efficient deliberation (Nelson and Banker 2007). Public sector scientists associated with universities and government agencies tackled the challenge of developing a risk assessment process that any nation could use to make decisions about GMOs through the GMO ERA Project. An environmental risk assessment (ERA)[16] is a logical tool to accomplish some of the analysis associated with GMOs, but it also has limitations. Most ERA models focus on science and ecosystem risk and do not address societal impacts, particularly social acceptance, economic factors, political influences, and ethical issues. Since most GMOs are solutions to a problem, it makes sense for the process to be grounded in a problem formulation process with reflection on alternatives that achieve similar goals. The project team recommends multi-stakeholder participation that engages the people most affected by the GMO decision in a deliberative process that integrates information and careful, reflective discussion about the problem and potential solutions (Nelson and Banker 2007). This process, known as the Problem Formulation and Options Assessment (PFOA) would become part of the standard ERA activity for GMOs.

In their pilot tests of the process in Brazil, Kenya, Malaysia, and Vietnam, project scientists learned that the process enabled a blend of expert and public voices to be heard and included in the discussion. Participants learned from and with each other as they moved through the process, and as a result, participants reshaped their views as they learned. Focusing on the problem they faced kept the group discussion on the realities of their context, and considering each alternative in a transparent process allowed interest groups to understand both the process and the recommendations the group made. This focus also enabled the groups to address the problems they face with creativity rather than limiting their considerations to the advantages and disadvantages of the GMO. The process is not simple or easy, however, and questions still confront the project organizers about how nations can develop the capacity to orchestrate the process and create recommendations that their regulatory bodies will accept.

The collaborative action component enables the group to implement their decisions, inform stakeholders of their progress, and make changes as necessary. This is generally the time at which those not directly involved in the process begin to see results. However, the success of this phase depends largely on the groundwork from stages one and two. During the reflexive monitoring phase, the group will set up strategies to track change, identify those components that require further investigation, and welcome critical reflection on their process and decisions.

In most examples of groups working to resolve socio-ecological conflicts, a positive outcome is linked to learning how to work together, establishing trust in each other and the process, collecting needed data together, incorporating disparate ideas and perspectives, and working toward a shared goal. The skills and processes of social learning, systems thinking, working with diverse stakeholders, and adaptive collaborative management may be essential features of a successful MSP. The example in Box 10.4 shows that this is especially true for issues being dealt with on a global scale.

Clearly, a multi-stakeholder process (MSP) is essential in understanding the problem and the possible consequences of each option the group selects to consider. The effectiveness of a process that includes people representing many different (and opposing) interests and experiences (from research scientist to farmer) will depend on developing trust and openness, practicing good listening and communication skills, building shared understanding, careful consideration and reflection. Understanding how to include opinion leaders of stakeholders, how to present information, how to convince people to attend meetings, and how to facilitate discussion requires understanding the motives and interests that encourage or discourage stakeholders to engage in social learning and to create a learning organization.

LEARNING ORGANIZATIONS

While the term ACM is often used in a natural resource context, business leaders often use the term **learning organization** to describe a similar model within an industry. Using the skills discussed above within the context of the workplace could help define an ethic of sustainability within the company. Decisions about which product to make, which budget to cut, or which problem to solve might be best answered by considering whom we need to hear from, what consequences have we not considered, what additional expertise can help, and how can we learn our way forward. In this section, we discuss the learning organization model and how change occurs within those organizations.

Developing the Ideal of a Learning Organization

There is little that is more motivating than a crisis. We are hard-wired to bolt at initial signs of potential danger—an inclination passed on by the ancestors who did not become lunch for a lion. While our abilities to leap to conclusions (a snapping twig might be a beast) and act (run without a backward glance) have clearly saved our lives for eons, the current sources of trouble are not so easily escaped. In fact, our intuitive reactions may be exactly the opposite of what is needed.

In the *Fifth Discipline,* Peter Senge[17] uses the experience of multi-national corporations and businesses to develop his suggestions of the skills that are needed to move us and our organizations toward sustainability. These skills are not easily acquired by the fight or flight responders. They must be learned and practiced over time, and they enable people to explore, dig deeply, and learn about problems and solutions together. Those who practice these skills talk about pausing, talking to each other, thinking together, and reflecting—a far cry from the snap decisions made in an emergency. When businesses, industries, and organizations value and nurture these skills, they evolve to become learning organizations. Senge describes learning organizations as sharing the following five disciplines:

Systems thinking—Rather than dividing a problem into parts, seeing a problem in the whole, and using systems thinking to understand the situation and see potential solutions.

Personal mastery—Becoming proficient at learning. This involves mastering the techniques of creating a vision, being patient, focusing energy, committing to a goal, and seeking truth. Where youthful optimism and idealism contribute greatly to this discipline, a seasoned workforce tends to be disgruntled and may lack the desire for mastery.

Mental models—Becoming skilled at understanding personal assumptions and rationale, that is, one's mental model, articulating that to others, and helping them understanding their mental models so that a shared model can be jointly constructed. These conversations involve balancing statements of advocacy with inquiry—promoting one's views and thoughts in such a way that different perspectives, faults, and contradictions are surfaced and explored.

Shared vision—Creating and sharing a powerful ideal of where the organization is moving and energizing commitment toward that vision that is not coerced but desired.

Team building—Building productive teams so that joint dialogue reflects exploration and learning. "Teams, not individuals, are the fundamental learning unit in modern organizations....Unless teams can learn, the organization cannot learn."[18]

The process of achieving change in the workplace, then, is a process of creating a learning organization—one where a systems perspective is used to understand important problems and situations, where teams of stakeholders work together toward a common vision or to resolve disputes, and where mental models are explored and challenged in an atmosphere of trust and acceptance. Good communication skills are vital for the development of shared visions and mental models. An understanding of behavior change, diffusion, misconceptions, and the role of advocacy can help the teams function more efficiently and honestly.

This does not happen overnight. Becoming a learning organization is a change in culture. A commitment by leadership to learning is often needed, as well as the ability to commit to change over time. After several years on this path, Harley-Davison President Jeff Bluestein was asked what was different in his company. He admitted it was not a massive change, but he thought it was significant. "I hear more and more people say, 'This is the way I am seeing things' rather than 'This is the way things are.'"[19]

Creating Change in a Learning Organization

One need not be a CEO to build the skills of a learning organization, although some level of support from leadership may be helpful. Within small units and offices, for example, these good practices can help people communicate clearly, address problems more effectively, and ask questions about the broader system. Taking the time to ask people for their opinions, establishing working groups and committees that investigate problems and make recommendations, and modeling and encouraging employees to work with stakeholders who share different views are ways we can move the office environment toward the practice of making more ethical decisions.

Another characteristic seems to be common to the people who work to shift the culture in their organization toward one of learning— they value and respect people. They know that people need and thrive on meaningful work, and finding meaning is more possible when people develop the skills associated with learning organizations. Supervisors who support creative new ideas—even when the experiments fail—help people grow, and human growth is a noble goal. These are the supervisors and companies more likely to tackle and succeed in moving into the unknown—sustainability.

Senge's work has been adopted by corporations and organizations in many different sectors. Staff at Unilever have created more meaningful work by gaining leadership skills in working with people and integrating more experiences in problem solving. Because their business relies upon fish, they have become involved in policies and the development of sustainable fisheries. In another example, several years ago Intel was developing a new facility for a new microprocessor. The leader of this large, stressful effort suffered a heart attack and returned to work with a new commitment to limit his work life to a more reasonable 50 hours a week and be home in time to eat dinner with his family.

He also made it clear that he expected the rest of the workforce to also take time for their families and hobbies. They used this opportunity to shift their culture to taking the time to work better, not harder. They become more engaged and even happier people. The new facility opened earlier than expected, eclipsing the original, demanding target.[20]

These and other businesses find that the work of their agency or industry is improved by valuing and respecting their employees— they solve problems and tackle unknowns with greater success. This bodes well for organizations that wish to move toward sustainability, as the issues are challenging and unknowns abound. We will need to create space to find joy in the many difficult trials that are ahead. The attributes of a learning organization suggest that these groups will be able to respond more adequately when the planet's warning lights start blinking.

CONCLUSION

It would be easier if we could simply have a scientific expert look at necessary data and make a decision regarding an issue or policy that would still satisfy competing values, differing perspectives, and ethical responsibilities to a wide range of stakeholders. But those experts are rare, if they exist at all. As a result, we need to engage a variety of people in making ethical decisions about sustainability. As the examples of the Frankfurt airport and the international GMO approval system suggest, decisions are not sustainable in the long term if they do not consider the varying perspectives of the environmentalists, the

rural poor, the neighbors, the unborn, and the nonhuman creatures on the planet. Considering all those elements requires groups of stakeholders and representatives who are probably not working for the same employer.

Implementing practices that lead toward sustainability in industries, businesses, government agencies, municipal offices, and schools will take a process of working together. Multi-stakeholder processes are one method for facilitating social learning where complexity and diverse perspectives are the rule. These groups will engage people with different experience and expertise who may not share the same vocabulary or biases. Communication within such groups begins with an agreement to try, a shared vision of the purpose and goal, and a trust that working together will result in something better than if everyone worked alone. As the world faces greater challenges in balancing environmental limits with economic necessity and social justice, it will not be hard to justify the importance of group efforts to design more sustainable products and practices.

The groups that focus on sustainability must include the ethical questions raised in Chapters 4 through 7 of this book. Perspectives on ethics can help people sort through the issues and weigh and compare various options. In some cases, we will miss alternative perceptions and need to challenge ourselves to always test assumptions and look for new considerations. We need to shed old ways of knowing and thinking in order to perceive options for sustainability. We also need to ask a series of questions that get at both the practical and the ethical dimensions of the problems. Is any outcome irreversible? Will future generations have the same resources and options we enjoy? Are all those who are affected by this technology or decision involved in the conversation? Are the costs of negative impacts included in the price? The process of discussing, debating, and deciding is not easy, but it is made more effective when groups deliberately use the strategies of social learning and learning organizations.

Convincing supervisors, colleagues, and laggards to adopt recommendations and new ideas, however, may be difficult. The skills of communication rest upon a foundation of understanding the motives and determinants of behavior, as well as the ways in which ideas move through a group. While these ideas have been perfected in the world of advertising and marketing, they are currently being used to affect health and conservation behaviors. It is only logical that they will also be used to make behavior more sustainable as well, as the next chapter will explore.

REFERENCES

Abelson, J., P-G. Forest, J. Eyles, P. Smith, E. Martin, and F-P.Gauvin. 2003. "Deliberations about Deliberative Methods: Issues in the design and evaluation of public participation processes." *Social Science and Medicine* 57(2):239–51.

Andrews, E., M. Stevens, and G. Wise. 2002. "A Model of Community-Based Environmental Education." In T. Dietz and P. C. Stern, Eds. *New Tools for Environmental Protection: Education, Information, and Voluntary Measures*. Washington, DC: National Academy Press, pp. 161–182.

Berkes, Fikret. 1998. "Indigenous knowledge and resource management systems in the Canadian subarctic." In F. Berkes, C. Folke, and J Colding, Eds. *Linking Social and Ecological Systems*. Cambridge: Cambridge University Press. pp. 98–128.

Berkes, F., J.Colding, and C. Folke. 2000. "Rediscovery of traditional ecological knowledge as adaptive management." *Ecological Applications* 10(5): 1251–1262.

Daniels, S. E. and G. B. Walker. 2001. *Working through Environmental Conflict: The collaborative learning approach*. Westport, CT: Praeger

Gertner, J. 2009. Why isn't the brain green? *New York Times*. Published April 16, 2009. Accessed August 12, 2009 from www.nytimes.com/2009/04/19/magazine/19Science-t.html?pagewanted=all.

Gunderson, L. H., C. S.Holling, and S. S. Light. 1995. *Barriers and Bridges to the Renewal of Ecosystems and Institutions*. New York: Columbia University Press.

Gunderson, L. H., Holling, C. S. Eds., 2002. *Panarchy: Understanding Transformations in Human and Natural Systems*. Washington, DC: Island Press.

Holling, C. S. 1978. *Adaptive environmental assessment and management*. London: John Wiley.

Janis, Irving. 1972. *Victims of Groupthink*. Boston: Houghton Mifflin.

Johannes, R. E. 1989. *Traditional Ecological Knowledge: A Collection of Essays*. Cambridge: World Conservation Union.

Keen, Meg, Valerie A. Brown, and RobertDyball. 2005. "Social Learning: A new approach to environmental management," InM. Keen, V. A. Brown, and R. Dyball, Eds. *Social Learning in Environmental Management: Towards a sustainable future*. London: Earthscan, pp. 3–21.

Leinhardt, G. 1992. "What research on learning tells us about teaching." *Educational Leadership* 49(7): 20–25.

Meister, Hans-Peter and Christopher Gohl. 2009. "Regional Dialogue Forum Airport Frankfurt." Available at http://portals.wi.wur.nl/msp/?page=1257and accessed on November 3, 2009.

Muro, M., and P. Jeffrey, 2008. "A critical review of the theory and application of social learning in participatory natural resource management." *Journal of Environmental Planning and Management* 51, 325–344.

Murray, C. and D. Marmorek. 2003. "Adaptive Management and Ecological Restoration." In P. Freiderici, Ed. *Ecological Restoration of Southwestern Ponderosa Pine Forests.* Washington D.C.: Island Press, pp. 417–428.

MSP Resource Portal (Multi-Stakeholder Processes Resource Portal). 2009. Wageningen University. Accessed November 3, 2009 at http://portals.wi.wur.nl/msp/.

Nelson, Kristen C. and Michael J. Banker. 2007. *Problem Formulation and Options Assessment Handbook.* St. Paul, MN: International Project on GMO Environmental Risk Assessment Methodologies.

Olsson, Per, Carl Folke, and Fikret Berkes. 2004. "Adaptive comanagement for building resilience in social-ecological systems." *Environmental Management* 34(1): 75–90.

Owens, S. 2000. "Commentary—Engaging the Public: Information and deliberation in environmental policy." *Environment and Planning A* 32(7):1141–48.

Renn, O., T. Webler, and P. Wiedemann. 1995. *Fairness and Competence in Citizen Participation: Evaluating models for environmental discourse.* Dordrecht: Kluwer Academic Press.

Robbins, Jim. 2007. "Saint UrsusMaritimus," *Conservation.* 8(4).Accessed on August 23, 2009 at www.conservationmagazine.org/articles/v8n4/saint-ursus-maritimus/.

Senge, Peter M. 2006. *The fifth discipline: the art and practice of the learning organization*, Revised ed. New York: Doubleday.

Sirianni, C. and L. Friedland. 2001. *Civic Innovation in America: Community empowerment, public policy, and the movement for civic renewal.* Berkeley, CA: University of California Press.

Slovic, Paul. 1987. "Perception of risk." *Science* 236(6): 280–285.

U.S. Department of Labor, Mine Safety and Health Administration. "Average of annual fatalities from 1996 to 2008." Accessed on May 21, 2009 at www.msha.gov/stats/charts/coalbystate.asp.

USEPA. 1998. *Guidelines for Ecological Risk Assessment.* EPA/630/R-925/002F, Washington, DC.

Walker, Brian, and David Salt. 2006. *Resilience Thinking.* Washington DC: Island Press.

Wondolleck, Julia M. and Steven L. Yaffee. 2000. *Making Collaboration Work: Lessons from Innovations in NaturalResource Management.* Washington, DC: Island Press.

ENDNOTES

1. Johannes (1989).
2. See for example, Berkes et al. (2000).
3. Keen et al. (2005); Muro and Jeffrey (2008).
4. Leinhardt (1992).
5. Gertner (2009).
6. See, for example, Abelson et al. (2003), Andrews et al. (2002), Daniels and Walker (2001), Owens (2000), Renn et al. (1995), Sirianni and Friedland (2001), and Wondolleck and Yaffee (2000).
7. Robbins (2007).

8. U.S. Department of Labor, Mine Safety and Health Administration.

9. Slovic (1987).

10. See Janis (1972).

11. A variety of resources and techniques are available to facilitators and organizers to think about the goals for the group, to win the trust and cooperation of group members, and to develop a process of critical reflection that results in a new idea for which there is broad agreement. For example, see the Multi-Stakeholder Process Resource Portal.

12. For a more thorough discussion of policy failures around the globe, see Gunderson et al. (1995).

13. See Walker and Salt (2006), Holling (1978), Gunderson and Holling (2002), and Murray and Marmorek (2003).

14. Olsson et al. (2004).

15. MSP Resource Portal.

16. The USEPA (1998) defines risk assessment as "a process that evaluates the likelihood that adverse ecological effects may occur or are occurring as a result of exposure to one of more stressors."

17. Senge (2006).

18. Senge (2006), page 10.

19. Senge (2006), page 187.

20. Senge (2006).

CHAPTER 11

Applying an Ethic of Sustainability

In response to demands by government and society that organizations and businesses be responsible for the conduct of their activities and their impacts on the environment and society, many have adopted sustainability as an approach for guiding decision making. In addition to its many other attributes, sustainability provides the advantage of "one-stop shopping." Rather than having to find one framework for addressing ecological system impacts, a second to cover community relationships, and perhaps even others to deal with climate change, fair trade, and impacts on future generations, sustainability can address all these concerns in a comprehensive, readily understandable, and implementable model. In this book, we suggest that shifting tracks to take advantage of the many benefits of sustainability requires the organization to internalize a set of values and principles that compose an ethic of sustainability.

As described in Chapter 1, sustainability is rarely used exactly as stated in the Brundtland definition as a guide to organizational change. Instead, a wide variety of sustainability frameworks with roots in the Brundtland definition have been developed for this purpose. In this chapter, we review the major concepts discussed in this book and describe a number of frameworks currently being used to translate these concepts into policies for companies and governments. We then take a closer look at the sustainability efforts of a large corporation and assess how an ethic of sustainability could have guided the adoption of sustainability and improved the resulting decision-making process. Rather than using an arbitrary selection of organizations for this purpose, the case study presented here is about an organization that has adopted sustainability to guide its actions.

MAKING ETHICAL DECISIONS FOR A SUSTAINABLE FUTURE: AN OVERVIEW

In this book, we have proposed several ethical principles of sustainability that provide the moral basis for opting for this framework as a means of guiding decision making, especially but not solely with respect to developing and deploying technology. Before we determine how to apply the ethics of sustainability, we will briefly recap the ethical principles that were described in the various chapters of the book.

Social Sustainability

In Chapter 4, we described four ethical principles that address the social aspects of sustainability.

The Golden Rule

Although the Golden Rule has many possible interpretations, in the context of sustainability, the Golden Rule means that, because we believe we have the right to have our basic needs met, we are obliged to extend this right to our local and global neighbors. In the context of futurity, the Golden Rule is also applied to future inhabitants of the Earth.

The Rights of the Vulnerable

Also referred to as *Care Ethics*, this principle obligates us to share responsibility for the welfare of the poor, weak, sick, and disenfranchised people of the world. Within the context of the Brundtland definition of sustainability, it squarely addresses "meeting the needs of the present" with the implication that these words are particularly directed at these vulnerable populations. This principle could also be extended to another population that is vulnerable to our contemporary behavior, namely future generations. The Rights of the Vulnerable Principle includes the concept of environmental justice, a response to environmental injustice, the presence of a disproportionate number of environmental risks in less well-off communities.

The Distributional Principle

Ensuring that both advantages and disadvantages, benefits and risks, are equitably distributed in society can be accomplished only if fair processes for sharing political and decision making power within the global community are developed.

Chain of Obligation (Expanded Community)

Sustainability extends the notion of distributional justice across temporal boundaries and confronts us with the lack of connection between current behavior patterns and the quality of life prospects for future generations. When the definition of community is expanded to include future generations as well, the Distributional Principle also addresses intergenerational justice, requiring a fair distribution of resources, ecological system function, and environmental amenity across time.

Ecological Sustainability

The environmental dimensions of sustainability were covered in Chapter 5 and two ethical principles were identified as being supportive of sustainability:

The Land Ethic

The Land Ethic provides a basic guideline by which people can judge the moral correctness of different attitudes and actions regarding nature. In the words of Aldo Leopold, "A thing is right when it tends to preserve the integrity, stability, and beauty of a biotic community. It is wrong when it tends otherwise." The Land Ethic calls for shift in thinking about land as a resource to land as a community in which human beings are merely members. Decisions must be made on the basis of what best preserves the ecological integrity of the community and not individual elements, including human beings. It calls for decisions that best preserve the integrity of nature above all other considerations.

The Rights of the Nonhuman World

While the Land Ethic proposes that we act in the best interests of ecosystem health rather than individual elements, the Rights of the Nonhuman World principle addresses how individual organisms (but most often animals) are treated. Human beings and animals have startlingly similar DNA, and we also seem to share much of the same capacity for feelings and pain. Consequently, it can be argued that animals have rights similar in most respects to those of human beings. Accepting this concept also requires consideration of the rights of other living species to include insects and plants and perhaps even the non-living world, such as geological formations.

Economic Sustainability

Four ethical principles that address the economic dimension of sustainability were described in Chapter 6, and include the following:

The Polluter Pays Principle

In addition to being a principle of an ethics of sustainability, the Polluter Pays Principle (PPP) is also a legal principle, ensuring the costs of pollution are justly allocated among those specifically causing the pollution. The PPP internalizes the cost of pollution by shifting the burden of responsibility and the costs of cleanup, mitigation, and abatement to the parties actually causing the pollution.

Extended Producer Responsibility

Based on the principle of Extended Producer Responsibility (EPR), manufacturers of products are held responsible for the entire life cycle of their products and are required to take back and recycle the product and its packaging. Rather than placing the burden of landfilled materials on society and future generations, EPR puts the onus for both appropriate design and materials selection on the manufacturer. In essence, EPR requires the redesign of the production system to eliminate waste, one of the major tenets of sustainability.

The Beneficiary Compensates Principle

The Beneficiary Compensates Principle (BCP) requires that those benefiting from the contribution of valuable natural systems or scenic landscapes by parties who would forgo income from such an action, compensate the parties who are making the contribution. For example, there is pressure to preserve large tracts of rainforest for biodiversity preservation and carbon sequestration, resulting in a quandary for the countries possessing these valuable tracts because they must forgo development and income to contribute to these laudable goals. In this case, the BCP would require that the beneficiaries, the international community, pay the countries who are protecting their forest for the income from timber harvesting that they have forgone.

Full-Cost Accounting

The objective of the Full-Cost Accounting principle is to ensure all the social and environmental costs of a product or process are identified and built into the price of the product or activity. These internalized costs can then be distributed to the parties who have been affected by the product or activity to compensate them for their losses or other effects.

Integrating the Dimensions of Sustainability

In Chapter 7, we discussed how to integrate the three legs of sustainability and two principles that are cross-cutting were described:

The Precautionary and Reversibility Principles

The Precautionary Principle requires that where there is scientific uncertainty regarding a technology or activity that is being implemented or being considered for implementation, society should take preemptory action to avert potential threats to health or the environment. Additionally, it is the proponent of the technology or activity that is responsible for the burden of proof. A subset of the Precautionary Principle, known as the Reversibility Principle, states that, in the event of scientific uncertainty, as a minimum, the ability to undo or reverse the consequences should be built into the technology or activity.

Transparency

Good governance is essential for balancing the many competing ends that challenges decision making in support of sustainability. Transparency means that nongovernmental organizations, citizens, elected officials, and others would have unencumbered access to information about decision making and hold each other accountable for following through on agreements. Among other things, the Transparency Principle supports good governance by requiring elected officials to stand behind their campaign promises through the publication of all arguments and meetings regarding legislation. It also means that corporations must report information about their products, processes, and decisions to the public to provide society insights into their financial, social, and environmental behavior. Transparency also applies to technology development and deployment, requiring that the components and ingredients of a product or process be made known, and that any potential negative consequences or uncertainty regarding a technology be made known to the public.

In addition to these concepts, concepts from the field of complex adaptive systems can help integrate the dimensions of sustainability. Viewing social-ecological systems as sets of nested systems helped to understand how systems interact across scales. We also looked at the concept of resilience as a way to frame decisions involving high uncertainty. Social-ecological systems with high diversity (in social, ecological, and economic contexts) will be better able to manage unexpected problems that arise. From this viewpoint, we can see the challenge of sustainability as the challenge of maintaining resilience in social-ecological systems across many scales of interaction.

CONTEMPORARY SUSTAINABILITY-BASED FRAMEWORKS

Sustainability is a broad concept upon which various frameworks can be constructed. The following sections describe three of these sustainability-based frameworks: The Natural Step, The Hannover Principles, and Corporate Social Responsibility.

The Natural Step

Developed by Karl Henrik Ròbert shortly after the publication of the Brundtland Report, The Natural Step (TNS) presented four principles of sustainability that provide a foundation for the framework. According to this framework, in order to achieve sustainability we must achieve these four objectives:

1. Eliminate our contribution to the progressive build-up of substances extracted from the Earth's crust (for example, heavy metals and fossil fuels)

2. Eliminate our contribution to the progressive build-up of chemicals and compounds produced by society (for example, dioxins, PCBs, and DDT)

3. Eliminate our contribution to the progressive physical degradation and destruction of nature and natural processes (for example, overharvesting forests and paving over critical wildlife habitat)

4. Eliminate our contribution to conditions that undermine people's capacity to meet their basic human needs (for example, unsafe working conditions and not enough pay to live on).[1]

The ecological focus here is evident. The chemical and physical impacts of human activities on environmental systems compose the focus of the first three objectives. The fourth objective, however, includes social and economic concerns as well.

In addition to the four objectives listed above, TNS provides a systematic approach to implementation by which corporations can progress to a point where they are essentially achieving the four objectives. Companies implementing this system can progress from Level 1 to Level 5. The five levels are outlined in brief here:[2]

Level 1: Implement a policy of year-by-year reductions in emissions of synthetic substances from the earth's crust, including solid waste, thereby avoiding local accumulation.

Level 2: Continue increasing the ratio of recycled to raw materials, decreasing dependence on materials extraction.

Level 3: Maximize resource efficiency and introduce analysis to assist in reducing the nonrenewable portion of the materials stream.

Level 4: Introduce Life Cycle Assessment (LCA) analysis to provide a more detailed understanding of the impact of production decisions.

Level 5: Set effective limits on materials extraction from the Earth's crust and the use of these materials. Consider use of land and set limits on the use of land for production.

TNS provides more of an educational than a practical framework for companies to use to progress toward sustainability. It sets limits that are difficult to determine much less attain. In spite of its shortcomings, TNS has become a very popular and well-recognized sustainability-based framework that provides insights on limits that society will have to face in order to avoid the consequences of ignoring them.

The Hannover Principles

In 1992, the city manager of Hannover, Germany, Jobst Fiedler, commissioned William McDonough, one of the early figures in the design of green buildings, to work with the city to develop a set of principles for sustainable design for the 2000 Hannover World Fair. The principles were not intended to serve as a how-to for ecological design but as a *foundation* for ecological design. One of the contributions that emerged from this relatively early attempt to articulate principles for the green building movement was a definition of **sustainable design** as the "conception and realization of ecologically, economically, and ethically responsible expression as part of the evolving matrix of nature." These principles, commonly known as the Hannover Principles, are listed in Table 1.1.[3]

In some respects the Hannover Principles could be said to extend the definitions of sustainability by explicitly addressing the nonmaterial world of spirit, describing the importance of design, and explaining how

---

TABLE 11.1   The Hannover Principles

1. Insist on the rights of humanity and nature to coexist.
2. Recognize interdependence.
3. Respect relationships between spirit and matter.
4. Accept responsibility for the consequences of design.
5. Create safe objects of long-term value.
6. Eliminate the concept of waste.
7. Rely on natural energy flows.
8. Understand the limitations of design.
9. Seek constant improvement by the sharing of knowledge.

---

designers have a responsibility for creating devices and objects that are culturally significant and of value to society. In this view, the problems being addressed by sustainability poor designs. At the 2007 meeting of the International Council of Societies of Industrial Design, Nathan Shedroff said, "Design is a big part of the sustainability problems in the world. Design has been focused on creating meaningless (often), disposable (though not responsibly so), trend-laden fashion items—all design. Graphic design is particularly bad, though paper materials, at least, have a huge potential to fix this problem."[4]

The Hannover Principles led to the development of sustainable design, which is now embedded in architecture and other areas of design such as landscape architecture, interior design, urban planning, and industrial design. Sustainable design can be described as an approach that recognizes that products and processes are interdependent with the environmental, economic, and social systems surrounding them and implements measures to prevent an unsustainable compromise to these systems.[5] It is a design approach that is often described as holistic, systems-based, and synergistic. The present day green building movement embraces sustainable design as central to the production of buildings, cities, and infrastructure that lower the impacts of construction and the consumption of resources associated with human-made structures.

Corporate Social Responsibility

Economist, Milton Friedman, famously said in 1962, "Few trends could so thoroughly undermine the foundations of our free enterprise society as the acceptance of a social responsibility other than to make as much money for their stockholders as possible."[6] Today, however, long-term business success requires a broader approach. There is a growing movement in the world of business to engage in the international dialogue about sustainability. The Exxon Valdez oil spill, the Bhopal disaster, the fraudulent financial reporting and subsequent collapse of Enron, Tyco, and Worldcom, the 2008–2009 collapse of financial industries, and the 2010 BP oil spill destroyed public trust and confidence in the corporate world, and affected the bottom-line performance of numerous companies because their behavior and financial reporting could not be trusted. Driven by this plague of environmental mishaps, fraud, and corporate scandals over the past three decades, the business world has embraced the notion of responsibility beyond mere financial performance.

The corporate sustainability movement, now termed Corporate Social Responsibility (CSR), attempts to apply sustainability to guide the behavior of business with respect to both society and the environment, as well as its responsibility to stockholders. In this new model corporations value their success not solely based on their financial bottom line but also on their environmental and social performance. Many refer to this broader definition of success as the triple bottom line.

Examples include some of the largest and most successful companies in the world. In 2000, Intel dramatically stepped up its support for education programs and now values its annual support for education programs supporting math, science and technology at $100 million through a combination of cash grants, equipment, and services. In 2008 Standard Chartered, a UK-based international bank with 75,000 employees operating in 70 countries, announced a $20 million global initiative, *Seeing Is Believing*, which aims to provide eye care to poor urban areas around the globe. Standard Chartered also has committed to making $500 million available for microfinance loans in developing countries, to educating a million people about HIV/AIDS over three years, and to operating a program called *Nets for Life* in Africa, which is working to curb the spread of malaria.

Xerox promotes the use of environmentally responsible paper that is sourced in certified, sustainably managed forests. They have partnered with the Nature Conservancy, giving the conservation organization $1 million to support researchers in developing better forest management practices. The drug maker, Wyeth, is leading efforts to make life-saving vaccines more accessible to the world's poor. Starbucks Corporation includes commitment to communities and environment as one of its six guiding principles. In addition to working with their suppliers to give bean growers better prices, they offer health-care and stock benefits even to part-time employees.

As these examples illustrate, companies applying CSR frameworks adopt more comprehensive approaches, addressing responsibilities beyond financial performance. The approach is not just more ethical. These companies show that a sustainability ethic can be good for business. Companies engaged in the CSR framework accrue significant benefits such as a better brand identity, lower levels of regulatory scrutiny, reduced liability, a better reputation among prospective employees, and a far greater probability of gaining a "license to operate" in communities where they propose to establish operations.

All of these social and environmental efforts by major corporations mark a significant departure from the traditional model of doing business and point to a trend toward incorporating sustainability thinking in business. Common CSR policies include:

- Adoption of internal controls reform in the wake of Enron and other accounting scandals

- Commitment to diversity in hiring employees and barring discrimination

- Management teams that view employees as assets rather than costs

- High-performance workplaces that integrate the views of line employees into decision-making processes

- Adoption of operating policies that exceed compliance with social and environmental laws

- Advanced resource productivity, focused on the use of natural resources in a more productive, efficient and profitable fashion (such as recycled content and product recycling)

- Taking responsibility for conditions under which goods are produced, directly or by contract, by employees domestically or abroad.

Many institutions have used the concept of corporate social responsibility to justify increased contributions to local communities and support of social values, such as worker benefits and investments in education rather than tobacco production. Some have incorporated environmental goals as well. One of the outcomes of the CSR movement has been new approaches to how companies report on their triple bottom line performance. Most prominent among the various reporting formats is the **Global Reporting Initiative** (GRI), which provides guidelines for CSR reporting by a wide variety of public and private sector organizations. Sustainability reports based on the GRI framework can serve a number of functions. First, they can provide benchmarks for organizational performance with respect to laws, norms, codes, performance standards, and voluntary initiatives. In addition, they can demonstrate organizational commitment to sustainable development and provide a measure for organizational performance over time. GRI promotes and develops a standardized approach to reporting to stimulate demand for sustainability information—which will benefit reporting organizations and those who use report information alike. Over 1,500 organizations from 60 countries use the GRI framework to report on their triple bottom line performance.

CSR has been criticized by some as a form of greenwashing, whereby companies adopt this framework as a strategy primarily to improve their public relations. The operations and products of some companies, for example chemical companies, oil companies, weapons manufacturers, and tobacco companies, to name but a few, seem to be incongruent with CSR and sustainability. Some critics argue that CSR is simply a means of allowing companies to reduce their social and environmental impacts voluntarily when what is truly needed are strong government intervention and regulation. The financial collapses of 2008–2009 are perhaps indicative of what can occur when the hand of government is removed and the interests of society at large are not addressed. On the other hand, some CSR proponents are optimistic that the widespread adoption of this framework will generally improve the well-being of society and instill a culture of responsibility in corporate boardrooms.

PUTTING IT ALL TOGETHER

As you have seen, there are a variety of ways for an organization, industry, or municipality to address and implement sustainability. Some choose to adapt the sustainability meta-framework by tailoring it to the functions of their organization. For example, medical organizations can adapt TNS for use in addressing the unique technology, waste, and social issues facing doctors in their daily work. Each of these existing or tailored frameworks results in a set of principles that are articulated to varying degrees. Alternatively, a corporation may adopt CSR as the framework best suited for their needs and then use the Global Reporting Initiative (GRI)[7] or ISO 14001[8] (Environmental Management Systems) to provide information on their progress to both internal and external stakeholders. Implicit in the GRI and ISO 14001 standards are principles, such as reducing energy and waste, increasing

stakeholder engagement, and increasing energy efficiency.

Numerous communities around the world have adopted Local Agenda 21 (LA21) as their sustainability framework and based their action plans and reporting on the very general guidance contained in the LA21.[9] None of these frameworks, including the sustainability meta-framework itself, explicitly requires the adoption of ethical principles. In each framework, however, ethics is implicit, whether expressed as "meeting the needs of the present . . ." as described in Brundtland or "reducing and eventually eliminating the systematic accumulation of materials from the earth's crust," as stated in TNS. It is our position that sustainability, in any of its various applications, can be successfully implemented only if a strong, coherent, and understandable ethics of sustainability underpins these efforts. In this section, we look at how these frameworks relate to the ethical concepts and decision-making principles covered in this book.

Sustainability Frameworks and Ethics

A careful, or perhaps cynical, reader will note that businesses can painlessly provide millions of dollars to a socially just cause and continue to invest in and support the exploitation of a fossil-fuel economy that maintains the existing power structure and does not lead the planet toward sustainability. We suggest this is evidence of a failure to base sustainability initiatives on an ethic of sustainability. Sustainability requires making decisions that reflect underlying ethical principles that support vulnerable and future populations of humans and nonhumans. This may explain, at least in part, the challenges faced by a variety of sustainability initiatives around the world. Sustainable Seattle, for example, one of the best-known sustainable community movements in the United States issued its well-known *Sustainability Indicators Report* in 1998 and has not issued another. Santa Monica, whose sustainability efforts were initiated by the city government, created a Sustainable City Task Force in 2003 and ended its activities in 2009. Santa Monica issued its Sustainable City Scorecard annually from 2005 to 2008 but has not continued this reporting. Perhaps the best-known sustainability movement in the United States was Chattanooga's Vision 2000, which kicked off in 1984 with an enormous effort by the community to envision its future. The result was a city transformed from what had been declared by the U.S. EPA in 1969 as American's most polluted city to one of America's 10 most enlightened cities, according to the Utne Reader.[10] However, the last community-scale effort in Chattanooga was Revision 2000, held in that year, and there has been very little sustainability-oriented activity in the city since that time. It is clear that "sustaining" a sustainability movement can be a difficult undertaking, particularly for community efforts because it is largely up to volunteers to make things happen.

While it takes time to take action on the decisions that come out of community meetings and activities, it is also essential that they include a long-term commitment for monitoring and discussion. We suggest that the inability to sustain these efforts is in large part the result of the need to articulate and internalize an ethic of sustainability as part of the process. Any complex undertaking by an organization requires strong values to propel it indefinitely. Sustainability is just that, a complex endeavor because it calls for significant shifts in behavior that would lead to, for example, the eradication of global poverty and the reduction of present-day impacts on the quality of life of future generations. This embedded notion of futurity demands commitment across decades and this clearly cannot occur without a strong ethical concept that supports it.

Picturing the Three-Legged Stool Model

As discussed in Chapter 1, the three-legged model of sustainability shown in Figure 11.1 is the most recognized means of graphically depicting this concept. Each of the three legs addresses strategies with which you are now familiar. Strategies at the outer focus only on that leg and do so in a traditional way. For example, traditional approaches in resource management typically address increasing

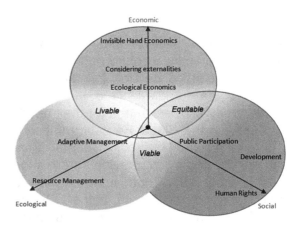

FIGURE 11.1 The three-legged sustainability model

yields by manipulating fertilizer, water, and pesticide applications, that is to say, manipulating the ecological elements with technology in support of increases in the resource. As resource managers become more aware of the consequences of their actions, they are more likely to consider the human health ramifications of pesticide use, for example, or even the environmental consequences of discounting the future. The framework of adaptive management recognizes that managers must monitor changes to the ecosystem as a function of management decisions and be ready to change the management regime to better maintain the system.

A team of resource managers could implement adaptive management by themselves, or they could invite local community members and investors to join the team in making decisions that reflect interests in all three axes. Doing so would place adaptive management closer to the center of the figure, or situate their activities in the shaded areas where two circles overlap. Similarly, neoclassical economics would be located at the outer edge of the figure, where ecological economics moves toward the center, and specifically toward the ecological axis. Areas within the diagram where two of the circles overlap are identified as well. Truly addressing sustainability requires an approach where all three circles overlap, the origin of our three-axis diagram.

Figure 11.2 provides a similar image, but this time it includes the tools and principles mentioned in this text that have defined traditional strategies and that bring the promise of addressing sustainability. One way of

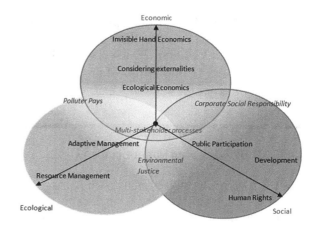

FIGURE 11.2 The three-legged sustainability model overlaid with tools and principles.

assessing an organization's approach to sustainability is by locating it on this kind if figure. For example, many companies implementing CSR focus primarily on their responsibility to the communities in which their partners, employees, and customers live. Hence we locate CSR in the social-economic portion of the figure. However, a program that also addresses the ecological impacts of the company might be placed within the center portion representing sustainability. Similarly, multi-stakeholder processes that engage representatives from each axes in meaningful dialogue are more likely to result in movement toward better understanding all three dimensions of sustainability. Polluter Pays is a tool that blends environmental consideration with the economy; Beneficiary Pays has the potential of addressing all three axes. Rights of the vulnerable and future populations originally reside in the social circle, until those rights are intertwined with biodiversity or labor, as they often are.

While some tools and principles are by design encompassing more than one aspect of sustainability (CSR and PPP), others will rely upon the users to implement them with sustainability in mind. Ethics will also play a role in the degree to which quality and sustainable decisions are made and implemented. In the meantime, this figure provides a way to remind ourselves of what can be important to consider and the tools we might use to do so.

CASE STUDY   The Ford Motor Company

The Ford Motor Company initiated its sustainability efforts in the late 1990s when Bill Clay Ford, Jr., the great grandson of Henry Ford, became the chief executive officer. Since that time the company has struggled with the classic conundrum of profit versus fully embracing sustainability. First impressions are always important, and when most people want to discover the sustainability orientation of an organization, they visit its website to determine if the organization values this concept and advertises its commitment to this way of thinking. Organizations that value sustainability, as well as any other concept, will state this on their home page, with links to current information about its various initiatives.

There is no mention of sustainability on Ford Motor Company's home page, and any mention of sustainability is at least two layers deep—that is, it cannot be reached directly from the home page. At the home page there are several tabs that guide the Internet surfer to information the company feels is important. The tabs are labeled *Vehicles*, *Purchasing Options*, *Owner Services*, *Innovations*, *Our Values*, and *About Ford*. Under the *Innovations* tab, there is a heading listed as *Greener Miles* which contains information on Ford's latest sustainability report, the increased level of recycled content in future Ford Explorers, how Ford is reducing water consumption, and several other green initiatives. Under the *Our Values* tab, there is a heading for *Environment* containing much of the same information as the *Greener Miles* heading. A link to sustainability information can be found under the *About Ford* tab, by clicking on *Company Information* where there is link to *Corporate Sustainability*, the location of its annual sustainability report. In contrast to Ford, Toyota Motor Company has a very prominent link to their sustainability programs on its home page.

According to its latest sustainability report, the 2009–2010, *The Future at Work: Blueprint for* Sustainability, Ford is making significant progress on many fronts related to sustainability, among them:[11]

- Developing and implementing a strategy to reduce CO_2 emissions and increase fuel efficiency, both by 30 percent, for all new U.S. and European models by 2020 compared to the 2006 base year
- Cutting global water use by 16.6 percent
- Reducing energy use at its global facilities by 44 percent since 2000
- Designing and manufacturing an array of new electric, hybrid, and plug-in hybrid vehicles
- Collaborating with major utilities and several U.S. cities to explore the implementation of infrastructure to support electric vehicles

Like many other major corporations, Ford has a company officer appointed to address sustainability, in this case, a group vice-president for sustainability, environment, and safety. This position is described as having responsibility "for establishing Ford Motor Company's long-range sustainability strategy and environmental policy," helping "develop the products and processes necessary to satisfy both customers and society," and serving "as Ford's chief liaison with global organizations seeking solutions to the challenges of sustainability, environmental stewardship and energy independence."[12]

Henry Ford and Fordism

Henry Ford, who founded Ford Motor Company in 1903, was the inventor of the assembly line, a novel approach to manufacturing that revolutionized the production of the automobile as well as all other products requiring assembly (see Figure 11.3). Rather than a single worker bolting and wiring together an entire car, each worker in the assembly line specialized in just a few tasks, dramatically increasing manufacturing efficiency and lowering costs and prices (see Figure 11.4). At peak production, a Model T could be assembled in 93 minutes and, because of the superb organization of the production lines, one Model T left the factory every three minutes (see Figure 11.5). The term Fordism was coined to describe this revolutionary approach to manufacturing. First applied to automobiles, it now refers to the ability to produce low-cost, affordable goods of all types.[13] It was the assembly line that made the Model-T Ford available to the average worker, then earning about $5 per day.

As a result of this major contribution to the Industrial Age, Ford was able to provide the average person with a degree of mobility that was previously impossible. The mass-produced automobile gave people the opportunity to travel much further with more ease, increasing the demand for roads and fossil fuels. The ability to manufacture efficiently and cheaply and move goods rapidly across the superior roads demanded by the automobile marked the advent of the age of consumerism. Lower manufacturing and transportation costs not only reduced prices, allowing people to acquire more material goods but also increased the productivity and wealth of the working class, and the United States became the dominant industrial power.

At its roots, Ford was oriented toward sustainability. In his book, "My Life and Work," Henry Ford revealed thinking that, at least in part parallels sustainability, "With all our fancied skill we still depend largely on natural resources and think they cannot be displaced. We dig coal and ore and they are gone; the trees cannot be replaced with a lifetime. We shall someday harness the heat that is all about us and no longer depend on coal—we may now create heat through electricity created by water power."[14] Henry Ford was a generous employer and well thought of by the Ford workforce. He was known for paying relatively high wages and for his efforts at producing automobiles that his workers could afford. Today's Ford Motor Company maintains much of this same historical emphasis on people and, as discussed later in this case study, Ford is considered one of the top companies when it comes to human rights and working conditions.

Ford Motor Company Today

Fast forwarding to the present, Ford is an enormous global conglomerate with manufacturing and distribution operations on six continents. It is the second largest automobile manufacturer in the United States

FIGURE 11.5 The Model-T was first produced in 1908 with a 20-horsepower engine and had a purchase price of $850. By the end of the first year of production, the price had dropped to about $550. Over 10,000 were produced in the first year, and by 1927, the last year of their manufacture, 15 million had emerged from Ford's factories. *(Photograph Courtesy of Ford Motor Company)*

FIGURE 11.3 Henry Ford with the first mass-produced V-8 engine *(Photograph Courtesy of Ford Motor Company)*

FIGURE 11.4 The assembly line was perhaps Henry Ford's major contribution to the industrial, allowing goods to be produced rapidly and cheaply to high quality standards. *(Photograph Courtesy of Ford Motor Company)*

and fourth largest in the world based on the number of vehicles sold annually. In 2008, it was the seventh largest U.S. company on the Fortune 500 list, with global revenues of $146.3 billion. In 2008, Ford employed about 213,000 employees at around 90 plants and facilities worldwide. During the Great Recession of 2008–2010, Ford's worldwide unit volume dropped from 5.5 million vehicles in 2008 to 4.8 million in 2009. In 2008 Ford lost $14.6 billion, the worst performance in its history. In spite of the drop in production, Ford had a net profit of $2.7 billion for 2009, reducing its liabilities significantly by swapping debt for equity. Alone among the three major American automobile companies (Ford, General Motors, and Chrysler), Ford managed to navigate the Great Recession without requesting government bailout money.

The company continues to prosper and appears to be resilient and well managed even in difficult economic times, announcing several recent technological advances that are reinforcing its strong position in the U.S. automotive marketplace. For example, the 2011 Ford Explorer equipped with a V-6 engine is 20 percent more fuel efficient than the 2010 model, and the 2011 equipped with a 2.0 liter V-4 engine is 30 percent more efficient, delivering energy performance of 26 mpg highway and 18 mpg city. This smaller engine delivers superior performance through sophisticated engine controls, the use of lighter materials, and powertrain improvements to the transmission and camshaft timing. Ford won the most awards in the J.D. Power 2010 Automotive Performance, Execution and Layout (APEAL) study that measures customer satisfaction in design, content, and vehicle performance. Simultaneously, Ford is marketing the fastest production car, the Shelby GT500, which has a 5.5 liter, supercharged V-8 engine with an estimated 23 mpg highway and 15 mpg city fuel performance. While Ford would laud this performance as being the best in its class, the class being powerful, behemoth, statement cars, the production of this type of vehicle can only be justified for profitability reasons.

The Evolution of Sustainability at Ford Motor Company

At least on paper Ford has, made significant commitments to a triple bottom-line approach in its business model. Ford started its journey to sustainability by introducing several environmental initiatives in 1989, notably the same year the Exxon Valdez ran aground in Prince Williams Sound in Alaska. Over the course of the next two decades Ford leadership announced a wide range of other initiatives that were designed to reengineer its image. Bill Clay Ford, Jr., who became chair of the board in 1998, has often expressed strong environmental and sustainability values. In 1998, he established the Environmental Strategy Review Committee to examine the company's product development and manufacturing operations for the purpose of establishing a corporate environmental perspective. It was clear to Bill Ford that it was necessary for the company to align itself with the emerging public consensus that, to be successful, good corporate citizenship had to be embedded in Ford's corporate psyche.

Ford sought to transform its organization, business practices, and products to better align them with the model of industrial ecology.[15] Rooted in the history of Ford's Model T (15 million were produced from 1908 to 1927) and the highly successful Model A (4.8 million were manufactured from 1927–1931), in 1999 Bill Ford announced that Ford would develop cars with a high level of ecological thinking, referred to by some as the Model E concept.[16] The Model E concept soon disappeared and the term E Concept reappeared in 2009, not as the line of ecologically friendly automobiles originally envisioned but as a turbocharged, 421-horsepower muscle car.[17]

Ford Motor Company endorsed the Global Sullivan Principles, met ISO 14001 environmental management certification requirements for all of its factories, started reporting its progress through corporate sustainability reports based on the requirements of the Global Reporting Initiative, and adopted the U.S. Green Building Council's Leadership in Energy and Environmental Design (LEED) green building rating system as a guide to the construction and renovation of many of its major facilities.[18] Following a massive explosion in 1999, Ford began the transformation of one of its largest truck building factories, the Ford Rouge Center in Dearborn, Michigan, into a LEED certified building. It is the largest brownfield redevelopment project undertaken in the world and has a 10.4-acre green roof, by far the largest green roof of any industrial building in the world (see Figure 11.6).

FIGURE 11.6 The largest green roof in the world is on the Ford's Rouge River Plant in Dearborn, Michigan. In this picture, workers are installing sedum on the roof of the plant, which at 10.4 acres is the largest green roof in the world. *(Photograph courtesy of the Henry Ford Museum)*

FIGURE 11.7 The Ford Excursion was first produced in 1999 and was the flagship of Ford's line of highly profitable SUVs. Weighing in at 7,190 lbs, it had a gas mileage of 8–10 miles per gallon in the city and 12–14 miles per gallon on the highway. The last Excursion was produced in the United States in September 2005 as rising gasoline prices began affecting sales. *(Photograph Courtesy of Ford Motor Company)*

The SUV Problem

Clearly many of these efforts were sincere and were in keeping with the often espoused values of Bill Ford and other key leaders of Ford. Ford issued its first sustainability report in 1999, *Connecting with Society*. Perhaps the most notable item in the 1999 report is the Sport Utility Vehicle Case Study in which Ford laid out the dilemmas it was facing because of the emergence of SUVs as its most popular vehicles, growing in sales from 540,199 units in 1990 to 766,743 in 1999. This latter figure accounted for more than half of Ford's vehicle sales in 1999. Ford acknowledged that without the SUV in its lineup, its profitability would suffer because it earned more profit per SUV than for any other vehicle, up to $14,000 per unit. They also admitted that (1) SUVs had relatively poor fuel economy and that the migration of customers to SUVs was increasing green house gas emissions, (2) they had higher emissions than cars because they are classified as trucks in U.S. regulations with more lenient emissions standards, (3) SUVs created safety problems for other drivers because of their increased weight and reduced visibility for car drivers as a result of their relatively large size, and (4) they could easily be driven off-road, resulting in increased damage to nature.

In this same report, Ford also described its approach to addressing these SUV problems: (1) substantially reducing SUV emissions, (2) increasing SUV fuel economy by offering smaller SUVs and developing hybrid electric models, and (3) making token efforts to reduce the danger of SUVs to cars by, for example, developing its BlockerBeam™ to prevent cars from sliding beneath the Ford Excursion SUV in a collision. Surprisingly, Ford actually quoted the Sierra Club's description of the Ford Excursion (see Figure 11.7):

> At a time of mounting concern over global warming, air pollution and oil exploration in fragile wilderness areas, the gas-guzzling SUV is a rolling monument to environmental destruction. The

nine-passenger Excursion is a suburban supertanker, stretching over 19 feet in length and slurping one gallon of gasoline for every 12 miles it travels. This 'suburban assault vehicle' spews as much global warming pollution into the air as two average cars."[19]

In spite of baring its soul with respect to the SUV, Ford did not renounce it for two reasons. First, it was the key to their profitability in 1999 and as a publicly traded corporation with its stockholders demanding the maximum returns on their investment, removing it from the product line was not, in their thinking, an option. Second, Ford maintained that if they did not make SUV's, some other manufacturer would fill the void and probably not try to lower the impacts as they were doing with the Excursion and Ranger.

Clearly the production of SUVs and other notorious large, energy-guzzling vehicles flies in the face of Ford's declared efforts to be sustainable. As is the case with most other automobile manufacturers, Ford chases the profitable segments of the industry, whether it be large pickup trucks, vans, or SUVs.

Ford's Business Principles

In the 2002 sustainability report, Corporate *Citizenship Report: Our Principles, Progress, and Performance*, Bill Ford is quoted as saying, "There are no shortcuts to sustaining our success for another century. To maintain the financial health that is essential for our survival, we are revitalizing our values as well as our business plans. That's what it will take for us to create greater value for all of our stakeholders and have an even more positive impact on the lives of people around the world in our next 100 years." In this report, Ford laid out seven business principles to guide them toward their objective of being a responsible corporation (See Table 11.2).[20]

Ford Motor Company's Key Performance Indicators

In its latest sustainability report for 2009/2010, Blueprint *for Sustainability: The Future at Work*, Ford reports progress on many fronts with respect to improving the performance of its operations. The executive summary of the report provides a Performance Overview in which several categories of key indicators of performance are detailed for the three year period 2007–2009: Economy/Quality, Environment, Society. Table 11.3 shows the trends in environmental performance indicators as stated in this report. In general, over even the short span of three years in the report, the indicators show continual progress for virtually all measured parameters.

TABLE 11.2   Ford Motor Company's Business Principles in 2002

1. Accountability – We will be honest and open and model the highest standards of corporate integrity.
2. Products and customers – We will offer excellent products and services.
3. Environment – We will respect natural environment and preserve it for future generations.
4. Safety – We will protect the health and safety of those who make, distribute, or use products.
5. Community – We will respect and contribute to communities around the world.
6. Quality of relationships – We will strive to earn the trust and respect of investors, customers, dealers, employees, unions, business partners, and society.
7. Financial health – We will make decisions with proper regard to long-term financial security of the company.

TABLE 11.3   Ford Key Indicators of Environmental Performance (2007–2009)

Ford Environmental Performance 2007–2009	2007	2008	2009
U.S. Fleet Fuel Economy, Total Cars and Trucks, miles per gallon**	25.3	26.0	27.1
U.S. Fleet CO_2 Emissions, Total Cars and Trucks, grams per mile*	352	340	326
European Fleet CO_2 emissions, grams per mile*			
Ford	149	146	139
Volvo	190	182	173
Worldwide Facility Energy Consumption, trillion BTUs*	65.6	61.0	51.5
Worldwide Facility Energy Consumption per vehicle, million BTUs*	10.8	12.2	11.2
Worldwide Facility CO_2 emissions, million metric tons*	6.1	5.4	4.9
Worldwide Facility CO_2 emissions per vehicle, metric tons*	1.02	1.09	1.05
North American Energy Efficiency Index (2000 base = 100%)*	74.4	69.9	65.3

*Lower is better
**Higher is better

Although Ford has made progress internally in both its fleet performance and operations, when stacked up against other automobile companies, Ford does not fare very well. In its 2010 automobile rankings, the Union of Concerned Scientists rated Ford as sixth out of the eight major automobile manufacturers whose performance was assessed using the Union's Fleet Average Environmental Scores. Ford was the highest rated American automobile manufacturer, but with a score of 108, was above the industry average of 100. (see Figure 11.8).[21]

Ford Motor Company's Workforce Relations

Ford's commitment to its workforce is strong, and they are responding to stakeholders they have engaged in the past 10 years who challenged them to take a leadership role in addressing human rights by creating sound working conditions in their facilities and throughout their supply chain. Ford applies the Ford Code of Basic Working Conditions, which they adopted in 2003, to their entire global enterprise and its $65 billion supply chain.[22] They are signatories to the United

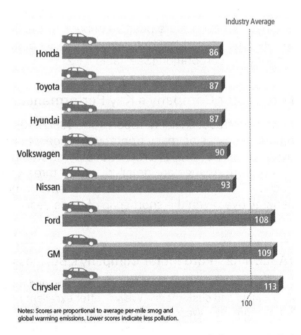

FIGURE 11.8 Based on the Union of Concerned Scientists Fleet Average Environmental Score index, Ford ranked sixth of the eight manufacturers rated and higher than the industry average. *(Illustration Courtesy of the Union of Concerned Scientists)*

Nations Global Compact and are participants in the Human Rights and Supply Chain Sustainability Advisory Groups convened by the Global Compact.[23]

Ford is working with its supply chain to address issues of human rights and working conditions in three ways: (1) engaging local suppliers through training and capability building for the purpose of solving problems with working conditions, (2) working with the corporate management of key suppliers to help them influence their own supply chains to ensure proper working and environmental conditions in their facilities, and (3) leading collaboration between the automotive industry and the supply chain concerning global working conditions. In 2010, *Corporate Responsibility Magazine* ranked Ford's human rights efforts first among companies included in the 100 Best Corporate Citizens list.[24] Also, in June 2010, Ford was recognized as one of the *World's Most Ethical Companies* by the Ethisphere Institute, the only automaker to receive either recognition.[25]

A FINAL CRITIQUE

The Ford Motor Company made a commitment to sustainability as a framework for decision making in the late 1990s and, at least publically, still maintains this commitment over a decade later. Ford is an interesting candidate for a case study because its leadership made strong statements about sustainability and, at least on paper, tries to remain faithful to the original pronouncements of its leadership, most notably Bill Clayton Ford, Jr., Yet it is an industry that is inherently difficult to reconcile with sustainability because the core of its survival, at least at present, is the consumption of nonrenewable fossil fuels.

In examining its record, it is fair to conclude that Ford does a very good job of addressing most of the social and economic issues that are considered de rigeur for corporate sustainability. Ford is well known for fair, and even generous, treatment of its workforce, as well as its commitment to global social equity. At the present time it is the most robust American automobile company and continues to gain strength due to technological innovations and financial strategy. However, it must also be noted that its record with respect to some other major aspects of sustainability is weak and indicates a gap between pronouncements and action. This is most evident in its product line of cars and trucks.

With respect to transparency, Ford produces an annual report that details its annual sustainability performance. Yet Ford's decision-making process is not transparent and produces results that fly squarely in the face of sustainability. How can a strategy that opts for the production of SUVs and muscle cars, for example, be considered consistent with sustainability? Why does Ford's product line lag in environmental performance and fuel efficiency when compared to the international market? It would appear that with respect to its products, sustainability is an afterthought. As noted in a 1999 study by the Houston Advanced Research Center:[26]

> Ford Motor Company is positioned between its successes—its huge commitment to its environmental programs and its position as the world's number one maker and seller of profitable sport utility vehicles. In fact, Ford is preparing to launch its Excursion, the 19-ft long, V-10 engine addition to its SUV product line. Simultaneously, Ford is moving ahead with plans to advertise its SUVs as certified low emission vehicles (LEVs) or better, which are setting the standard for Ford's competitors and positioning Ford exceptionally well in the high-profile California market.

Although somewhat dated, this statement reveals the conundrum that Ford faces as an automobile manufacturer. While Ford may green its operations and the material content of its products, it is fundamentally impossible to produce a sustainable fossil-fuel-burning automobile. And in spite of publicity about its commitment to sustainability, Ford has consistently followed the direction of the market, refusing to forgo the production of unsustainable large, gas-guzzling vehicles like the Excursion, SUVs, and pickup trucks. Only when the price of gasoline began a climb to over $4.00 a gallon between 2007 and 2008 did Ford (and the other U.S. manufacturers) become serious about offering more fuel efficient vehicles. Unlike Toyota and Honda who long ago made strategic decisions that were more aligned with sustainability, the American manufacturers responded only when their market share was

threatened. The lesson that has not been learned by the Americans is that the main reason for the success of their Japanese competitors is their commitment to sustainability! Ford's public commitment to sustainability contrasted with its lack of a vision as to how to be the world leader in low-impact, energy-efficient vehicles is clearly contradictory. As Timothy Luke noted in 2001, "Ford's innovations are noteworthy, but its approach falls short of what is needed from big business to help create a more ecological society."[27] This remains true today.

As noted above, Ford does have an admirable track record of being ahead of the curve in its treatment of its workforce. Yet along with the other American automakers, it has reduced wages, pensions, and other benefits to survive both the vast economic down and the impacts of its poor strategic decision planning, especially with respect to the environmental impacts and efficiency of its fleet. Ford is reducing the operating costs and resource consumption of its plants and indications are that the energy input per dollar of output is falling and continues to fall. It is the strongest U.S. automotive survivor of the Great Recession of 2008–2010. One could say that with respect to the three-legged model of sustainability, the stool legs for Ford have measurably different lengths. On social issues and economic issues Ford does very well. However, it is falling far short in its efforts to produce sustainable products. It ranks first among U.S. automotive companies in its environmental performance but behind all its foreign competitors. While Ford claims a leadership role in sustainability in its industry segment, it does not have a strategic plan for a future product line that makes sense. Ford is likely a victim of being a publicly traded corporation in the United States, burdened with short-term performance requirements that results in a myopic vision. It is also a victim, in a sense, of historically and artificially low energy prices, indicating the added danger of a national policy that subsidizes unsustainable energy resources: It provides no motivation to the automobile companies to design truly energy efficient cars.

The question remains whether Ford will wake up to the need for a decision making process based on sustainability regarding its development of technology. The history of American automobile manufacturing indicates a pattern of reacting to crises rather than planning strategically. Ford now produces a line of automobiles that recently won the most Top Safety picks by the Insurance Institute for Highway Safety. However, they and the other manufacturers were motivated to design safe automobiles only after Ralph Nader, in 1965, raised the red flag about the Ford Pinto's unsafe gas tank design. The record is that Ford and the other manufacturers fought the Federal government for years about changes to gas tanks that were cheap and would save lives. In 1979, then Chrysler CEO, Lee Iacocca, successfully lobbied Congress for a $1 billion dollar bailout. The reason? The rising gasoline prices of that era motivated buyers to switch to fuel-efficient Japanese and German models which had the added advantage of having higher quality. Clearly Ford had an enormous opportunity to seize the advantage it had created by advocating for sustainability over a decade ago. It could have focused on producing energy-

efficient cars that were world class, that is, they would have competed with the best of class (here in the sense of the typical the passenger car) automobiles of any manufacturer. The added advantage would have been that Ford would have thus aligned all its actions, including the design of its product line, with its avowed declaration of being a sustainable corporation. The likely outcome, however, based on past behavior, is that they will not take advantage of this opening and will continue to shrink in size, along with the other American manufacturers. In spite of their own problems, Toyota and Honda, which have made strong, consistent commitments to sustainability, will likely gain market share at the expense of the Americans, in large part because they are committed to sustainability. What the Japanese understand is that designing and producing highly efficient cars, not what is fashionable today, are the key to success. They understand that though difficult to instill, sustainability is a competitive advantage. As noted earlier in this chapter, the first mention of sustainability on the Ford Motor Company website is three clicks away from the home page. Toyota Motor Company has a large link to sustainability directly on their home page. Clearly Toyota views sustainability as a higher priority than Ford and its product line reflects this difference. However within Ford itself, there appears to be a strong internal movement that cuts across all units and departments as evidenced by their most recent sustainability report that weighs in at 518 pages. Toyota's report, while impressive and detailed in its own right, is 96 pages in length.[28] Although the mass of a sustainability report is not the only arbiter of the company's motivations, the report does indicate that Ford's commitment to sustainability remains intact if uneven.

Ford's inability to fully grasp the competitive advantage of sustainability is a function of a lack of the truly deep commitment that is needed to make this paradigm work. We suggest that this deep commitment can only be attained by realizing that sustainability starts with ethical principles and that unless these become part of the organizational culture and unless all decisions are screened against these principles, adopting sustainability to guide decision making is likely to bring, at best, only limited results and success. By understanding and applying the ethical principles that frame sustainability, Ford and other organizations can have the dual benefit of doing the right thing and gaining a competitive edge. The question is how to create this realization and shift from superficial approaches to strategies that are rooted in these very important ethical concepts.

REFERENCES

De Grazia, Victoria. 2005. *Irresistible Empire: America's Advance Through 20th-Century Europe*. Cambridge: Belknap Press of Harvard University Press.

Ford, Henry. 1922. *My Life and Work*, Garden City: Garden City Publishing Co., Inc.

Ford Motor Company 1999. *Connecting with Society: 1999 Corporate Citizenship Report*.

Ford Motor Company. 2002. *Corporate Citizenship Report: Our Principles, Progress, and Performance*. Available online at www.ford.com/doc/2002_sustainability_report.pdf.

Ford Motor Company. 2010. *Blueprint for Sustainability: Our Future at Work*. Available online at www.ford.com/microsites/sustainability-report-2009-10/default.

Foss, Michelle Michot, Eduardo Gonzalez and Halyk Noyen. 1999. Ford Motor Company, in Corporate Incentives and Environmental Decision Making. The Woodlands: Center for Global Studies. Available online at http://files.harc.edu/Projects/Archive/Reports/EnvironmentalDecisionMaking.pdf.

Hastings, Marilou. 1999. *Corporate Incentives and Environmental Decision Making: A Case Studies and Workshop Report*, The Woodlands: Center for Global Studies. online at http://files.harc.edu/Projects/Archive/Reports/EnvironmentalDecisionMaking.pdf.

Luke, Timothy W. 2000. "From analogue to digital Fordism: Toward a critique of the political economy of internationalization." Available online at www.2.cddc.vt.edu/digitalfordism/index.html.

Luke, Timothy W. 2001. "SUVs and the Greening of Ford: Reimagining Industrial Ecology as an Environmental Corporate Strategy in Action," *Organization & Environment*, 14(3), September, pp. 311–335. Available online at http://oae.sagepub.com/cgi/reprint/14/3/311.

ENDNOTES

1. The Natural Step organization's U.S. branch has a website at www.naturalstep.org.
2. From Upham (2000).
3. The Hannover Principles: Design for Sustainability, is available at the McDonough and Partners website, www.mcdonough.com/principles.pdf.
4. The ICSID/IDSA Conference was held in San Francisco October 17-20, 2007. A link to the events of the conference can be found at

www.designverb.com/2007/10/30/design-is-the-problem-in-sustainability

5. As described at the US Department of Energy website at www.gsa.gov/portal/content/104462

6. As stated in Friedman (1962).

7. The Global Reporting Initiative provides guidelines for sustainability reporting for various sectors, including automobile manufacturing. The G3 Guidelines provide general guidance and there are sector supplements that provide specific reporting requirements for automobile manufacturing and other major activities. The G3 Guidelines and sector supplements can be found at www.globalreporting.org.

8. The International Standards Organization (ISO) developed ISO 14001, Environmental Management Systems, to provide companies with guidance for identifying their environmental impacts, continually improving their environmental performance, and establishing targets for environmental performance. In Europe, third-party certification to ISO 14001 is the norm and it is often required by, for example, automobile manufacturers, that their suppliers also be certified to ISO 14001, ensuring the supply chain is continually reducing its impacts. In the United States, most companies, such as Ford, opt for ISO 14001 registration, that is, the third-party certification body records the certification in its client register. In general, ISO 14001 is an effective approach for automobile manufacturers to use for ensuring progress in reducing resource consumption and environmental impacts.

9. Local Agenda 21 is the commonly used name for Chapter 28 of Agenda 21, the report issued by the 1992 Rio Conference, and it addresses the role of local authorities in the effort to promote sustainable development.

10. The UtneReader recognized Chattanooga's enlightened status in its May/June 1997 issue, which can be found online at www.utne.com/1997-05-01/Americas10MostEnlightenedTowns.aspx.

11. A summary of Ford's 2009–2010 sustainability report can be found at www.ford.com/doc/sr09-blueprint-summary.pdf.

12. From the Ford Motor Company website at http://media.ford.com/article_display.cfm?article_id=7334. The press release which describes this position announced the appointment of the current holder, Susan M. Cischke, on April 1, 2008.

13. In her book *Irresistible Empire: America's Advance Through Europe in the 20th Century* (2005), Victoria DeGraza described Fordism as "the eponymous manufacturing system designed to spew out standardized, low-cost goods and afford its workers decent enough wages to buy them."

14. See Ford (1922).

15. The information about Ford's behavior in attempting to adopt Industrial Ecology as a model is well described in Timothy W. Luke's (2001) excellent article in the online version of *Organizational Behavior*.

16. As described by Timothy Luke (2000).

17. The 2009 E Concept car had the full name of F6 E Concept and was introduced into the Australian market in 2009.

18. LEED is an acronym for "Leadership in Energy and Environmental Design," a suite of building rating systems for assessing the degree to which a building is green. Through the implementation and acceptance of LEED as a guiding factor in design and construction, the U.S. Green Building Council has been highly successful in transforming building industry. In addition to a rating systems for new construction (LEED-NC), the suite of LEED rating systems addresses existing buildings, homes, neighborhood development, and specific building types such as schools and retail stores.

19. From a Sierra Club press release dated February 25, 1999.

20. From Ford's Corporate Citizenship Report (2002).

21. The report of the Union of Concerned Scientists that rates automobiles based on their environmental impacts is titled *Automaker Rankings 2010: The Environmental Performance of Car Companies*. It is available at www.ucsusa.org/assets/documents/clean_vehicles/2010-automaker-report.pdf.

22. The Ford Code of Basic Working Conditions states, among other things, that child labor or forced labor will never be used by Ford or companies in its supply chain, calls for engagement with stakeholders and indigenous peoples, and states that collective bargaining is a right of the workforce. www.ford.com/microsites/sustainability-report-2007-08/issues-humanrights-ford-code.

23. The U.N. Global Compact is an initiative for businesses that agree to follow 10 principles that address four broad categories: human rights, labor, environment, and anti-corruption. In addition to following these principles, the 7700 participating businesses agree to support the Millennium Development Goals (MDG), which focus on the eradication of poverty globally. The Global Compact website is www.unglobalcompact.org/ and the MDGs can be found at www.un.org/millenniumgoals/.

24. The Corporate Responsibility Magazine's "100 Best Corporate Citizens List for 2010" can be found at www.thecro.com/files/CR100Best.pdf.

25. The Ethisphere Institute's announcement of Ford Motor Company as one of the World's Most Ethical Companies can be found at http://ethisphere.com/ford-wme-award/.

26. As stated in Foss (1999).

27. As stated in Luke (2001).

28. Ford's 2009/2010 Sustainability Report is located at http://corporate.ford.com/doc/sr09.pdf and Toyota's is located at www.toyota-global.com/sustainability/sustainability_report/pdf_file_download/10/pdf/sustainability_report10.pdf.

Index

For these and other Wiley books on sustainable design, visit www.wiley.com/go/sustainabledesign

Environmental Benefits Statement

This book is printed with soy-based inks on presses with VOC levels that are lower than the standard for the printing industry. The paper, Rolland Enviro 100, is manufactured by Cascades Fine Papers Group and is made from 100 percent post-consumer, de-inked fiber, without chlorine. According to the manufacturer, the use of every ton of Rolland Enviro100 Book paper, switched from virgin paper, helps the environment in the following ways:

Mature trees	Waterborne waste not created	Water flow saved	Atmospheric emissions eliminated	Soiled wastes reduced	Natural gas saved by using biogas
17	6.9 lbs	10,196 gals.	2,098 lbs.	1,081 lbs.	2,478 cubic feet

Printed in the USA/Agawam, MA
October 7, 2020

762412.022